Metric Manipulations in Haydn and Mozart

OXFORD STUDIES IN MUSIC THEORY

Series Editor Richard Cohn

Studies in Music with Text, David Lewin

Music as Discourse: Semiotic Adventures in Romantic Music, Kofi Agawu

Metric Manipulations in Haydn and Mozart: Chamber Music for Strings, 1787–1791, Danuta Mirka

Metric Manipulations in Haydn and Mozart

Chamber Music for Strings, 1787–1791

DANUTA MIRKA

OXFORD
UNIVERSITY PRESS

2009

OXFORD
UNIVERSITY PRESS

Oxford University Press, Inc., publishes works that further
Oxford University's objective of excellence
in research, scholarship, and education.

Oxford New York
Auckland Cape Town Dar es Salaam Hong Kong Karachi
Kuala Lumpur Madrid Melbourne Mexico City Nairobi
New Delhi Shanghai Taipei Toronto

With offices in
Argentina Austria Brazil Chile Czech Republic France Greece
Guatemala Hungary Italy Japan Poland Portugal Singapore
South Korea Switzerland Thailand Turkey Ukraine Vietnam

Published by Oxford University Press, Inc.
198 Madison Avenue, New York, New York 10016

www.oup.com

Library of Congress Cataloging-in-Publication Data
Mirka, Danuta.
Metric manipulations in Haydn and Mozart: Chamber Music for Strings,
1787–1791 / Danuta Mirka.
p. cm. — (Oxford studies in music theory)
Includes bibliographical references and index.
ISBN 978-0-19-538492-5
1. Musical meter and rhythm. 2. Chamber music—18th century—Analysis,
appreciation. 3. Chamber music—18th century—History and criticism.
4. Haydn, Joseph, 1732–1809—Criticism and interpretation. 5. Mozart,
Wolfgang Amadeus, 1756–1791—Criticism and interpretation. I. Title.
MT140.M67 2009
785'.70922—dc22 2008049384

Publication of this book was supported by the Lloyd Hibberd Publication
Endowment Fund of the American Musicological Society.

9 8 7 6 5 4 3 2 1

Printed in the United States of America
on acid-free paper

ACKNOWLEDGMENTS

This book grew very slowly over the course of several blissful years of work supported by various research scholarships. I started working on it at Indiana University, Bloomington, during my Fulbright Senior Research Grant in 2001–2 and continued in 2002–6 at the University of Freiburg, Germany, as research fellow of the Alexander von Humboldt Foundation and Deutsche Forschungsgemeinschaft. I wish to express my thanks to all three foundations for their generous support. My special thanks to Eugeniusz Knapik, the rector of my former home institution, the Music Academy in Katowice, Poland, who allowed me to take a sabbatical leave of unprecedented length. Senior academic colleagues who read an earlier version of my manuscript are Kofi Agawu and Floyd Grave. I am most grateful to both of them for their thoughtful comments and for persuading me to publish the results of my research on eighteenth-century rhythm and meter before extending it to hypermeter and phrase structure. Had I pursued my original idea of a book covering both these areas, it would not have seen the light of day for many years to come. I am also grateful to two anonymous reviewers at Oxford University Press for further critical comments, which resulted in significant improvements of my manuscript, and to James Webster for explanations regarding details of dynamics and articulation in Haydn's string quartets Op. 50 and Op. 54/55.

All modern musical examples and graphics included in this book were prepared by Guillermo Brachetta. I wish to thank him not only for correctly setting all notes and symbols but also for his sympathy for and interest in this project. I thank further Martha Ramsey for copyediting the manuscript and the editors at Oxford University Press—especially Suzanne Ryan, Madelyn Sutton, and Liz Smith—for safely shepherding it through various stages of the publication process. Chapters 2 and 6 draw on material from Danuta Mirka, "Metre, Phrase Structure and Manipulations of Musical Beginnings," chapter 4 of Danuta Mirka and Kofi Agawu, eds., *Communication in Eighteenth-Century Music*, copyright Cambridge University Press 2008, reproduced with permission.

CONTENTS

Introduction ix

Note on Terminology, Language, and Musical Examples xv

1 Musical Meter between Composition and Perception 3

1.1 The Concept of Meter in the Late Eighteenth Century 3
1.2 The Revival of the Hierarchical Concept of Meter in the Twentieth Century 13
1.3 Toward a Dynamic Model of Meter 17
1.4 Borrowing from a Different Model 23

2 Finding Meter 31

2.1 Statistical Parameters 39
2.2 Harmony 50
2.3 Streaming and the Role of Bass 57
2.4 Cadence (Structural Accent) 69

3 Sustaining Meter—Challenging Meter 93

3.1 *Metrum* and Regularity of Beats 93
3.2 Missing Beats 99
3.3 General Pauses 101
3.4 Fermatas 116
3.5 Syncopations 122

4 Changing Meter I: Change of Period 133

4.1 *Imbroglio* 135
4.2 Submetrical Dissonance 151
4.3 Hemiola 159

5 Changing Meter II: Change of Phase 165

5.1 Chains of Rhythmical Dissonances 165
5.2 Other Parameters in Displacement Dissonances 174
5.3 Imitation 189

5.4 *Ligaturae*, Retardation, Anticipation 198
5.5 Syncopated Accompaniment 204
5.6 A Remark on Subliminal Dissonances 205

6 Changing Meter III: Change of Tactus 209

6.1 Changes of *Taktteile* in Compound Meters 209
6.2 Changes of *Taktteile* in Double Measures 217
6.3 Perceptual Factors 232
6.4 *Taktteile* and the Tactus 241

7 Analyses of Long-Range Metrical Strategies 249

7.1 Haydn, String Quartet in C Major, Op. 50 No. 2, First Movement 254
7.2 Haydn, String Quartet in F Minor, Op. 55 No. 2, Finale 275

8 Wit, Comedy, and Metric Manipulations in Haydn's and Mozart's Personal Styles 295

8.1 Haydn 295
8.2 Mozart 301
8.3 Haydn's Earlier and Later String Quartets 305
8.4 Inconclusive Conclusion 308

Bibliography 311

Index of Compositions by Haydn and Mozart 321

General Index 323

INTRODUCTION

Among the most remarkable developments in the music theory of recent decades have been the rapid advances in the study of meter and rhythm. After the pioneering works by Cooper and Meyer (1960), Cone (1968), Komar (1971), and Yeston (1976), this area of study received a new impulse from *A Generative Theory of Tonal Music* by Lerdahl and Jackendoff (1983), and a stream of publications followed, including books by Lester (1986), Kramer (1988), Rothstein (1989), Hasty (1997), Krebs (1999), and London (2004). In many of these publications, theoretical arguments are illustrated with examples from eighteenth-century music. But apart from a handful of articles, metric manipulations characteristic of this music have not received any systematic study. This book is designed to fill this gap, yet it differs from those by earlier authors in that I take as my point of departure historical music theory of the late eighteenth century. At that time in Germany, a new theory of meter emerged. It was first presented in *Allgemeine Theorie der schönen Künste* by Johann Sulzer (1771–74) and was further elaborated in handbooks of composition by Johann Philipp Kirnberger (1771–79) and Heinrich Christoph Koch (1782–93). Continued in the nineteenth century by such authors as Gottfried Wilhelm Fink, Gottfried Weber, and Simon Sechter, this theory was rejected at the end of the century by Hugo Riemann, only to be revived in the twentieth century by the American authors mentioned earlier. As I will demonstrate in chapter 1, the eighteenth-century concept of meter originating with Sulzer's encyclopedia is compatible with the one adopted by most of these authors. One might venture a hypothesis that it was the return to this very concept that made the recent advances in the study of meter and rhythm possible. Consequently, twentieth- and twenty-first-century theory of meter can be viewed as a further development of eighteenth-century music theory. It is this view that substantially informs this book.

A rapprochement of historical and contemporary perspectives on meter and rhythm is further justified by the strong cognitive component of eighteenth-century music theory, which can be fruitfully combined with recent approaches in the field of cognitive musicology and cognitively oriented music theory. To be sure, the eighteenth century did not yet have a full-fledged theory of music cognition, but authors of composition handbooks expressed numerous intuitions concerning the mechanism of metric perception and factors that affect it. Several of these intuitions have been experimentally confirmed and assimilated into theoretical and computational models of metric perception. These models can thus be used not only to explain the perceptual effect of eighteenth-century metric manipulations on twentieth- and twenty-first-century listeners but also their effect on historical listeners as intended by eighteenth-century composers. To this end, it would be easiest to avail oneself of one of the existing models. Yet many of them have the disadvantage of being partial, in that they include only one or a few factors of metric perception, and most of them are static, hence not able to account for some manipulations of meter encountered in the eighteenth century. In order to analyze such manipulations, I propose a dynamic model of metric perception referring to the theory of Fred Lerdahl and Ray Jackendoff (1983) and based on Jackendoff's model derived from it (1991). This model emerges gradually in the course of chapter 1 from my comparison of the eighteenth-century concept of meter with Lerdahl and Jackendoff's Metrical Well-Formedness Rules (MWFRs). It is then supplemented with elements of metric theory by Christopher Hasty (1997). In chapter 2, the model provides the framework for further comparison between intuitions of eighteenth-century music theorists and factors of metric perception that Lerdahl and Jackendoff include in their set of Metrical Preference Rules (MPRs). At the same time, this model is analytically applied to various examples of metric manipulations. In chapter 2, all these manipulations take place in the phase of metrical induction at the beginning of a piece. It is in this phase that the influence of individual factors can be most easily demonstrated. Subsequent chapters are devoted to metric manipulations that take place in the further course of a piece, where factors of metric perception interfere not only with each other but also with the listener's sense of meter inherited from an earlier passage. Chapter 3 deals with the antimetrical effect of single pauses and syncopations. Chapters 4 and 5 reflect on longer series of antimetrical phenomena displaying their own regularity and hence generating a new metrical structure imposed on that of the notated meter or leading to changes of meter concerning its phase or period. These last phenomena have been recently described by Harald Krebs (1999) in his theory of metrical dissonance, but their earliest descriptions come from the eighteenth century. The way eighteenth-century authors conceive of them reveals both similarities and differences between their concept of meter and ours, and consequently it suggests how the theory of metrical dissonance could be adapted to eighteenth-century music. Conversely, this last theory offers a conceptual framework with which to systematize metric manipulations, and provides tools for analytically dealing with more sophisticated cases not discussed in eighteenth-century composition handbooks addressed to beginners.

Yet the eighteenth-century theory of meter is not completely coextensive with the contemporary theory. Clearly, authors of eighteenth-century composition handbooks were not primarily supposed to theorize about meter and metric perception but to teach a beginning composer how to correctly notate music. This entailed teaching rules as to which musical events should be assigned to strong and weak parts of the measure. The consistency of these rules throughout the eighteenth century strongly suggests that they belonged to the body of common knowledge normally transmitted to beginning composers by their composition teachers. It may have also suggested to both parties that these rules are natural. Indeed, they were claimed by eighteenth-century authors to originate in the nature of human "ears" (*Ohren*) or "hearing" (*Gehör*). Yet this claim is not confirmed by cognitive studies. The rules are not natural but conventional. But this does not stipulate that they are irrelevant. Rather, it is only in light of these rules that one can gain analytical insights into some of the most sophisticated manipulations of meter exercised by eighteenth-century composers. These manipulations, discussed in chapter 6, consist in changes of the so-called parts of the measure (*Taktteile*). In contrast to other metric manipulations, which were accessible to all attentive listeners of the eighteenth century, including less competent ones (*Liebhaber*), changes of *Taktteile* could be appreciated only by listeners equipped with adequate theoretical knowledge (*Kenner*).

The accessibility of metric manipulations to different groups of listeners and their assignment to different levels of listening experience is most succinctly illustrated by the relationship between the eighteenth-century concept of *Taktteile* and the concept of tactus in the theory of Lerdahl and Jackendoff. Whereas tactus is the central level of metrical hierarchy inferred from the musical surface by the unconsciously working mechanism of metric perception, *Taktteile* have to be consciously identified by the listener on the basis of the theoretical knowledge of compositional rules. One could thus say that the former is a matter of *cognition* and the latter of *recognition*; or, with Jerry Fodor (1983), that the level of processing involved in the former concept is "modular" and in the latter "central." I draw the distinction between *Taktteile* and tactus in chapter 1, continue to discuss it in chapter 2, and return to it in chapter 6, where I explain that tactus and *Taktteile* need not be located on the same metrical level and that, in the course of a given piece, their changes may or may not coincide. At the end of chapter 6, this discussion leads toward what I propose to call a future theory of metrical consonance. It comes close to hypermeter, yet it does not cross this threshold. Although the idea of higher metrical levels was anticipated in the eighteenth century, several aspects of hypermeter are related to phrase structure and hence belong to a segment of eighteenth-century music theory (*Taktordnung*) that is different from the theory of meter (*Takt*). Apart from practical considerations—a book including a thorough discussion of both phenomena would far exceed a standard size—this is the most important reason to postpone the discussion of hypermeter to another study. There, I hope to address the issue of displacements in compound meters identified by Floyd Grave (1984, 1985) and to build further on the foundation laid down by William Rothstein in his *Phrase Rhythm in Tonal Music* (1989). Even if references to Rothstein are virtually absent from this book, it should be clear that his combination of eighteenth-century music theory with the theory of Lerdahl and Jackendoff was one of the most important catalysts of this study.

The practical purpose of eighteenth-century music theory as handmaiden of composition is the source of an even more important difference between historical and contemporary theories of meter. Whereas the recent advances in the area of meter and rhythm have come at the price of divorcing it from other areas of music theory, in the eighteenth century meter formed only one aspect of compositional métier and was closely connected to others. The nature of these connections was clarified by the metaphor of music as language: music, like language, had its grammar and rhetoric. In the late eighteenth century, musical rhetoric embraced mainly the questions of form and design, including tonal processes and distribution of musical themes, but it extended to the style—high, middle, or low—of musical discourse, as well as its conventional subjects, represented by musical topics. Grammatical rules of music were the rules of harmony and counterpoint. Musical meter had its counterpart in poetic meter but was related to grammar in the sense that strong beats, as strong syllables, were called "grammatical" accents. Metric manipulations could thus be compared to disturbances on the phonetic and syntactical level of language. Yet they were not unrelated to rhetoric. Indeed, their rhetorical effect frequently forms their motivation. Within the conceptual horizon defined by the metaphor of music as language, eighteenth-century playing with meter was a dimension of play with musical form and its topical decorum.

This wider conceptual horizon opens up in chapter 7, where I include analyses of long-range metrical strategies embracing entire movements. In this chapter, it will become clear that this study has points of connection not only with other theories of meter but also with historically informed approaches to other aspects of eighteenth-century music. Interestingly enough, this last stream of American musicology and music theory, inspired by Leonard G. Ratner (1980) and continued by Wye J. Allanbrook (1983), Janet Levy (1982, 1992), Gretchen Wheelock (1992), Elaine Sisman (1993), Mark Evan Bonds (1991a, 1991b), and Karol Berger (1992, 1996), among others, increasingly converges with cognitively oriented approaches to eighteenth-century melodic-harmonic schemata represented by Leonard B. Meyer (1973) and Robert O. Gjerdingen (1988, 2007). That these two streams meet in the eighteenth century testifies to the strong cognitive component of eighteenth-century music theory mentioned earlier, which motivates my own historically informed and cognitively oriented approach to meter and rhythm. Even more important, both these streams are driven by a common impulse "to approach the music and musical precepts of the 18th century in much the same way a listener of that time would have done" (Ratner 1980: xvi). Although this impulse has been criticized for its "naïveté" (Christensen 1993), it need not be taken naïvely. To be sure, we probably cannot hear eighteenth-century music the same way it was heard by its historical listeners (even if we could, we wouldn't know it), but we can try to reconstruct the "historical listener" of the eighteenth century—one equipped with the theoretical knowledge of the time (which can be learned from historical treatises) and with a cognitive mechanism supposedly not different from that of today's listeners (which thus can be studied empirically and modelled theoretically). We can also propose this reconstruction as an alternative mode of listening to eighteenth-century music. While this mode may be more demanding than those inherited from the nineteenth and twentieth centuries, it may be also more rewarding, as it turns today's listener from a passive consumer into an active partner of the eighteenth-century composer in a game played with the compositional rules of the time.

This last remark explains the choice of musical repertory analyzed in this study. In the late eighteenth century, the role of listeners as partners in a game proposed by a composer was particularly prominent in the string quartet. In this genre, which predominantly addressed *Kenner*, at least part of the audience could have reasonably been expected to possess the theoretical knowledge necessary to participate in such a game with understanding and delight. This is why

I illustrate metric manipulations in late eighteenth-century music with examples from Haydn's and Mozart's chamber music for strings. Within this repertory, I concentrate on compositions from 1787–91. They include Haydn's string quartet collections Op. 50, Op. 54/55, and Op. 64, and Mozart's "Prussian" Quartets, String Quintets K. 515, 516, 593, and 614, as well as the Divertimento for String Trio K. 563. While both sets of compositions are clearly delineated in their composers' chamber music—Haydn's middle string quartets, Mozart's late period of string chamber music—at the same time they display numerous stylistic affinities, pointing to presumably intense contacts between Haydn and Mozart in this period of their acquaintance and friendship in Vienna. So far, those affinities have not been much explored; most authors have concentrated instead on connections between Haydn's quartets Op. 33 and Mozart's "Haydn" Quartets (Einstein 1945; Steinbeck 1984; Bonds 1993; Irving 1998). Connections between Haydn's later quartets and Mozart's "Prussian" Quartets and quintets have been accounted for in terms of their form, texture, and thematic ideas (Rosen 1971; Schick 1994), if at all. Meter and rhythm feature prominently neither in the comparison of these works nor in analyses of individual pieces. The analyses included in this study are thus meant not only to illustrate a theoretical argument but also to cast light onto an insufficiently recognized aspect of otherwise famous works and in this way to extend a bridge from music theory to style analysis. The role of metric manipulations in Haydn's and Mozart's personal styles is summarized in chapter 8. Yet this conclusion is inconclusive. On the one hand, to understand the role of metric manipulations performed by Haydn and Mozart would require analytically applying theoretical concepts developed in this book to string chamber music from other periods and to other genres cultivated by these composers. On the other hand, this role cannot be fully appreciated within the confines of music theory. If playing with meter is frequently motivated on the rhetorical level by play with topics and form, this last level of play may have its motivation in a quasi-theatrical play enacted by means of chamber music. In relation to Haydn, this phenomenon was insightfully described by Wheelock (1992). Her concepts frame my discussion in chapter 8. But with this further widening of the conceptual horizon, I ultimately step out of the area of music theory and into that of aesthetics. While this step was customarily taken by eighteenth-century music theorists, it is only rarely risked by music theorists today. I leave this thread loose as a temptation to myself and an invitation to others to undertake it in the future.

NOTE ON TERMINOLOGY, LANGUAGE, AND MUSICAL EXAMPLES

In the course of this book I frequently refer to eighteenth-century German terminology concerning meter. Many of these terms are hardly translatable into English. If translated, they must be rendered as longer expressions rather than single words, which makes the translation cumbersome. Furthermore, their translations in modern English editions of historical treatises by Kirnberger, Koch, and Türk are incongruent. The most natural solution to these problems is to preserve the terms in their original German forms. This leads to occasional amendments in passages quoted from existing English translations. All references to translations are followed by references to the original sources in square brackets to enable the reader to consult the German text. For passages not yet translated into English, the original text is provided in the notes.

My usage of gender-specific pronouns is partly conditioned by the realities of eighteenth-century musical life. Since eighteenth-century composers and performers of string quartets were to my knowledge almost exclusively male, I refer to them with masculine pronouns while reserving feminine pronouns for listeners, even though eighteenth- and twenty-first-century listeners to string quartets were and are both female and male.

The texts of musical examples from Mozart's string chamber music are based on *Neue Mozart Ausgabe* (*NMA*; Mozart 1961, 1967, 1975) and from Haydn's Op. 64 string quartets on *Joseph Haydn Werke* (*JHW*; Haydn 1978). For examples from Haydn's Op. 50 and Op. 54/55, which at the time of preparing my manuscript for publication were not yet available from *JHW*, I rely on the new Peters edition (Haydn 2003, 2004).

Metric Manipulations in Haydn and Mozart

CHAPTER One

Musical Meter between Composition and Perception

1.1. The Concept of Meter in the Late Eighteenth Century

The eighteenth century was a time of change in conceptualizing musical meter.[1] The older concept of meter, predominant early in the century, was based on the principle of division. Its point of departure and hence the central level of metrical hierarchy was the measure. Duration represented by a rhythmical value equivalent to one measure was subdivided into shorter durations. By recursively applying this operation to lower metrical levels, music theorists were able to account for various metrical hierarchies encountered in individual pieces. This concept of meter, indebted to the earlier mensural theory, was most authoritatively advocated by Johann Mattheson. Yet in the further course of the century, it was gradually dissolved by such authors as Johann Adolph Scheibe, Friedrich Wilhelm Marpurg, and others.[2] What crystallized in their writings was a new concept of meter that was destined to dominate the scene of music theory from the late eighteenth century until well into the nineteenth. Its accounts come first from Johann Philipp Kirnberger and his pupil Johann Abraham Peter Schulz, who penned articles about music in Johann Georg Sulzer's *Allgemeine Theorie der schönen Künste* (1771–74). Both writers authored the article "Rhythmus" in the fourth volume of Sulzer's encyclopedia. The article "Takt," from the same volume, was written by Schulz alone.[3] These general formulations were subsequently

1. This change is discussed by Wilhelm Seidel (1975) in terms of transition between two opposite principles called by him Division and Progression. In the terminology adopted in my study, the latter term corresponds to grouping.
2. Details of this process and its consequences for different interpretations of 4/4 meter in the course of the eighteenth century are traced by Nicole Schwindt-Gross (1989).
3. The division of labor between Sulzer, Kirnberger, and Schulz in writing articles about music is described by Sulzer in the preface to the second volume of the original edition. In his account, articles from the first volume (letters *A–K*) were written by himself and Kirnberger. Schulz wrote all articles from the letter *S* until the end and helped with earlier articles in the second volume spanning

elaborated by Kirnberger in his comprehensive handbook of composition, *Die Kunst des reinen Satzes* (1771–79). One decade later, the discussion of *Takt* was undertaken once again by Heinrich Christoph Koch, in the second volume of his *Versuch einer Anleitung zur Composition* (1787).

In all these writings, the point of departure for defining musical meter is not a single duration but a series of equal and equidistant beats (*Schläge*). In the article "Rhythmus," Kirnberger and Schulz illustrate them with images of completely undifferentiated tones produced by regularly falling raindrops, hammer beats, drumbeats, or tones of one string: "To return to the image of drumbeats, when we imagine a succession of equal beats following each other in equal time intervals as points of equal size set in equal distances from each other [as shown in Example 1.1], then we have the concept of the simplest order in the succession of things: the lowest and weakest degree of rhythm [*Rhythmus*]."[4] According to Kirnberger and Schulz, such beats could be counted as an infinite series of numbers: one–two–three–four–five–six and so on. As the further course of the argument makes clear, however, their regularity is not yet meter at all. For meter to arise, a second-order regularity must be superimposed on the otherwise undifferentiated beats. This is achieved through accents recurring at regular time intervals within the original series: "Now, if one wanted to introduce one more degree of order, this would have to happen in such a way that the beats are not equally strong but the stronger and the weaker beats alternate according to some constant rule.... Thus one would notice that, apart from the order of the equal time intervals, the beats also follow always in pairs—one strong and one weak—like these points [in Example 1.2]. Here begins already what in music we call meter."[5] Meter in the proper sense of the word is therefore a "double uniformity" (*doppelte Einförmigkeit*) as it forms a hierarchical interconnection of two regular series to be counted by means of cyclically recurring shorter series of numbers, in this case one–two, one–two, one–two.

from the letter *L* up to *R*. Schulz himself offers a more specific account of his contribution in a later article he published in *Allgemeine musikalische Zeitung* (1800). According to him, Sulzer entrusted him with the task of helping Kirnberger to order his thorough theoretical knowledge in written form. "From the article 'Preludiren' up to the letter S—apart from the article 'System,' which was already finished, and the first half of the article 'Recitativ'—Sulzer had only little contribution to the musical articles" ("Von dem Artikel Preludiren bis zu dem Buchstaben S hat Sulzer, ausser dem Artikel System, der schon fertig war, und der ersten Hälfte des Artikels Recitativ, nur noch wenigen Antheil an den musikalischen Artikeln") (Schulz 1800: cols. 277–78).

4. "Wenn wir uns also, um wieder auf die Schläge der Trommel zu kommen, eine Folge von gleichen Schlägen nach gleichen Zeittheilen auf einander kommend, unter dem Bilde gleichgroßer und in gleicher Entfernung von einander gesetzter Puncte vorstellen, [Example 1.1]: so haben wir einen Begriff von der einfachsten Ordnung in der Folge der Dinge, den untersten und schwächesten Grad des Rhythmus" (Kirnberger and Schulz 1794: 92).

5. "Wollte man nun hier einen Grad der Ordnung mehr hineinbringen, so müßte es dadurch geschehen, daß die Schläge nicht gleich stark wären, die stärkern und schwächern aber nach einer festen Regel abwechselten.... Alsdenn würde man außer der Ordnung der gleichen Zeitfolge auch die bemerken, daß die Schläge immer paarweise, ein starker und ein schwacher folgten, wie diese Punkte [Example 1.2]. Hier fängt nun schon das an, was wir in der Musik den Takt nennen" (Kirnberger and Schulz 1794: 92).

Example 1.1. Kirnberger and Schulz, "Rhythmus," 92.

Example 1.2. Kirnberger and Schulz, "Rhythmus," 92.

From the quotation above, it follows that Kirnberger and Schulz require accents to be of a phenomenal character. In other words, the beats of a series must display acoustical differences of intensity that make the second-order regularity perceivable for the listener. Kirnberger and Schulz emphasize this by stating that "in fact, it would not yet be a real meter, were it not that something in the beats themselves is felt to give rise to this division into groups of two, three, or more parts."[6] The same opinion is implicit in Schulz's article "Takt" (1794: 491) but not in Kirnberger's discussion of meter in *Die Kunst des reinen Satzes*. On the view exposed there, no phenomenal accent is absolutely necessary for the listener to have a sense of meter. In an undifferentiated series of beats, subjective accents will arise by virtue of the cognitive mechanism that tends to impose a mental organization on otherwise unorganized stimuli: "If one hears a succession of equal pulses [*Schlägen*] that are repeated at the same time interval, as in [Example 1.3], experience teaches us that we immediately divide them metrically in our minds by arranging them in groups containing an equal number of pulses; and we do this in such a way that we put an accent on the first pulse of each group or imagine hearing it stronger than the others. This division can occur in three ways, as shown in [Example 1.4]." (Kirnberger 1982: 383 [1776: 114–15]).

Example 1.3. Kirnberger, *Die Kunst des reinen Satzes*, vol. 2, sec.1, 115.

Example 1.4. Kirnberger, *Die Kunst des reinen Satzes*, vol. 2, sec. 1, 115.

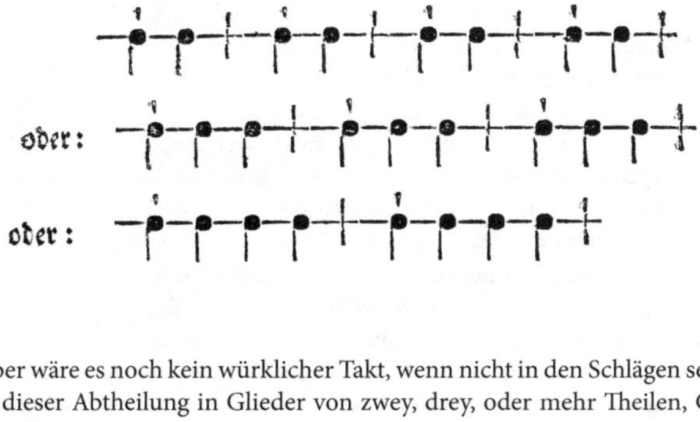

6. "In der That aber wäre es noch kein würklicher Takt, wenn nicht in den Schlägen selbst etwas gefühlt würde, das zu dieser Abtheilung in Glieder von zwey, drey, oder mehr Theilen, Gelegenheit gäbe" (Kirnberger and Schulz 1794: 94).

The existence of such a cognitive mechanism was assumed also by Koch (1787). Because Koch claims that this mechanism resides "in the nature of our senses and our powers of imagination"[7]—in other words, that it is an inherent, cognitive mechanism of human perception—he would presumably endorse Kirnberger's interpretation above. Yet in contrast to Kirnberger, he illustrates the working of this mechanism in an example drawn from the area of visual perception:

> Suppose that one looks at a certain number of objects of the same species and type, for example a rope of pearls of the same color and size, or a certain number of billiard balls that adjoin at more than one point. If one wants not merely to contemplate these objects blankly but, for example, to count them, one will not be able to do so as long as one imagines certain resting points [*Ruhepuncte*] through which to draw a distinction between a certain number of them and the others. This single example can suffice to convince us that, if several objects of one and the same species and type act upon one of our senses in such a manner that from their particular combination our imagination cannot extract a resting point in order to draw a distinction among them, we are then required to imagine ourselves such resting points [*Ruhepuncte der Vorstellung*], through which we are enabled to draw distinctions among them and reflect upon them.[8]

The reference to vision rather than to audition is connected to the different position taken by Koch in his discussion of meter. Kirnberger takes the position of the listener confronted with a series of identical beats as acoustical stimuli, whereas Koch takes the position of a performer—singer or player—in front of a stave showing a series of identical notes that he or she is supposed to execute.[9] According to Koch, such identical notes form a graphical object analogous to a rope of pearls; it will thus be organized in the performer's mind by means of resting points of the imagination (*Ruhepunkte der Vorstellung*). The resting points will, in turn, manifest themselves acoustically in the performance as stress (*Nachdruck*) or weight (*Gewicht*): "As soon as one looks, for instance, at the following six quarter notes

7. "In der Natur unserer Sinnen und unserer Vorstellungskraft" (Koch 1787: 278).
8. "Man betrachte eine Anzahl Gegenstände einerley Art und Gattung, z. B. eine Schnur angereiheter Perlen von gleicher Farbe und Größe, oder eine gewisse Anzahl Billiardkugeln die einander an mehr als einem Orte berühren; will man diese Gegenstände nicht gedankenlos ansehen, sondern sie z. B. zählen, so ist man dieses zu thun nicht eher im Stande, bis man sich in den Gedanken gewisse Ruhepuncte vorstelle, durch welche man eine gewisse Anzahl derselben von den andern scheidet. Dieses einzige Beyspiel kann hinreichend seyn uns zu überzeugen, daß, wenn mehrere Gegenstände einerley Art und Gattung dergestalt auf einen unserer Sinne würken, daß unsere Vorstellung bey der Art ihrer Vereinigung keine Ruhepuncte gewinnen kann, sie von einander zu unterscheiden, wir alsdenn genöthigt sind, uns selbst solche Ruhepuncte der Vorstellung hinzu zu denken, durch welche wir sie zu unterscheiden und zu betrachten vermögend sind" (Koch 1787: 278); the English translation of this quotation is based, in part, on Hasty (1997: 27).
9. In his discussion of Koch's metric theory, Hasty (1997: 26–31) misreads this part of Koch's argument, presenting it as if it concerned the listener and her ability to group beats of an acoustically undifferentiated series in the way postulated by Kirnberger. This misreading was subsequently adopted by London in the entry "Rhythm" in *The New Grove Dictionary* (2001: 280) and in his recent book *Hearing in Time* (2004: 15).

[Example 1.5] with the intention of performing them, that is, when one wants to sing or play them, one is forced to select among them certain resting points of the imagination [*Ruhepunkte der Vorstellung*], and so to mark this or that tone as such a resting point, which means also to give it a certain weight [*Gewicht*] or a certain stress [*Nachdruck*] in the performance, [a stress] that is lacking from the other tones that do not form such resting points of the imagination."[10]Although later in his treatise Koch characterizes resting points (*Ruhepunkte*) as points of division (*Abteilungspunkte*), he uses the word "division" in a different sense than does Mattheson earlier in the century, in that Koch's sense applies not to a single duration of a measure (*Takt*) but to a series of consecutive beats.[11] From the perspective of those beats, *Ruhepunkte* are a means not of division but of grouping. They group beats into measures (*Takte*). Koch refers to this operation when he says that, in a given measure, beats are united "under the perspective of" one *Ruhepunkt* (282). Several possible types of metric organization imposed on beats by resting points are represented by Koch in the following series of musical examples (Example 1.6).

Example 1.5. Koch, *Versuch einer Anleitung zur Composition*, vol. 2, 279.

Example 1.6. Koch, *Versuch einer Anleitung zur Composition*, vol. 2, 280–81, figs. 1–4.

10. "Sobald man z. B. folgende sechs Viertelnoten [Example 1.5] in Absicht auf Vortrag betrachtet, das ist, wenn man sie singen oder spielen will, sobald ist man auch gezwungen, sich unter denselben gewisse Ruhepuncte der Vorstellung zu denken, und also diesen oder jenen Ton als einen solchen Ruhepunct zu bezeichnen, das heißt, ihm auch ein gewisses Gewicht oder einen gewissen Nachdruck bey dem Vortrage zu geben, welcher den übrigen Tönen mangelt, die nicht solche Ruhepuncte der Vorstellung ausmachen" (Koch 1787: 279–80).
11. For an exhaustive discussion of this difference see Seidel (1975: 90–91).

In spite of the new relationship between beats and measures, based on grouping, Koch refers to beats contained in measures as *Taktteile* (parts of the measure), thus paying tribute to the older concept of meter based on division. The difference between *Taktteile* that carry *Ruhepunkte* and those that do not is rendered by Koch in the following equivalent pairs of concepts, which he compiles from many eighteenth-century treatises: *Thesis* and *Arsis*, "good" (*gut*) and "bad" (*schlecht*), "intrinsically long" (*innerlich lang*) and "intrinsically short" (*innerlich kurz*), downbeat (*Niederschlag*) and upbeat (*Aufschlag*).[12] This difference also applies to beats of the lower metrical levels, called by Koch members of the measure (*Taktglieder*) and notes of the measure (*Taktnoten*). In his musical examples, accented and unaccented beats of those levels are represented by the prosodic symbols — and ◡, derived from the poetic feet of Latin verse. Owing to the existence of lower levels, the primary hierarchical interconnection between *Takte* and *Taktteile* extends down into a broader metrical hierarchy.[13] Despite the fact that the relationships of accented and unaccented beats occur on all levels of this hierarchy, individual levels are nevertheless not equivalent to each other. The eighteenth-century metrical hierarchy is centered around the level of *Taktteile*. It is only to this level that *Ruhepunkte* properly apply. As primitive beats of the original series, *Taktteile* are grouped by *Ruhepunkte* into *Takte*, but for themselves, they do not arise from the grouping of lower-level beats. Rather, the lower-level beats arise through divisions of *Taktteile* into *Taktglieder* and *Taktglieder* into *Taktnoten*. This last process bears similarity to the older concept of meter represented by Mattheson and others. Yet the operations of grouping and division—marking two directions of the metrical hierarchy, upward and downward, from the centrally situated *Taktteile*—are of different importance for the new concept of meter. The lower metrical levels are secondary, in that changes concerning the ratios of divisions through which they arise do not entail a change of meter.[14] Instead, the ratio of grouping, which determines the interconnection of *Taktteile* and *Takte,* is constitutive for meter and forms the basic criterion in classification of meters (*Taktarten*), which come into being through the assignment of different rhythmical values to the level of *Taktteile*.

The classification of meters shown in Table 1.1 combines classifications presented by Kirnberger and Koch in their composition handbooks.[15] Although both authors depart from the same set of basic theoretical premises and elaborate them into the same concept of meter, it is in the details of these classifications that differences between them come to the fore. The first difference concerns the range

12. The genesis of these various pairs of concepts is explained in Houle (1987: 78–84).
13. Descriptions of such metrical hierarchy graphically represented by means of prosodic symbols — and ◡ occur already in Schulz (1794) and Kirnberger (1776), but these authors do not elaborate any terminology comparable in clarity and consistency with Koch's. The level corresponding to that of *Taktteile* is termed by them alternately *Zeiten, Zahlzeiten*, or *Hauptzeiten*; lower metrical levels have no proper names. Although the terms used by Kirnberger and Schulz suit the new concept of meter better than Koch's *Taktteile,* for the sake of uniformity throughout this study I follow Koch's terminology.
14. This point is emphasized by Seidel (1975: 111).
15. Kirnberger's classification of meters is equivalent to that presented earlier by Schulz in the article "Takt" (1794), which was most likely written under Kirnberger's influence.

Table 1.1 Classification of meters by Kirnberger (1776) and Koch (1787)

Simple duple meters		Simple triple meters		Simple quadruple meters (Kirnberger)	
Ordinary	Mixed (Koch) Tripled (Kirnberger)	Ordinary	Mixed (Koch) Tripled (Kirnberger)	Ordinary	Tripled
2/1 (ϕ)	6/2	3/1	9/2		
2/2 (Ç)	6/4	**3/2**	9/4	4/2 (o)	12/4
2/4	**6/8**	**3/4**	**9/8**	4/4 (c)	12/8
2/8	6/16	**3/8**	9/16	4/8	12/16
		3/16	9/32		
Compound duple meters		Compound triple meters			
4/2 (c) = 2/2+2/2		6/2 = 3/2 + 3/2			
4/4 (c) = 2/4+2/4	**12/8 = 6/8 + 6/8**	**6/4 = 3/4 + 3/4**			
4/8 = 2/8 + 2/8	12/16 = 6/16+6/16	**6/8 = 3/8 + 3/8**			
		6/16 = 3/16 + 3/16			

of rhythmical values assigned to *Taktteile*: The conservatively minded Kirnberger gives a full account of all meters known to the earlier generation of composers—with the values of *Taktteile* reaching from sixteenths to whole notes—even if some of them, as he himself admits, are no longer in practical use. Koch, oriented mainly toward the modern, galant style of instrumental music, lists only meters used by his contemporaries. (In Table 1.1, the meters mentioned by Koch are shown in bold print.) The second difference between classifications of meters by Kirnberger and Koch originates in a theoretical controversy concerning the number of beats that can be grouped according to one accent or, in Koch's parlance, "united under one perspective." As shown earlier in Example 1.4 and explicated in the accompanying commentary, Kirnberger assumes a natural grouping of two, three, or four beats by a single accent. Consequently, he acknowledges two classes of simple even meter (*einfache gerade Taktart*)—duple and quadruple—in addition to one class of odd (*ungerade*) triple meter. For Koch, instead, one *Ruhepunkt* can unite only two or three *Taktteile*. Consequently, he accepts only duple and triple meters as simple: the former as the only representative of even meters and the latter as the only representative of odd meters. His view was more popular in the eighteenth century, as it corresponded with the opinions of most other music theorists, including Mattheson, Scheibe, and Marpurg.[16] Quadruple simple meters, described by Kirnberger and represented in the right column of Table 1.1, are not included in Koch's classification.

Among simple meters, both Kirnberger and Koch distinguish a special group of meters characterized by the triple subdivision of *Taktteile* into *Taktglieder*. In Kirnberger, they are described as meters of triple beats or tripled meters (*triplierte Taktarten*). Koch, following Marpurg, calls them mixed meters (*vermischte Taktarten*). The existence of this class requires explanation in light of my earlier remark that the ratio of the division under the level of *Taktteile* has no bearing on metric classification. Indeed, as Koch admits, *Taktglieder* arising from a triple division of *Taktteile* could be notated as triplets under an ordinary time signature, such as 2/4, but in practice this is acceptable only when the triplet motion is consistent throughout the piece. In cases when *Taktglieder* are divided further into *Taktnoten* or when, conversely, they are occasionally joined together into triplet quarters or, finally, when *Taktglieder* and *Taktnoten* make up dotted rhythms, the result is a notation that would be confusing for the performer. In order to avoid this confusion, it suffices to endow rhythmical values of *Taktteile* with a dot: in 2/4 this would mean to write them as dotted quarters instead of quarters. Yet, since dotted-rhythm values of *Taktteile* cannot be directly indicated by denominators of time signatures, these denominators, in the case of mixed meters, must refer to the level of *Taktglieder*. In this way, in Koch's classification, 2/4 turns into 6/8. Similarly, the ordinary simple meter 3/4 turns into mixed 9/8.[17]

16. For a detailed discussion of various classifications of meters in the earlier half of the eighteenth century in Germany and beyond, see Houle (1987: 35–61).

17. The explanations concerning mixed meters summarized in the foregoing passage occur in Koch (1787: 322–28).

In addition to simple meters—whether ordinary or mixed—a separate class discussed by Kirnberger and Koch is that of compound meters (*zusammengesetzte Taktarten*; shown in the lower part of Table 1.1). Every measure of such meters is made up of two simple measures. Consequently, one notated measure of compound meters contains two accents. As is explained by both authors, the rationale behind compounding measures is to avoid an excessive number of bar lines. This process "does not change anything about the nature of individual measures" because accents falling at the beginnings of two simple measures contained in one compound measure are equal. "It therefore does not matter whether one avails himself of a simple or compound meter to represent a given melody."[18] Apart from this "notational" type of compound meter, Kirnberger describes a different type in which accents are *not* equal: "In duple as well as in triple meter, there are melodies in which it is obvious that whole measures are alternately strong and weak, so that a whole measure is heard as only one beat. If the melody is of such a nature that the entire measure is felt as only one beat, two measures must be grouped together to form just one, whose first part is accented and the other unaccented" (Kirnberger 1982: 398 [1776: 131]). On the one hand, this "hierarchical" type of compound meter—not known to Koch—is a conservative trait of Kirnberger's theory of meter, in that it retains elements of Mattheson's theory (see Schwindt-Gross 1989). On the other hand, it can be considered progressive because it contains a germ of the idea of hypermeter, which was to be systematically developed by music theorists in the nineteenth century (Rothstein 2008). Since I postpone my discussion of hypermeter to another study, in the further course of this study the hierarchical type of compound meter will not play any significant role. Interestingly enough, although Kirnberger admits the existence of quadruple simple meters, he does not allow for compound meters arising from them. Tripled versions of triple meters yield compound meters in neither Kirnberger's nor Koch's classifications.

It should be noted that all time signatures of compound meters occur in other slots of the table in reference to simple meters. Among the meters discussed by Koch, this concerns in particular 6/8, which may be considered either as compound, with every notated measure comprising two simple 3/8 measures, or as a mixed meter derived from ordinary 2/4. Although these meters feature the same size of notated measures and the same structure of the metrical hierarchy, they differ as to the rhythmical values assigned to the level of *Taktteile*. In the compound 6/8 meter, the *Taktteil* is the eighth note, as is indicated by the denominator of the time signature; in the simple (mixed) 6/8 meter, the *Taktteil* is the dotted

18. "Die Ursache dieses Verfahrens mag entweder seyn, nicht nöthig zu haben, allzuviele Tactstriche zu schreiben, oder sie mag seyn, bey Tonstücken, bey welchen der Gewohnheit zu Folge der Tact gegeben wird, dem Director das allzu öftere Tactschlagen zu überheben, so wird durch dieses Zusammensetzen zweyer einfachen Tacte, in die äußerliche Form eines einzigen Tactes nichts in der Natur des Tactes selbst abgeändert, so lange man dabey nicht ausser Acht läßt, daß jeder Tact einer solchen zusammen gesetzten Tactart zwey Tacte einer einfachen Tactart enthält. Es ist daher völlig einerley, ob man sich zur Vorstellung einer Melodie einer einfachen oder zusammen gesetzten Tactgattung bedienet" (Koch 1787: 332).

quarter. The difference between the two versions of 6/8 is thus analogous to that between 2/2 and 4/4, which normally bear the different time signatures ¢ and c.[19] In Kirnberger's classification, an additional equivocation concerns 4/4 (c) and its tripled version 12/8 as either compound or simple meters. Although the rhythmical values of *Taktteile* are identical in both versions of these meters, the difference between them concerns the level of composed *Takte* and, consequently, the number of accents occurring in one notated measure. In measures of simple 4/4 and 12/8, there is only one accent falling on the first *Taktteil*. In compound 4/4 and 12/8, two accents fall on the first and the third *Taktteil*, respectively, of every measure, marking the strong beats of the simple measures 2/4 and 6/8 contained in them.[20]

Because in eighteenth-century music theory meter was defined by the interconnection of *Taktteile* and *Takte*, each occurrence of a given time signature in Table 1.1 indicates a different meter. Learning to distinguish between them and to use them properly in notation was part of the fundamental training of every beginning composer. As I will show later in this study, equivocations between different meters bearing the same time signature were also an important aspect of some of the compositional strategies employed by the masters. If contemporary music theory became oblivious to these distinctions, this has to do with the change in the status of music theory that took place between the late eighteenth century and the present day, turning theory from the handmaiden of composition into an independent discipline dealing primarily with music analysis and perception. Because the differences—residing in the levels of *Taktteile* and/or *Takte*—between meters indicated by the same time signature cannot be ascertained perceptually, they were judged to be irrelevant.[21] Consequently, the level of *Taktteile*, central for the eighteenth-century metrical hierarchy, was eliminated from the contemporary concept of meter. Only the concept of metrical hierarchy as such was retained.

19. Sometimes the same time signature c is used for both meters, however, as was pointed out by Koch (1787: 295). In addition, Schulz (1794) and Kirnberger (1776) distinguish between "large" (*der grosse*) and "small" 4/4 meter (*der kleine Viervierteltakt*). The former is "suited primarily to church piece, choruses and fugues" (Kirnberger 1982: 391 [1776: 123]), whereas the latter can be used in all styles. Although both of them can be indicated by c, in order to distinguish the former from the latter, the authors suggest the signature 4/4 for the "large" and c for the "small." Schulz remarks (1794: 496) that some composers indicate the "large" 4/4 meter with 4/2 instead of 4/4. This meter is, however, of no practical relevance in this study.
20. Apart from the main accent on the downbeat, Kirnberger (1982: 392 [1776: 124]) assumes an additional, subordinated accent on the third beat in simple quadruple meter. His opinion differs from that of his pupil, Schulz (1794: 497), who emphasizes that all weak beats of quadruple simple meter must be performed equally, without any accentuation whatsoever. According to Schulz, an accent on the third beat is proper only in compound meter. As a matter of fact, the pattern of accentuation specified by Kirnberger for simple quadruple meter is identical to that of his "hierarchical" type of compound meter discussed above.
21. Characteristic in this respect is the opinion expressed by Richard Cohn: "A measure of 'compound' 6/8, two measures of 'simple' 3/8, and a measure of 'simple' tripled 2/4 all manifest [2 3] relation and, more importantly, are indistinguishable to perception" (1992a: 195 n. 23). The bracketed factors, which form integral part of the preceding quotation, indicate ratios between neighboring metrical levels.

1.2. The Revival of the Hierarchical Concept of Meter in the Twentieth Century

The twentieth-century renewal of music-theoretical interest in meter and rhythm brought a revival of the hierarchical concept of meter characteristic of the eighteenth century. In two books that became seminal for the study of meter and rhythm in American music theory of the last few decades—*The Rhythmic Structure of Music*, by Grosvenor Cooper and Leonard B. Meyer (1960), and *The Stratification of Musical Rhythm*, by Maury Yeston (1976)—the authors follow clearly in the footsteps of Kirnberger, Schulz, and Koch, referring to the image of an infinite series of equidistant beats and defining meter as arising from a second-order regularity superimposed on such a series by accents.[22] This is perhaps most evident in Yeston. Apparently unaware of his close connection with the eighteenth-century authors, Yeston in fact retraces their line of argument and, in part, even their examples. His representation of the infinite series of beats to be counted by means of an infinite row of numerals (Example 1.7) closely corresponds with that offered two centuries earlier by Kirnberger and Schulz (Example 1.1). In turn, the double series counted as an alternation "one–two, one–two" (Example 1.8) is equivalent to the representation shown by Kirnberger and Schulz in Example 1.2. Remarks concerning the nature of meter made by Yeston in his commentary parallel those that an interested reader of the eighteenth century could find under the entry "Rhythmus" in Sulzer's encyclopedia: "The fundamental logical requirement for meter is therefore that there be a constant rate within a constant rate—at least

Example 1.7. Yeston, *The Stratification of Musical Rhythm*, 65.

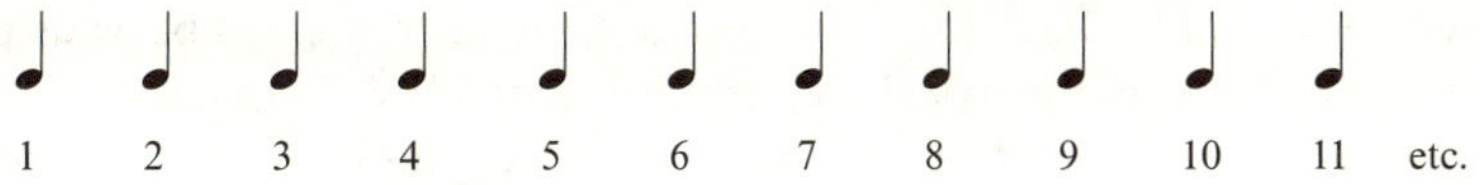

Example 1.8. Yeston, *The Stratification of Musical Rhythm*, 66.

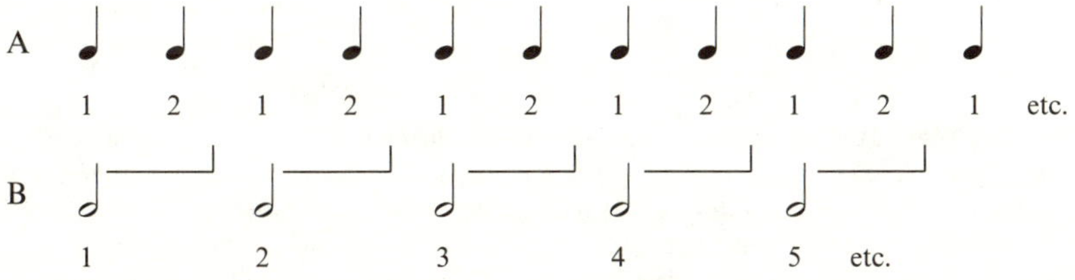

22. Two other books published in the same period, in which rhythm and meter take an important place, are Edward T. Cone's *Musical Form and Musical Performance* (1968) and Arthur Komar's *Theory of Suspensions* (1971). Komar's definition of meter begins not from an image of equidistant beats but from a duration divided into a whole number of equal portions. In so doing, it is close to the early eighteenth-century position represented by Mattheson. Cone does not formulate any definition. The most significant contribution of his book to the study of meter is the notion of "hypermeasure," which—as already indicated—will be further explored in a separate study.

two rates of events of which one is faster and another is slower. . . . Meter is an outgrowth of the interaction of two levels—two differently-rated strata, the faster of which provides the elements and the slower of which groups them" (Yeston 1976: 65–66). Clearly, the "constant rate within a constant rate," postulated by Yeston in this passage as the fundamental requirement for meter, is merely a modern version of Kirnberger and Schulz's idea of "double uniformity" (*doppelte Einförmigkeit*).[23]

In the series of valuable publications following Yeston's book, a special place belongs to Fred Lerdahl and Ray Jackendoff's *A Generative Theory of Tonal Music* (1983). In this ground-breaking volume, *metrical structure* is only one of four components theorized by the authors, the others being *grouping structure*, *time-span reduction*, and *prolongational reduction*.[24] The influence of Yeston and—through his (perhaps unconscious) mediation—the eighteenth-century authors on Lerdahl and Jackendoff's generative theory of tonal music (GTTM) is apparent in their assumption that "it is the interaction of different levels of beats (or the regular alternation of strong and weak beats at a given level) that produces the sensation of meter" (68). As did the eighteenth-century authors, Lerdahl and Jackendoff relate metrical accent, or "strong beat," to the idea of metrical hierarchy. But whereas in the eighteenth-century theory of meter, accents—whether phenomenal or mental—made the hierarchy of metrical levels possible, for Lerdahl and Jackendoff it is the metrical hierarchy that generates accents: "For beats to be strong or weak there must exist a metrical hierarchy—two or more levels of beats. The relationship of 'strong beat' to 'metrical level' is simply that, if a beat is felt to be strong at a particular level, it is also a beat at the next larger level" (19). This metrical hierarchy is graphically represented by Lerdahl and Jackendoff as a hierarchy of dots (Example 1.9). As they point out, the superiority of the dot format over the traditional prosodic notation of metrical accents by means of the symbols — and ◡ lies in the fact that dots better represent beats as points in time. Moreover, every metrical level is represented here as one row of dots. It is interesting to observe that, although the prosodic notation was most common in the eighteenth century, by introducing the dot format Lerdahl and Jackendoff actually turn back to the original representation of beats as dots by Kirnberger and Schulz (Example 1.1).

23. Although Yeston's definition of meter became most influential, it does not essentially differ from definitions offered by other authors. Cooper and Meyer define meter as "the measurement of the number of pulses between more or less regularly recurring accents" (1960: 4). For Carl Schachter, "it is a truism that meter arises out of the interaction of strong and weak beats. That means that meter will never result from a single string of equal time spans. At least two series must be present, coordinated so that all points that demarcate the longer spans at higher levels simultaneously mark off shorter spans at all lower levels" (1976: 5). Frank Samarotto clearly echoes Yeston when he defines meter as "regular pulse grouped by another regular pulse" (1999b: 48). Most recently, Yeston's graphical representations have been adopted by London in his study of psychological aspects of meter (2004: 17).

24. As was pointed out independently by Jonathan Kramer (1988: 98) and Richard Parncutt (1994: 411), the distinction drawn by Lerdahl and Jackendoff between grouping structure and metrical structure involves a terminological problem because meter, too, is a kind of grouping. At times in the course of this study this problem will be palpable.

Example 1.9. Lerdahl and Jackendoff, *A Generative Theory of Tonal Music*, 19, ex. 2.7.

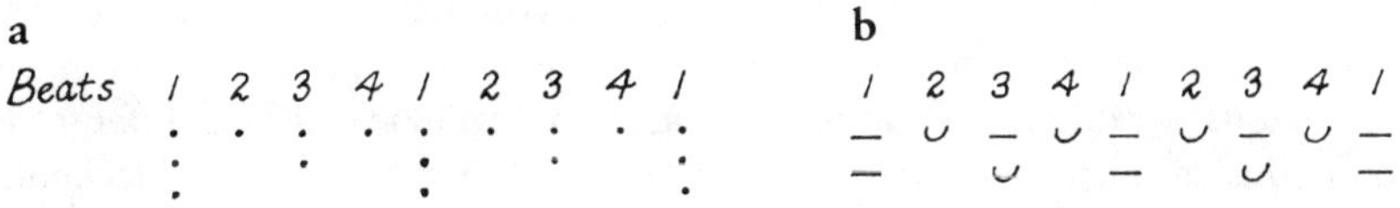

The formal characteristics of the metrical hierarchy underlying the idiom of tonal music are summarized by Lerdahl and Jackendoff in the set of Metrical Well-Formedness Rules (MWFRs). These include equal spacing of beats on a given metrical level (MWFR 4), hierarchical interconnection of levels (MWFR 2), and spacing of higher-level beats two or three beats apart on the next lower level (MWFR 3). According to MWFR 1, "every attack point must be associated with a beat at the smallest level of metrical structure." Although Lerdahl and Jackendoff include this rule in their list of MWFRs, it has a different status in that it refers not to the formal characteristics of metrical structure as such but to the correspondence of metrical structure with a given musical surface.[25] The metrical hierarchy emerging from these tentative formulations of MWFRs, similar as it is to the eighteenth-century metrical hierarchy, differs from the eighteenth-century one in that it has no central level. Because the relations between levels determined in MWFR 3 are recursive across the metrical hierarchy, all levels are equivalent to each other and can be constructed uniformly: either upward, by the grouping together of two or three beats of lower levels, or downward, by the dividing of higher-level time spans into two or three parts. Acknowledging the inadequacy of such a view of meter, which is thus seen "as though each metrical level is as salient as every other" (1983: 71), the authors revise MWFRs so as to introduce one privileged level of beats, called the *tactus*. Since this Latin term, borrowed from the mensural theory of the Renaissance, was translated into German in the early eighteenth century as *Takt,* one might think that it would correspond to "measure." Yet this is not what it means for Lerdahl and Jackendoff. Rather, the tactus is defined by them as "the minimal metrical level that is required to be continuous throughout the piece" (71). On the basis of this definition and the central position this level has in the metrical hierarchy, one might, again, be inclined to identify beats of the tactus with *Taktteile*, the series of equidistant beats that is fundamental to the late eighteenth-century concept of meter. Indeed, in many cases the tactus may correspond with what the eighteenth-century theorists would indicate as the level of *Taktteile*. Yet this need not always be so. For in reality, these two concepts are quite different. Whereas the concept of *Taktteile* has a theoretical character and applies to the level assumed a priori as central by the composer, the level of tactus is perceptual and derived from the musical surface by the listener. In choosing the term *tactus*, Lerdahl and Jackendoff were guided not so much by its connotations

25. The difference between MWFR 1 and other MWFRs can be accounted for in terms of the distinction between "correspondence rules" and "formation rules," as introduced by Jackendoff (1987: 220 n. 1) in relation to Grouping Well-Formedness Rules (GWFRs). According to him, GWFR 1 is a "correspondence rule," whereas the other GWFRs are formation rules.

in different historical periods of music theory as by its close connection with the familiar activity of "beating the time."[26] This becomes clear from their alternative definition of tactus as "the level of beats that is conducted and with which one most naturally coordinates foot-tapping and dance steps" (71). Not only can such a level occasionally differ from that of *Taktteile*, it can even be assigned differently to the same musical surface by different listeners. This is why Lerdahl and Jackendoff sometimes assume two alternative levels of tactus. Curiously enough, this happens in examples whose time signatures in the eighteenth century allowed for two different levels of *Taktteile*, thus inviting two different interpretations of a given meter as either simple or compound.[27]

The psychological orientation of Lerdahl and Jackendoff's metric theory comes even more to the fore in their discussion of Metrical Preference Rules (MPRs). Although many possible metrical structures fulfilling MWFRs can be assigned to every musical surface, it is MPRs that decide which metrical structure will actually be heard by the listener. These rules, which I will discuss in detail in the next chapter, embrace factors of both innate (universal) and learned (idiom-specific) character that cause a given beat to be heard as strong. The elaboration of the comprehensive set of MPRs makes Lerdahl and Jackendoff's theory of meter a theoretical model of metric perception. To the extent that this model is compatible with the late eighteenth-century concept of meter, it can account not only for manipulations of metric perception encountered in eighteenth-century music but also for the way these manipulations were construed by eighteenth-century composers. The model has, however, one disadvantage in fulfilling this task: MPRs are applied all at once to a given musical section and assign to it only one metrical structure, emerging near its end as the result of a certain cognitive process. Lerdahl and Jackendoff openly declare as much: "Instead of describing the listener's real-time mental processes, we will be concerned only with the final state of his understanding. In our view it would be fruitless to theorize about mental processing before understanding the organization to which the processing leads" (1983: 4). As a result of this methodological option, the model of meter developed by Lerdahl and Jackendoff is inherently static. The only aspect of metrical manipulations it can capture is the difference between *clear* and *vague* sensation of meter. Clear meter arises if the cues provided from the musical surface are regular and mutually supportive. "If there is little regularity to these cues, or if they conflict, the sense of metrical accent becomes attenuated or ambiguous" (17). But this does not suffice to account for all metric manipulations to be discussed in the course of this study, since many of them induce the listener to develop several representations of one musical passage successively. To provide just one analytical description of a passage when in fact the listener hears the passage in

26. The Latin term *tactus* means literally "beat" (Houle 1987: 1) and denotes "a unit of time measured by a movement of the hand" (Brown and Bockmaier 2008).

27. For instance, in the theme of Mozart's K. 331/i, notated in 6/8 meter, Lerdahl and Jackendoff (1983: 71–72) propose either eighths or dotted quarters as the tactus. Although recent psychological experiments (Parncutt 1994; Drake et al. 1997) demonstrate that the metrical level tapped by listeners can occasionally be that of measures, Lerdahl and Jackendoff never admit measures as the tactus. Instead, they clearly try to coordinate the tactus with metrical units. This suggests that even if they define tactus in purely psychological terms as "a perceptually prominent level of metrical structure" (71), their idea of this level is guided to some extent by theoretical considerations as well.

different ways as it continues results not only in obscuring a very important aspect of the listener's experience but also in ignoring a crucial part of the composer's strategy. What is needed for the description of such metrical manipulations is a dynamic theory of musical processing as an extension of Lerdahl and Jackendoff's model. As Jackendoff put it: "A theory of musical processing based on this theory [the GTTM] must show how the principles of the listener's internalized musical grammar can be deployed in real time to build musical representations. In particular, it must show that the rules used for idealized final-state analyses can actually be used to account for listeners' experiences as they hear a piece over time" (1992: 52).

1.3. Toward a Dynamic Model of Meter

The prospect of such a theory opened up when Jackendoff incorporated the GTTM into the theoretical perspective offered by the modular theory of mind espoused by Jerry Fodor. Fodor's *Modularity of Mind* was published the same year as Lerdahl and Jackendoff's work (1983) and had not influenced their original formulations. The assimilation and elaboration of Fodor's views into a broad theory of perception and cognition was accomplished by Jackendoff in his subsequent book *Consciousness and the Computational Mind* (1987). The assumption that the perception of music is analogous to the perception of language, which had already informed the conceptual background of the GTTM, eventually led to the conclusion that music perception, like language perception, is modular and that individual components of GTTM—among them metrical structure—correspond with modules that are responsible for various aspects of music perception in the tonal idiom.[28] To account for the internal workings of these modules, Jackendoff sketched in his book a model of a processor, which he developed in more detail in his later article "Musical Parsing and Musical Affect" (1991) and illustrated there with an analytic example from a Bach chorale.[29]

In the course of his analysis, Jackendoff observes that in deriving the abstract structure of this piece in real time, the processor confronts many points of indeterminacy that cannot be resolved until considerably later in the music. For instance, the two chords in Example 1.10 can form a succession of strong–weak, weak–strong, or two weak beats. In order to account for the way the processor deals with such situations, Jackendoff put forth three models based on linguistic parsers—processors designed to model analysis of sentences by the hearer: the *serial single-choice model*, the *serial indeterministic model*, and the *parallel multiple-analysis*

28. Jackendoff (1987: 262–65) calls these modules "integrative processors." He also postulates the existence of "translation processors," whose function is to make a representation elaborated in one module available to the other.

29. An abridged version of this article appeared the following year under the title "Musical Processing and Musical Affect" (1992). The fact that in the further course of this chapter I refer mostly to the 1992 version has to do with the change of terminology signaled in the title. Whereas in the original version Jackendoff called his model a "parser" and described its activity as "parsing," in the abridged version he uses the terms "processor" and "processing," which have since become commonly accepted in the cognitive study of music.

model. On closer inspection, the first two of these displayed logical problems: the choice of the best analysis—whether made after each piece of information, as in the serial single-choice model, or after a larger portion of information, as in the serial indeterministic model—entails comparison of several analyses that these processors by definition do not elaborate.[30] Hence only the parallel multiple-analysis model is a viable one. As Jackendoff explains, the idea behind this model is that "when the processor encounters a choice point among competing analyses, processing splits into simultaneous branches, each computing an analysis for one of the possibilities" (1992: 62). Such choice points may be encountered several times during a given musical passage, resulting in the processor elaborating a number of metric analyses in conformance with the set of MWFRs. By the end of the first measure of Bach's chorale, the processor will have elaborated the five analyses shown in Example 1.11. As illustrated by Jackendoff in a series of further examples, each of these analyses can receive a musically plausible continuation.

Example 1.10. Jackendoff, "Musical Parsing and Musical Affect," 204, fig. 3.

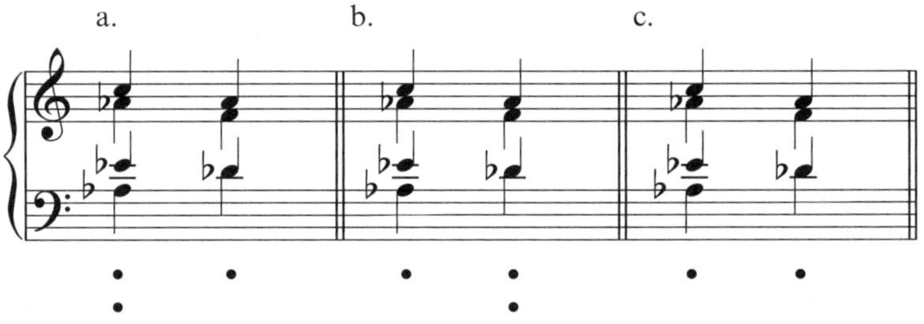

Example 1.11. Jackendoff, "Musical Parsing and Musical Affect," 207, fig. 10.

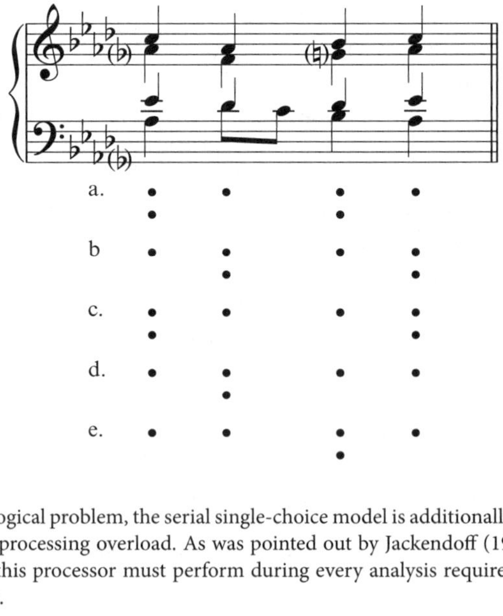

30. Apart from this logical problem, the serial single-choice model is additionally involved in the practical problem of processing overload. As was pointed out by Jackendoff (1991: 213), the amount of backtracking this processor must perform during every analysis requires an implausibly high processing speed.

Out of these analyses, however, only one will be consciously experienced by the listener. The reason for this lies in the *selection function*, postulated by Jackendoff as "a device that continuously evaluates the currently active analyses for relative plausibility and designates one of them as the currently most salient" (1992: 63). This evaluation is carried out on the basis of MPRs. As soon as enough evidence is collected by the selection function, it selects only one analysis. "This selected analysis will be the single one that appears in awareness as *the* structure of the music at this point" (63). But this analysis will not appear as if it started only at this point in a piece. Rather, it will be heard by the listener as if it "has been there" from the very beginning, for indeed, it was elaborated by the processor from the very beginning of a piece, albeit in parallel with other, alternative analyses. This perception is possible in every case when the process of selection is completed within the span of the short-term musical memory (STMM), during which all percepts and sensations are simultaneously available to attention, perception, and cognitive processing.[31]

What makes the parallel multiple-analysis model particularly apt for modeling playful manipulations of meter is the fact that it incorporates *prospective hearing* and *retrospective hearing. Prospective hearing*, which parallels the predictive analyses of language, accounts for "musical expectation or implication" (1992: 64). In using these terms, Jackendoff refers expressly to the implication–realization model postulated by Meyer (1973) and Narmour (1977). At the exact same moment that the selection function surfaces one analysis to consciousness, it faces its metrical grid both backward to the beginning of a piece and forward to the future. In Jackendoff's words, "the strong preference for a constant meter (Metrical Well-Formedness Rule 4) projects the existing metrical structure beyond the portion of the musical surface that has already been heard" (65). This statement suggests that the graphic representation of the metrical structure might be slightly modified in comparison with Example 1.9, by joining the dots of individual metrical levels with arrows (Example 1.12). Although Jackendoff himself does not adopt this notation, this is how Lerdahl and Jackendoff's representations are to be understood in every case in which meter has already been established. The arrows are equivalent to the time spans that Lerdahl and Jackendoff (1983) symbolize by brackets but represent time spans temporally activated and thus turned into projections that guide the listener's expectations concerning when further events should occur. Hierarchical levels of projections determine, in turn, the relative salience of events the listener expects to occur at different beats of the metrical grid.

Example 1.12. Metrical hierarchy as projective hierarchy.

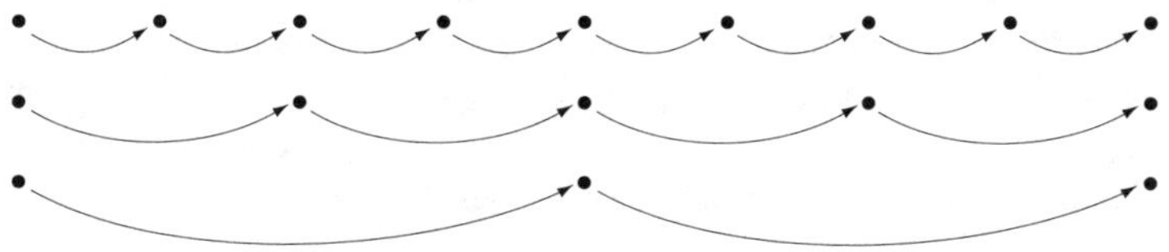

31. The STMM (Jackendoff 1987: 242) is the musical equivalent of what psychologists have described on various occasions as "span of consciousness" (Wundt 1874), "specious present" (James 1890), or "psychological present" (Fraisse 1963). Its average duration is estimated as ca. 4 seconds, with experimental results spanning 2–8 seconds (see Pancutt 1994: 450–51).

When these expectations, as generated by the selected analysis, are confirmed, the metric perception of the listener will be one of "hearing the music without effort." When, instead, these expectations are challenged by the lack of an expected event or by an unexpected event whose salience does not correspond with its position in the grid, the result will be surprise. It is the possibility of surprise that most convincingly confirms the perceptual reality of prospective hearing. Surprise may, in turn, lead to revision of the selected analysis, in this way revealing the phenomenon of *retrospective hearing*. From the cooperation of prospective and retrospective hearing, three situations can arise in the course of metric processing at the beginning of a piece. Jackendoff's discussion suggests that they form sequences of different states of metrical representation—either a clear or a vague sensation of meter—which the processor assigns, one after the other, to the same musical passage:

1. "Retrospective analysis" takes place when, for a relatively longer time, there is insufficient evidence for the selection function to decide between analyses, so that the meter of a piece is determined some distance from the beginning. Because this distance is longer than in the case of "hearing the music without effort," the sensation of "ambiguity or vagueness" (Jackendoff 1987: 243) originally arises, before being replaced by a sense of clear meter.
2. "Retrospective reanalysis" takes place when one analysis has been selected by the processor and generates expectations, yet a surprising event makes the selection function change its choice. The change happens between two clear metric representations, one of them unmasked as false and replaced by the true meter. Jackendoff figuratively calls this "changing horses in midstream."
3. "Bewilderment" or "losing one's bearings" occurs when an analysis has been selected by the processor and generates expectations, but then a surprising event arrives "that is inconsistent with *all* the analyses being considered, so the selection function has no alternative to fall back upon" (243–44). This third situation is the reversal of the first, because a clear sense of meter is replaced by metric "ambiguity or vagueness."[32]

The possibility of "retrospective reanalysis" is based on the assumption that after the selection function has entered, nonpreferred analyses will still continue for some time. If not, then there would be no possibility for the processor to "fall back on" one of them. Retrospective reanalysis happens precisely in the temporal span between that moment when the selection function has already chosen one analysis for consciousness and the moment when the nonpreferred analyses are abandoned. This observation raises two important methodological questions concerning Jackendoff's model: First, when does the selection function make its choice? Second, when are nonpreferred analyses discarded?

32. I follow Jackendoff's description of these situations in *Consciousness and the Computational Mind* (1987). In his later article (1991) and its abridged version (1992), "retrospective analysis" under point 1 is replaced by "hearing the music without effort"; and "bewilderment" under point 3 is defined as a situation in which no analysis of a passage is chosen by the selection function at any stage of its processing.

As to the first question, it is assumed that the selection function needs to collect enough evidence in order to decide between analyses. But what amount of evidence is enough? This question cannot be answered unequivocally. This is because the preference rule approach adopted by Lerdahl and Jackendoff in the GTTM does not allow for a sharp distinction between clear and vague sensations of meter.[33] Whereas the ideal case of the former is an absolute congruence and regularity of cues at the musical surface and the ideal case of the latter is the total disparity and irregularity of such cues, most situations confronted in actual musical compositions fall between these two poles, in a continuous gradation of stronger and weaker metric articulations. In this respect, the GTTM aptly mirrors perceptual reality, in which a very weak sensation of meter and a sensation of no meter flow smoothly into each other. As a consequence, "retrospective analysis," "retrospective reanalysis," and "bewilderment"—which form sequences of clear and vague sensations of meter—cannot be cleanly delineated. Even so, one can ask another question concerning the selection function: If all evidence speaks consistently in favor of one analysis, when will this analysis be selected? This question is not answered by Jackendoff either. Yet without answering it, one cannot distinguish between "hearing the music without effort" and "retrospective analysis," because the latter, as assumed by Jackendoff, implies a longer time before an analysis is selected than occurs in the former. Neither can one speak about "retrospective reanalysis," because there would be no clear reason why the selection function should make a premature choice instead of waiting for more evidence before making its decision. Without a clear criterion concerning the earliest moment at which the selection function can enter, one is not even able to distinguish Jackendoff's "bewilderment," where the earlier-selected analysis is shaken by a surprising event, from a state of total metrical anarchy in which no selection is ever made.[34] In order to propose such a criterion, a methodological refinement of Jackendoff's model is necessary. I will return to this question in section 1.4.

As to the second question, Jackendoff suggests that "cadenced group boundaries are points when less stable analyses are 'pruned'" (1991: 214).[35] The assumption that the nonpreferred analyses are discarded at cadential closures mirrors experimental evidence in the study of language, which demonstrates that it is at a clause or sentence boundary that irrelevant syntactic analyses are discarded (1991: 218). Obviously, the boundary of a sentence (clause) or phrase creates the threshold between short-term memory and long-term memory.[36] Beyond this point, there is thus no possibility of

33. The authors admit as much when they write: "We have not completely characterized what happens when two preference rules come into conflict. Sometimes the outcome is a vague or ambiguous intuition; sometimes one rule overrides the other resulting in an unambiguous judgment anyway" (Lerdahl and Jackendoff 1983: 54). In the further course of their discussion, they reflect on the possibility of assigning numerical values to individual rules, as is the case with computational models of visual and aural perception, but reject this solution as premature and simplistic.
34. This last sense of "bewilderment" is adopted by Jackendoff in his articles (1991, 1992). See note 32.
35. Jackendoff credits Lerdahl (personal communication) with this suggestion.
36. That the "psychological present" is framed by the size of a phrase is assumed by many authors. See, for instance, Brower (1993), Parncutt (1994), and Temperley (2001). Fraisse (1982) and Dowling (1984) take phrase lengths as evidence for the duration of the psychological present.

revision in the form of "retrospective analysis," "retrospective reanalysis," or "bewilderment." To be sure, in a new phrase a meter may change or become corrupt, yet this will not affect the fixed understanding of the earlier phrase.[37]

The assumption that, after meter has been found by the selection function, other analyses are discarded at the next cadence is of consequence for the activity of the processor after this moment. Although Jackendoff expresses no opinion about this issue, there is no reason to suppose that alternative analyses will start being elaborated again in the subsequent phrase, if the selected analysis is confirmed by further information coming from the musical surface. After all, the function of meter is to provide a cognitive matrix for rhythmic patterns in order to make their understanding possible. If a given analysis performs this task in a satisfactory way, why should the processor produce analyses as an alternative to it? It is more likely that it will maintain only this one analysis and limit itself to monitoring its match with the musical surface. If this reasoning has merit, the processor's activity consists of two different phases or functions: (a) looking for meter, and (b) monitoring meter. These correspond to two phases of metric cognition distinguished by Justin London in his "dynamic model of meter," for which he draws from the psychological phenomenon of "entrainment":

> The first [phase] involves a rather high processing load, as every event [has] an equal amount of significance (or potential significance).... Once the meter has been recognized the cognitive load drops considerably. Now the listener is entrained and needs relatively little information to maintain the metric pattern. Indeed, as is well known, we will continue to maintain the chosen pattern even when confronted with a fair amount of contradictory information (e.g. an extended passage of syncopation, or a series of stressed weak beats, etc.). In order to break or shift an established metric pattern we must be presented with a strong and continuing series of cues in order to achieve a metric reconfiguration. (1993: 10)

In his most recent development of this model, London (2004) labels these two phases, respectively, "finding the meter" and "keeping the meter going." As he remarks elsewhere, they differ as to the direction in which the sense of accent is transmitted between the musical surface and the metrical grid: "At some times a sense of accent flows from the musical surface to the emerging metre, and at other times from the metre to the unfolding musical surface" (2001: 283). This explains the difference, pointed out earlier in this chapter, between Kirnberger

37. A question arises about situations in which cadential closure does not occur until later in the piece. Since it is unlikely that many nonpreferred analyses will be continued by the processor for a long time, one might hypothesize that some of them will be discarded before the cadence. In Jackendoff's words (1992: 62), "when a particular branch [of analysis] drops below some threshold of plausibility, it is abandoned." On the other hand, Brower (1993: 22) suggests that "if the phrase is so long or complex that it exceeds our capacity for short-term retention, we may have difficulty processing it as a single unit, and be forced to break it up into smaller units." Intriguing as it is, this question has little significance in the musical repertory of the late eighteenth century, in which a clear articulation of melodic units by different types of cadential closures, especially at the beginning of a piece, was considered obligatory.

and Schulz on the one hand, who consider accent an indispensable condition for the existence of meter, and Lerdahl and Jackendoff on the other hand, who treat accent as an effect rather than a cause of metrical hierarchy. In the passages quoted, these two pairs of authors actually refer to two different types of accent—*phenomenal accent* and *metrical accent*—and to different phases of the processor's activity. In Lerdahl and Jackendoff, the discussion of metrical accent occurs in the context of MWFRs, and the concept of phenomenal accent is introduced by them in the context of MPRs. Phenomenal accent will be a subject of thorough discussion in the next chapter.

Note that the processor responsible for metric perception displays characteristics of the parallel multiple-analysis model, properly speaking, only in the phase of looking for meter. In the phase of monitoring meter, it "hibernates." This means that Jackendoff's model concerns only the first phase. In other words, it is a model of *metrical induction*. Playful manipulations of meter at the beginning of a piece are represented by the three situations described by Jackendoff. But metrical induction is not constrained to the initial section of a piece. The parallel multiple-analysis processor can "wake up" again, if necessary, when the single analysis maintained by it in the phase of monitoring meter stops providing a satisfactory account of the metric organization of the musical surface. This happens when a certain event (or events) challenges the metrical grid projected by the processor. Such situations, confronted by the processor after the meter has already been established, can be classified according to the relationships between the metrical structures elaborated by the processor before and after the challenge. This, in turn, depends on the number and pattern of challenging events. Again, three situations are possible:

1. *Challenge to meter:* The parallel multiple-analysis processor has restarted, but the analysis it finds is a continuation of the preceding analysis. This happens when there are only one or two challenging events, which by definition cannot create any regular pattern and which the processor normally accommodates to the old grid.
2. *Change of meter:* The processor has restarted, and the new analysis differs from the one projected earlier. As London correctly notes, this situation arises if there is a regular series of challenging events on the musical surface.
3. *Dissolution of meter:* The processor starts over but for a longer time cannot select any analysis; hence the sense of meter is "vague" for the listener. This happens if there is a disorderly series of challenging events or if the previous meter is not sufficiently sustained on the musical surface.

1.4. Borrowing from a Different Model

Before embarking on my analyses of metric manipulations in Haydn's and Mozart's string chamber music, it is necessary to pose one more methodological question, which concerns the ways in which the processor elaborates individual analyses at the stage of looking for meter. What role does information from the musical surface play in this process, and how does the processor approach it? Does it *wait* (without any anticipation) or *await* (with anticipation)?

The stance taken by Jackendoff in his analysis of a Bach chorale is that the processor *waits* for information. Only after a new tone attack occurs can the processor match it with a certain metrical structure. If this were the case, then the processor's retrospective orientation in the phase of looking for meter would contrast with its prospective orientation in the phase of monitoring meter, when the metrical structure is projected onto the future, anticipating upcoming events. This option is not the only one possible, though. There is nothing in Jackendoff's model that would preclude the assumption that, already in the phase of looking for meter, the processor actively *awaits* further information on the basis of the information collected earlier. This could be done by projecting the time interval between two earlier attacks into the future, so as to anticipate the moment of a third attack (Example 1.13).

Example 1.13. Projection.

Note that this assumption about the processor's activity corresponds better with its function in the phase of looking for meter. If meter is regularity, then looking for meter means looking for equal time intervals between attacks on the musical surface. The precision with which given intervals are judged as equal or unequal increases when—rather then comparing them with each other after both have already occurred—one assumes their equality as a working hypothesis and awaits the end of the second time interval at a certain moment in the future, that is to say, at the moment when the third attack should occur.[38] On this view, in the phase of looking for meter, projection would thus be a hypothesis of regularity based on empirical data from the past portion of the musical surface (the time interval between the two attacks), which is either confirmed or proven wrong by further data (the third attack).[39]

If this assumption is right, the processor works essentially the same way in both the phase of looking for meter and that of monitoring meter. The difference between these two phases consists only in the fact that in the phase of looking for

38. These two attitudes correspond to what Hasty (1997: 184) calls "judgment of equality" and "projective repetition," respectively.

39. For Fodor, every analysis conducted by a module is a perceptual hypothesis (Fodor 1983: 68–110; DeBellis 1995). The same is true of analyses elaborated by the parallel multiple-analysis processor, whether it works via the mechanism of projection or not. What this mechanism presupposes is that, in the framework of hypotheses concerning the metrical structure of the music heard thus far, the processor automatically develops hypotheses about the moment of future attacks.

meter, the projection is developed without any commitment being made from the side of the processor. As long as this projection has not been realized and selected for consciousness by the selection function, it does not have the status of expectation, which otherwise characterizes a realized and selected projection in the phase of monitoring meter. This is in line with perceptual reality, which shows a difference between an imperceptible effect of a "denied" projection at the beginning of a piece and the often startling effect of surprise that is caused by a denied projection in the course of a piece, after the meter has become established. The difference in the status of projections is mirrored graphically as the difference between the solid arrows in Example 1.12 and the dotted arrows in Example 1.13. Related to this difference is another one, concerning the persistence of projection. In the phase of looking for meter, if the projection is not realized by further attacks, it is discarded. Because in this phase several projections are usually being elaborated simultaneously, a denial of one projection will give more chances to others. In the phase of monitoring meter, instead, the projection that is characteristic of the selected analysis is the only one that the processor maintains. Consequently, that projection is more "stubborn" and not discarded so easily, even in the absence of one or more further attacks.

The assumption that projection is the mechanism by which the processor generates analyses provides us with the missing criterion for determining the earliest moment when a given (preferred) analysis can be surfaced by the selection function. Because meter is regularity, it is necessary to have a confirmed hypothesis of regularity, as represented by a realized projection. Moreover, because meter is regularity on at least two levels of beats, there must be realized projections of at least two, hierarchically interconnected levels. This situation is shown in Example 1.14. In this example, the moment when the analysis is chosen for consciousness coincides with the attack at which the higher-level projection is realized; this moment is shown in the graphical representation by the change from dotted to solid arrows. If the lower-level projection is that of metrical units and the higher-level projection that of measures, then two complete measures are necessary in order for a meter to be established. To this end, the evidence collected by the selection function must be clearly in favor of this analysis. If the evidence is unclear, the analysis will be selected at a later time, if at all. It is here that the difference between "hearing the music without effort" and "retrospective analysis" lies.

Example 1.14. Projection on two hierarchical levels.

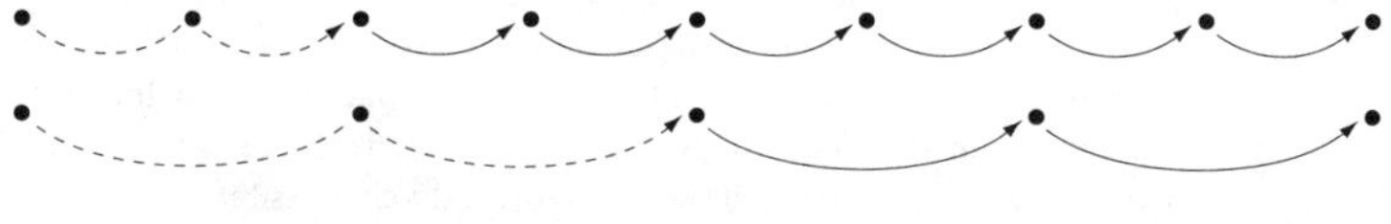

Apart from the unification of both phases of the processor's activity, the mechanism of projection gives a more economical account of this activity in the phase of looking for meter. According to the GTTM, strictly speaking, the processor should elaborate all well-formed metrical structures in a given musical passage.

This would mean to elaborate an extremely high number of analyses, including quite improbable ones; for instance, thoroughly syncopated analyses of a given passage.[40] Note that MWFR 1, which requires coordination of attacks with beats of "the smallest metrical level present at that point in the piece," does not exclude such analyses. In practice, however, Lerdahl and Jackendoff never deal with them. Nor does Jackendoff, in his analytic sample from a Bach chorale, consider such improbable analyses. The syncopated analysis in Example 1.15 is introduced by him only after the third event—the eighth note—and would not have been invoked at all had the music continued in quarters. Although he does not state it explicitly, his processor is guided by the "principle of economy" (Povel 1984): It tends to organize data in the simplest possible way; it chooses a grid that directly matches the maximum number of attacks and that accounts for other attacks with the greatest possible ease. In the GTTM, the economy principle is included in the MPRs as a preference for a metrical structure in which attacks coincide with strong beats (MPR 3).[41] According to this rule, two attacks will be preferably interpreted as two consecutive beats at the same metrical level. The analytic result of this preference is thus identical with that of the mechanism of projection, which requires two attacks as generators of a potential metrical level. In contrast, the mechanism of projection has the advantage of not needing to refer to MPRs at this stage of the processor's activity. Rather, it automatically yields only the best analyses in terms of the "principle of economy" without dealing with other, less economical ones.[42] At the same time, it answers better the question of the origin of individual analyses. If the processor were to work in the way assumed by Jackendoff, that is, by matching several metrical structures with the musical surface, then one would need to

40. This is observed by Longuet-Higgins and Lee (1982: 117): "Phrase structure grammars by which meters are most naturally represented generate certain impossible musical structures, such as rhythms beginning with a series of tied notes, or rests followed by just one note . . . and there seems to be no obvious way of constraining the grammatical rules so that they fail to generate such structures." Their solution to this problem is analogous to the idea of projection, even if not labeled as such. Yet the computer models of Longuet-Higgins and Lee (1982), as well as Lee (1991), are serial single-choice models. Consequently, they are involved in the practical and logical problems of the kinds of models indicated by Jackendoff (see note 30 above).
41. The coordination of beats with attacks, as a preference rule guiding the selection between several possible analyses, occurs in several other models of metrical induction, such as those by Longuet-Higgins and Lee (1984), Povel and Essens (1985), Rosenthal (1992), and Parncutt (1994).
42. On the other hand, it presupposes that the "retrospective reanalysis" of a totally syncopated passage is not possible because a corresponding analysis was not elaborated by the processor. This may create a problem in analyzing certain musical examples. Yet the same problem is inherent in Jackendoff's model. Although Jackendoff points to one example of a piece starting with syncopations—Schumann's song "Dein Bildnis wunderselig" from *Liederkreis* Op. 39—he dismisses this problem by stating that two syncopated events are "a highly unlikely possibility at the beginning of a piece" (1991: 205) and does not include the analysis reproduced in Example 1.15 into the set of analyses elaborated by the processor by the end of the first measure (Example 1.11). Significantly, Example 1.15 and the accompanying commentary are removed from the abridged version of his article (1992). The problem can only be solved if one assumes that—within the confines of the STMM—the selected analysis can be extended backward beyond the point when it started being elaborated. If the length of a syncopated passage exceeds the span of STMM, this operation is obviously not possible.

clarify separately where these structures come from. In the process of meter finding via projection, instead, every metrical structure is generated directly from the surface by the pattern of attacks. In other words, the attacks provide the necessary input for analyses.[43] In this perspective, MPR 3 should be treated not as just one preference rule among others but as the *sole* "generative" rule of meter.

Example 1.15. Jackendoff, "Musical Parsing and Musical Affect," 206, fig. 9.

On the other hand, not every attack must participate in some projection that is constitutive of every given analysis. This solves the problem of attacks resulting from very small and/or irregular metrical divisions. In Lerdahl and Jackendoff's theory of meter this problem is elicited by MWFR 1, which establishes a relation of beats to attacks such that "every attack point must be associated with a beat at the smallest level of metrical structure." This rule was subsequently revised by the authors so as to incorporate changes of metrical divisions; for instance, between regular eighth notes and eighth-note triplets. Yet even with this revision, the authors were forced to postulate further a special class of *extrametrical* events. Because, as already noted, MWFR 1 does not properly belong to the set of MWFRs and, as shown above, is not helpful in avoiding improbable metrical analyses, it can be easily eliminated without any harm being done to either Lerdahl and Jackendoff's metric theory or the processor model I propose in this study.[44]

Readers familiar with current developments in the study of meter will have already noticed that the idea of projection proposed above is borrowed from a different model of meter: the one elaborated by Christopher Hasty in his book *Meter as Rhythm* (1997). Hasty defines projection as "the process in which a mensurally determinate duration provides a definite durational potential for the beginning of an immediately successive event" (84). In the course of this process, the earlier, *projective* duration is thus *projected* into the future (Example 1.16). Like all processes performed by modules, this operation is automatic and mandatory,

43. This is assumed in a number of other models in which metric "clocks" or templates are induced by events (Povel 1981; Povel and Essens 1985; Parncutt 1994: 434). Another possible solution to this problem is to postulate several templates preexisting in the cognitive mechanism of the listener, which are subsequently attuned to the periodicities at the musical surface. This is the hypothesis underlying the work on so-called oscillators (Large and Kolen 1994; Large and Jones 1999; Large and Palmer 2002; Toiviainen 2001).

44. In his book elaborating computational models of musical perception based on the GTTM, David Temperley (2001: 36) proposes, similarly, to eliminate MWFR 1.

and therefore can be incorporated into Jackendoff's model of a parallel multiple-analysis processor. In my proposed model, however, the role of "projection" differs in many ways from the role Hasty assigns to it. This is so because the axiom of Hasty's theory is not an attack point imagined as a durational instant but is instead a gradually growing duration. The solid arrow in Example 1.16 is thus not meant as an expectation that the first attack will be followed by the second attack; rather, it symbolizes the growing size of duration as the listener's attention "travels" with it, from the beginning of the first sound until the beginning of the second sound. For this reason—and different from Example 1.13—an arrow is assigned to the first duration, but not to the second. The arrow is solid because the first duration is already past, whereas the second lies in the future. The reason the beginnings of these durations are marked not by dots but by short lines is that they are not durationless instants, as the following commentary makes clear:

> To actually be a beginning, this point that is before sound and before duration will have to have become past. Thus, it is only by *becoming* past that tn *becomes* a beginning. Although there is a point tn before there is duration, there is no tn as a point of beginning before there is duration. We might say that tn has become t0—a point of beginning from which duration can be measured now that there is duration to be measured. But in this case, even if tn and t0 are in some sense the same, it will have taken time for t0 to be a beginning. (Hasty 1997: 70)

Example 1.16. Hasty, *Meter as Rhythm*, 84, ex. 7.1.

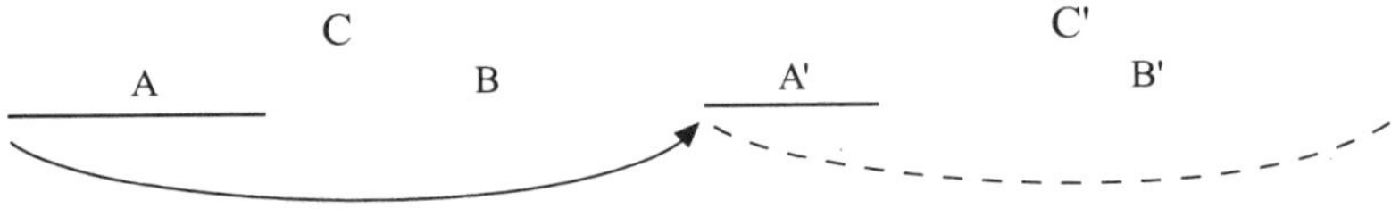

This passage is indicative of the epistemological background of Hasty's metrical theory in Bergson's philosophy and phenomenology.[45] The idea of continuity of experience (*Erlebnis*), so fundamental to phenomenological thought, presupposes continuous unfolding of sound in the psychological time of the listener. This continuous unfolding cannot be captured in a series of durationless instants analogous to points, which are characteristic of the physical time postulated in classical scientific doctrine. This is why Hasty's book constitutes such a severe critique of the theoretical tradition, from the eighteenth century until now. That tradition construes meter as a regularity of timeless points in time—its prime contemporary manifestation being the theory of Lerdahl and Jackendoff. To this Hasty opposes his own theory of "meter as process."

The opposition between Lerdahl and Jackendoff's metric theory on the one hand and Hasty's theory on the other is clear so long as the former is taken in

45. The phenomenological background is clear in Hasty, although his book contains only one short remark about Husserlian "time-consciousness" (1997: 38). For the most part, he draws his philosophical insights from the work of Alfred North Whitehead.

its original version as presented in *A Generative Theory of Tonal Music* (1983), according to which meter is construed as a "product" or "final state of understanding." Yet, as already observed, the later developments of this theory by Jackendoff are motivated precisely by the need to account for metric perception as a dynamic process. It is therefore proper and needful to inquire into the relation between his parallel multiple-analysis processor model and Hasty's theory. This question is particularly interesting, given the present study's refinement of Jackendoff's theory, which makes use of projections.

In pursuing the differences between the two authors' theories of meter, it should be observed that, even if Jackendoff speaks about a theory of musical processing, he nevertheless concentrates on representations (products), which arise as the results of such processing. This is so because, in Jackendoff's view, only these products are accessible to consciousness. Although the processor is working in time, the temporal dimension of its activity can be witnessed by the listener only if, during a given musical passage, it results in changes of representations or, occasionally, changes between different states of metric representation (clear meter) and nonrepresentation (vague meter). The inner working of the processor, which results in a number of alternative analyses, is irrelevant unless one of the analyses is subsequently selected. By contrast, for Hasty this inner working is more than relevant, going so far as to capture his entire interest. One could say that for Hasty, "meter as process" means "meter as processing." All of the analyses presented in his book are designed to reveal intermediary stages of this processing by bringing to light the projections of which it consists. From the way Hasty uses projections, however, one can infer that he assumes the serial single-choice model of processor: He allows different projections to be elaborated in parallel only when they are nested in one another, thus forming a projective hierarchy. Because projections cannot overlap, for him the choice of one projection means the automatic discarding of an earlier projection that is noncongruent with that choice. To put it the other way around: If one projection is chosen and not discarded, then alternative noncongruent projections are not elaborated. In Hasty's analyses, such choices are made by the processor starting from the earliest stage of processing, which is in line with Jackendoff's description of the serial single-choice model. Given the logical problems of this model, as pointed out by Jackendoff, it is both advisable and possible to reinterpret Hasty's analyses in terms of the multiple-analysis model, as reflecting fluctuations of preference between individual analyses in the course of their being elaborated by the processor and evaluated by its selection function. If this reinterpretation is valid, then it is these fluctuations—which thus would or, at least, could in principle be perceived by the listener—that, for Hasty, constitute the content of metric experience (*Erlebnis*). And it is this "experience" as a mental process emulated by music that he properly calls "meter." Because "meter" in this sense of the word is determined by the ensemble of all projective potentials along with their realizations or nonrealizations, which in their turn are determined by the rhythmic configuration of attacks at the musical surface, it is identical with "rhythm." This is what the title of Hasty's book essentially says.

It is no surprise that Hasty's theory of meter concerns the side of the processor's activity that is opposite to that dealt with by Jackendoff. Whereas Lerdahl and

Jackendoff are heirs of the eighteenth-century theory of meter discussed earlier, Hasty refers to a different tradition in the study of meter, initiated in the nineteenth century by Moritz Hauptmann and continued in the twentieth century by Friedrich Neumann, which considers meter not as a property of the musical surface but as the listener's ability to measure and compare durations. What is surprising is, rather, that Hasty's approach turns out to be compatible with Jackendoff's model of the metric processor and that both approaches can fit into the framework of the parallel multiple-analysis model I propose in this study. It is in this framework, which draws on Fodor's modular theory, that the question can be raised as to the applicability of Hasty's approach to the eighteenth-century musical repertory. Put crudely, the question is whether (and if yes, to what extent) the "metric experience" described by Hasty could become part of the experience of historical listeners in the eighteenth century. According to Fodor, intermediary stages of processing in the module are for the most part inaccessible to consciousness; or, better, they are "accessible at a price: you can get at them, but only by imposing special demands upon memory or attention" (1983: 60). Indeed, Hasty accesses them at the expense of attention, in that he requires from the reader a close (inner) hearing of his musical examples in order to verify the details of their analyses. Such a way of hearing music can be compared with hearing language in ways used by researchers in phonetics, by which they access raw acoustic materials before the module turns them into phonemes and segments them into lexical items. As Fodor emphasizes, it is in fact no "innocent hearing" but, rather, a "*super*sophisticated perceptual achievement" that requires extra training (1983: 54). Since the close hearing postulated by Hasty is not reported in eighteenth-century music theory treatises, there is no reason to suppose that listeners of the time underwent the training necessary to acquire it. Yet this is not to say that the phenomenon of close hearing could not arise spontaneously under certain conditions. The first of these conditions is a relatively slow tempo. Because a process guided by attention takes more time, the effect of tempo is of great importance. Indeed, a moderate or slow tempo is suggested in most of Hasty's analytical examples. Second, the attention of the listener will be heightened when the articulation of meter is very weak. It is not unlikely that to provoke close hearing was one of the composer's intentions in such musical passages. The advantage of the processor model proposed in this study is that it makes it possible for one to give an account of this side of metric manipulation without committing the sin of methodological impurity. Although I will mostly describe metric manipulations "from the outside," in Jackendoff's manner, I will take a look "from the inside" à la Hasty here and there, if it promises an interesting analytic insight.

CHAPTER Two

Finding Meter

Theorists of the eighteenth century were aware of the cognitive role of meter in the understanding of rhythmic patterns; therefore, they took it for granted that meter should be established very clearly from the outset of a musical piece. Yet their instructions how to accomplish this are rather scant. In fact, the only few remarks having to do directly with this issue occur in the discussion of *Rhythmus* by Kirnberger in *Die Kunst des reinen Satzes*.

In Kirnberger's terminology in his composition handbook, the term *Rhythmus* refers not just to rhythm in the contemporary sense of the word but, more specifically, to a rhythmic group or segment of the musical surface.[1] In this sense, it is synonymous with *Einschnitt* (incise) and *Satz* (phrase) and is used interchangeably with them. The relationship between *Rhythmus,* so defined, and *Takt* is equivalent to Lerdahl and Jackendoff's distinction between grouping and meter. In conformance with this distinction, Kirnberger admits that *Rhythmus* can begin with any metrical position, yet he prefers certain positions over others: "The beginning of a phrase, and hence its end as well, is not restricted to any point within the measure; not only can they fall on any beat [*Zeit des Tackts*] but also on any small part of the beat [*kleinen Theil der Zeiten*]. However, to compose in the easiest and most comprehensible way, one begins either on the downbeat [*Niederschlag*] or upbeat [*Aufschlag*]" (Kirnberger 1982: 413 [1776: 147]). It is noticeable that the preference for downbeat and upbeat as points at which to start a *Rhythmus* expressed in the last sentence of the quotation is motivated cognitively by reference to the comprehensibility of a rhythmic group. Whereas this quotation applies to any *Rhythmus,* notwithstanding its location at the beginning of a piece or in its further course, slightly later in the same passage Kirnberger refers explicitly to beginnings of pieces and describes as "unusual" such situations as when a *Rhythmus* starts "with the second, third, or fifth eighth in 4/4 meter or the second or third eighth in 3/4 meter" (1982: 414 [1776: 149]).

1. In another sense, *Rhythmus* denotes relationships between sizes of rhythmic groups in the course of musical composition. These two senses of the word are explicitly distinguished by Kirnberger in a note (1982: 403 n. 8 [1776: 137]).

Although the "point within the measure" on which the first attack falls certainly has bearing on the composer's process of establishing meter and the listener's process of finding it, it does not, by and of itself, guarantee its success. On the one hand, as Kirnberger himself admits, starting with a less usual metrical position does not preclude a successful metrical induction. On the other hand, it is possible to imagine a *Rhythmus* starting with the downbeat or upbeat that nevertheless does not yield a clear sense of meter. That Kirnberger does not provide any more definite instructions is because they were superfluous. For his eighteenth-century readers, it was a matter of course that in order to introduce meter (*Takt*), one needed to articulate its constitutive beats (*Taktteile*). The fundamental role of *Taktteile* in eighteenth-century music was not only theoretical—as the central level of the metrical hierarchy from which all other levels are derived—but also quite practical: The procession of *Taktteile* had to be articulated by attacks on the musical surface. This assumption, implicit in Kirnberger's remarks, was stated explicitly by other theorists before and after. In *De Rhythmopoeia oder von der Tactordnung* (1752), the first volume of the monumental composition treatise *Anfangsgründe zur musicalischen Setzkunst,* Joseph Riepel emphasizes that "in music motion must be continuously heard, that is, when one or two voices rest, the others must move."[2] In the examples with which he illustrates this principle, the regular motion takes place on the metrical level corresponding either with *Taktteile* or *Taktglieder*. Because the *Taktglieder* are subdivisions of the *Taktteile*, all *Taktteile* are articulated by attacks in either case. The same principle was confirmed and systematically elaborated by Koch, as will be seen from the detailed discussion at the beginning of the next chapter. For the listener of the time, the fundamental condition of finding meter was thus to find *Taktteile* as a regular series of attacks on the musical surface.[3]

It is here that the metric theory of the eighteenth century comes together with the parallel multiple-analysis model of processor I described in the preceding chapter. As already explained, the mechanism of projection, on which this model is based, works like a hypothesis of regularity. For this mechanism to start, there must be two attacks on the musical surface with the time interval between them falling within the confines of durational determinacy delimited by Hasty as around 0.2–2 seconds.[4] Given such an interval, the processor projects it onto the

2. "Inzwischen muß in der Musik stets eine Bewegung vernommen werden, das ist: wenn eine oder zwei Stimmen ruhen, so müssen sich die übrigen rühren" (Riepel 1752: 17).
3. This regular series of attacks was one of the factors securing aesthetic unity in eighteenth-century musical composition. As was observed by Seidel, "the unifying musical factor in question is nothing else than the primitive series of beats underlying the theory of meter [exposed for the first time in Sulzer's *Allgemeine Theorie der schönen Künste*]. Koch turns Sulzer's theory into compositional instructions" (1975: 115).
4. Hasty assumes that projective durations under 0.2 second can be felt, even if he does not consider "such fine-grained perceptions" in his study (1997: 108 n. 2). His view can be questioned on the grounds of recent psychological experiments demonstrating that 0.2 second is the lower limit of the range within which we can hear beat or pulse (London 2004: 27–47). As noted by Brower, "listeners do not perceive individual durations below the level of the pulse, but only the rhythmic pattern created by those durations" (1993: 25). This has to do with the reaction time. With durations under 0.2 second, the time necessary to project them ahead would be longer than the projection itself.

future from the second to the hypothetical third attack. If the third attack occurs on schedule, the projection is realized, and a hypothesis of regularity is confirmed on one metrical level. If not, the projection is discarded. In keeping with the idea behind the parallel multiple-analysis model, a number of projections can be generated simultaneously. Depending on the pattern of attacks on the musical surface, several of these projections—different as to their period (duration) or phase—can be realized. To be sure, projective durations do not need to be initiated at the first attack only. New projections will start at subsequent attacks. Nor do projective durations need to arise only between consecutive attacks. Rather, the second attack may be separated from the first by other attacks. The same applies to the realization of projection by the third attack. In the model just proposed, it is assumed that such intervening attacks do not disturb the realization of a given projection, even though they may give rise to or realize other projections.

The assumption that projective time spans do not necessarily need to arise between consecutive attacks makes it possible for certain higher-level projections to be built on lower-level projections. Periods of higher-level projections can be accounted for by the number of beats—two or three (MWFR 3)—of a lower level that elapse between beats of a higher level. Because they are not measured by the processor in absolute time values but in terms of lower-level beats, projections of higher levels are not constrained by the upper time limit of the durational determinacy indicated above.[5] As various projections of lower levels may differ from each other, so also various higher-level projections built on the same lower-level projection can differ in respect to either their period or their phase. An interconnection between a given higher-level projection with its underlying lower-level projection forms the germ of "projective hierarchy," and a realized projection of the higher level results in one metric analysis of a given passage. If at the moment of its realization this analysis is preferred by the selection function, it will be selected for consciousness. However, a single level of projection does not count as metric analysis. If it is not hierarchically interconnected with some other level, it will be discarded, unless no other analysis is at hand.

These principles of the processor's inner workings, when applied to the opening measures of the first movement of Haydn's String Quartet in D major, Op. 50 No. 6 ("The Frog"), lead to interesting analytical results (Example 2.1). The time signature c refers here to Kirnberger's simple quadruple meter with the quarter note as *Taktteil*. The first confirmed projection is, however, not that of *Taktteile* but of *Takte*. Indicated by the time interval between the onsets of the dotted half notes E and G in mm. 1 and 2 of the melody, it is confirmed in m. 3 by the E. *Taktteile* are found in the course of a much longer process. The time interval of a quarter note between the D at the beginning of the sixteenth-note series in m. 1 and the subsequent G fails to establish any regularity because it is

5. According to Hasty, the confines of durational determinacy 0.2–2 seconds apply only to "simple (noncomposite, unmodulated) events" (1997: 108). On higher levels of projective hierarchy, "projective potential is not simply a time-span (measurable by a clock), but a measured duration—that is, a duration measured by the coordination of many projections" (188).

not followed by the third attack in an equal interval. The same happens to the quarter note between F♯ and E (mm. 2–3). The first confirmed projection under the level of whole notes is that of the half note between E and D in m. 3, and only afterward the quarter note between D and C♯ in the same measure. Both these projections are confirmed by the arrival on D at the beginning of m. 4, at which the busy accompaniment in eighths starts. Thus it is only at this D that the meter is established.

Interestingly, the same D brings the ultimate consolidation of the D-major key after the unusual beginning of this movement on the dominant. This has to do with the formal trick performed by Haydn: The movement begins with a cadence, which in itself is a closing gesture, and it does so, so to say, before its beginning.[6] Although several authors have made note of this trick,[7] they have usually seen the crux of this manipulation in its tonal dimension. As it turns out, it has a metrical dimension as well. The process of establishing the syntactical matrix of meter and key is delayed in both dimensions, and the arrival of this process marks the structural beginning of the sonata form.[8]

Example 2.1. Haydn, String Quartet in D major, "The Frog," Op. 50 No. 6/i, mm. 1–4.

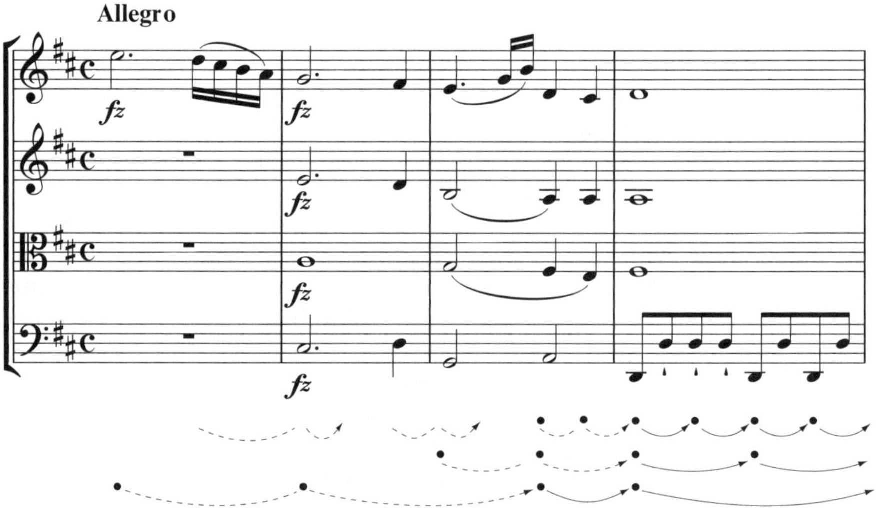

6. Similar tricks occur in the opening movements of Haydn's Op. 33 No. 4, Op. 33 No. 5, Op. 50 No. 1, Op. 71 No. 1, Op. 71 No. 3, and Op. 74 No. 1.
7. See Rosen (1971: 128) and Sutcliffe (1992: 100).
8. One might argue that the subdivision of the whole-note duration, established at this moment, determines in retrospect the virtual subdivision of the same duration in mm. 1–2 so that, after all, the piece is understood by the listener to be in 4/4 meter from the beginning. In order to accept this argument, one must assume that the selection function not only surfaces and extends a given analysis backward within the confines of the STMM but also complements it with levels not originally elaborated by the processor. The proposed model of the processor is open to this assumption. Nevertheless, in the example discussed, the late clarification of meter is at the core of the manipulation executed by the composer.

Although the meter is established "some distance from the beginning," this does not cause the sense of metrical vagueness that characterizes Jackendoff's "retrospective analysis." This is because the opening of "The Frog" quartet yields only one analysis after all. The higher-level projection (*Takte*) is realized here before the lower-level projection (*Taktteile*) so that the former, rather than being built on the latter, provides ready-made slots into which the lower-level projection must fit itself. Such a reversed order of projections arises only when *Taktteile* are not articulated by attacks from the very beginning of the piece. Inventing his formal trick, Haydn apparently allowed himself to ignore this fundamental requirement of eighteenth-century music theory. In pieces that observe this requirement, the series of *Taktteile* will cause the processor to generate higher-level projections corresponding to *Takte* of all periods (duple or triple) and phases possible on the basis of the MWFRs. Such a full set of projections is shown in Example 2.2. To represent it graphically in analyses, however, would be too cumbersome. It would also be redundant, because the same set of projections arises every time. For these reasons, in the examples analyzed in the rest of this chapter, I show only those projections that play a role in the metrical strategy of the composer, that is to say, those that are chosen for consciousness at some stage of the processor's working or, as the case may be, that hinder each other in being selected.

Example 2.2. Projections of *Takte* arising upon a complete series of *Taktteile*.

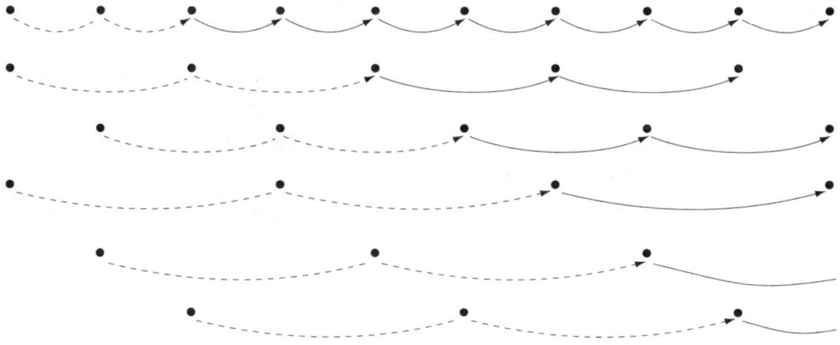

As was explained in the preceding chapter, the choice of some analysis for consciousness is made by the processor's selection function on the basis of MPRs. Jackendoff characterizes the evaluation of analyses by the selection function in terms of collecting evidence from the musical surface, but this does not apply in every case. In experiments on "subjective rhythmization," in which subjects are presented with series of equal and equidistant beats, no such evidence is at hand, yet subjects nevertheless have a sense of metric organization. The factors that give rise to meter in the absence of evidence from the musical surface, or in the face of confounding evidence, concern both phase and period of projection.

Concerning the phase, projections started at the first attack are preferred. In their MPRs, Lerdahl and Jackendoff include this preference—called the "primacy effect" in the psychological literature (Parncutt 1994)—as MPR 2 ("strong beat early").

Kirnberger demonstrates his intuitive recognition of this phenomenon in the passage quoted at the beginning of this chapter, where he considers downbeat and upbeat the most likely places to begin a piece: If a piece starts with the downbeat, the first attack initiates the projection on both levels—*Taktteile* and *Takte*—constitutive for meter. If a piece starts with the upbeat, the first attack initiates the projection of *Taktteile,* though not *Takte.* In other cases, mentioned by him as less usual, some later attacks turn out to start the projections on the levels of both *Taktteile* and *Takte.*[9]

As concerns the period, duple projections are preferred to triple projections. A plausible explanation of this preference, given in MPR 10 ("binary regularity"), is that a duple projection is realized sooner, which gives it an advantage at the start. Hasty discusses the greater cognitive difficulty involved in the perception of triple meter under the concept of "deferral." According to Hasty, who argues in terms of the serial single-choice model, in triple meter an earlier duple projection is denied and replaced by triple projection. In the framework of the parallel multiple-analysis model of processor postulated in this study, the nature of deferral can be explained as resulting from a superposition of two different analyses carried out by the processor in parallel. Although the duple projection is realized sooner, the triple projection is selected for some other reason. According to this explanation, the duple analysis is not discarded, though. While nonpreferred, it will nevertheless be carried further and, under favorable circumstances, may still come back into play before it is ultimately discontinued by the processor at the phrase boundary.[10]

Clearly, duple projection will be realized soonest of all, if started at the first attack. By combining the two subjective factors of preference, the preferred analysis will thus be equivalent to duple meter started with the downbeat. This analysis is actually preferred in experiments on "subjective rhythmization."[11] At the beginning of their discussions of meter (see Examples 1.4 and 1.6), Kirnberger and Koch designated the same analysis as the first of many possible ways to organize a series of quarter notes. Because both these eighteenth-century authors assume that the

9. In order that the rhythmic pattern may be understood from the beginning of a piece, metric representation elaborated by the processor on the basis of the projections started at later attacks must in such cases be stretched back to the silence before the first attack. This corresponds to the idea of the "silent beginning" of a projection postulated by Hasty (1997: 125). Yet this last idea is misleading: Projection cannot start from a silence. Clearly, the source of this methodological problem in Hasty is his rejection of the distinction between the projection as a mechanism of metric processing and the representation resulting from this processing.
10. From the point of view of the parallel multiple-analysis model, the triple projection will arise in every case, even if the selection function has already selected the duple projection. This is a further point differentiating this model from Hasty's theory.
11. Subjective rhythmization has a long history in experimental psychology. In various experiments, consisting of the subjects' tapping with a series of identical and isochronous tones or clicks, grouping by twos and fours has been found more common than by threes (see Handel 1989: 386). Grouping by fours arises as a combination of duple grouping on two levels so that subjective accents occur on every second attack. As hypothesized by Parncutt (1994: 444), one of the reasons for the preference for duple grouping is the ability to establish a "deeper" projective hierarchy of metrical levels characterized by periods of one, two, and four beats. Other reasons, traditionally mentioned by music theorists, include the human heartbeat, bipedalism, and breathing (see Rothstein 1989: 34).

organization of the quarter notes arises in virtue of a cognitive mechanism, they actually describe the phenomenon of "subjective rhythmization," whose existence and characteristic inner bias they have thus correctly intuited. Haydn also apparently intuited this bias, and he uses it ingeniously in the finales of his quartets Op. 50 No. 6 and Op. 64 No. 3 to lead the listener into error (Examples 2.3 and 2.4). In both examples, the false phase of the duple projection—shifted by an eighth note backward in comparison to the notation—is induced owing to the "primacy effect," only to be challenged by further events. In Op. 50 No. 6, this event is the quarter note

Example 2.3. Haydn, String Quartet in D major, "The Frog," Op. 50 No. 6/iv, mm. 1–4.

Example 2.4. Haydn, String Quartet in B-flat major, Op. 64 No. 3/iv, mm. 1–4.

G in the melody, which, from the point of view of the shifted meter, would form a syncopation. (The backward arrow indicates that the longer rhythmical value of this note will be perceived by the listener only in retrospect.) In Op. 64 No. 3, the tied F (mm. 2/3) seems at first to confirm the false meter but is unmasked as a syncopation by the subsequent bass entrance in m. 3. Either of these events occasions the selection function to "change horses in midstream" and switch to an analysis corresponding to the notated meter. The examples thus illustrate "retrospective reanalysis" as discussed by Jackendoff.

What these examples also clearly illustrate is that however important *subjective accents* may be at times as factors of preference in metric perception, they will not survive in the face of evidence to the contrary coming from the musical surface. All kinds of such evidence are called by Lerdahl and Jackendoff *phenomenal accents*: "By phenomenal accent we mean any event at the musical surface that gives emphasis or stress to a moment in the musical flow. Included in this category are attack points of pitch-events, local stresses such as sforzandi, sudden changes in dynamics or timbre, long notes, leaps to relatively high or low notes, harmonic changes, and so forth" (1983: 17). One correction must be introduced to this list of phenomenal accents as a consequence of the discussion in the preceding chapter. As was stated there, the processor builds individual analyses on attacks at the musical surface. If so, then, strictly speaking, "attack points of pitch events" are not phenomenal accents. They do not weight in favor of one analysis over others but rather enable analyses to be elaborated in the first place. Their exclusion from the set of phenomenal accents, suggested here, corresponds to the exclusion of MPR 3 as the preference rule concerning the relationship between attacks and strong beats from the set of MPRs. I will assume in this study that phenomenal accents are effectuated not by attacks as such but by salient characteristics of sound events initiated at certain attacks. For the sake of the following discussion, it will be helpful to sort them into two categories, in accordance with Leonard B. Meyer's distinction between statistical and syntactical parameters (Meyer 1989, 1998).[12] The former category includes events characterized by salient values of loudness (*dynamic accent*), duration (*durational* or *agogic accent*), and pitch (*melodic accent*).[13] As a statistical parameter, pitch relates to contour and register and can be accounted for in terms of sheer differences between "higher/lower" tones by analogy to "louder/softer" dynamics and "longer/shorter" duration. As a syntactical parameter, pitch forms the basis of tonal organization and underlies a separate category of phenomenal accents, including harmonic change and harmonic stability. Apart from phenomenal accents, Lerdahl and Jackendoff distinguish *structural accents*, which they relate to the cadence. Obviously this factor has much in common with harmony, but it takes a special place among the MPRs, as will be shown in due time.

Further factors relevant to metric perception are *grouping* and *streaming*. Although grouping structure and metrical structure are in principle independent,

12. In his earlier publications, Meyer (1967, 1973) describes these two groups of parameters as "primary" and "secondary."

13. The role of timbre in producing the sense of accent is debatable. At any rate, this parameter is largely irrelevant in string quartets.

Table 2.1 Factors of metric perception

Subjective accents		Initial accent Binary regularity	MPR 2 "strong beat early" MPR 10 "binary regularity"
Phenomenal accents	Statistical parameters	Dynamic accent Durational or agogic accent Melodic accent	MPR 4 "stress" MPR 5 "length" MPR 5a–e, MPR 2 "strong beat early"
	Syntactical parameter (harmony)	Harmonic change Harmonic stability Harmonic salience	MPR 5f, MPR 8 "suspension"
Structural accent		Cadence	MPR 7 "cadence"
Grouping		Initial accent Terminal accent	MPR 5a–e, MPR 2 "strong beat early"
Streaming		Textural accent	MPR 6 "bass"
Parallelism			MPR 1 "parallelism"

Lerdahl and Jackendoff nevertheless admit an influence of grouping on meter. Grouping, in turn, is influenced by pitch, duration, and loudness, factors listed above as belonging to phenomenal accents. In fact, as I will demonstrate, some of these factors influence metric perception not directly but with the mediation of grouping. Consequently, the discussion of grouping is interwoven in the section devoted to phenomenal accents. Streaming is discussed in a separate section (2.3). The last factor is *parallelism*. Crucial as it is for metric perception, parallelism will not be discussed in this chapter but is thoroughly discussed in chapter 4.

Table 2.1 shows all factors that influence metric perception. The right column shows the MPRs corresponding to these factors in the GTTM. Empty slots in this column suggest further possible preference rules with which to supplement Lerdahl and Jackendoff's list, as I will indicate in the course of the following discussion. This discussion will also clarify some peculiar couplings of MPRs, as well as a few new terms contained in Table 2.1.[14]

2.1. Statistical Parameters

As Lerdahl and Jackendoff (1983: 85) point out, loudness, duration, and pitch are equivalent to prosodic features that differentiate between strong and weak syllables in language. For the differentiation of strong and weak beats in music, only the first two factors are of fundamental importance. They are listed among the MPRs as stress (MPR 4) and length (MPR 5). Pitch, although not without relevance, is

14. Apart from Lerdahl and Jackendoff, comprehensive lists of factors that influence metric perception have been elaborated by Wallace Berry (1976: 335–45) and Joel Lester (1986: 18–40). In the following discussion, I rely on Lerdahl and Jackendoff but refer to other authors when the need arises.

not subsumed under any separate MPR. The privileged role of stress and length in metric perception was commonly recognized in the eighteenth century. This is understandable if one realizes that they correspond to the prosodic features underlying the modern German and the classical Latin. For eighteenth-century music theory, based on the metaphor of music as language, it was only natural to treat them as the two chief acoustic markers of metrical accent.

2.1.1. Stress (Dynamic Accent)

Dynamic accent, or stress, corresponds to the qualitative principle of the German language based on alternation of stronger and weaker syllables. In the series of equal and equidistant beats presented by the eighteenth-century theorists in their discussions of meter, stress offered in fact the only possibility of acoustic differentiation. In Kirnberger and Schulz's article "Rhythmus," referred to at the beginning of chapter 1, it is precisely the alternation of stronger and weaker beats that creates meter. The same point is even more pronounced in Schulz's article "Takt":

> As we have shown elsewhere [in the article "Rhythmus"], meter [*Takt*] takes place even when no differentiation between higher and lower or faster and slower tones yet occurs; however, accents [*Accente*] are necessary for this, because without them the hearing would have no opportunity to divide the succession of tones into equal and equivalent groups. Thus when we set a series of tones equal in height and duration, as [in Example 2.5a], then, if the hearing should have the sensation of meter [*Takt*] and rhythm [*Rhythmus*], this series must be divided into equal and equivalent groups through accents, as [in Example 2.5b].[15]

Example 2.5. Schulz, "Takt," 491–92.

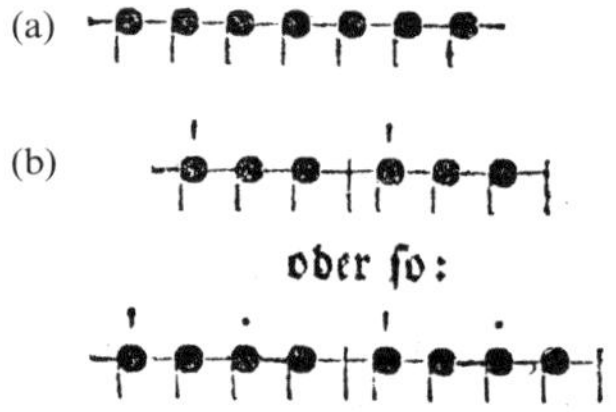

15. "Der Takt hat, wie wir schon anderswo gezeiget haben [S. Rhythmus], schon statt, wo noch keine Verschiedenheit der höhern und tiefern, oder der geschwindern und langsamern Töne vorkommt; nothwendig aber werden dazu die Accente, weil ohne sie das Gehör keine Veranlassung hätte, die Folge von Tönen in gleiche un gleichartige Glieder einzutheilen. Wenn wir also eine Reihe gleichhoher und gleichanhaltender Töne setzen, als: [Example 2.5a] u. s. f. so muß nothwendig, wenn das Gehör einen Takt und Rhythmus darin empfinden soll, diese Reihe durch Accente in gleiche und gleichartige Glieder eingetheilt werden, als: [Example 2.5b]" (Schulz 1794: 491–92).

Clearly, dynamic accent is accent *sensu proprio*.[16] The decisive role it plays in establishing the strong metrical position of a beat in a measure resulted in the transference of the word "accent" onto this position as such. In Koch's terminology, this is reflected in the distinction between accented (*accentuierte*) and unaccented (*unaccentuierte*) notes (1787: 282). By the same token, in an established meter, the strong metrical position of a given beat creates an effect of subjective accent even when no phenomenal accentuation takes place. When speaking about metrical "accent," contemporary music theorists draw conclusions from this eighteenth-century insight.

The close connection between metrical accent and dynamic accent was of consequence for eighteenth-century performance practice.[17] As already observed, Koch assumes that metrical accents, which he called *Ruhepunkte der Vorstellung*, will spontaneously manifest themselves as "stress" or "weight." Later, in the entry "Accent" in his *Musikalisches Lexikon* (1802), he was to label this kind of discrete stress given by a performer to a beat in virtue of its strong metrical position "grammatical accent" (*grammatischer Accent*) and oppose it to more emphatic "oratoric accents" (*oratorische Accente*) and "pathetic accents" (*pathetische Accente*) not related to any particular position in a measure. Koch's remarks are corroborated in greater detail by Daniel Gottlob Türk in *Klavierschule oder Anweisung zum Klavierspielen* (1789). Türk indicates the gradation of stress to be assigned to individual beats in Example 2.6.[18] As he points out, this accentuation is to be taken for granted by the performer in every case when no other particular interpretation is explicitly indicated on the score. "If the composer does not wish this kind of realization in certain places, then he must expressly specify the opposite" by means of dynamic markings. Yet deviations from the rule regarding patterns of metric accentuation can also take place without being indicated in notation. "In general, the above rule is only valid for as long as no indication of *forte* and *piano*, etc., appears, or until an exception becomes necessary for other reasons" (1982: 325 [1789: 336]). These reasons, illustrated in Example 2.7, can be given by "a variety of single tones which must be played with emphasis. To these, other than appoggiaturas...belong especially those intervals which are dissonant with the bass (*a*), or through which (by means of a tie) dissonant intervals may be prepared (*b*), further, syncopated notes (*c*), intervals which do not belong to the diatonic scale of that key, by means of which one has modulated (*d*), those tones which

16. All other types of accents are such only in metaphorical sense, because they create a perceptual effect similar to dynamic accents. As famously formulated by Cooper and Meyer (1960: 4), this effect consists in being "marked for consciousness."

17. An extensive discussion of the role dynamic accent played in the articulation of meter in Germany and beyond can be found in Houle (1987: 124–34). As he emphasizes, "the dynamic accent became the predominant means of distinguishing between good and bad notes in the second half of the eighteenth century" (124) and replaced the older practice of *notes inégales* (discussed in the next paragraph).

18. In a note accompanying Example 2.6, Türk admonishes the performer that the dynamic markings are to be realized "not entirely in the given degrees of strength, because this manner of playing would otherwise take on a 'limping' character" (1983: 505 n. 10 [1789: 335]).

are distinguished by their length, highness, and lowness (*e*), the intervals which become important because of the basic harmony (*f*), and so forth" (326 [337]). This list does not exhaust all possible exceptions from the usual pattern of metric accentuation. As Türk concludes, "besides the notes which have been specified here, there are still a variety of others which should be accented and for which it would be difficult to establish rules" (327 [338]). While sometimes such "anti-metrical" accents are explicitly marked by composers, in most cases they are left to the discretion of performers, who thus have to identify them and decide how to coordinate them with metrical accents.

Example 2.6. Türk, *Klavierschule*, 335.

Example 2.7. Türk, *Klavierschule*, 337.

2.1.2. Length (Agogic or Durational Accent)

Whereas stress had its equivalent in the modern German language, length referred to the quantitative principle governing the ancient Latin verse, with its differentiation between long and short syllables. In late eighteenth-century music theory this factor was less favored than stress, as it could not be applied to a series of equal and equidistant beats underlying the theoretical discourse about meter. Nevertheless, it played a significant role in real music. Kirnberger clearly considers stress and length to be equiponderant factors of metrical position: "This transformation of a mere [ametrical] stream of notes into a [metrical] melody resembling speech is accomplished in part by accents [*Accente*] that are given to a few notes, and partly by the difference of their durations [*Länge und Kürze*]" (1982: 382 [1776: 113]).

Like the word "accent," "duration" was transferred from the phenomenal property of a given tone onto a position in the measure to account, in turn, for the subjective effect of elongation or abbreviation attached to it in the established meter. A century earlier, Wolfgang Caspar Printz (1696) had already taken this step: "The position in the measure has a particular power and virtue which cause notes equal to one another, according to the time signature, to seem [somewhat] longer or [somewhat] shorter.... The apparent different length of notes that are equal according to their time or value is called *Quantitas Temporalis Intrinseca*, or the inner duration" (1696: 18, quoted in Houle 1987: 80–81). In the late eighteenth century, Printz's *quantitas intrinseca* was a commonly accepted music-theoretical concept. Schulz refers to it when he writes about "innerliche Quantitäten" (1794: 498). Koch translates it more colloquially as "innern Werth" (intrinsic value), which is represented by intrinsically long (*innerlich lange*) and intrinsically short (*innerlich kurze*) *Taktteile*, and which must be distinguished from the "äussern Werth" (extrinsic value) of a note, indicated by its rhythmical value (1787: 270–341). Where Koch contends in the following passage that of two equal tones, the tone in strong metrical position will be heard as subjectively longer than the tone in weak metrical position, he overtly pays tribute to Printz, even if his remark in parenthesis indicates that he prefers to interpret intrinsic length in more modern terms of accent: "Experience teaches us that, if two tones of equal duration were sung or played after each other, one of them would nevertheless be perceived by the hearing as longer (that means actually, with more stress) and that hence one of them would express more intrinsic value than the other."[19]

In accordance with this theoretical standpoint, lengthening a note could substitute for or supplement stress in performance. This older practice of metric articulation, which Koch does not mention, was nevertheless cultivated in the German-speaking area until the late eighteenth century, after the fashion of the French *notes inégales*. For Johann Joachim Quantz (1752), lengthening was still the only method of enhancing a metrically strong beat. Türk considers it as an alternative to stress, "which is to be used much less often and with great care" (1982: 327 [1789: 338]). As stress itself, lengthening can be applied both to metrically accented notes and to other important events illustrated in Example 2.7. When the rhythmical value of a given note is longer than that of the following ones, it is not necessary to lengthen it because "the longer note accents itself without assistance" (328 [339]).[20]

It must be emphasized that in the eighteenth century the extrinsic value or length is always considered to be an effective duration. This is also how length is defined by Lerdahl and Jackendoff in the first version of their MPR 5. More recently, Richard Parncutt (1994) substitutes this concept of length in Lerdahl and Jackendoff's list of phenomenal accents with one of duration interpreted as intraonset interval (IOI),

19. "Die Erfahrung lehre uns, daß, wenn zwey Töne von gleicher Dauer nach einander gesungen oder gespielt würden, dennoch einer derselben von dem Gehöre länger (das heißt eigentlich, mit mehr Nachdruck) vernommen würde, und daß daher einer derselben mehr innern Werth äussere als der andere" (Koch 1787: 273).

20. French and German practice of *notes inégales* is discussed by Houle (1987: 86–91).

that is, time interval between consecutive tone attacks.[21] In so doing, Parncutt refers to psychological experiments conducted by Povel and Okkerman (1981) in which subjects were presented series of tones separated by two different IOIs. The results of these experiments indicate that the following tones are heard as accented, or perceptually marked: (a) relatively isolated tones, (b) the second tone of a cluster of two notes, and (c) the initial and final tones of a cluster consisting of three or more notes.[22] From the fact that all tones were of equal length and that, at the same time, all beats followed by longer IOIs were perceived as accented, Parncutt concludes that it is IOI, rather then effective duration, that plays the role of durational accent. It seems, however, that the same results can be interpreted more correctly as illustrating the influence of grouping on meter. According to Lerdahl and Jackendoff, one of the two main factors influencing grouping is proximity. In their set of Grouping Preference Rules (GPRs), it is included under GPR 2. Long IOI, represented by a pause, is therefore a natural group boundary. What the experiments demonstrate is that in such a group, the first and the last attacks are heard as strong. Note that the effect of the first element corresponds to the "primacy effect" accounted for by MPR 2, whose application to the first attack of a piece has already been discussed earlier in this chapter. In the set of MPRs, it is precisely this rule—"weakly prefer a metrical structure in which the strongest beat in a group appears relatively early in the group" (Lerdahl and Jackendoff 1983: 76)—that establishes the relation between grouping and meter. In the light of the experimental results obtained by Povel and Okkerman, this rule requires revision, in that only the first attack arouses the sensation of a strong beat. Further attacks inside a group—whether early or late—do not have this effect at all. On the other hand, MPR 2 requires supplementation by a rule that would acknowledge the effect of the last element in a group.[23] In groups of only two elements, where these two rules collide, the latter actually takes precedence over the former. Note that the effects of the first and the last element in a group cannot be classified as phenomenal accents. On the basis of the definition assumed in this study, phenomenal accents must be elicited by salient characteristics of sound events, whereas tones used in the experiments by Povel and Okkerman were all identical. Accents produced by grouping are thus subjective.[24] This assumption accords with my classification of the "primacy effect" related to MPR 2 under subjective accents earlier in this chapter.

Although in the first version of MPR 5 Lerdahl and Jackendoff consider length to be simply the effective duration of a single sound event, in their revised version

21. This interpretation was subsequently adopted by Temperley and Sleator (1999; Temperley 2001) in their computational model of meter-finding that draws on the GTTM.
22. These experimental results form the basis of a model of metric perception elaborated and further tested by Povel and Essens (1985).
23. This effect is observable only in fast tempi (Parncutt 1994: 427).
24. Parncutt (1994) describes the effect of IOIs at the same time as "subjective accents" and "phenomenal accents." This demonstrates that although Parncutt takes this last term from Lerdahl and Jackendoff, he understands it in a different way: not as accents that have their motivation in phenomena of the musical surface but rather, in a more Kantian way, as events that manifest themselves to the listener "phenomenally" as accented.

of the same rule they extend the concept of length to a series of events that share some common characteristic—pitch, rhythmical values,[25] dynamics, or harmony—or are joined by a slur. In two successive series of different lengths, the relatively strong beat will be perceived as falling on the first event of the longer series. But the comparison of lengths, which alleges to be the proper content of this rule, is in reality only one of two factors of preference involved. What is implied in this rule in the first place is an even more fundamental observation that in a series of events sharing some common characteristics—be it long or short—the first event is perceptually marked. This means that the revised version of MPR 5 rests on grouping. But whereas in the aforementioned experiments by Povel and Okkerman grouping is an effect of proximity, here it results from similarity of sound events. In the set of GPRs, similarity is included under GPR 3, as the second main factor influencing grouping. Indeed, all characteristics of sound events enumerated by Lerdahl and Jackendoff under MPR 5—with the exception of harmony and slur—correspond to those that determine grouping on the basis of GPR 3.[26] That the accent is perceived on the first event in a group follows from MPR 2 in its more precise formulation proposed above. By contrast to groups based on proximity, however, groups based on similarity seem to have no accent falling on the last event. At first glance, it might seem that the contrast between these two types of groups concerns, further, the status of accents produced by them. If in groups based on proximity these accents are subjective, in groups based on similarity the accent falling on the first event of a new group coincides with a change of characteristics—pitch, rhythmical value, or dynamics—relative to the last event of the preceding group. From this point of view it would thus be phenomenal. But, as was observed earlier, phenomenal accents are ascribed to more salient events in terms of a given statistical parameter, whereas the beginning of a group may equally coincide with a change to a less salient event, for example from louder to softer dynamics, from longer to shorter rhythmical values, or from higher to lower pitch. For this reason it will be more proper to admit that grouping, in and of itself, produces *subjective accents*. The phenomenal component of accents in groups based on similarity constitutes, instead, the indispensable condition that a group boundary may arise. In other words, it is not a result of grouping, but rather its cause.

In contemporary music theory, William Caplin (1978) has recognized the effect of a subjective accent attached to the first event in a group sharing some common characteristics. Caplin refers to it by the term "initial accent" (*der Akzent des Anfangs*), which he derives from the metric theory of the nineteenth-century German author Moritz Hauptmann. Curious as it may seem, intuitions concerning initial accent reach even further back, into the late eighteenth century. The example with which Caplin illustrates this accent in a series of pitch repetitions (Example 2.8) is already anticipated by Kirnberger and Schulz in

25. Although Lerdahl and Jackendoff speak about "pattern of articulation" (MPR 5d), their example 4.29 (1983: 82) makes clear that this expression is meant as pattern of attacks determined by rhythmical values.

26. Harmony is not a preference factor of small-scale but only large-scale grouping (GPR 7); slur belongs under GPR 2 (proximity).

their article "Rhythmus," where it is designed to show how the sensation of meter arises in a series of beats performed on different pitches (Example 2.9). In the commentary, the authors write that the same metrical effect would arise in a series switching between the different dynamic levels *piano* and *forte*. (One such switch to *piano* is actually indicated by them in the middle of the example.)

Example 2.8. Caplin, "Der Akzent des Anfangs," 19, ex. 8.

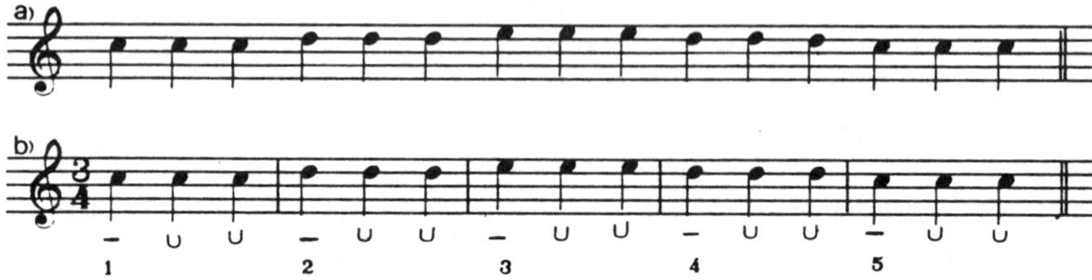

Example 2.9. Kirnberger and Schulz, "Rhythmus," 101.

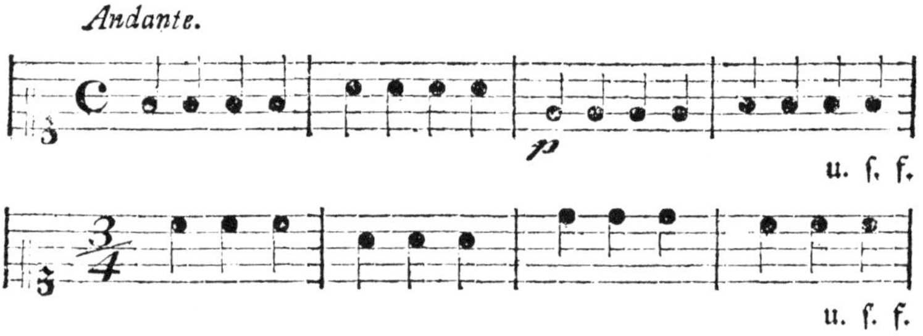

The effect of initial accent was also recognized by Türk, as can be seen in Example 2.10. As he notes, "everyone feels that in *a*, of each group of two notes, and in *b*, of each group of three notes, the first note is the most important" (1982: 90 [1789: 91]). He supplements this observation with the following remark in a note: "It would not be difficult also to have added the bar lines at the appropriate places if I had not already given the meter signature" (446 n. 100). What is interesting about Türk's example is that, in contrast to that of Kirnberger and Schulz, it shows not only sheer pitch repetitions but includes a prolongation of a pitch by means of its neighbor note at the beginning of Example 2.10b and a passing note between two pitches of the same chord at the end of this example. In this way Türk anticipates the application of the "length" rule by Lerdahl and Jackendoff to duration of pitch events and harmony on higher levels of time-span reduction (MPR 5e–f).

Example 2.10. Türk, *Klavierschule*, 91.

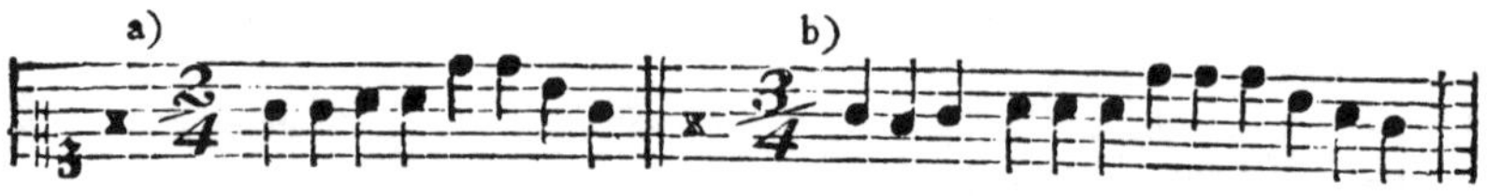

2.1.3. *Pitch (Melodic Accent)*

Although the examples above show that eighteenth-century theorists were not insensitive to the role pitch could occasionally play in metric perception, in principle this parameter was not considered by them to be capable of producing metrical accents. In this respect, their standpoint corresponds to that of Lerdahl and Jackendoff. All the more interesting in this context is a remark made by Kirnberger and Schulz in their article "Rhythmus" that suggests the possibility of melodic accent being treated as a substitute for dynamic accent. This remark occurs in a passage in which the authors, pointing to the origins of musical meter in different kinds of regular behaviors accompanying the work of craftsmen, abandon their original image of drumbeats for that of hammer beats: "The cooper who drives a hoop [onto a barrel], [or] the coppersmith who hammers a kettle soon takes it into his head to perform his beats not singly in a completely identical way [as in Example 2.11a]; [rather] he will soon beat them [as in Examples 2.11b or 2.11c] in order to slightly differentiate the strength or the pitch [*Ton*] of the three or four beats going on one measure, so that the division of groups may become perceptible to the ear."[27]

Example 2.11. Kirnberger and Schulz, "Rhythmus," 97.

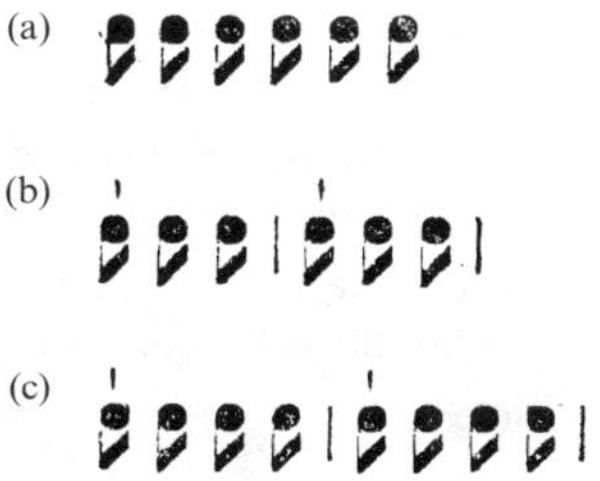

If *Ton* in this quotation is indeed meant as pitch, the intuition of these eighteenth-century authors squares with the experimental results of contemporary music psychology that demonstrate that, in a series of repetitions divided by a less frequent pitch, this last will be perceived as stronger (Handel 1989: 387). But the concept of melodic accent goes far beyond this simple observation. From a survey by David Huron and Matthew Royal (1996), it follows that melodic accent is used in three different senses having to do with changes of pitch height, pitch interval, or pitch contour. In the first sense, tones in either the highest or the lowest register are accented. The former normally are more salient in the melody, the latter in the bass. Huron and Royal call them *registral extreme accents*. Note that in the eighteenth century such tones were to be accented by the performer. They are actually included by Türk under letter (*e*) in Example 2.7. Further

27. "Der Faßbinder, oder Böttcher, der einen Reifen antreibt, der Kupferschmied, der einen Kessel hämmert, fällt gar bald darauf, seine Schläge nicht einzeln in völliger Gleichheit so zu thun [Example 2.10a] u. s. f. er wird bald so schlagen: [Example 2.10b] u. s. f. oder so: [Example 2.10c] u. s. f. um die Stärke oder den Ton der drey, oder vier auf einen Takt gehenden Schläge etwas abzuändern, damit die Eintheilung in Glieder dem Ohr merklich werde" (Kirnberger and Schulz 1794: 97).

conceptions concerning melodic accent point to pitches following large intervals (*interval size accent*) and pitches creating a change in melody direction (*contour pivot accent*). To be sure, these conceptions overlap considerably, and it seems that only instances of melodic accent that result from such overlapping have a more pronounced perceptual effect. In fact, "leaps to relatively high or low notes," listed by Lerdahl and Jackendoff among phenomenal accents, represent an overlap between intervallic skip and registral extreme. After a skip, the melodic line usually changes direction and follows in stepwise motion.[28] In such instances, the note achieved by a skip is also the contour pivot (Example 2.12).

Example 2.12. Lerdahl and Jackendoff, *A Generative Theory of Tonal Music*, 75, ex. 4.12.

It is worth observing that Lerdahl and Jackendoff explain the effect of intervallic skips in these examples by reference not to a separate preference rule for melodic accents—which, as already indicated, they do not have—but to grouping. Because skips mark group boundaries (GPR 3a), pitches following skips are first events of groups. The above examples are thus closely related to the examples of initial accents in series of pitch repetitions. Still, it seems that the last pitches of groups shown in Example 2.12 are also plausible candidates for a metrical accent, especially since they are the highest pitches achieved by stepwise ascents. This relates these groups to those based on temporal proximity of sound events. Indeed, similarity of pitches can be considered to be pitch proximity and an intervallic skip to be a pitch equivalent to a longer IOI. Even so, whereas in groups delineated by IOI there is a tendency toward the last as stronger, in groups delineated by skips the first element dominates.

Contrary to what might be inferred from the examples so far, however, grouping generated by pitch patterns is not constrained to repetitions of the same pitch or consistent stepwise lines. Melodic groups can form more complex patterns as well. Stephen Handel (1989: 408–9) lists the following patterns that can be perceived as melodic groups: identical (111), alternating (1212),[29] ascending (123), or descending (321). Accordingly, group boundaries can be defined not only by change of pitch (111222) and by intervallic skip combined with change of direction but also separately by jumps in pitch (123 567), changes of direction (123321, 12321), or changes in alternation (12122323). In every case, melodic grouping will influence metric perception due to the accent falling on the initial note in a pattern. Yet it seems that the proliferation of melodic patterns weakens the effect of melodic accent at

28. This follows from the traditional practice of voice-leading. The observation that an intervallic skip is followed by a stepwise melodic progression in the opposite direction lies at the basis of "gap-fill melodies" identified by Meyer (1973).
29. Lerdahl and Jackendoff (1983: 83–84 ex. 4.32) consider alternating patterns as pitch repetition in the relevant level of time-span reduction (MPR 5e).

the same time. In a melodic line of an average complexity, competitive patterns will result in mutually exclusive groupings, and so melodic accents arising from them will annihilate one another. This surmise is consistent with recent experimental results that demonstrate that pitch information is of negligible influence on metric perception (Snyder and Krumhansl 2001). Presumably, this information plays a role only in the absence of other information and only if melodic contour is completely univocal. The effect of melodic accents seems to be strongest in solo lines of equal rhythmical values performed with a high velocity.[30]

In light of the discussion devoted to grouping in paragraphs 2.1.2 and 2.1.3, it is curious to see how this factor of metric perception informs the results of an analytical exercise undertaken by Koch in the course of his composition handbook. Koch's objective in this exercise is to teach the beginning composer the proper metric notation of a melody. He shows his exemplary melody at first without bar lines (Example 2.13), thus in a format strikingly similar to that employed by Lerdahl and Jackendoff in their discussion of MPRs. Koch indicates two possible locations of downbeats with asterisks and circles. Notation of the melody in conformance with one or the other location is shown, respectively, in Examples 2.14 and 2.15.

Example 2.13. Koch, *Versuch einer Anleitung zur Composition*, vol. 2, 385.

Although Koch does not offer any further comments to justify his metrical analyses of the melody, it is immediately apparent that the preference factor that is crucial in both of them is grouping arising from the alternation of two types of rhythmical values: eighth notes and sixteenth notes. In the analysis indicated by circles, the downbeat falls on the first sixteenth note, and in that indicated by asterisks on the first eighth note. The analysis indicated by asterisks also makes use of melodic grouping, because its first downbeat falls on the initial C in a series of pitch repetitions. The second downbeat falls in this analysis on the F, which, apart from its melodic salience as the highest pitch event (melodic accent), marks the beginning of the alternating pattern of the falling third F–D. Both patterns—the repetition of C and the alternation of F–D—form segments that are equal to

30. Huron and Royal (1996: 504) observe that melodic accents are most evident in solo passages. The hypothesis that their effect is restricted to fast tempi is posited by analogy to the subjective accents occurring in groups arising through temporal proximity of elements (see note 23).

half notes and thus longer than the segments of the melody between them. The preference for this analysis over the one indicated by circles can thus be explained by reference to the revised version of Lerdahl and Jackendoff's "length" rule (MPR 5). The other interpretation is no less likely, because it is supported by harmony—the factor of preference to which we now turn.

Example 2.14. Koch, *Versuch einer Anleitung zur Composition*, vol. 2, 386.

Example 2.15. Koch, *Versuch einer Anleitung zur Composition*, vol. 2, 387.

2.2. Harmony

Apart from phenomenal accents relying on statistical parameters of intensity, duration, and pitch, harmony is the most important factor influencing metric perception. As already indicated, the effect of harmony on meter has two aspects: harmonic change and harmonic stability. The former is much stronger and, certainly for this reason, has long since established itself in the awareness of music theorists. The latter is relatively weak. Its existence has been a matter of disparate opinions over the entire course of the theory of tonal harmony.

2.2.1. Harmonic Change

Change of harmony underlying a given musical passage is commonly considered the most powerful factor influencing meter. The pattern of such changes is termed "harmonic rhythm." Surprisingly, Lerdahl and Jackendoff have no separate preference rule for harmony. In their set of MPRs, harmony is included under the "length" rule (MPR 5) along with dynamics, pitch, rhythmical values, and slur. As already observed, this rule implies that beats coinciding with changes in any of these parameters are perceived as stronger than beats without such changes. From this point of view, harmonic changes would constitute one more type of initial accent. Indeed, this is how they are conceived by Joel Lester. In *The Rhythms of Tonal Music* (1986) Lester classifies harmonic changes as "new events" along with other pitch changes. As he explains, "the change from one harmony to another is a change from one constellation of pitch relationships to another. The point at which this change occurs is always a point of accent in relation to the sustained portion of that harmony and of any preceding harmony" (26). Still, this view obliterates an important difference between harmony and the other parameters subsumed by Lerdahl and Jackendoff under MPR 5: Changes in those parameters influence meter via grouping, which is a relatively weak factor of preference. Instead, harmonic changes are not considered by Lerdahl and Jackendoff to be a factor of grouping and do not appear under GPR 3. The influence of harmony on metric perception is direct and therefore of far greater impact. Whereas one can easily imagine a metrical grid out of phase with grouping—it is this possibility that motivates the distinction between grouping structure and metrical structure, a fundamental distinction for the GTTM—it is much more difficult to imagine such a grid out of phase with harmonic rhythm. "When harmonic changes occur on weak beats or weak beat divisions and there are no factors supporting the notated beats, the continuation of the meter may be itself in question" (27–28). In other words, a pattern of harmonic changes that consistently contradicts the notated meter will likely evoke a new metric perception.

In eighteenth-century music theory, the awareness of the close correlation between harmonic rhythm and meter is manifest in instructions concerning proper location of chords in measures. According to Kirnberger, every new measure should start with a new harmony. More specifically, no metrically strong beat should pass without a harmonic change, if such a change took place on the preceding weak beat or beat subdivision: "Except at the beginning of a piece, one must never use the same chord on an accented beat that was just used on the preceding unaccented beat, because the progression to a different chord, which the ear expects, is thereby obscured, and a faulty monotony is produced" (1982: 307 [1776: 32]). One logical consequence of this instruction was the strict regulation concerning the metrical location of suspensions. Kirnberger includes this issue, which has a very long tradition in the history of counterpoint, in his *Harmonielehre* under the rubric of nonessential dissonances (*zufällige Dissonanzen*). Following the tradition, Kirnberger requires that nonessential dissonances occur on accented beats, being prepared and resolved on unaccented beats. In the GTTM, the strong metrical position of suspensions on the strong beat is the subject of a separate preference rule (MPR 8), but in reality, as is rightly pointed out by Caplin (1978), it can be considered a special case of the initial accent in application to harmony. This is so because the entrance of the dissonance coincides with the harmonic change. It is precisely due to this change that a note sustained from the preceding chord becomes dissonant in relation to the new chord.[31] The dissonance and its resolution thus belong to one and the same harmony—different from that of the preparation—whose inception, according to Kirnberger's instruction, must fall on an accented beat.

2.2.2. Harmonic Stability

Harmony exerts an influence on the process of metrical induction through not only sheer change but also stability. The theoretical foundation of this hypothesis was laid by Lerdahl and Jackendoff (1983) and then developed by Lerdahl in his more recent book *Tonal Pitch Space* (2001). As exposed by Lerdahl, an analogy exists between meter and key, in that both of them form hierarchies of more or less stable elements—beats on the one hand; tones, chords, and regions on the other. The stability of a chord can be accounted for as its relation to the tonic, the most stable being the tonic itself. Given a cognitive tendency to correlate elements that are stable in terms of these two hierarchies, perception of the tonic in the phase of looking for meter should thus foster the perception of metrical downbeat.[32]

The correlation between the tonic and the downbeat was hinted at in a more or less overt way by several theorists. Caplin (1983) provides a useful survey of opinions expressed on this issue by authors from Rameau to Riemann and beyond. Yet, as Caplin indicates, these opinions have never consolidated into any firm consensus. Whereas some authors have posited the existence of such correlation to varying degrees and in different contexts, others have denied it or had nothing to say about this matter. Because German theorists of the late eighteenth century are not included in Caplin's report, one might think that they belonged to the latter group. In this context it is all the more interesting to observe the way Kirnberger intuits the correlation of the tonic with the metrical downbeat at the beginning of the piece. The clue is indirect and certainly for this reason went unnoticed by Caplin. It occurs in Kirnberger's instruction concerning the need for harmonic change at the downbeat, quoted in the preceding paragraph. In this quotation, an exception is made for the beginning of a piece. This exception makes sense in connection with another, seemingly

31. Caplin (1978) credits Gottfried Weber (1821) with this observation, but Weber's remarks do not bring anything substantially new to the view already exposed quite clearly by Kirnberger. For Kirnberger, the very purpose of nonessential dissonances is to form a close association between two consonant chords or, in his words, "to allow them to flow into one another" (1982: 43 [1771: 29]) by prolonging one or more notes of the preceding chord over the following chord. That he understood the latter chord as starting along with the entrance of the dissonance is obvious from the following passage: "Simply the notion of making harmony somewhat more exciting on occasion or of arousing the listener's desire for this excitement may have been the reason for allowing the harmony to be sounded incomplete directly above the bass note, and the missing note to be reinstated immediately thereafter to the listener's even greater satisfaction" (41 [27]).

32. The opposite will be true if meter is established earlier than key: In such cases, the perception of metrical downbeat will foster the perception of the tonic. Accordingly, Jean-Philippe Rameau, in *Nouveau système de musique théorique* (1726), treats the downbeat as the indicator of the tonic in passages based exclusively on consonant triads (Caplin 1983: 3).

unrelated instruction that occurs at a different point in his treatise: that the first chord of a piece must be its tonic (1982: 110 [1771: 91]).[33] In a piece starting with the metrical upbeat, the tonic harmony introduced on this upbeat may—in fact, should—thus be repeated on the following downbeat. This nicely fits the hypothesis of cognitive correlation between the tonic and the downbeat presented above. If a less stable chord than the tonic occurred on the first downbeat of a piece, the metric stability of the downbeat would be contradicted and the metric perception obliterated.

This can be verified analytically at the beginning of the String Quartet in E major, Op. 54 No. 3, by Joseph Haydn (Example 2.16), where Kirnberger's instruction is not observed. The tonic harmony from the upbeat is not repeated on the following downbeat. Instead, it returns again on the weak second and fourth quarters in m. 1. Reinforced by dynamic accents, the tonics thereby support a metric analysis shifted one quarter back in comparison to the notated bar lines. If this analysis were preferred, it would be selected for consciousness at the moment of the realization of the half-note projection, which coincides with and is strengthened by the entrance of the first violin—just in time for the full chord of m. 2 to surprise the listener and throw her into the proper meter reflected in the notation. That this chord does not really surprise is because the harmonic stability of the tonics conflicts with the grouping indicated by the slur, which supports the notated meter. Although grouping is a weak factor of preference, it will prevent the false meter from establishing itself clearly in perception. At the same time, it will not be strong enough to clearly articulate the notated meter from the beginning of the piece.

Example 2.16. Haydn, String Quartet in E major, Op. 54 No. 3/i, mm. 1–4.

33. The requirement to start a piece with the tonic is formulated already by Riepel (1755: 32–36). Violations to this rule motivated by unusual character of a piece are called by Riepel "ex abrupto," by analogy to an unexpected opening of an oration.

Haydn similarly ignores Kirnberger's instruction in the trio of the minuet of "The Frog" quartet Op. 50 No. 6 (Example 2.17). The slightly misleading effect of this manipulation is developed, however, in a far more fanciful manner and with recourse to the most disparate means, among which harmonic change and suspension play a privileged role. As in Example 2.16, the tonic stands on the upbeat and moves to the dominant on the following downbeat. The notated meter is articulated by the slur in the three lower voices, but this weak articulation is obliterated by the uniform chain of parallel thirds that stretches from the upbeat D–F♯ to G–B at the beginning of m. 34. The diatonic stepwise motion of this descent not only levels the effect of grouping, it also affects the process of metrical induction due to its unclear harmonic implications. In m. 33 the thirds seem to create a prolongation of the dominant, so that, after A–C♯ has been reached, the listener expects a resolution to the tonic, which would clearly mark the downbeat by virtue of the harmonic change. Instead, the descent continues down to G–B, thereby revealing itself as an independent principle relatively unconstrained by harmonic considerations. The only sensible scenario is that it will lead further down to F♯–A, but the bass stops on the dissonant chord resulting from the superposition of the high A

Example 2.17. Haydn, String Quartet in D major, "The Frog," Op. 50 No. 6/iii, mm. 33–44.

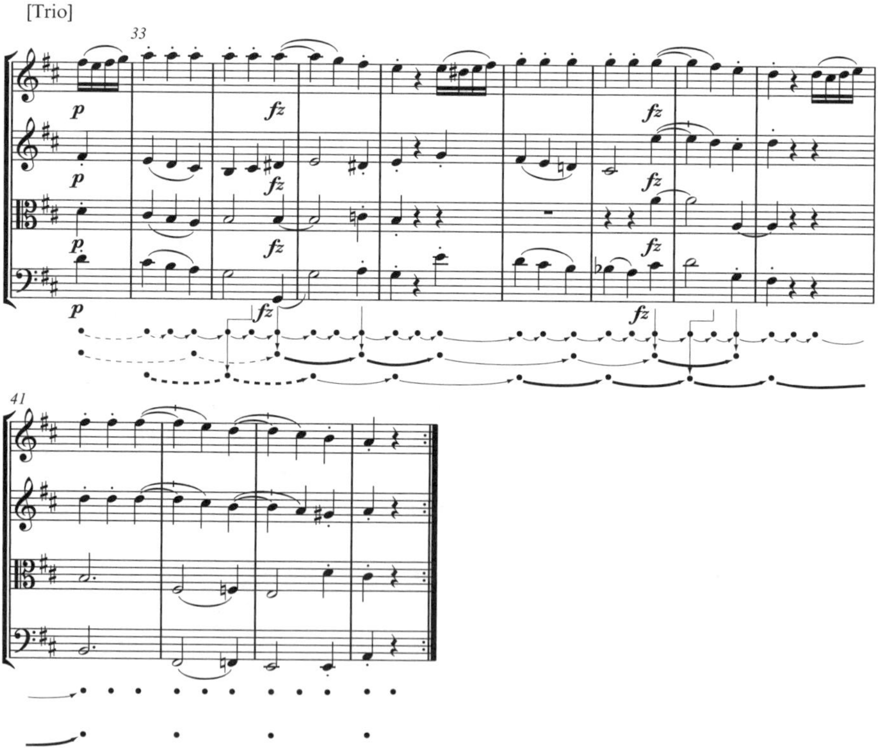

in the first violin and the third G–B. Although the harmonic sense of this sonority at first remains mysterious for the listener, the longer rhythmical value (durational accent) in the bass allows her to recognize that it marks the downbeat. Observe that this recognition ensues not immediately at the inception of G–B but only in retrospect, after the expected step down to F♯–A fails to materialize. The hypothetical downbeat assigned to G–B links back to the beginning of the first notated measure marked by the only clear harmonic change thus far and by the subjective accent assigned to A, which initiates the series of pitch repetitions in the melody. Taken together, these two attacks form the most preferred projection on the level of *Takte* up to this point—a projection that happens to coincide with the notated meter. Yet, before this projection is realized at the downbeat of m. 35, the powerful chord emphasized by the *forzando* dynamic accent subverts this order of preference elaborated by the selection function. Harmonically, this moment yields one more eccentric twist of expectations: After the C♯ in the second violin has turned the preceding sonority into what might be a third-inversion dominant ninth, the listener expects its resolution to the tonic triad in first inversion. Accordingly, C♯ as the leading tone should go up to D. Instead, this tone misleads the listener by going up to D♯, while the other three voices remain in place. The resulting dissonant formation, G–B–D♯–A—even more eccentric in the framework of eighteenth-century harmonic syntax than the chord of the preceding downbeat—behaves subsequently like a nonessential dissonance: the two dissonant tones D♯ and A in the violins resolve by steps to E and G over the sustained notes in the two lower instruments, in the end crystallizing as the E-minor triad. In this unorthodox way Haydn actually accomplishes the modulation to the key of the second degree. Yet a nonessential dissonance should fall on the downbeat, whereas here it is notated on the upbeat. Note that the tie in the first violin does not join the dissonance with its preparation but rather prolongs the dissonance, introduced on the upbeat, until its delayed resolution to G. Its underlying harmony, lasting for three beats, thus enhances a projection shifted by one quarter relative to the notated meter, which links back to the projection initiated by the improper upbeat tonic and forward to the subsequent harmony of the diminished seventh. Yet in the face of the contradictory evidence collected up to this point and the resolution of the diminished seventh in m. 36, the selection function is not likely to choose this projection for consciousness, and so at the end of the first phrase the listener is left with no reliable sense of meter.

In the second phrase, which forms a transposition of the first by a step down, a couple of adjustments are undertaken in order to avoid the same upsetting outcome. The effect of the *fz* in m. 38 is harmonically disarmed in comparison to that of m. 34 because it does not coincide with a nonessential dissonance. Rather, the suspension arises regularly on the following downbeat, thereby providing stronger evidence in favor of the previously preferred projection. The ties in the violins are quite regular this time, in that they join the preparation on the upbeat to the dissonance on the downbeat. Consequently, the sense of the notated meter is more clearly established, even though at the last moment it is slightly put into question by the tied A in the viola. (Note, incidentally, that this tie makes it possible to interpret the third-inversion dominant seventh in m. 39

as a triple appoggiatura to the following first-inversion tonic in m. 40, a possibility not arising at the corresponding point of the first phrase.) The ultimate consolidation of metric perception comes about in the third phrase due to its clear harmonic rhythm. An echo of the earlier perturbations can be heard here only in the ties of the two violins.

The above examples seem to cast a favorable light on the hypothesis that perception of the tonic fosters perception of the metrical downbeat. (Further examples that demonstrate the effect of the tonic on metric perception will be given below: see Examples 2.26 and 3.24.) Although, as already indicated, this hypothesis draws on the metric and tonal theories of Lerdahl and Jackendoff, curiously enough these authors themselves do not consider tonal function as a factor in metric perception.[34] By way of supplementing the list of MPRs, one more preference rule can thus be proposed. In the parlance used by Lerdahl and Jackendoff, it can be formulated as follows: "Prefer a metrical structure in which the perceived tonic falls on strong beats." Easy as it sounds, the practical application of this rule in music analysis may be quite difficult. The first difficulty lies in that the rule applies not to the actual *tonic* of the piece but to the *perception of the tonic*, and the two are not always identical. Sometimes a chord may be tentatively perceived as a tonic, even if this interpretation is subsequently changed. Thus, in evaluating the perception of tonic function, it is not sufficient merely to follow the score; one must reconstruct the process of key induction carried out by the listener.[35]

The second difficulty has to do with the feedback between key induction and metrical induction. The existence of this feedback, in which perception of tonal function influences metrical accent but at the same time perception of metrical accent influences tonal function, regularly impedes computational models of metrical and tonal induction elaborated in the field of cognitive research.[36] For a human analyst, however, this need not end up in a vicious circle if she succeeds in determining the actual direction of influence between meter and key at every given moment of these interrelated induction processes.

One more difficulty lies in that, as already noted, the tonal function is a very weak MPR. It is undoubtedly here that the disparity of opinions among the different authors Caplin quotes has its origin. The effect of this rule comes to the fore only in theoretically prepared examples, where harmonic function is the only factor influencing metric perception. In real musical excerpts, if it acts in congruence with other factors, its influence is rather difficult to prove; if incongruent with other factors, it is

34. Although MPR 9 accounts for harmonic stability as a factor of metric perception, the remarks and examples offered by Lerdahl and Jackendoff indicate that the authors refer here only to the inner stability of chords in different inversions rather than to their outer stability as represented by tonal function.

35. This may best be done along the lines sketched by Lerdahl in *Tonal Pitch Space* (2001: 193–201) as the method of "finding the tonic."

36. See, for example, Temperley (1999). The problem of mutual influence between meter and key in interpretation of experimental results is discussed in Vos (2000).

overridden by them. In point of fact, the perception of the tonic as a metrical factor seems to be even weaker than the subjective accentuation supplied by the processor on the basis of an earlier metrical grid in the phase of monitoring meter. This is why it plays a role only in the phase of looking for meter. As soon as the meter is established, the tonic can occur anywhere in the measure without disturbing it.

A particularly intriguing theoretical problem concerning harmonic stability is that, in the process of metrical induction, harmonic stability may be countered by harmonic salience. Although harmony is a syntactical parameter, it can incorporate the effect of salience as so-called "sensory dissonance." In his recent work Lerdahl (2001: 151, 321) uses this concept as synonym for "surface tension" or the inner tension of a given sonority resulting from the position of the upper voice and bass and from the collection of nonharmonic tones contained in it. According to his "surface tension rule," the most salient sonorities are strong dissonances additionally destabilized by inversions. In contrast, "sensory consonance" denotes harmonic stability as the inner characteristic of a consonant chord. So construed, harmonic stability is thus distinct from the "outer" relation of a chord to the tonic. At the same time, the inner and outer dimensions of harmonic stability are related to each other in that the tonic must be a consonant chord. Since harmonic stability and harmonic salience form a direct opposition, it is only logical that they are always out of phase with one another. This being so, a striking dissonance can bring to consciousness a given beat more strongly than the tonic would do, and so override the effect of harmonic stability in a given musical context. This is all the more plausible in light of eighteenth-century performing practice, according to which salient harmonic events such as strong dissonances, suspensions, chromatic tones, and deceptive resolutions should receive dynamic stress. Türk includes them in his list of exceptions to the rule of metrical accentuation and illustrates them in Example 2.7 under letters (*a*), (*b*), (*d*), and (*f*). Often stress is also bestowed on a surprising dissonant chord in the notation. One such example is the eccentric sonority falling on the third beat of m. 34 in the above excerpt from the trio of Haydn's Op. 50 No. 6 (see Example 2.17). The effect of harmonic salience caused by this and similar strong dissonances might be called *harmonic accent* and proposed as a separate factor of preference to be included in the original set of MPRs. It was intuited by Wallace Berry, for whom "dissonance in a given harmonic event...contributes, by virtue of intensity and instability, to its accentual value" (1976: 341). However, this factor is the least known of all the factors influencing metric perception. Much more experimental study will be needed before any reliable theoretical generalizations may be formulated.

2.3. Streaming and the Role of Bass

Although important experimental results concerning stream segregation had already been obtained in the 1970s, the systematic exposition of this phenomenon did not come until the publication of the monumental volume *Auditory Scene Analysis* (1990) by Albert Bregman. This is probably why Lerdahl and Jackendoff left the problem of streaming outside the scope of their immediate theoretical interest. A brief paragraph about streaming appears in Lerdahl's *Tonal Pitch Space* (2001: 32–34), but it is David Temperley who properly deserves credit for having assimilated streaming into Lerdahl and Jackendoff's theory: In his book *The Cognition of Basic Musical Structures* (2001), which presents a series of computational models corresponding to individual elements of the GTTM, streaming is included under the name "contrapuntal structure."

In music perception, sorting out tones into streams forms the vertical dimension of grouping. Both operations are based on analogous factors of preference: similarity and proximity. They also occur simultaneously. Even so, streaming is logically more fundamental than grouping. Whereas it is possible for streaming to arise without grouping, grouping without streaming could not properly materialize. Indeed, all the formal characteristics of grouping structure listed under Lerdahl and Jackendoff's GWFRs apply only if grouping is built on a prior stream segregation. If music perception as such proceeds in streams, it is only logical to assume that the same is the case with metric perception. The consequence of this assumption for the processor model proposed in this study is that patterns of attacks are perceived and individual analyses are generated by the mechanism of projection relatively separately in different auditory streams. The parallel multiple-analysis model is "parallel" in this sense also. At the same time, the coordination of attacks between streams obviously has bearing on the evaluation of analyses by the selection function. If attacks of different streams coincide, the beat marked by them will be perceived as stronger on a given metrical level. This observation is a candidate for another MPR to supplement Lerdahl and Jackendoff's list. It is also quite new in the field of music theory influenced by the GTTM. Although Lerdahl (1989, 2001: 320) includes density (number of simultaneous attacks) among his salience conditions, and Temperley makes note of it,[37] for both of these authors it is essentially unimportant whether such attacks are divided between different streams or not. In contrast, the rule proposed above presupposes that, even if the number of simultaneous attacks is identical, their effect on metric perception will be greater if they occur in different streams. This rule corresponds with the concept of "textural accent" defined by Lester as an accent "caused by attacks in many or all voices of a texture" (1986: 29). Even before Lester, streaming as a factor in metric perception was acknowledged by Berry, who observed that "accompanying voices or other voices may influence the feeling of accentual impulse" (1976: 341).

This leads us to the question what an auditory stream actually is. In psychological experiments, streams are usually lines containing one pitch per stream at a given attack. The same is assumed in the computational model of streaming developed by Temperley.[38] In this strict sense, streaming would apply only to polyphonic

37. "The more event-onsets at a time-point, the better a beat location it is" (Temperley 2001: 33).

38. For the sake of this model, Temperley makes this assumption in Contrapuntal Well-Formedness Rule 2. In his general discussion, however, he treats it as a preference factor (2001: 91). Further, Lerdahl admits that one stream may contain not only single pitches but also "chords (especially consonant ones) and mixed orchestral timbres" (2001: 33).

music, as reflected in the terms "polyphonic grouping" and "contrapuntal structure" given to streaming by Lerdahl and Temperley. Although the preference for a given stream to contain only one simultaneous pitch at a given attack is important, it is not absolutely strict. It collides with another preference: to minimize the number of streams (Temperley 2001: 91). Indeed, it seems unlikely that the listener can process a very high number of streams simultaneously. Simultaneous attacks fulfilling the criteria of pitch proximity and similarity therefore tend to be perceived together as chords in the same stream. In addition, several substreams can join into one higher-level stream.[39] This assumption is of fundamental importance for the homophonic texture of eighteenth-century music, in which there are normally only two auditory streams: one represented by melody, the other by accompaniment. In eighteenth-century harmonic theory, informed by the *Generalbasslehre,* accompaniment is, in turn, identified with bass, of which the inner voices are more-or-less necessary vertical extensions. Only rarely can inner voices be advanced to the role of independent perceptual streams.

The role played by the melody and the bass in metric perception is not equal, though. The reason for this lies, first of all, in their relationship to harmony. In melody alone it is very difficult to identify harmonic changes. On the one hand, the same pitch may belong to two different harmonies.[40] On the other hand, one harmony can underlie not only tones that belong to it but also tones that do not. The discrimination between harmonic and nonharmonic tones is particularly difficult in the principal voice, where nonharmonic tones can fall with equal probability either on strong or weak metrical positions. This is well illustrated in Koch's earlier examples (Examples 2.14 and 2.15), where two different locations of bar lines presuppose different harmonic interpretations of the group of sixteenth notes. In Example 2.14 this group still belongs to the tonic. C and E are thus harmonic tones, whereas one of the two Ds forms an appoggiatura and the other is an irregular passing note. In Example 2.15, where the same melodic turn starts a new measure, this turn presupposes a harmonic change to the dominant, in keeping with Kirnberger's instruction prohibiting prolongation of a harmony over the bar line. The two Ds are now harmonic tones, while C and E play the roles of neighbor note and passing note, respectively. Harmonic equivocations of an unaccompanied melody, resulting from the syntactical dimension of pitch, thereby add to the significantly convoluted problem of melodic accent discussed earlier in this chapter.

In the bass, on the other hand, harmonic changes are very clear, because—along with the other voices of the accompaniment—the bass presents harmony as a vertical entity. Even in a single bass line, harmonic changes are usually easily identifiable. One can hypothesize that this is so because nonharmonic tones occur in the bass, if at all, only at weak metrical positions. Nonharmonic tones at strong metrical

39. This is suggested by Temperley (2001: 366 n. 5).

40. If such harmonies follow each other, it is not possible to pinpoint the moment of their change with certainty. In other cases harmonic sense of a certain pitch is revealed only a posteriori (Yeston 1976: 57). The attendant recognition of meter is thus retrospective as well. An interesting demonstration of harmonic equivocations involved in an unaccompanied melody occurs in Hasty (1997: 162).

positions—such as suspensions or irregular passing notes—are unique in the bass. The same applies to anticipations. From this point of view, the privileged role of the bass in metric perception would be explainable as stemming from its idiom-specific connection with harmony. Yet other evidence points to the privileged role of the bass also in a non-idiom-specific sense. This follows from experiments in which the bass does not go along with any harmonic changes (Povel and Essens 1985, experiment 3). The results of these experiments can be explained on the basis of the rule proposed above concerning the coordination of patterns of attacks across streams. Because the bass is usually slower than the melody, its attacks enhance some of the projections generated by the processor on the basis of the melody alone. This phenomenon underlies a remark made by Kirnberger in reference to an unidentified symphony by C. P. E. Bach that starts with many thirty-second notes in a row: "With such note values, the three beats of this meter must be indicated most clearly in the other voices; otherwise the melody would remain fuzzy and incomprehensible to the listener" (1982: 394 [1776: 127]). Of "the other voices," it is in practice almost always the bass that is entrusted with this function.

In the GTTM the role of the bass forms the content of MPR 6 ("prefer a metrically stable bass"). Commenting on this rule, Lerdahl and Jackendoff note that "in tonal music, the bass tends to be metrically more stable than the upper parts: when it plays isolated notes, they are usually strong beats; when it plays sustained notes, they are much less likely to be syncopated than an upper part is, and so forth" (1983: 87–88). As a matter of fact, already the very entrance of the bass at the beginning of a piece constitutes the most significant event from the point of view of metrical induction—not only because it carries the initial accent but also because, when the melody enters before the bass, the bass entrance marks the first attack at which these two streams are synchronized. For this reason the bass normally starts with the downbeat. If it enters on an upbeat or afterbeat, metrical confusion is likely to arise. This could be observed in Example 2.17, from "The Frog" quartet, where the bass starts with the upbeat in the two first phrases of the trio. Only in the third phrase does it begin with the downbeat, which greatly contributes to the consolidation of meter.

Examples discussed earlier in this chapter in which the bass enters on the upbeat are those from the finales of Op. 50 No. 6 (Example 2.3) and Op. 64 No. 3 (Example 2.4). In the former, the upbeat in the bass is a result of an imitation between the melody and the bass. In the latter, the bass enters on the upbeat along with the melody. It is worth noting that the effect of the bass entrance in the latter example is combined with that of harmony: The dissonant chord with which Haydn opens this finale, thereby violating Kirnberger's explicit instruction to start a piece with the tonic, is a triple appoggiatura in the tonic triad over its root, B♭. Yet the metrical position of this appoggiatura is incorrect. As a nonessential dissonance, this sonority should fall on a strong beat, while Haydn notates it on the weak beat and so violates another of Kirnberger's instructions. This reveals that the metric manipulation leading to the false metric perception on the side of the listener was carefully planned by the composer. Further factors involved in this manipulation include melodic accents (highest pitches) falling on the notated weak beats, and the contrast between *legato* and *staccato*, the latter annihilating in performance the durational accents of the eighth notes appearing in notation. As can be seen from these remarks, the subjective accents resulting from the natural bias of the processor toward starting with the strong beat (MPR 2), indicated previously as the proper source of the metric manipulation in this example, go hand in hand with several clues at the musical surface. It might also be interesting to add that the dissonant chord opening this finale is slightly changed by Haydn near the end, where it receives the root F, thereby turning into a dominant seventh. The metric position of this dominant on the upbeat is perfectly correct, and its resolution to the tonic forms a typical closing gesture, which Haydn actually uses in this functional role in the coda—and with a playful exaggeration in the last occurrence (Example 2.18). As it turns out, the metric manipulation contained in the first measures is related to Haydn's favorite trick of opening a movement with a gesture that serves subsequently as its close.

Example 2.18. Haydn, String Quartet in B-flat major, Op. 64 No. 3/iv, mm. 236–39.

Bass entrances on afterbeats are even weirder than those on upbeats. In the minuet of Haydn's quartet in G major, Op. 64 No. 4 (Example 2.19), the bass enters on "two," thereby suggesting that all the preceding eighths in the melody form an upbeat. This suggestion is all the stronger as the first stroke of the bass coincides with the longest rhythmical value and a dynamic accent in the melodic line.[41] On the other hand, the bass entrance is not necessarily heard as the downbeat if it does not come along with an attack in the melody. This demonstrates that the "bass rule" of Lerdahl and Jackendoff, rather than being an independent factor of preference, in reality rests on the rule of stream correlation. One can convince oneself of this by observing the eccentric effect of the metrical opening of the minuet from

41. The correction of metric perception in this example comes *before* the realization of the projection characteristic of the false meter (m. 3). It nevertheless results in "retrospective reanalysis," because this projection has already been selected earlier on the basis of parallelism. As I will explain in chapter 4, parallelism allows for an earlier crystallization of meter than is possible on the basis of either phenomenal or subjective accents.

Mozart's String Quartet in G major, K. 387, in his earlier "Haydn" collection. A further illustration occurs in the minuet of Haydn's Op. 64 No. 3 (Example 2.20). The manipulation taking place at the beginning of the trio is reversed in comparison to the preceding example: the bass enters here regularly on "one" yet is heard as if it were entering on "two" because its strokes fall during long notes in the melody that weight strongly in favor of the downbeat. This way of hearing the melody seems not only perceptually plausible but also stylistically justified in eighteenth-century music. When, at the beginning of a piece or section, the melody marks the metrical downbeat with a rhythmical value longer than the *Taktteil,* the bass entrance is frequently delayed to the weak second *Taktteil* or *Taktglied.* This is illustrated by two examples reproduced in the next chapter (Examples 3.2 and 3.6), which are shown by Koch as most typical beginnings.[42] The fact that the manipulations in Op. 64 No. 4 and Op. 64 No. 3 both take place in minuets suggests that Haydn's purpose was to mislead the listener as to the moment when "to take the first step." Although minuets in string quartets are not designed for dancing, historical evidence bespeaks the internalization of the pattern of steps characteristic of this dance by eighteenth-century listeners to such an extent that they mentally recreated them during minuet movements.[43] When the notated meter is revealed slightly later, forcing the listeners to "change the step," this arouses an effect of a physical disturbance of the sort that has been discerned in Haydn's other minuet movements by Gretchen A. Wheelock (1992).

Example 2.19. Haydn, String Quartet in G major, Op. 64 No. 4/ii, mm. 1–4.

42. In minuets, bass strokes of the accompaniment falling on "two" can be found, for instance, in the trio from Mozart's K. 465/iii and in Haydn's Op. 76 No. 6/iii.
43. Such evidence is provided by Abbé Georg Joseph Vogler (1778). See my further remarks in chapter 8.

Example 2.20. Haydn, String Quartet in B-flat major, Op. 64 No. 3/iii, mm. 59–65.

The difficulties involved in deriving meter from an unaccompanied melody, observed earlier, shed light on compositional strategies that aim to attenuate the sense of meter at the beginning of a piece by postponing the bass entrance to a considerably later moment. This method is exploited by Mozart in the minuets of his two string quintets.

In the String Quintet in C major, K. 515, the minuet starts with a chain of parallel thirds joined by a slur (Example 2.21).[44] As long as this chain forms a stepwise diatonic series played in equal rhythmical values, it does not offer any cues as to the position of the downbeats. The strategy of depriving the listener of acoustic information necessary to derive the meter from the musical surface is realized by other means as well. The unusually long slur joining as many as seven quarters over two bar lines stifles any variations of dynamics and timing that would normally result from bowing, and the *crescendo* prevents the performers from applying the usual pattern of accentuation shown in Example 2.6. The processor's inherent bias toward binary regularity (MPR 10) and the fact that the harmonies represented by the consecutive thirds alternate between two chords—the dominant and the tonic—render duple projection slightly more

44. The following analysis has tangential points of congruence with the analysis Frank Samarotto (1999b: 81–94) elaborated in the framework of his theory of temporal plasticity. The most important difference is that Samarotto discusses individual plasticity conditions one by one beginning from the series of uninterpreted pitches included in the melodic line of the upper voice. When taken in isolation from the lower voice, the melody of the first violin implies the key of D minor. Yet this implication does not arise when the melody is accompanied by the second violin, because the two voices, taken together, yield the diatonic pitch collection of C major. It is the tonal hierarchy of the latter—not the former—key that informs the process of looking for meter in the minuet. If Samarotto's analysis can be described as "logical," mine is "chronological" because it accounts for the process of metric perception as it takes place in real time.

likely than triple, yet the phase of this projection remains equivocal. On the one hand, the "primacy effect" supports the metric analysis that has the downbeat falling on the first attack, especially since it initiates the slur at the same time. On the other hand, this very first attack represents the dominant harmony, which resolves to the tonic in the next step, so that harmonic stability weights in favor of the analysis that starts with the upbeat. (Even though the tonic occurs regularly on the downbeat, the preceding dominant nevertheless violates the rule of starting a piece with the tonic chord. It is interesting to observe that, while going against Kirnberger's instructions, this harmonic progression does so in an opposite way to that exercised by Haydn in Examples 2.16 and 2.17.) In the face of two equally plausible phases of the duple projection, the selection function is not likely to choose either of them. This delay will result in heightening the attention of the listener, and make her more sensitive to the minute fluctuations of probabilities between these analyses in light of further cues. The first cue comes with the skip by a third down in m. 2 from A–F to F–D. As the contour pivot, the third A–F receives a melodic accent. Moreover, the two thirds A–F and F–D combine into one harmony that is longer than any other thus far. Both these facts indicate that A–F is the downbeat. Note, however, that the listener recognizes this only after F–D occurs. This late recognition is indicated in Example 2.21 with a backward arrow. The location of the downbeat on A–F does not yet explain the notated meter, though. That the meter is actually 3/4 is clarified only in m. 3, due to the change of the bow indicated by the slur boundary between E and D in the melody, the rather peculiar return to *piano* after the earlier *crescendo*, and the longer rhythmical value of D–B. From this point, the selection function thus performs the "retrospective analysis" of the entire passage back to its beginning. The analysis is retrospective in another sense of the word also, because again the perception of the longer duration comes only after it is retained at the second beat.[45] To be sure, this delay in recognizing D–B as the downbeat would not take place if the bass entrance happened simultaneously. From this point of view, the afterbeat entrance of the bass on "two" instead of "one" is slightly misleading. Yet, as in Example 2.20, it does not in itself suggest the downbeat. Rather, coming in the course of the half note played by the two violins and prolonging the dominant harmony introduced by them, it is immediately understood as the weak second beat.

The metric manipulation just described can be better appreciated in the broader context of the entire quintet cycle. Because in the Artaria first edition the minuet occurs immediately after the opening Allegro, one might suspect that the original suggestion of duple projection along with the *legato* articulation—the latter otherwise quite atypical in minuets—was designed by Mozart to mislead the listener into believing that she is hearing the beginning of a slow movement. The quarter notes of the Allegretto could be taken in this interpretation for the eighths of an Adagio

45. Note that this retrospective effect characterizes every durational accent. It may be considered a particularly evident application of Hasty's observation, quoted in chapter 1, that the beginning becomes a beginning only after it has become past (1997: 70).

Example 2.21. Mozart, String Quintet in C major, K. 515/iii, mm. 1–4.

or Larghetto. If the listener swallowed the gudgeon, the retrospective analysis in m. 3 would bring not only the delayed discovery of the proper notated 3/4 meter but also the recognition of the movement type she is attending to.

A diatonic chain of parallel thirds also opens the minuet of the String Quintet in E-flat major, K. 614 (Example 2.22). As in Example 2.21, both phases of the duple projection are possible: Whereas the first third B♭–G attracts the metrical downbeat due to the initial accent and the melodic accent falling on it, the third G–E♭ features a longer rhythmical value and a greater harmonic stability. These last two factors gain significance in the further course of the descent. On the one hand, the quarter note G–E♭ turns out to be the first element in a series of equal rhythmical values. (The initial accent in groups based on similarity is assigned to an attack only in retrospect.) On the other hand, the harmonic progression implied by the parallel thirds is most economically heard as containing resolutions of appoggiaturas in the dominant (E♭–C to D–B♭) and the tonic (C–A♭ to B♭–G), respectively. As a result, the analysis starting with the upbeat is slightly preferred. The upbeat entrance of the accompaniment changes this order of preference because in the first moment it sounds like the downbeat. This perception is, in turn, corrected by the longer rhythmical values immediately following in the three upper voices and the longer duration of harmony.[46] Once again, however, the effect of durational

46. Instead, the slur of the second viola contributes to the misleading effect of the bass entrance on the preceding downbeat.

accents is retrospective, so that the recognition of the downbeat at the beginning of the notated m. 3 comes only after the inception of the second quarter in this measure. Even so, the meter could still be duple. It is the subsequent durational accent and the parallelism of the bass motives (see the brackets in Example 2.22) that ultimately allow the listener to recognize the notated 3/4 meter.

Example 2.22. Mozart, String Quintet in E-flat major, K. 614/iii, mm. 1–4.

Although the means of deception used by Mozart in K. 614 are strikingly similar to those in Example 2.21, they serve to imitate a different topic. If the false duple meter in the minuet of K. 515 faked the beginning of a slow movement, here it alludes to march. This is conditioned by the dotted rhythm as well as the undifferentiated *forte* dynamics and the *detaché* bowing. After the courtly gavotte in the slow movement, the minuet with elements of military style turns closer to the hunting style of the opening movement of K. 614, with which it also shares the key of E-flat major. Incidentally, this key indicates one further commonality of these two topics: the use of brass instruments. Whereas the most remarkable effects in the opening movement are the violas' imitations of horns, the two violins at the beginning of the minuet resemble a pair of trumpets, and the descending parallel thirds they play are actually a literal quotation of their first entrance in the opening movement. But the compositional strategy of the minuet, inscribed into a complex web of cross-movement connections, will succeed only if these connections are realized by the performers. If they unthinkingly apply the usual bowing technique[47] and overemphasize the usual pattern of accentuation shown by Türk (see Example 2.6), the topical allusion to march will easily be spoiled.

It is worth noting that the role of the uniform chains of parallel thirds in both of these examples from Mozart is analogous to that observed earlier in Haydn's Op. 50 No. 6 (See Example 2.17). Parallel thirds occur also at the beginning of Example 2.16 from Op. 54 No. 3. In the absence of durational and dynamic accents, a uniform stepwise motion along a diatonic or chromatic scale—whether realized as a single line or as a chain of parallel intervals or chords—is metrically neutral in that it admits of any grouping into measures.[48] In this respect it is like the series of pitch repetitions in equal quarter notes shown by Kirnberger and Koch in their composition handbooks, while at the same time it is more tractable as melodic material for real compositions. Interestingly enough, when Koch retraces his discussion of meter in *Musikalisches Lexikon*, he replaces his original example of pitch repetition with a new example of stepwise motion and demonstrates that such motion can take on any type of metric organization in either duple or triple meter (Example 2.23).[49] Further examples of a uniform stepwise motion used for the sake of attenuating metric perception follow in section 2.4.

Example 2.23. Koch, *Musikalisches Lexikon*, cols. 1473–76.

(continued)

47. The most important eighteenth-century school of violin playing was that of Leopold Mozart (1756), who in his instructions about bowing follows Georg Muffat (1698). According to these instructions, the first note in a triple measure consisting of three equal notes must always be a down-bow, the second always an up-bow, and the third either an up-bow or a down-bow, depending on the tempo and the desired effect of execution. For a detailed discussion of stringed-instrument bowing techniques and their role in the articulation of meter, see Houle (1987: 103–9).
48. Of course, this can also be true about other pitch successions. London (2004) characterizes such metrically neutral phenomena as "metrically malleable." At the same time, he emphasizes that they need not be metrically ambiguous. Rather, metrically malleable melodies will be ambiguous only in deadpan performances. "However, when malleable melodies are performed by musicians who see them notated in a particular meter, the performer's use of expressive variations of timing and dynamics will usually serve to disambiguate them" (79–80).
49. Stepwise motion is also considered metrically neutral by Samarotto (1999b: 43) and in this regard is comparable with succession of equal durations (46). Yet, as Samarotto observes, the degree of neutrality in such a series varies, in that "pitches internal to the series are the most neutral, beginning and ending pitches less so" (43). This observation accords with my earlier remarks about initial and terminal accent in groups based on pitch proximity.

Example 2.23. cont.

A special case from the point of view of the relationship between streams is represented by the introduction (Larghetto) to the first movement of Mozart's String Quintet in D major, K. 593 (Example 2.24). This is so because here the bass enters before the upper voices and does not continue simultaneously with them. The role of the isolated cello arpeggiation in m. 1 is initially unclear for the listener. The phrase starts for her properly with the entrance of the upper stream. Nonetheless, the time interval of two quarters, staked out by the stream entrances, influences the metric perception of the upper stream: the listener tends to hear it in 2/4 meter with the downbeat falling on the first attack. This perception receives further support from the harmonic rhythm, in which the tonic harmony is prolonged by the first two chords and changes to the dominant at the third chord. The moment of the harmonic change is additionally enhanced by the large melodic skips of the two violins. Supported by all the available factors of metric perception, the 2/4 meter is selected for consciousness at the beginning of the notated m. 3. Only in mm. 3–4 is it put into question. In m. 3 the cue is rather weak as it concerns merely the change of bow indicated by the slurs in the violin parts. More confusing is the fact that the phrase does not yet come to its end here, as a regular four-measure phrase in 2/4 meter should do. The ultimate counterevidence against 2/4 meter is brought by the two dominant chords in m. 4, of which the first must receive the downbeat. As indicated by the backward arrow, however, it is only the second chord that makes this fact clear in retrospect. This means that the notated 3/4 meter is clarified by the very last event of the phrase. At the same time, it completely subverts the previous understanding of the phrase structure. In 3/4 meter the initial cello arpeggiation counts as the proper beginning of the phrase, which turns out, after all, to have a regular length of four measures.

The repetition of the phrase in mm. 5–8, starting from the second degree of the scale, features an analogous distribution of the metrical cues, such that 3/4 again receives evidence from the musical surface only in the second part of the phrase. In both phrases, the notated meter is thus consolidated by the cadence. This is a significant observation, which leads us into the topic of the last section.

Example 2.24. Mozart, String Quintet in D major, K. 593/i, mm. 1–8.

2.4. Cadence (Structural Accent)

Apart from *metrical accents,* defined as strong beats of a given metrical level, and *phenomenal accents,* defined as events at the musical surface that provide perceptual input to metrical accents, Lerdahl and Jackendoff distinguish a third kind of accent, which they call *structural accent.* "Structural accents articulate the boundaries of groups at the phrase level and all larger grouping levels" (1983: 30). As such, structural accents mark *structural beginnings* and *structural endings* of phrases. In this respect, structural accents correspond with the initial and terminal accents in groups at smaller grouping levels that I have discussed earlier in this chapter but, in contradistinction to them, do not necessarily coincide with the first and last attack of a phrase. Rather, they represent the point of departure and the goal of a tonal motion within a phrase. Of these two, the structural ending, marked by the cadence, plays a particularly important role in metric perception. Lerdahl and Jackendoff admit that, even when surrounding metrical evidence is in conflict, "the cadence is decisive in settling on a preferred metrical structure" (89). This observation is elevated by them to the status of a preference rule (MPR 7).[50]

50. Structural beginning is without further significance for the process of metrical induction because, to be identified as the structural beginning, an event must be heard as metrically strong. Although not stated explicitly by Lerdahl and Jackendoff, this follows from their example 2.18 and from the assertion that "a structural beginning may occur shortly after the onset of a group, especially if there is an anacrusis" (1983: 30). In other words, metrical structure is a factor in finding the structural beginning, and not vice versa.

The theoretical substantiation of this rule is possible in the framework of the parallel multiple-analysis model of the processor responsible for metric perception. As I pointed out in chapter 1, phrases represent the level of grouping at which groups turn into fixed objects and are transferred from the short-term to the long-term musical memory. In this respect they are comparable with sentences or clauses in language. Consequently, a phrase boundary, marked by the cadence, acts like a clause boundary, in that it marks the point at which the processing of a phrase is completed and the nonpreferred analyses are discontinued by the processor. The information coming at this point has a particular weight because it cannot be "undone" by any further information. The following remarks by Kirnberger, which betray a surprisingly modern view of linguistic and musical processing, reveal that this line of reasoning was present already *in nuce* in the eighteenth-century metaphor of music as language:

> In speech one comprehends the meaning only at the end of a sentence [*Satz*] and is more or less satisfied by it depending on whether this meaning establishes a more or less complete statement. The same is true in music. Not until a succession of connected notes reaches a point of rest [*Ruhepunct*] at which the ear is somewhat satisfied does it comprehend these notes as a small unit; before this, the ear perceives no meaning and is anxious to understand what this succession of notes really wants to say. However, if a noticeable break does occur after a moderately long succession of connected notes, which provides the ear with a small rest point and concludes the meaning of the phrase [*des Satzes*], then the ear combines all these notes into a comprehensible unit [*Satz*]. (1982: 404 [1776: 138])

The difference between this description and the theory of metric processing implied by the parallel multiple-analysis model lies in that, according to the latter, understanding of a given phrase is not postponed until its cadence.[51] In most cases the selection function has already chosen one metric analysis before the cadence. Consequently, the cadence can stand in different relationship to the perception of meter in the earlier course of the phrase. Normally, the cadence confirms this perception. In other cases, however, the cadence may change the perception of meter, if the information it brings collides with the evidence the selection function has collected earlier ("retrospective reanalysis"). Alternatively, if the earlier evidence has been muddled, the cadence clarifies the meter ("retrospective analysis"). The only eighteenth-century author who did not shrink from speculating about such less standard cases was Riepel. In *De Rhythmopoeia* (1752) he offers an example bearing a curious double time signature that reflects the metrical switch from a Larghetto in 6/8 to a minuet in 3/4 taking place at the cadence owing to the harmonic rhythm in m. 4 (Example 2.25). In the earlier course of the phrase the melodic stepwise motion admits of either triple or duple grouping of eighths. Considering their metrically neutral character, one might wonder why, according to Riepel, the perception of 6/8 should arise in the first place. The likely answer is that it arises

51. Kirnberger's description accords with the serial indeterministic model of processor Jackendoff advances yet rejects on the basis of logical difficulties, as was explained in chapter 1.

from the "grammatical accents" being provided by the performer to the first and fourth eighth of every measure in accordance with the notation.

Example 2.25. Riepel, *De Rhythmopoeia*, 61.

Whereas the idea of a fake slow movement at the beginning of a minuet resembles the playful manipulation detected in Mozart's K. 515, the relationship of the meters 6/8 and 3/4 in Riepel's example corresponds with that found at the beginning of the slow movement "The Dream" in Haydn's String Quartet in F major, Op. 50 No. 5 (Example 2.26a). The character of this movement, to which the entire quartet owes its nickname, arises in part from a very weak articulation of meter. The long-lasting notes in the first violin and cello stifle the cues coming from the inner voices. In the inner voices, the sense of meter is attenuated, again, by chains of parallel thirds, as well as the complete uniformity of dynamics, rhythm, and articulation (*legato*). Under these circumstances the only factor exerting influence on metric perception in the first measure is harmonic stability. Yet this factor is used by the composer in a misleading way. The distribution of harmonic and nonharmonic tones in the chain of parallel thirds is such that, after the first and second eighth of the measure, the consonant tonic triad emerges again on the fourth eighth note, in this way encouraging the perception of 6/8 meter, contrary to the time signature 3/4. It will be noted that the perception of 3/4 is here particularly unlikely because it would render the tones E♭–C on the third quaver as "irregular" or "accented passing notes," that is, as passing notes located on a beat or division of the beat that is stronger than the following harmonic tones. This phenomenon was quite rare at the time and was used particularly sparingly at the openings of pieces. The false metric perception is further maintained in m. 2 by the rhythm of the violoncello and the slurs of the second violin and viola. In addition, the second violin—the most prominent melodic voice under the long-lasting high F—contributes to this perception, with its large melodic skip between the third and fourth eighth notes. In m. 3 the first violin and viola move for the first time only at the fourth eighth note, and at the same moment the first harmonic change in this measure takes place, whereas no harmonic change occurred on the third eighth note, as might be expected in a 3/4 measure. Not until the following half cadence is the alleged 6/8 swept away, and the proper 3/4 meter clarified: the precadential sixth-chord, the cadential six-four chord, and the dominant, which follow in equal quarter-note motion.

Yet the notated meter is not settled by the cadence once and for all. Throughout the movement it is obliterated again and again by uniform chains of parallel sixth-chords, the first of which occurs already at the beginning of the next phrase in mm. 5–6. Because the melody emphasizes the first and the fourth eighth notes of m. 5, the scale of 6/8 meter outweighs that of 3/4, and it is only later in m. 6, when the uniform parallel motion of the accompaniment slows down from eighths to quarters, that 3/4 reemerges at the musical surface. After the following cadence consolidates this metrical status quo, another chain of parallel sixth-chords starting in m. 8 weakens it yet again, even if it does not weight for 6/8 meter. Apart from the obliteration of meter, the effect of the parallel motion here and elsewhere in this movement is the attenuation of tonal relationships between chords, which further contributes to the "dreamy" character of the music.

Interestingly enough, the alternation between 6/8 and 3/4 meter is brought one step further by Haydn during the thematic return (Example 2.26b). When the cadence in m. 29 is evaded and the music starts modulating in an initially unforeseen direction, the pendulum neighbor-note motion prolonging the harmonies in mm. 29–31 at first sustains the sense of 3/4 meter, yet then factors of metric perception are reshuffled so as to yield a pattern characteristic of 6/8 meter in m. 32. The harmony splits the measure into two halves embracing, respectively, the dominant with its resolution to the tonic and the precadential sixth-chord prolonged by its secondary dominant in contrary motion. The contour of the outer voices favors the fourth eighth note of the measure, owing to the pivot C in the melody and the large skip between the B♭ and the E♭ in the bass, whereas the part of the second violin reflects 6/8 directly by slurs. The 3/4 is restored by the half cadence in m. 33, which at the same time denounces the false modulation by returning to the key of B-flat major from which it departed. It is worth noting that, by constantly switching between 3/4 and 6/8, Haydn plays not only with the listener but also with the metric theory of the time, in which the distinction between these two meters was drawn with greatest care. In the article "Takt" in Sulzer's *Allgemeine Theorie der schönen Künste* the reader could have found the following remark by Schulz, illustrated with Example 2.27: "After what has been said about the inner quantity [*der innern Quantität*] of the *Taktteile,* it requires no further evidence that 6/8 is infinitely different from 3/4 due to a different [distribution of] metrical weight [*Taktgewicht*], although both meters comprise in themselves the same number of identical note values."[52]

Notably, in the examples by Riepel and Haydn as well as that from Mozart's K. 593 (Example 2.24) the factors that clarify meter within cadences are harmonic rhythm and the bass motion. This indicates that MPR 7 is, in point of fact, no independent rule. Rather, its sense boils down to investing other preference rules with a particular weight in cadential areas. That is precisely how its content is explicated by Lerdahl and Jackendoff: "Strongly prefer a metrical structure in which cadences are metrically stable; that is, strongly avoid violations of local preference rules within cadences" (1983: 88). In particular, MPR 7 posits no strict assignment

52. "Nach dem, was von der innern Quantität der Taktheile angezeigt worden, bedarf es wol [*sic*] keines Beweises, daß ... der 6/8 von dem 3/4, obgleich beyde Takte dieselbe Anzahl einerley Notengattungen in sich begreifen, durch das verschiedene Taktgewicht unendlich von einander unterschiedlich sind" (Schulz 1794: 499).

Example 2.26. Haydn, String Quartet in F major, "The Dream," Op. 50 No. 5/ii, mm. 1–8 (a) and 28–33 (b).

(a)

(b)

Example 2.27. Schulz, "Takt," 499.

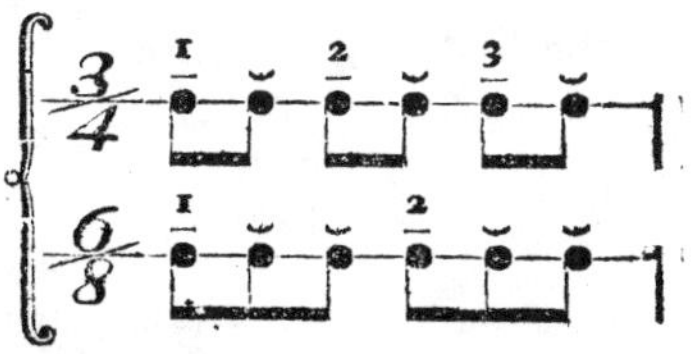

of the individual chords making up the cadence to specific metrical positions. This is a consequence of the fundamental independence assumed in the GTTM between grouping and meter. The final chord of a cadence can fall either on a metrically strong or a metrically weak beat. This theoretical position adopted by Lerdahl and Jackendoff allows them to preserve the distinction drawn in contemporary harmony handbooks between "masculine" and "feminine" cadences. For the very same reason, however, it diverges from the position taken by the eighteenth-century authors, according to whom the final element of the cadence—the caesura note (*Cäsurnote*) or, in short, caesura (*Cäsur*)—must fall on the metrical downbeat.

The placement of the caesura on the metrical downbeat was considered obligatory throughout the eighteenth century.[53] Already Riepel (1752: 48–49) had every reason to treat it as long since established among the rules of the compositional métier. In the characteristically jovial style of his treatise, written as a dialogue between a teacher, Praeceptor, and a pupil, Discantista, Riepel derides the incompetence of an imaginary composer by putting in the mouth of Praeceptor the following denunciation: "I admit I had to chuckle about one or another amusing cadence [*Cadenz*], at which he brought the final note either on the second or on the fourth quarter of the measure, for instance [as in Example 2.28]. Because in my opinion such cadences would sound very nice in a music to a *Policinello* or puppet play in the Kreutzer comedy."[54]

Example 2.28. Riepel, *De Rhythmopoeia*, 65.

The rule concerning the metrical placement of the caesura is repeated with unabated emphasis by Kirnberger (1982: 390 [1776: 122]) and Koch. For Koch, the rule that "the caesuras of melodic sections should properly always fall on the strong part of the measure [*Theil des Tactes*]" (1983: 19 [1787: 385]) is of fundamental importance in his teaching of proper metric notation. Notation of a melody in which caesura falls on the weak beat is considered by him a serious mistake. He illustrates this with two examples, each notated at first incorrectly (Examples 2.29a and 2.30a) and then corrected so as to comply with the rule (Examples 2.29b and 2.30b).

In the further course of his discussion, Koch refers to the caesura as a criterion that allows him to ultimately disqualify one of the two possible metric notations of the melody shown earlier in Examples 2.14 and 2.15. By completing this melody with a cadence, he demonstrates that in the first notation (Example 2.31a), forming

53. Apart from the authors mentioned below, the caesura-placement rule was exposed by Mattheson (1739) and Marpurg (1760–63). Exceptions from this rule were permitted in certain dances, including the polonaise (Marpurg 1760–63: 2:18), English and Scottish dances (Kirnberger 1982: 398 [1776: 131]), and minuets, as well as "some choraic and melismatic things" (Mattheson 1981: 322 [1739: 147]). For a detailed discussion of national differences regarding caesura placement in the eighteenth century, see Rothstein (2008).

54. "Ich gestehe es: ich mußte heimlich lachen über eine und andere poßirliche Cadenz, wobey er die Endnote entweder auf das zweyte oder auf das vierte Viertel des Tactes brachte, z. E. [Example 2.28]. Denn dergleichen Cadenzen müßten meines Erachtens recht artig lauten in einer Musik beym *Policinello*- oder Puppen-Spiel in der Kreutzer-Comödie" (Riepel 1752: 65).

Example 2.29. Koch, *Versuch einer Anleitung zur Composition*, vol. 2, 309.

Example 2.30. Koch, *Versuch einer Anleitung zur Composition*, vol. 2, 310 (a) and 311 (b).

the continuation of Example 2.14 and corresponding with the metrical interpretation indicated in Example 2.13 with asterisks, caesura note falls on the downbeat, whereas in the second notation (Example 2.31b), indicated with circles in Example 2.13 and carrying further the notation of Example 2.15, the caesura falls on the weak beat. With this cadence, only the first notation is thus acceptable, whereas the second is incorrect.

In his commentary to the above examples Koch justifies the rule concerning the metrical position of the caesura on the downbeat by referring to the fact that caesuras, as points of division (*Abteilungspunkte*) of phrases, are analogical

Example 2.31. Koch, *Versuch einer Anleitung zur Composition*, vol. 2, 388, fig. 3 (a) and fig. 4 (b).

to downbeats as points of division (*Abteilungspunkte*) of measures. Consequently, as do the latter, so also the former receive inner emphasis. "If the caesura note of cadences [*Tonschlüsse*], phrases [*Absätze*], and incises [*Einschnitte*] were introduced on the weak part of the measure [*Theil des Tactes*], a contradiction would arise between the nature of such a caesura note, which has an inner emphasis as a point of division [*Abtheilungspunct*], and the nature of the measure, which is only capable of this emphasis on the downbeat. In most cases, this offends our feelings in a very perceptible way" (1983: 20–21 [1787: 387–88]). In the broader context of Koch's treatise, the analogy between caesuras and downbeats is reflected further in the term *Ruhepunkt* (resting point).[55] Whereas in the course of his discussion of meter Koch uses this term in application to downbeats (*Ruhepunkte der Vorstellung*), in his discussion of melody he introduces it again in reference to caesuras (*Ruhepunkte des Geistes*), following Kirnberger in this, as can be seen from the passage quoted at the beginning of this section.

Convincing as it might appear at first glance, in reality Koch's analogy between caesuras and downbeats is faulty. The failure originates in that although their function as "points of division" is analogical, it concerns division (grouping) in two completely different senses of the word. In one sense, grouping of beats into measures forms the foundation of meter; in another sense, grouping of tones into phrases yields grouping proper in the sense attached to this term by Lerdahl and

55. The fact that *Abteilungspunkte* and *Ruhepunkte* are treated by Koch as synonyms is attested by the fact that in the immediate context of the above quotation, Koch motivates the inner emphasis of *Abteilungspunkte* in the sense of metrical downbeats by reference to an earlier section of his treatise (1787: sec. 50, 273–82) where he speaks about *Ruhepunkte*.

Jackendoff.[56] In these different kinds of groups, the location of points of division is different: whereas downbeats fall at the beginnings of measures, caesuras mark the ends of phrases or other musical sections.[57] Thus, the origin of the caesura-placement rule is grounded in a fallacy of confounding meter and grouping, a fallacy that Lerdahl and Jackendoff deserve credit for clarifying. That this rule finds no justification in the mechanism of metric perception can be ascertained from the earlier examples of improper metric notation offered by Koch (Examples 2.29a and 2.30a), which actually do not "offend the feelings" of the contemporary listener. That Example 2.31b does offend our feelings is not so much due to the metrical position of the caesura as to the harmonic rhythm: the tonic harmony implied in the melodic line of m. 5 is prolonged to m. 6 over the bar line and, inside m. 6, is shorter than the dominant harmony introduced on the weak second beat. The metric analysis reflected in the notation of Example 2.31b would thus be rejected by Lerdahl and Jackendoff on the basis of MPR 5f, whose particularly strict observation in the cadence is required by MPR 7.

Although the rule concerning the strong metrical position of the caesura is rightly excluded by Lerdahl and Jackendoff from the content of MPR 7, it must nevertheless be included in a study of metric manipulations in eighteenth-century music, because at the time it informed the intentions of the composers and the responses of their historical listeners. This rule is, however, of a different order than the MPRs discussed so far because it relies on the knowledge that is not accessible to the module represented by the metric processor. This knowledge can be acquired through explicit instruction, not through exposure, as the module otherwise acquires knowledge, and is accessible not automatically, as the knowledge in the module is, but through an act of conscious attention characteristic of central processing. Difficult as it might appear to a novice today, this way of attending to music was apparently habitual for a knowledgeable listener of the eighteenth century, as can be inferred from the remarks of Riepel's Praeceptor. Even though not based on any natural mechanism, as the theorists of the time tended to think, it could easily become the listener's "second nature."

What follows is that the cadence as a metrical factor in the music of the eighteenth century combines two distinct rules, one *perceptual*, covered by MPR 7, and one *theoretical*, regarding the obligatory metrical position of the caesura on the downbeat. The difference between these two rules concerns not only their different status but also the metrical level to which they properly apply. Whereas MPR 7—like all other MPRs—is operative at every level of metrical hierarchy, the rule concerning the metrical position of the caesura is uniquely attached to the level of *Taktteile*. This is the case because it requires the caesura note of the cadence to fall not just on a strong beat of some metrical level, but on a strong *Taktteil*. In so doing, the caesura note indicates the level of *Taktteile*. As already observed in the preceding chapter,

56. See note 24 in chapter 1 here.

57. The difference between beginning-accented meter and goal-oriented phrases has been succinctly described by William Rothstein (1989: 28) and more recently labeled "head/end ambiguity" by Michael Spitzer (2004: 247–48). See also Allanbrook (2008) for an interesting discussion of how this problem is reflected in several analyses of the first eight measures of Mozart's Piano Sonata in A major, K. 331.

this level cannot be identified perceptually with any certainty. For this reason it lies beyond the scope of the metric theory contained in the GTTM and beyond the reach of the model of the metric processor proposed in this study. Indeed, in certain earlier analyses the two hierarchically interconnected levels of projections—forming the minimum requirement for there being a metric analysis—were not those of *Taktteile* and *Takte,* whose interconnection is constitutive for meter in the eighteenth-century music theory. In Examples 2.3, 2.4, and 2.16, the projections rely on lower metrical levels of *Taktglieder* and *Taktteile.* If in other examples the processor picked up *Taktteile* and *Takte,* it did so because no level of projection lower than *Taktteile* was available on the musical surface. As the theoretical component of the eighteenth-century metrical hierarchy, the level of *Taktteile* must be identified by using a theoretical criterion, this criterion being the caesura.

The role played by the caesura as the criterion in identifying the level of *Taktteile* and, consequently, in determining the meter of a given composition was commonly recognized in the eighteenth century in reference to simple and compound meters of the same size of notated measure. In Koch's classification this concerns the compound meters c and 6/8.[58] As already observed, for each of these meters an equivalent simple meter exists in which *Taktteile* are assigned to a higher level of the metrical hierarchy. For the compound c (4/4) meter, with the quarter note as the *Taktteil,* it is ¢ (2/2) meter whose *Taktteil* is the half note. For the compound 6/8 meter, with the eighth note as the *Taktteil,* it is the mixed 6/8 meter arising from tripled 2/4 whose *Taktteil* is the dotted quarter. The distinction between compound and simple meters in every pair is possible due to the positions taken in them by the caesura note of the cadence. Because simple meters have only one strong *Taktteil* located at the beginning of the measure, it is only on this position that the caesura can fall. Instead, as noted by Koch, "because every measure of a compound meter consists of two measures of a simple meter, it must necessarily contain two strong and also two weak *Taktteile,* and hence the caesuras of the resting point of the spirit [*Ruhepuncte des Geistes*] in every compound meter must be allowed to fall both on the first and on the second half of the measure; and this last [position] is particularly the indication that beginners must follow in order to distinguish compound meters from simple ones."[59]

58. In the framework of Kirnberger's classification of meters, the criterion of caesura allows one also to distinguish between simple and compound quadruple meters bearing the time signature c, although in both of them *Taktteile* are represented by quarter notes (1982: 398 [1776: 132]).

59. "Weil jeder Tact einer zusammen gesetzten Tactart aus zwey Tacten einer einfachen besteht, so muß er nothwendig zwey gute und auch zwey schlechte Tacttheile enthalten, und die Cäsuren der Ruhepuncte des Geistes müssen daher bey jeder zusammen gesetzten Tactart sowohl auf die erste als auch auf die zweyte Hälfte des Tactes fallen können; und dieses lezte [*sic*] insbesondere ist das Kennzeichen, an welches sich Anfänger halten müssen, um die zusammen gesetzten Tactarten von den einfachen zu unterscheiden" (Koch 1787: 333). An earlier author, referring explicitly to caesura as the criterion of distinguishing compound from simple meters, is Marpurg (1760–63: 1:107–8). In the quoted passage, Koch actually retraces Marpurg's argument.

In order to properly understand this indication, however, one must be aware of the eighteenth-century distinction between two different types of ending formulas—*Kadenz* and *Absatz*—subsumed under the overarching concept of the "cadence" in the contemporary harmony handbooks.[60] The difference between them lies in the definitiveness of closure they effectuate and hence in the type of phrase (*Satz*) to which they apply. While *Absatz* closes internal phrases (*Absätze*), *Kadenz* is the ending formula of closing phrases (*Schlußsätze*) that conclude periods (*Periode*).[61] Consequently, the *Kadenz* is suitable to close a whole composition. In compliance with this formal function, it forms the harmonic progression from the dominant (or dominant seventh) to the tonic, both chords in root position. The tonic must also have the root in the uppermost voice. This caesura note of the *Kadenz* does not tolerate any decorations. Even if some further material follows the caesura—called overhang (*Überhang*) when it is kept within the confines of one measure; called appendix (*Anhang*) when it extends itself into the following measure or measures—it does not cause the caesura note to change its metric position on the strong *Taktteil.* This last characteristic of the *Kadenz* makes it an ideal indicator of meter. Nevertheless, *Kadenz* is of little practical importance for the listener in the phase of looking for meter, because it normally arrives when the meter has long since been established.

For the identification of meter at the beginning of a piece, the *Absatz* is far more important.[62] Harmonically, it can represent either *Grundabsatz* or *Quintabsatz.* The former closes with the local tonic, the latter with the dominant. In contradistinction to the *Kadenz, Grundabsatz* does not need to contain the root of the tonic triad in the melody, although there are *Grundabsätze* in which the caesura note is the root. Furthermore, unlike the *Kadenz,* the caesura note of an *Absatz* may receive different decorations. It is due to these decorations that its metrical position may become obliterated. Koch divides decorations of the caesura note into three types:

1. *Nachschlag* (afterbeat): This type of decoration consists in attaching, after the caesura note, one more note based on the same harmony. The skip between these two notes may be realized as a more decorative arpeggiation

60. These two types of ending formulas are already carefully distinguished by Riepel (1755). The most elaborated and clear theory of endings is offered by Koch in the second volume of his *Versuch* (1983: 19–40 [1787: 384–424]), where he concentrates on melodic aspects of *Absätze* and *Kadenze.* He discusses harmonic aspects of the *Kadenz* separately in the first volume (1782: 240–44).

61. A peculiarity of the eighteenth-century German terminology is that an ending formula and the section closed with such a formula are denoted by the same word. *Absatz*—in its two harmonic variations *Grundabsatz* and *Quintabsatz,* discussed below—refers thus equally to an (internal) phrase and its ending. The same is true for *Einschnitt,* or incise (see the following note), which denotes a component part of a phrase and its ending formula. Even *Kadenz* is used occasionally to refer to the section closed with the *Kadenz.* In the further course of my discussion, I retain the original German terms for ending formulas and use their English translations for melodic sections.

62. An ending formula that can occur even before an *Absatz* is called the *Einschnitt.* As Koch remarks, "the punctuation figures of incises [*Einschnitte*]...are not essentially different from those of phrases [*Absätze*], because both can end only sections of the whole" (1983: 22 [1787: 390–91]). For this reason, he does not separately discuss *Einschnitte* in his treatise.

of the underlying harmony or filled with passing notes. As a result, the *Absatz* receives an overhang (*Überhang*) or feminine ending (*weiblicher Ausgang*). The feminine ending in the sense attached to this term by Koch is different from the "feminine cadence" of today's harmonic theory, in that the final harmony of the *Absatz* is introduced regularly on the downbeat. Only its melodic line reaches to the following weak *Taktglied* or *Taktteil*. The distinction between the eighteenth-century "feminine ending" and the "feminine cadence" may be obscured, however, when the former is accompanied "improperly" (*uneigentlich*) by a harmony different from that on which the *Absatz* is actually made.[63] Such exceptional cases are illustrated by Koch in Example 2.32b. Still, the dominant arising before the last tonic is not considered by him a chord in its own rights but an auxiliary harmony replacing the tonic of Example 2.32a. Accordingly, the caesura falls on the downbeat in every case, as Koch indicates with a square.

Example 2.32. Koch, Versuch einer Anleitung zur Composition, vol. 2, 400.

(a)

(b)

2. *Vorschlag* (appoggiatura) or *Vorhalt* (suspension): This type of decoration is made by a dissonant note entering on the downbeat and resolving to the caesura note only on the following weak beat—*Taktglied* or *Taktteil*. As in the case of *Nachschlag*, the harmony underlying this process enters "properly" on the downbeat, unless the appoggiatura receives an "improper" harmonization "for more harmonic variety" (1983: 33 [1787: 407]). In Example 2.33

63. One may guess that improperly harmonized "feminine endings" form one source of the concept of "feminine cadences" in contemporary music theory. The other source is the position of caesuras in the middle of a measure in compound meters. The inability to recognize compound meters makes many authors believe that such caesuras fall on weak beats.

this results in a harmonic succession with the dominant on the downbeat and the tonic on the weak beat, thus creating the impression of a "feminine cadence." But again, as in Example 2.32b, the dominant is considered only an auxiliary harmony and, from the point of view represented by Koch, does not affect the rule concerning the strong metrical position of the caesura.[64]

Example 2.33. Koch, *Versuch einer Anleitung zur Composition*, vol. 2, 408, fig. 12.

3. The third type of decoration is not given any proper name, but the description and example of it offered by Koch (Example 2.34) make clear that it is equivalent to the "lead-in" of today's musical terminology. It consists in filling the space between the caesura note of the *Absatz* and the first tone of the following phrase with a rapid series of notes. The result of this decoration is the "connecting of two phrases [*Zusammenketten zweyer Sätze*]" (1983: 34 [1787: 411]). Because the final harmony of the *Absatz* is always introduced "properly" on the downbeat, no equivocations comparable with those discussed in connection with *Nachschlag* and *Vorschlag* arise.

64. In most examples from the musical literature, the dominant used for the "improper harmonization" of a *Grundabsatz* is reached on the weak beat in the preceding measure and repeated on the subsequent downbeat. A good illustration of this typical case is found in m. 8 of the earlier Example 2.24 from Mozart's String Quintet K. 593. Because—as I mentioned in paragraph 2.2.1—such a repetition of a chord was otherwise prohibited, it indicates clearly that the second dominant counts as a harmonic appoggiatura to the tonic. The example shown by Koch (Example 2.33) is exceptional, in that the dominant is introduced for the first time only on the downbeat. This may lead to a theoretical problem in analytically applying the criterion of the caesura for discrimination of compound and simple meters. Happily, we will not encounter such problematic cases in the following analyses, but it will be necessary to return to Koch's example in connection with some analyses included in chapter 6.

Example 2.34. Koch, *Versuch einer Anleitung zur Composition*, vol. 2, 411, fig. 2.

While Koch discusses the typical function of the caesura as a criterion in the identification of meter, in the compositional practice of the time it could also be used atypically as a tool of metric manipulation. In contrast to the examples of metric manipulations discussed earlier, such manipulations involve not cognition but the recognition of meter. Consequently, they could be appreciated only by listeners who possessed an adequate theoretical knowledge. One such manipulation takes place in the opening movement of Haydn's String Quartet in E-flat major, Op. 64 No. 6 (Example 2.35). In this example the level of *Taktteile* can be determined by a knowledgeable listener already before the caesura on the basis of another criterion derived from the eighteenth-century requirement concerning the articulation of *Taktteile* by attacks at the musical surface. From this requirement, invoked at the beginning of this chapter and corroborated by Koch in the course of a long discussion to be summarized in the subsequent chapter, it follows that the level of *Taktteile* must correspond with some level of the projective hierarchy elaborated by the processor in the course of its analysis. In other words, a metrical level that is lower than the lowest level of projection cannot be that of *Taktteile*. Because at the beginning of Example 2.35 the lowest level of projection is represented by half notes, these rhythmical values are to be interpreted as *Taktteile* of 2/2 or alla breve meter, in compliance with the time signature ¢ used by Haydn. Metrical interpretation in the compound 4/4 meter (c) is not possible because in m. 1 quarter notes are not articulated. When they occur from m. 2, they do so only as *Taktglieder*. But in alla breve, caesura notes of *Absätze* and *Kadenze* are allowed to fall exclusively on the beginnings of notated measures. Instead, the *Quintabsatz* occurs in the middle of m. 4, and the same happens with the *Kadenz* in m. 8. What takes place here is a sort of metrical modulation, which Haydn carries out in the course of the first and then, again, in the course of the second phrase from the simple 2/2 to the compound 4/4 meter. As a result of this modulation, the quarter notes are advanced from the initial role of *Taktglieder* to that of *Taktteile*, and the half notes, originally taken for *Taktteile,* turn out to represent the level of projection corresponding with the real 2/4 measures (*Takte*) that are contained in every notated measure of 4/4. The shift of *Taktteile* to a lower metrical level is clearly perceivable because of the diminution of rhythmical values at the musical surface and the gradual acceleration of the harmonic rhythm.

Example 2.35. Haydn, String Quartet in E-flat major, Op. 64 No. 6/i, mm. 1–8.

Note that the existence of a corresponding level of projection as the criterion for the identification of *Taktteile* in Example 2.35 allows for metrical modulation only from the simple to the compound meter. It is not effective for the metrical change going the other way around. This is so because the level of *Taktteile* in a simple meter is higher than in its equivalent compound meter. If a level of the projective hierarchy exists corresponding to that of the *Taktteile* of compound meter, the projection of the *Taktteile* of the simple meter arises automatically. In such cases, interpretation of a given passage in both meters 2/2 or 4/4 is equally possible, and the caesura, rather than changing the meter, clarifies it in the first place.[65] In view of these remarks, one can better appreciate the exceptionality of the manipulation accomplished by Haydn in his B-minor quartet, Op. 64 No. 2 (Example 2.36), in which the first phrase begins in the compound 4/4 meter but ends in the simple alla breve. Haydn is able to realize this modulation because he takes his cue, as it were, from the phrase structure (*Satzbau*). After the opening D, whose function remains at first unclear for the listener, the repeated eighth-note motive, indicated by the brackets, will be most naturally understood by her as an imperfect incise. One of the most popular types of the four-measure phrase (*Vierer*) in eighteenth-century compositions starts with a repetition—exact or varied—of an imperfect incise (*unvollkommener Einschnitt*) of one measure followed by a perfect incise (*vollkommener Einschnitt*) of two measures.[66] Had this scenario been carried through by Haydn, the phrase would have likely continued as shown in Example 2.37. The size of the imperfect incises allows a knowledgeable listener to determine the meter as 2/4, which can be notated as compound 4/4 in keeping with the time signature c used by Haydn on the score.

65. This is confirmed by Koch (1787: 294), who shows an example containing four quarter notes in every notated measure. In the commentary, he points out that these rhythmical values can be interpreted either as *Taktteile* of compound 4/4 meter or as *Taktglieder* of simple 2/2 meter.

66. See Koch (1983: 14 [1787: 373]). Nancy Kovaleff Baker translates *unvollkommener Einschnitt* as "incomplete incise" and *vollkommener Einschnitt* as "complete incise." This translation not only is linguistically imprecise but also obliterates the fact that, for Koch, all incises are by definition incomplete (*unvollständig*).

Yet the actual continuation of the phrase takes a different course and, by doing so, forces the listener to revise her conjecture concerning the meter. The *Quintabsatz* of m. 4, with the appoggiatura falling on the first half of the measure and its resolution reaching to the second half, clearly indicates alla breve. Further cues pointing to the change of meter in the course of the phrase are the two half-note values in mm. 3 and 4, which interrupt the articulation of quarters as *Taktteile* of the compound c meter. (Note that, in and of themselves, these interruptions would not testify to the change of meter because the articulation of quarter notes at the beginning of the phrase does not univocally indicate 4/4. Rather, as explained above, it admits of either 2/2 or 4/4.) It is interesting to observe that the projection equal to the half note was initiated already by the opening D before the projection of quarters. Whereas, in the context of the two following incises, it was interpreted as representing the level of *Takte* in 2/4 meter preceding the projection of *Taktteile* in the way similar to that observed in Example 2.1, in 2/2 meter it turns out to announce the level of *Taktteile* that is ultimately explained only at the end of the phrase by its *Absatz*. As a further consequence, the change of meter attested to by the *Absatz* also clarifies the role of the opening note D as the actual beginning of a four-measure phrase (*Vierer*) in 2/2 meter. The structure of this phrase, which is highly unusual from the point of view of the eighteenth-century *Satzbau*, serves the purpose of the metrical modulation and therefore can be understood only in light of it.[67]

Another peculiarity of this phrase is the change of key from D major, suggested by its beginning, to B minor, coming at its end. Whereas this tonal manipulation has been recognized by virtually all authors writing about Haydn's string quartets,[68] the metrical change from 4/4 to 2/2 apparently has escaped their attention. In point of fact, the two changes constitute two sides of the same trick, which aims at producing a surprising twist in the expressive character of the theme: from a contredanse in D major and 2/4—announcing a thematic idea proper for a quick finale rather than an opening movement—to what Wye J. Allanbrook (1983) would call an "exalted march" in B minor and 2/2. The moment of this twist can be precisely indicated. It happens when the dominant seventh enters in the middle

67. This is why the otherwise valuable analysis by William Rothstein (1989: 170–73) remains nevertheless incomplete. Rothstein does observe the metric ambiguity at the beginning of Op. 64 No. 2 resulting from the conflict between the opening note D and the motivic parallelism in mm. 1–2—"does the meter begin at the beginning, or with the second half of m. 1?"—and he astutely points out that the resolution of this conflict happens in mm. 3–4, so that "retroactively, the meter is understood to have begun with the first note of the piece" (170); but he does not relate these observations to the change of meter from 4/4 to 2/2. Rather, he analyzes the whole phrase in compound 4/4 meter. Indeed, this last meter returns from m. 9 and underlies a series of phrases whose structure Rothstein correctly describes in the further course of his analysis. Yet, as he points out, "Haydn is rarely one to neglect the potential of his material" (170), and so Haydn continues to exploit the metric ambiguity of the theme throughout the movement by switching between the two meters announced at the beginning. If 4/4 is restored immediately after the theme, 2/2 will come back into play slightly later; most notably from m. 83 (see Example 3.9).

68. Among others, by Tovey (1949: 62) and Rosen (1971: 140). For both authors, this was the reason to link Op. 64 No. 2 with the B-minor quartet Op. 33 No. 1, which contains the same trick.

Example 2.36. Haydn, String Quartet in B minor, Op. 64 No. 2/i, mm. 1–4.

Example 2.37. Recomposition of the opening of Haydn's Op. 64 No. 2/i.

of the phrase (mm. 2/3), interrupting the realization of the scenario reconstructed in Example 2.37 simultaneously in its metrical and tonal dimension. The effect of this chord is enhanced by the sudden change from *solo* to *tutti* and from *piano* to *forte*.

A particularly complex case of metric manipulation in two stages takes place in the finale of Haydn's String Quartet in B-flat major, Op. 55 No. 3 (Example 2.38). While the caesura plays an important role at the second stage, the first stage makes use of perceptual factors represented by MPRs so that the entire intrigue involves both modular and central processing. At the beginning of the theme, melodic accents falling on the highest first notes within uniform sixteenth-note runs determine the perception of the meter, with bar lines shifted by one eighth note backward in comparison with the notation. Within every run, the duple grouping of sixteenths is indicated by slurs, which establish rhythmical values of eighths as the lower level of projection. The slurs also give support to the higher-level projection, represented by dotted quarters, in that they join the two first pairs of notes but not the last pair. The first notes of the first slurs thus receive initial accents coinciding with the melodic accents on B♭, G, and E♭. According to the revised version of MPR 5, initial accents also fall on the first *staccato* notes after the slurs, but their effect is incomparably weaker, because the *legato* segments are longer than the *staccato* ones.

Having been selected by the processor at the E♭, which realizes the higher-level projection near the end of m. 1, this analysis is put into question in m. 2, during the third run, which is played in unison by all four instruments. The first cue pointing to the necessity of retrospective reanalysis is the change of articulation from *legato* to *staccato*. This happens already on the second pair of notes, C–B♭, which the listener expects to be slurred. The surprise produced by this failed expectation and the initial accent occasioned by the change of articulation mark this moment for consciousness. The C becomes more salient than the earlier E♭ also because the series of *staccato* notes turns out to be much longer than the single slur. The second cue is the prolongation of the descending scale by two notes, F–E♭. As a result, the next beat of the higher-level projection, falling on F, while articulated by an attack, receives no support from any factor of preference. Instead, such support is clearly received by the following D: because it not only is a melodic contour pivot but also initiates the new zigzagged melodic pattern in the first violin and the series of eighths in the three lower parts. At this moment the original analysis is thus revised, and the analysis corresponding with the notated meter is imposed retrospectively on the earlier portion of music.

Yet even the revised analysis does not answer the question which of the interconnected levels of projection—eighths or dotted quarters—is that of *Taktteile* and, consequently, whether 6/8 is meant here as compound or simple meter. Only

Example 2.38. Haydn, String Quartet in B-flat major, Op. 55 No. 3/iv, mm. 1–8.

the half cadence (*Quintabsatz*) arriving at the beginning of the notated m. 4 brings the answer to this question. Because this *Absatz* is clearly felt as the closure of a regular four-measure phrase (*Vierer*) started with the D in the middle of the notated m. 2, it reveals that the 6/8 meter is compound, its every notated measure comprising two real measures of simple 3/8. That the caesura note of this *Absatz* falls on the first half of the notated measure and not on the second half, as is normally the case with regular phrases in compound meters, has to do with the fact that the *Vierer* begins in the middle of m. 2, being preceded by a huge anacrusis of more than three real measures of 3/8, which is not counted to its length and whose function remains unclear to the listener at this stage of her understanding.

This understanding is immediately challenged, though, by the material following the caesura. Whereas one would expect a single stroke of the dominant chord in m. 4, this chord is repeated many times and, in the course of these repetitions, provided with a double appoggiatura, which ultimately resolves to the plain dominant on the second half of the notated measure. If the real meter were 3/8, this resolution would fall already on the subsequent downbeat after the deleted bar line. This means, in turn, that the material following the caesura would extend beyond the limit of one measure permitted for an overhang (*Überhang*). According to Koch, "it is beyond doubt that the caesura of an *Absatz* must fall only on one strong *Taktteil*. Although the *Absatz* itself can end with a feminine ending, that means, be prolonged until the weak *Taktteil*,...the ending of an *Absatz* can never take two measures, that is, two strong and two weak *Taktteile*."[69] The manipulation performed by Haydn corresponds, in fact, to an example of incorrect notation provided by Koch (Example 2.39a). The conclusion drawn by him is that this example is not really in 3/8 but, rather, in the simple (mixed) 6/8 derived from 2/4, and its correct notation should appear as it does in Example 2.39b. The same conclusion applies also to Haydn, with the difference that he does not commit any notational mistake. Although the 3/8 meter, recognized at first by the listener on the basis of the caesura, must be corrected to 6/8 in the face of its overhang, the composer writes the whole passage in 6/8, which provides a comfortable framework for both meters.

Example 2.39. Koch, *Versuch einer Anleitung zur Composition*, vol. 2, 320, fig. 1 (a) and 324, fig. 3 (b).

(continued)

69. "Es ist ja eine ausgemachte Sache, daß die Cäsur eines Absatzes nur auf einen guten Tacttheil fallen muß, und daß zwar der Absatz selbst sich gleichsam mit einem weiblichen Ausgange endigen, das ist, bis in den schlechten Tacttheil hinüber gezogen werden kann,...aber niemals kann die Endigung eines Absatzes zwey Tacte, das ist, zwey gute und zwey schlechte Tacttheile einnehmen" (Koch 1787: 305–6).

Example 2.39. cont.

Observe that the caesura falls not only in the fourth measure of 3/8 counting from the D in m. 2 but also in the fourth measure of the simple 6/8 counted from the beginning of the theme. The revision of meter, forced by the overhang, thus results in the entire first phrase of the theme turning into a *Vierer* that is aligned with the notated bar lines on the score and that incorporates in its structure the initial sixteenth-note runs. From this point of view this metric manipulation is a true stroke of genius, bringing all the puzzles of this peculiar opening into a logical pattern in the end. Again, as in Op. 64 No. 2 (Example 2.36), the complexity of this pattern reflects the complexity of the process through which the phrase comes into being. But Haydn's game with the listener is not over yet. Its final stage takes place during the repetition of the phrase in mm. 5–8. Because this time the phrase ends not with the *Quintabsatz* but with *Kadenz,* it includes one more chord, the tonic, which falls in the middle of m. 8, in this way univocally attesting to 3/8 meter notated in compound 6/8. The simple 6/8 does not arise here at all. The entire second phrase, started at the D in m. 6, is a five-measure one (*Fünfer*), preceded by an eccentric three-measure anacrusis that is not taken into account in determining the phrase's length.

Whereas Haydn's manipulations involving the caesura notes of *Absätze* and *Kadenze* consist in shifts of the metrical level of *Taktteile* and in attendant changes or modulations between simple and compound meters, Mozart makes use of caesuras to a completely different end. One of two curious examples comes from the finale of his String Quintet in G minor, K. 516 (Example 2.40). Although notated with an upbeat, the theme of this finale is heard clearly as starting with the downbeat. This perception—with bar lines shifted by half a measure in comparison with the notated meter—is supported univocally by all factors of preference, including the bass entrance, octave transfers in the bass, and the harmonic changes in the middle of mm. 41 and 45. In the context of the perceived meter, the caesuras of the *Absätze,* notated on the downbeats of mm. 42 and 46, are thus heard as falling incorrectly on weak beats. Clearly, Mozart's intention was to create an impression of blatant mistakes while at the same time providing for himself an alibi in the apparently correct notation. The effect of this joke on the knowledgeable listener of the eighteenth century must have been similar to that reported by Riepel's Praeceptor in reference to mistakes committed by an incompetent composer: more like the clownery of the puppet theatre than a serious composition. In its quality, even if not in its extent, it thus comes close to the jokes that appeared soon afterward in the *Dorfmusikanten-Sextett*, K. 522, entitled by Mozart *Ein musikalischer Spass*.[70] Other signs of compositional incompetence typical of a folk band include the unsophisticated harmonization of the theme by prolongation of the tonic harmony for the entire three measures and the dynamic accents in the middle of mm. 39 and 43, which lead the players to emphasize—in the way characteristic of bad musicians—the melodic accents on the high B. The fact that such clownish music occurs in the finale of K. 516 and that it directly follows the startling complaint of the introduction sheds a rather peculiar light on this work that is commonly considered the deepest and most personally felt expression of tragedy in Mozart's oeuvre.[71]

Parenthetically, the fact that Mozart sought to secure the location of caesuras on the notated downbeats by starting the theme with an incomplete first measure demonstrates that he considered 6/8 in this finale as a simple meter. In compound meter this concern would be superfluous since both positions of the caesura—whether on the first or on the second half of the measure—are correct. Indicative of simple meter in this example are also the slow harmonic rhythm and the bass, whose strokes clearly mark successive *Taktteile*. Although—as it will be explained in chapter 6—neither of these factors is absolutely reliable in determining the level of *Taktteile*, their common occurrence in fast tempo fosters the perception of simple meter and in this way makes the joking effect of the "incorrectly" positioned caesuras possible.

Example 2.40. Mozart, String Quintet in G minor, K. 516/iv, mm. 39–46.

70. The dates of composition of K. 516 and K. 522 are only one month apart: the former is dated 16 May 1787 and the latter 14 June 1787.

71. The shift of meter by half a measure in the finale of K. 516 is also noted by Ratner (1980: 253–54). Although Ratner does not elaborate on this observation and his metrical scansion of the theme (ex. 4–14) differs from mine, his identification of the *Ländler* topic supports my reading of the finale as a musical comedy consisting in a parody of folk band musicians.

One more falsely positioned caesura occurs in Mozart's last string quartet—that in F major, K. 590 (Example 2.41)—but the metrical manipulation it brings about is quite different from the one in K. 516. It does not serve as a joke in a sparkling finale but occurs in the opening movement, where it adds to the curiosity of the movement's principal theme. This theme is composed of two irregular three-measure incises, the first of them played in unison by all four instruments. At its beginning, the melodic motion in half notes bears witness to alla breve meter (¢), thus contradicting the time signature c.[72] The projection generated in m. 1 by F and A is realized in m. 2 by C but then fails twice. First, there is no attack at the expected moment in the middle of m. 2. The next attack D enters too late, and in the uniform series of sixteenth notes it initiates, the attack articulated by E at the beginning of the notated third measure does not receive support from any factors of preference. Not only is it not more salient than any other tone of the series, it is far outweighed by the last tone A, which receives the terminal accent, in accordance with the aforementioned experimental results obtained by Povel and Okkerman (1981). Earlier I observed a similar case in the finale of Haydn's Op. 55 No. 3 (Example 2.38), where the F in m. 2 is outweighed by the later D. The similarity of Haydn's manipulation to Mozart's is all the more striking, since it, too, takes place in the course of a sixteenth-note run played in unison by the entire quartet. The question whether Mozart actually drew an inspiration from Haydn may be left open here.[73] In any case, their manipulations also display an important difference: Whereas in Haydn the D throws the listener into the metric perception corresponding with the notated meter, in Mozart the A ultimately shakes the notated meter that has been crystallizing from the beginning of the piece. Although the projection on the level of *Taktteile* has already been realized, after two successive failures it is again dissolved. The projection on the level of *Takte* is not properly realized at all.

In the second incise of the theme, where the unison is replaced by the more common homophonic texture, the process of metrical induction is facilitated by the accompaniment. The projection on the level of *Taktteile,* which failed previously at the equivalent moment of m. 2, is now articulated in the middle of m. 5 by the intervening attack of the second violin and at the beginning of m. 6 by the dominant chord of all three accompanying instruments. The same chord realizes the projection on the level of *Takte*. Yet, immediately after having finally been established, the meter is challenged by the resolution of the dominant to the tonic. This harmonic progression, following the pre-dominant sixth chord over the

72. In contrast to Haydn, who uses time signatures ¢ and c, in Examples 2.35 and 2.36, to indicate the meter playfully suggested at the beginning of phrases, the intention behind Mozart's time signature c is less clear. Not only does the 4/4 meter not crystallize in the course of the opening phrase, the entire movement is actually kept in alla breve without any switches to 4/4 whatsoever, even though such switches are otherwise characteristic of Mozart's opening movements, as will be indicated in chapter 6. Similar inconsistencies in Mozart's use of time signatures ¢ and c are observed by Maurer Zenck (2001: 209–11).

73. This is certainly not unlikely, considering that Haydn's Op. 55 No. 3, composed probably in the autumn of 1788, was published in Vienna only in 1789, just a couple of months before the composition of Mozart's K. 590 in June 1790.

fourth degree of the scale (ii^6), bears all the characteristic traits of the *Kadenz* in the sense ascribed to this notion by the eighteenth-century music theory, except that the final tonic does not fall on the downbeat. Still, in contrast to the falsely positioned caesuras of *Absätze* in the finale of K. 516, which appear to fall on weak *Taktteile,* the caesura note of this *Kadenz* falls on a weak *Taktglied*, represented in alla breve by the second quarter. This determines its effect of harmonic syncopation: Because the tonic is followed by pauses, it virtually continues until the end of the measure and, consequently, is longer than the dominant introduced on the downbeat. The effect of syncopation is reinforced by the greater harmonic stability of the tonic over the dominant and by the terminal accent falling on F as the last attack of a rapid isochronous series in the melody, by analogy to that attached to A in the first incise.

Example 2.41. Mozart, String Quartet in F major, K. 590/i, mm. 1–6.

However inappropriate the metrical position of its caesura, in other respects the *Kadenz* of m. 6 constitutes the only proper *Kadenz* in the course of the entire opening movement of K. 590. The later *Kadenz* of mm. 28–31 has no proper bass and is weakened through dynamic and harmonic manipulations. The *Kadenz* of mm. 60–63 is garbled through a surprising dynamic change to *piano* and an unexpected continuation both in melodic and harmonic sense. In addition, it is stifled by its elision with the closing section, which leads smoothly back to the beginning of the movement and, at the repeat of the second reprise, to the coda. The coda, in its turn, does not contain any real *Kadenz* at all. The movement not so much closes but rather ceases. The peculiar manipulation of its beginning thus is of consequence for its entire course.

This last statement is true not only for Mozart's K. 590. As Charles Rosen remarked about the openings of Haydn's compositions, "they express an immediate conflict, and the full play and resolution of the conflict is the work" (1971: 120). This general remark proves particularly illuminating in reference to openings containing conflicts of meters in which one meter supersedes another. Such metrical manipulations are never left without consequences by the composers (neither by Haydn nor by Mozart, even if Mozart introduces them far less often). Rather, they serve as announcements of more or less elaborated metrical strategies that are realized throughout the rest of the movements, during which the same conflict is usually exposed more clearly as a change of meter. In the following chapters I will refer back to some of the examples I have discussed in this chapter when I analyze later episodes of strategies initiated by them.

CHAPTER Three

Sustaining Meter—Challenging Meter

3.1. *Metrum* and Regularity of Beats

As soon as one analysis is selected and the others discarded by the selection function, the processor enters into the phase of monitoring meter. In this phase the selected analysis determines expectations of further attacks occurring at certain future moments indicated by its constitutive projections. One way of challenging meter is thus through the absence of an expected attack. This, in turn, weakens the projection. Although projection is more stubborn in the phase of monitoring meter than in the phase of looking for meter, it nevertheless cannot survive for a long time without receiving steady confirmation from the musical surface. In the eighteenth century the necessity of sustaining meter by attacks was discussed most extensively by Koch. This discussion is included in the first chapter of the third volume of his composition handbook (1793), entitled "Von dem Metrum oder dem Taktgewichte,"[1] which was reprinted with minor changes under the entry "Metrum" in *Musikalisches Lexikon* (1802). The reason for this placement lies in Koch's two innovations concerning the concept of *Metrum* and its continuity in the course of a musical composition.

The concept of *Metrum* was inherited by the music theory of the eighteenth century from an older theoretical tradition that derived the variety of musical rhythms from the various poetic feet (*Füsse*): the trochee, iamb, spondee, pyrrhic, dactyl, anapest, amphibrach, and others. In accordance with the quantitative principle of Latin verse, every such foot was a fixed succession of long and short syllables. In music these feet could most naturally be realized as successions of longer or shorter rhythmical values. This is how musical feet (*Klangfüsse*) are interpreted by Mattheson in his classical teaching of *Metrum* in *Der vollkommene*

1. In the English translation of Koch's treatise by Nancy Kovaleff Baker (1983), *Metrum* is rendered as "meter," the same word that otherwise is used for *Takt*. Consequently, the title of this chapter is translated rather improperly as "Meter and Metrical Stress." To avoid confusion, in the following discussion and quotations I retain the original German term.

Capellmeister (1739). Yet the distinction drawn by Printz (1696) between *quantitas intrinseca* and *quantitas extrinseca* made it possible to relate the length of syllable in a given foot not only to a note's extrinsic value but also to its intrinsic value, determined by its position in the measure. This possibility was first realized by Printz himself, then by Scheibe (1745) and Marpurg (1760–63),[2] but it was only Koch who pushed it to its ultimate consequences. In his examples of musical feet (*Tonfüsse*), long and short syllables are correlated consistently with intrinsically long (*innerlich lange*) and intrinsically short (*innerlich kurze*) *Taktteile*. This indicates the direct dependence of *Metrum* on *Takt* and motivates Koch's definition of *Metrum* as motion of the parts of the measure (*Bewegung der Taktteile*). Although in some of his examples the lengths of syllables correspond with the extrinsic values of notes as well, in others, long and short syllables are often rendered in equal rhythmical values or are even reversed with respect to these values, so that a long syllable is represented by a note shorter than the note corresponding to the short syllable. In this way Koch completes the change taking place in eighteenth-century music theory from the quantitative principle of Latin verse, based on length, to the qualitative principle of German verse, based on stress or weight.

The second of Koch's innovations concerns the continuity of *Metrum*. This issue belonged traditionally to the very idea of a poetic foot. As repetitions of a given foot or combination of feet—poetic meter—govern the entire verse in poetry, so also in music a given foot should be repeated in an entire piece or, at least, in a longer section thereof. For earlier authors such repetitions were necessary to secure the aesthetic unity of a composition.[3] Continuity of *Metrum* is also taken for granted by Koch, although for him it is motivated not so much by aesthetic considerations as by cognitive ones: "Now, when a composition begins with such a *Metrum*, that is, with such a fixed movement of the divisions of the measure [*der Teile des Taktes*], our feeling accepts this type of movement very easily and, as it were, settles itself in it. It is, however, immediately offended when this movement is interrupted in its flow by another dissimilar one, because it must then accommodate itself to another movement too quickly and too unexpectedly" (Koch 1983: 69 [1793: 19]). Yet analysis of the examples with which Koch illustrates his discussion reveals that he does not understand continuity of *Metrum* as the uninterrupted

2. In their accounts of musical feet, these authors combine extrinsic and intrinsic values of notes. For a survey of theoretical positions concerning the problem of *Metrum* in the eighteenth century, see Maurer Zenck (2001: 141–49). Seidel (1975) and Houle (1987: 62–77) refer to this aspect of metric theory as *Rhythmopoeia*, but this term was not used by the authors whose theories they summarize. Even if in the seventeenth and early eighteenth centuries some of these authors characterized musical feet as *Rhythmi*, in the later eighteenth century the term *Rhythmopoeia* was applied not to musical feet as such but to relations between lengths of segments containing one or more feet. This sense of the term was established by Riepel in the first volume of his composition handbook *Anfangsgründe zur musicalischen Setzkunst*, entitled *De Rhythmopoeia oder von der Tactordnung* (1752). Koch was aware of it (1802: col. 1256) but preferred to use the German equivalent *Taktordnung*, also included in Riepel's title.

3. They did not have to be exact, though. In the course of a piece, a given foot could be decorated by diminutions of its component tones. This is acknowledged by Koch (1983: 69 [1793: 19]), who treats such decorations as the main point of difference between *Metrum* in poetry and in music.

repetition of a foot. In these examples, feet are repeated only at the beginnings of successive melodic sections: incises (*Einschnitte*) and phrases (*Sätze*). If a given foot does not continue throughout such a section, it is complemented by Koch with free material. This demonstrates that, while on the one hand Koch relates *Metrum* to *Takt*, on the other he relates it to phrase structure, which is the chief issue of his *Melodienlehre*. The relationship between *Metrum* and phrase structure explains why the chapter devoted to *Metrum* appears in the section entitled "The Connection of Melodic Sections, or the Structure of Periods," which is included in part 2 of his handbook under the heading "The Mechanical Rules of Melody."[4]

If a given foot constitutes the initial segment of melodic sections and its tones are assigned to fixed metrical positions, to continue *Metrum* presupposes starting successive sections at the same point within the measure. As this follows logically from Koch's theory of *Metrum*, it is not discussed by Koch himself, but one can find it elaborated at some length by Kirnberger in *Die Kunst des reinen Satzes* in the context of his discussion of *Rhythmus*, a term synonymous with *Einschnitt* and *Satz*. Although in the passage quoted at the beginning of the preceding chapter Kirnberger writes that "the beginning of a phrase, and hence its end as well, is not restricted to any point within the measure," in another passage he emphasizes that several *Rhythmen* in succession have to begin at the same point: "Otherwise the unity of the melody requires that all periods begin on the same beat throughout the piece. It would completely disrupt the feeling of unity if they were sometimes to begin on the upbeat and at other times on the downbeat" (1982: 406–7 [1776: 140]). In the further course of Kirnberger's argument it becomes clear that this requirement holds, strictly speaking, only for short pieces; however, in long compositions also the original *Rhythmus* should be repeated most often (414 [149]).

The issue Koch focuses on in his long discussion of the continuity of *Metrum* is, instead, the continuity of the motion that is characteristic of it. According to Koch, this motion is always based on a certain metrical level. From his definition of *Metrum* it follows that this level is normally that of *Taktteile*: "Because a measure is divided into a certain number of sections [*Theile*] which determine the *Metrum* through their motion [*Bewegung*], it follows necessarily that these sections can be of no greater value than the so-called metrical units [*Tacttheile*]" (1983: 71 [1793: 23]). Occasionally the level of motion constitutive for *Metrum* can be smaller than *Taktteile*. As Koch remarks, in slow tempo *Metrum* is often based on *Taktglieder* (71 [23]). In either case, all beats of the metrical level constitutive of *Metrum* must be consistently articulated by attacks: "When the melody of the main part does not preserve the accepted *Metrum* perceptibly enough, or deviates from its movement too much, then either the bass or one of the subsidiary parts present can and must maintain the similarity of this movement" (70 [20]).

4. The connection between Koch's theory of *Metrum* and *Melodienlehre* deserves a separate discussion, especially since so far it seems to have gone unrecognized. According to Maurer Zenck (2001: 149), by complementing musical feet in his examples with free material, Koch gives up his own requirement of the continuity of *Metrum* and leads the very idea of *Metrum* ad absurdum. This imputation must be abrogated when one realizes that in such cases a foot is nevertheless supposed to be repeated at the beginning of the subsequent melodic section.

As I mentioned at the beginning of chapter 2, a similar instruction had already been formulated by Riepel. But Riepel did not relate it to *Metrum*. That Koch subsumes the consistent articulation of *Taktteile* or *Taktglieder* under the continuity of *Metrum* can be viewed as his way of compensating for the fact that he no longer conceives of this continuity as an uninterrupted repetition of a given foot. The possible deviations of melody from the motion that is characteristic of *Metrum* are divided by Koch into three categories: (1) rests (Example 3.1); (2) rhythmical values longer than those of *Taktteile* or *Taktglieder*, depending on the metrical level on which *Metrum* is based (Example 3.2); and (3) syncopations arising when a strong (intrinsically long) *Taktteil* or *Taktglied* is tied to an immediately preceding weak (intrinsically short) one (Example 3.3). In each of these situations an attack of "the bass or one of the subsidiary parts" must be supplied. Because Koch illustrates his instructions with examples containing only melody and bass, the omission of an articulation in the former is always filled by an attack in the latter.

Example 3.1. Koch, *Versuch einer Anleitung zur Composition*, vol. 3, 22.

Example 3.2. Koch, *Versuch einer Anleitung zur Composition*, vol. 3, 25, fig. 1.

Example 3.3. Koch, *Versuch einer Anleitung zur Composition*, vol. 3, 26–27, fig. 4.

It is worth noting that, according to Koch, not all syncopations present a challenge to *Metrum*. If a given syncopation does not result in suppression of an attack on the metrical level constitutive of *Metrum,* it is not harmful to it and thus does not require compensation in another voice:

> In [Example 3.4], for instance, the *Metrum* is defined through the quarter note; thus our feeling cannot be offended although the ties of sixteenth notes in the third measure are not supported by the bass. It is enough that the movement is maintained by the striking of a tone in every metrical division. In [Example 3.5], on the other hand, the same figure of notes is found in the third measure as in [Example 3.4]. But because in this phrase the *Metrum* is based upon the eighth note, the bass must necessarily sound with the tying of these sixteenth notes. (1983: 73 [1793: 29–30])

Example 3.4. Koch, *Versuch einer Anleitung zur Composition*, vol. 3, 29, fig. 1.

Yet the instruction to consistently articulate the metrical level constitutive of *Metrum* does not need to be observed in every case. As Koch admits, there are exceptional cases when an interruption of *Metrum* has a good effect. In one of the two examples with which he illustrates this point there is a pause between two phrases that is not filled by the bass (Example 3.6); in the other an attack is missing in the course of a phrase during a syncopation in the melody (Example 3.7). Koch explains in his commentary to the first example that, not only is it not offensive, but in fact "this lack of a unit in the metrical progress between two phrases can please our feeling, because no dissimilar motion hinders it from filling this small gap itself" (1983: 76 [1793: 33]).[5] He elaborates on this idea in the commentary to the second example: "Once accustomed to this metrical motion and not confused through any constraining motion, our feeling itself compensates for this omission" (76 [33]). This remark attests to Koch's awareness of the psychological phenomenon of entrainment discussed by London. What Koch means is clearly that an entrained projection will mark a beat for consciousness, even if this beat is not articulated at the musical surface. It is precisely the contrast between the mental articulation and the absence of phenomenal articulation that makes for the particular effect of the interruption judged by Koch as "pleasing."

Example 3.5. Koch, *Versuch einer Anleitung zur Composition*, vol. 3, 30, fig. 2.

Example 3.6. Koch, *Versuch einer Anleitung zur Composition*, vol. 3, 32–33.

5. Exceptions from the rule of continuous motion are also permitted by Riepel and illustrated by him with an example (1752: 17).

Example 3.7. Koch, *Versuch einer Anleitung zur Composition*, vol. 3, 34, fig. 2.

fig. 2.

3.2. Missing Beats

Similar interruptions occur in Haydn's quartets. In the String Quartet in F major, Op. 50 No. 5 (Example 3.8), they take place in the course of the principal theme of the opening movement. The "fault" in this case belongs to the accompaniment, which does not provide the missing strokes between individual incises of the melody played by the violins. But how many strokes of the accompaniment are actually missing during every pause? One or two? The answer to this question depends on whether *Metrum* is based on *Taktteile* or *Taktglieder*. Although Koch does not provide any independent criterion to identify the metrical level constitutive of *Metrum,* his very requirement that this level must be consistently articulated by attacks presupposes that it must belong to the projective hierarchy. From the examples provided by Koch, one can further infer that it is the lowest level of this hierarchy. Whenever *Metrum* is indicated by him as being based on *Taktteile,* as in Examples 3.1, 3.2, 3.3, and 3.4, the rhythmical values of *Taktteile* also form the lowest level of projection consistently articulated by attacks. When Koch indicates in two cases that *Metrum* is based on *Taktglieder,* as in Example 3.5, it is the *Taktglieder* that constitute the lowest level.[6] In the Haydn example this means that *Metrum* is based on the metrical level of *Taktglieder* represented by eighth notes.

6. Koch gives another example with *Metrum* based on *Taktglieder* (1983: 71 ex. 211 [1787: 24]). While he does not show examples in which the lowest metrical level consistently articulated by attacks is that of *Taktnoten,* from his discussion it follows that he would not allow for *Metrum* based on that level. This might imply that he intuitively acknowledged the lower limit of durational determinacy. As was indicated in chapter 2, note 4, durations approaching this limit (0.2 second) do not create projections and hence cannot form a level of projective hierarchy. At the same time, Koch's remark about the metrical level of *Metrum* in slow movements being often based on *Taktglieder* might suggest that the eighteenth-century foundation of musical motion represented by his concept of *Metrum* is related to what Lerdahl and Jackendoff call the tactus. For a further commentary on this issue, see note 57 in chapter 6.

This was clearly Haydn's conclusion, too, judging from the way, starting from m. 5, he fills the pauses with two eighth-note attacks in the bass. Logically, as many as two attacks in a row are also missing in the preceding pauses, and these attacks are actually provided by Haydn when the theme returns in the recapitulation (mm. 102–5). This suggests that the interruptions of *Metrum* caused by the pauses are stronger than that demonstrated by Koch in Example 3.6, where only a single attack is missing.[7] Furthermore, these interruptions occur in the course of the phrase, which further strengthens their effect in comparison with Koch's example, where the pause intervenes between phrases. Strikingly, when the bass finally enters in m. 5, it does so with a dissonant pitch, C♯, which sounds out of tune in the diatonic context of F major that has been established in the preceding measures. In fact, the listener cannot even be sure whether this pitch is to be understood as C♯ or D♭. Only the subsequent D explains its spelling as C♯ by resolving the implied dissonance.[8]

Example 3.8. Haydn, String Quartet in F major, "The Dream," Op. 50 No. 5/i, mm. 1–8.

An effect of interruption stronger than that of Koch's examples also occurs in the first movement of the String Quartet in B minor, Op. 64 No. 2 (Example 3.9). It is stronger because the pause of mm. 85–86 contains a missing downbeat. Clearly, the lead-in of the violoncello (m. 83–84), preceding the first incise of the melody, should be repeated before its second incise. In its absence, the downbeat of m. 86 is "empty," and the articulation of the following upbeat is further attenuated by the absence of the accompanying voices. Here, however, only one attack is missing. Because the

7. In Example 2.36 from Haydn's Op. 64 No. 2, three attacks are missing during the half note in m. 3, because *Metrum* is based there on the level of eighths, taken originally for *Taktglieder* of the feigned 2/4 meter. This drastic interruption of *Metrum* is clearly designed to emphasize the surprising twist in the tonal and metrical course of the theme brought by the dominant seventh. By contrast to Example 3.8, however, this interruption is effectuated not by a pause but by a longer rhythmical value. In this respect it is analogous to Koch's Example 3.7.
8. This awkward bass entrance becomes an agent of a tonal plot pursued by Haydn throughout the movement (see Sutcliffe 1992: 94; Grave and Grave 2006: 234–36). Metrical aspects involved in this plot will be discussed in connection with Examples 3.27 and 5.12.

lowest metrical level otherwise consistently articulated by attacks is that of half notes representing *Taktteile* in alla breve meter, it is on this level that *Metrum* is based.[9]

Example 3.9. Haydn, String Quartet in B minor, Op. 64 No. 2/i, mm. 83–87.

If Koch confines himself to relatively modest examples of interruptions in his composition handbook, this is motivated not by his conservatism but rather by the didactic purpose of this publication, addressed to beginners. In *Musikalisches Lexikon,* not constrained by this purpose, he extends his discussion onto several more striking cases. He does so, however, in the entries devoted not to *Metrum* but to the general pause and fermata.

3.3. General Pauses

In the entry from *Musikalisches Lexikon*, Koch defines general pause as "a pause in all existing voices of a piece that amounts to more than one *Taktteil*, with the result that the *Taktgewicht* is stopped for a short time, but the movement of the measure [*Bewegung des Taktes*] is not suspended or interrupted."[10] The logical connection of this definition to the discussion in *Versuch* is apparent in that it indicates the effect of a general pause on *Taktgewicht*, Koch's synonym for *Metrum*.[11]

9. Despite the time signature c, the composed meter of Op. 64 No. 2/i alternates between 4/4 and 2/2. How this metrical strategy of the movement is announced already by its theme was explained in my commentary to Example 2.36. That alla breve is the composed meter in mm. 83–87 is also assumed by Rothstein (1989: 172–73 ex. 5.26d).

10. "Generalpause. Eine Pause in allen vorhandenen Stimmen eines Stückes, die mehr als einen Taktheil beträgt, wobey zwar das Taktgewicht auf eine kurze Zeit gehemmt, die angenommene Bewegung des Taktes aber nicht aufgehoben und unterbrochen wird" (Koch 1802: cols. 659–60).

11. That *Taktgewicht* is a synonym of *Metrum* is implied by Koch in the title of the chapter "Von dem Metrum oder dem Taktgewichte" and throughout his discussion in *Versuch*. In *Musikalisches Lexikon,* he makes this point explicit by referring to *Metrum* as the phenomenon "welches man auch das Taktgewicht nennet" (1802: col. 957). This clause is missing at the corresponding place in the composition handbook.

This effect is stronger because, in contrast to the examples from the composition handbook, which demonstrate each time a single missing *Taktteil*, general pauses presuppose two or more successive *Taktteile* not articulated by attacks at the musical surface. In practice they last at least one entire measure, which implies, in turn, that they contain the metrical downbeat. But even more fundamental than the lack of articulation, which otherwise can also take place during a long note, the effect of a general pause has to do with the lack of sound. As a result, it affects the listener's most basic expectation that the music will continue until it reaches a convincing closure. For this reason general pauses are among the greatest challenges given to meter. Their startling effect, far removed from the discreet wittiness of the examples I have presented so far, is aptly characterized by Riepel: "Such an unexpected general pause is successful in attracting the attention of even those hateful listeners who chatter and argue with each other during the music as impetuously (I cannot say as reasonably) as the old women on the cow market."[12]

Riepel's remark about unsophisticated listeners sheds an interesting light on the effect of general pauses in string quartets. In this genre for *Kenner,* their effect "offended the feelings" of the listeners not only as a cognitive surprise, in the sense customarily attached to this expression by Koch, but as a challenge to their cultivated taste. Certainly this is why the general pause was so very attractive for Haydn. His breaking of the rules of stylistic etiquette was particularly effective in his minuets, where general pauses stand alongside such contrivances as drones, yodeling melodies, and stomping syncopations, all of which subvert the courtly decorum of this dance. Another important aspect of general pauses, indicated by Wheelock in her illuminating study of Haydn's jesting strategies, is their effect of physical disturbance, breaking into the established pattern of steps and figures. As she notes, "such surprises have a somatic force in minuet movements, where regularity of pace and pattern is the rule" (1992: 76). In other quartet movements Wheelock relates the effect of general pauses to the metaphor of conversation and interprets it as a parody of common malfunctions in everyday communication—the speaker's interruption and distraction (93). The metaphor of conversation also allows her to take an alternative view of the general pause as a musical equivalent to the rhetoric pause (Wheelock 2003). Which of these aspects is most pronounced in a given context depends on several musical characteristics, including on the one hand those indicative of the *Affekt*, such as tempo, key, topic, or melodic figures, and on the other hand the relation of the general pause to phrase structure and form. Whereas the former defy any systematic account and so determine the individual character of general pauses in their different occurrences, the latter constitutes the basis of the following classification into four types.

12. "Eine solche unvermuthete General-Pause ist vermögend auch sogar diejenigen verhassten Zuhörer aufmerksam zu machen, welche währender Musik so heftig (ich darf nicht sagen so vernünftig) miteinander schwätzen und streiten, als die alten Weiber auf dem Kuh-Markt" (Riepel 1752: 58).

3.3.1. The General Pause as an Interruption

The first type of general pause is one that intervenes in the otherwise smooth course of the music. This can happen either *between* or *within* phrases. It is the former situation that is referred to by Riepel, as follows from Example 3.10, with which he illustrates the remark quoted earlier. In Haydn an equivalent example occurs in the opening movement of the String Quartet in C major, Op. 54 No. 2 (Example 3.11), where general pauses separate phrases of the principal theme. The rustic air of this theme is further enhanced by long-lasting chords and drones in the accompaniment.

Example 3.10. Riepel, *De Rhythmopoeia*, 58.

Example 3.11. Haydn, String Quartet in C major, Op. 54 No. 2/i, mm. 1–12.

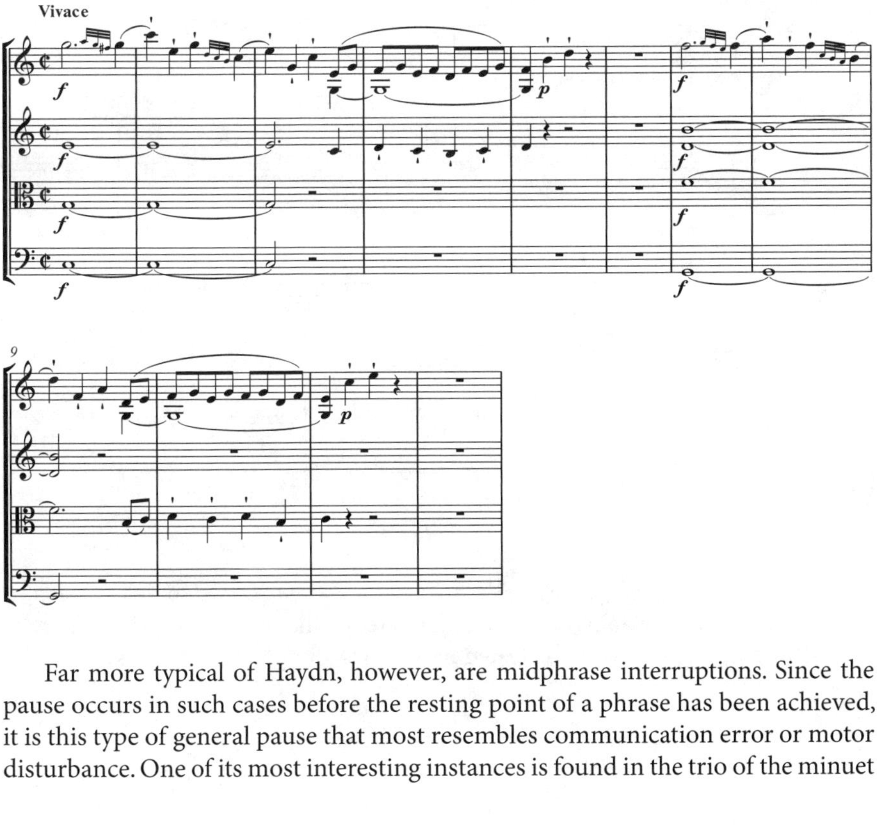

Far more typical of Haydn, however, are midphrase interruptions. Since the pause occurs in such cases before the resting point of a phrase has been achieved, it is this type of general pause that most resembles communication error or motor disturbance. One of its most interesting instances is found in the trio of the minuet from Op. 50 No. 2 (Example 3.12). The thematic return in the second reprise is interrupted by two general pauses, which results in repetitions of the theme's opening incise. Only after this incise is transferred to the cello in m. 73 does the thematic return ultimately succeed. Yet, while helping to overcome the impasse, the cellist skips over the upbeat, which thus far has invariably started all incises of the trio. In this way he playfully ignores Kirnberger's requirement that in short compositions every *Rhythmus* should start at the same point within the measure. As a result, the second pause surprises the listener not only by its very occurrence but also by its size in comparison with the first pause, which was followed by the complete incise started with the upbeat. Even more than a dancer's frozen gestures, the series of mechanical repetitions that occurs between the general pauses sounds like a barrel organ that has got jammed, due to the characteristic figures of the accompaniment and its standard harmonic substance, based on the diatonic stepwise descend of the bass.[13] The disturbance brought by the general pauses forms the only point of metrical irregularity in the otherwise perfectly regular succession of square four-measure phrases in this trio.

Example 3.12. Haydn, String Quartet in C major, Op. 50 No. 2/iii, mm. 64–75.

By contrast, general pauses in the trio of Op. 50 No. 6 (Example 3.13) occur in the course of an elaborated metrical strategy whose first episode—the process of finding meter—was illustrated earlier in Example 2.17. As I explained in

13. To the extent a human agency is felt behind these gestures, they illustrate what Janet Levy calls "something mechanical encrusted on the living" in her article of the same title (1992).

the accompanying commentary, this process extends onto two out of the three phrases that make up the first reprise. In the second reprise these two phrases return with all their metrical complexities (mm. 57–64), but the third phrase, which brought the explanation of the metrical puzzle and accomplished the modulation from the tonic to the dominant in the first reprise, is now postponed. While the viola and the cello step back, the two violins play the unaccompanied opening motives of the preceding phrases in parallel thirds. The sudden change of texture and register indicates that this section is a parenthesis. Although inserted between phrases, it does not form a complete phrase itself.[14] Rather, the two imperfect incises, based on the tonic and the subdominant, respectively, are

Example 3.13. Haydn, String Quartet in D major, "The Frog," Op. 50 No. 6/iii, 57–77.

14. Parenthesis can occur either in the course of a phrase as a means of phrase expansion or between phrases. Whereas in the former case it is the size of an incise, in the latter case it normally forms a complete phrase (Koch 1983: 53–54, 160–62 [1787: 451–52; 1793: 218–22]). I will need to say more about parentheses in connection with my analysis of the first movement of Haydn's C-major quartet Op. 50 No. 2 in chapter 7.

suspended on the B–D representing the third and the fifth of the subdominant triad and followed by a general pause of two measures (mm. 67–68). The third phrase, starting after the pause, is transposed up a fourth in comparison with the first reprise so as to return in the tonic rather than the dominant key. The parenthesis and the general pause thus help to unnoticeably change the harmonic connection between the second and the third phrase. In addition, the parallel thirds of the parenthesis ingeniously mediate between the end of the former and the beginning of the latter phrase, during which the two violins consistently play in tandem. With the *Kadenz* at m. 72, corresponding to m. 44 of the first reprise, the structural goal of the second reprise is achieved, but the music continues with a second parenthesis. This time the motives of the first parenthesis are played by two pairs of instruments alternately in lower and higher registers. After the second general pause, intervening in mm. 77–78, the third phrase starts once again, yet its route toward the final cadence is almost tantalizing for the listener, due to a curious harmonic loop and a long chain of syncopations. This last phrase, shown in Example 5.6a, will be discussed in connection with metrical displacement dissonance in chapter 5.

3.3.2. The General Pause as a "Question Mark"

Another type of general pause is one that enters after surprising harmonic events. A general pause is felt in such cases not so much as the proper reason of surprise but more as a reaction to it. Its character of a musical "question mark" is even more enhanced if the surprising harmony is dissonant, yearning for resolution. While general pauses occurring in other contexts were cultivated with greater or lesser dedication by several eighteenth-century composers, this type of general pause was peculiar to Haydn and was already recognized as such by his contemporaries. The Englishman Thomas Robertson wrote in 1784 about "abrupt and unexpected stops upon Discords, the application of which he [Haydn] has greatly extended, if not invented" (quoted in Wheelock 1992: 76). Two representative cases of such stops are found in the minuets of the string quartets Op. 64 No. 3 in B-flat major (Example 3.14) and Op. 64 No. 2 in B minor (Example 3.15). The general pauses intervene here, again, in the course of the thematic return after, respectively, a half-diminished and a fully diminished seventh chord. Whereas in the former case the resolution of the dissonance follows after the pause, in the latter case the diminished seventh does not receive any proper resolution at all or, in any case, not immediately. The broken harmonic thread is resumed only in m. 37, when the high A♯ from m. 33 is taken up by the first violin in the lower octave, and in m. 38 the diminished seventh is restituted through a chromatic adjustment C–C♯ in the second violin, leading to the cadence. These consecutive steps explain the first-inversion C-major chord from mm. 35–36 as the "Neapolitan" of B minor. At first, however, this seemingly unrelated chord and the abrupt change of dynamics and register create an impression that the pause broke not only metric continuity but also any logical connection between the music before and after it.

Example 3.14. Haydn, String Quartet in B-flat major, Op. 64 No. 3/iii, mm. 83–100.

Example 3.15. Haydn, String Quartet in B minor, Op. 64 No. 2/iii, mm. 27–42.

A special subtype of musical "question mark" includes general pauses after deceptive cadences. In the finale of the String Quartet in E-flat major, Op. 64 No. 6, such a pause after vi is immediately followed by another one after V^6_5 (Example 3.16).

Example 3.16. Haydn, String Quartet in E-flat major, Op. 64 No. 6/iv, mm. 170–84.

The wit of what happens after the second pause is related to two earlier moments in the course of the finale (mm. 83 and 142) where thematic returns were preceded by the dominant seventh and a general pause. For the so "conditioned" listener, the general pause after V^6_5 becomes a clear signal for an imminent entrance of the theme. The theme does indeed enter in m. 178, but it does so in a manner of a slow-motion picture, as if the composer were provocatively asking the audience, "Is this what you are waiting for?" Only after this provocation does he provide the proper version of the theme.

The function of "question mark" may be performed by a general pause not only in local contexts—as a reaction to a surprising harmonic twist—but also in the global context of a formal process whose further course is at some point put into question. To be sure, this global context forms an additional dimension of all the earlier examples I have discussed. In each of them the harmonic surprise—coming in the course of the thematic return near the end of the second reprise—subverts the formal expectations of the listener concerning the regular course of events until the end of the piece. But the global dimension may be also separated from the local one, when an event perfectly regular in its harmonic context nevertheless proves surprising from the point of view of the formal process. In the eighteenth century, whose concept of form is determined by the sequence of cadential closures realized in the course of a given movement according to a certain harmonic plan, this happens when a given type of closure occurs at a wrong moment or in a wrong key. In light of musical rhetoric, such situations are comparable to an argument running into a dead end. Intervention of a general pause at the same time provokes the listener to and gives her time for guesses about what will come next.[15] Alternatively, the attempt to figure out the way the music should continue may be projected by the listener onto the composer. In such cases, the music is perceived as a sort of pantomime with the composer as its subject occupied with the question "What to do next?" Of course, this pantomimic effect is equally inherent in the first type of general pause. At the beginning of the development, interruptions effected by general pauses can be interpreted by the listener as portraying the hesitance of the composer about the course to be taken in this least determined section of the sonata form.

In the minuet of Op. 55 No. 3 (Example 3.17a) the thematic return is expected to lead to the final tonic. This could be easily done by repeating the content of the

Example 3.17. Haydn, String Quartet in B-flat major, Op. 55 No. 3/iii, mm. 29–42 (a) and recomposition of mm. 37–41 (b).

(a)

(b)

15. This point is made by Wheelock (1992: 109). In terms of Fodor's modular theory, one can explain this by saying that the shock produced by a general pause is transferred from the modular level to the central level and initiates a certain process in the listener's consciousness. As emphasized by Fodor (1983: 69–70), central processing requires considerably more time than modular processing.

first reprise (mm. 1–12) while replacing the *Quintabsatz* of its third phrase with a *Kadenz*. Instead the third phrase arrives at the dominant seventh. How and when will the piece achieve its conclusion? This is the question that will be posed by the listener in the course of the following general pause (m. 36–37). Curiously, the answer brought by the closing phrase is interrupted by another general pause in m. 39. Compared to the sheer interruptions demonstrated earlier, this pause is particularly sophisticated in that it constitutes a part of an insertion in the course of the phrase. After the six-four chord achieved in m. 39, the music is expected to proceed directly to the dominant seventh of m. 40, thus taking the course reconstructed in Example 3.17b. The insertion thus embraces not only the pause but also the single chord on the downbeat of m. 40. It is because this chord is devoid of the upbeat, expected by the listener by analogy to the two previous incises, that the pause arises. As in Example 3.12, Haydn playfully offends against Kirnberger's rule quoted earlier, that *Rhythmus* must consistently start at the same point within the measure. The effect of this offense is even more striking because the upbeat expected by the listener is longer and more characteristic.

*3.3.3. General Pauses after the Half Cadence (*Halbkadenz*)*

If not that it occurs in an improper formal context, the first of the two general pauses in Example 3.17 would illustrate a playful prolongation of caesura between the half cadence and the thematic return. This is, in fact, an additional dimension of Haydn's trick. Although the thematic return has already taken place in m. 25, the four measures of standing on the dominant, preceding the pause, make one expect another thematic return, and the closing phrase of the minuet, entering after the pause, actually alludes to the beginning of the theme.

It must be emphasized that Koch's instructions concerning consistent articulation of *Taktteile* or *Taktglieder* by attacks are not always observed after caesuras of large formal sections. One such caesura is the one following a half cadence (*Halbkadenz*).[16] In the sonata form it normally occurs in the middle of the exposition and before the thematic return starting the recapitulation.[17] The half cadence pre-

16. The term *Halbkadenz* or *halbe Kadenz* is used throughout the eighteenth century by several authors, among them Quantz (1752), Kirnberger (1771), and Türk (1789). In Koch's classification of ending formulas, all half cadences are treated simply as *Quintabsätze*, their formal function notwithstanding. *Halbkadenz* has for him a specific meaning: it denotes *Quintabsatz* at the end of a piece preparing another piece that follows *attacca* (1983: 49 [1787: 443]). Koch adopts the more common eighteenth-century meaning of the term in his *Musikalisches Lexikon*, where he defines *Halbkadenz* as an ending formula based on the dominant "with which one usually does not close a musical piece but only separates one part of a main period from the other" ("womit gewönlicher Weise kein Tonstück geschlossen, sondern nur ein Theil einer Hauptperiode von dem andern abgesondert werden kann") (1802: col. 712). In Koch's terminology, the first main period of the sonata form is the exposition.
17. In terms of James Hepokoski and Warren Darcy's "sonata theory" (1997, 2006), the former of these locations marks the so-called medial caesura. In fact, the missing beat in Koch's example showing an exception from his own rule (Example 3.6) occurs after what Hepokoski and Darcy would call I:HC MC of a miniature sonata form.

ceding the thematic return is equally characteristic of minuets and corresponds to the half cadences before the returns of the refrain in rondos. After the arrival of the dominant harmony, normally consolidated by a longer standing on the dominant, the interruption of metric continuity by a pause is very usual. Its effect becomes playful only when it is prolonged by an extra measure or two. This type of general pause occurs, for instance, in the finales of Haydn's Op. 54 No. 2, Op. 55 No. 1, and Op. 64 No. 3. Because the listener expects the entrance of the theme at a precise moment after the pause, to prolong the pause means at the same time to challenge this expectation and to heighten the tension toward the thematic return. This effect arises, however, only when the general pause causes hypermetrical irregularity. If such irregularity does not arise, the general pause after the half cadence has no interruptive effect. Rather, it completes a hypermeasure started at the dominant arrival.

*3.3.4. The General Pause after the Cadence (*Kadenz*): "False End"*

The other type of caesura marking large formal sections is the *Kadenz*. In a subordinate key it concludes the exposition and in the main key the recapitulation of the sonata form. If the *Kadenz* in the main key is properly prepared and occurs in a plausible formal context, it is thus interpreted by the listener as the end of the movement. This is so even if no general pause occurs. It suffices that the resolution to the tonic is followed by a regular caesura. This effect is used by Haydn in a tricky way to fake the end of the first movement in Op. 50 No. 5 (m. 133).[18] If the caesura is prolonged by a general pause, the false ending is even more convincing. It is interesting to observe that the effect of such a general pause is reversed in comparison with general pauses prolonging caesuras after the half cadence. What is surprising this time is not the pause—taken at first for the silence after the piece—but rather the fact that, after the pause, the music continues.

The most famous example of the "false end" faked by general pauses is certainly that from the finale of the "Joke" quartet, Op. 33 No. 2. Haydn's later collections of string quartets contain more jokes of this sort, some of them even more perfidious, although less known. In the finale of the String Quartet in B-flat major, Op. 50 No. 1, the end is faked as many as five times in a row before it actually arrives (Example 3.18). Only the first time is it suggested by a general pause (mm. 223–24); the subsequent *Kadenze* are followed by simple caesuras.[19] To be sure, "false ends" in finales are particularly suggestive because they fake the ending of the entire multimovement piece. But Haydn also employs this trick in the opening movement of Op. 50 No. 3 (mm. 112–13) and in the minuet of Op. 64 No. 3 (mm. 48–49). In the second movement of Op. 55 No. 2—which constitutes the

18. This *Kadenz* has an equivalent in the exposition (m. 24), where it playfully offends against the formal principle "not to conclude any period but the last in an entire piece with the principal tonic" (Kirnberger 1982: 406 [1776: 139]). Sutcliffe (1992: 96) reports that mm. 20–23, cementing this cadence by means of a quasi-codetta, were added by Haydn as an afterthought in the autograph of Op. 50 No. 5, but Sutcliffe interprets the significance of this addition in a different way.

19. They capitalize on the effect of the *Kadenz* located in m. 16 of the exposition.

Example 3.18. Haydn, String Quartet in B-flat major, Op. 50 No. 1/iv, mm. 220–45.

equivalent of the proper opening movement transferred in this unusual quartet cycle to the second position after the opening set of variations—and in the finale of Op. 64 No. 2 Haydn's strategy is an opposite one: Having quite implausibly placed general pauses earlier in the course of these movements, he has aroused the listener's mistrust of prolonged silences so that, when the actual end arrives, the listener is not inclined to believe it and expects a continuation. The fact that in each case the pauses in the last measures are carefully written out on the score suggests that the performers should contribute to the joke by keeping the listener in suspense for some time after the movement is already over.

From the classification above it appears that the position relative to the phrase structure and form determines not only the effect of general pauses representing different types but also, more specifically, the amount of surprise elicited by them. Strongest are certainly general pauses intervening in the course of phrases. This concerns midphrase interruptions included under the first type as well as general pauses of the second type, because phrases ended with a deceptive cadence or another harmonic twist are not yet complete. Among general pauses occurring between phrases, those after the half cadence—which presupposes continuation—are stronger than those after the full cadence.[20] Within individual types the strength of general pauses can be further differentiated by reference to their purely metrical context. It is commonly acknowledged that the strength of a pause's effect is proportional to the strength of the metrical position on which it falls. Accordingly, the effect of "loud pauses" (Cooper and Meyer 1960; London 1993) presupposes that a pause falls on the metrical downbeat. This insight can be further refined by observing that, of two pauses falling on the same beat, stronger surprise characterizes the pause preceded by the attack falling on a weaker beat. From this point of view the surprise of pauses can be accounted for as a skip up in the metrical hierarchy. In Example 3.12 from Op. 50 No. 2 the last attacks before the pauses belong to the level of eighths so that the skip up to the downbeats contained in the pauses spans two metrical levels. Still, the surprise of these pauses is not equal. The second of them is clearly stronger, because the distance from the last attack in m. 71 to the downbeat of m. 72 is smaller. One might bring these observations together by saying that the amount of surprise occasioned by pauses depends on the distance from the preceding attack to the strongest beat contained in the pause measured in the vertical as well as horizontal dimension of the metrical hierarchy. The larger the former and the smaller the latter, the greater the surprise. This formulation corresponds with the account of *metrical attractions* developed by Lerdahl (2001) on the analogy to melodic attractions. Just as attractions between individual pitches depend on their stability and proximity in tonal pitch space, attractions between beats also depend on *stability* and *proximity*, represented, respectively, by the vertical and horizontal dimensions of the metrical hierarchy (Lerdahl 2001: 290). In Lerdahl's "Metrical Attraction Rule," however, proximity as the horizontal distance plays a very limited role because this rule is designed to calculate attractions only between adjacent beats of a given metrical level. My formulation can be considered an elaboration of the "Metrical Attraction Rule" in order to account for attractions between nonadjacent beats.[21]

It is not by chance that the examples illustrating interruptions of *Metrum* from the beginning of this chapter until now have come exclusively from Haydn. Indeed, such interruptions—whether by means of ordinary or general pauses—are the trademark of Haydn's personal style. In Mozart they occur much less frequently.

20. These observations accord with experimental results obtained by Margulis (2007). In her experiments, Margulis assessed the musical effects of acoustic silences, including their perceived tension and salience in various tonal contexts, especially in relation to tonal closures marking phrase boundaries. She did not evaluate their metrical contexts (discussed below).

21. In contrast to Lerdahl, I do not endeavor to turn it into any formula for quantification. As Lerdahl has admitted in reference to both "melodic attraction" and "metrical attraction," "quantificational details may require modification should the future empirical evidence demonstrate the need. It is the explanatory factors embodied in the rule, stability and proximity, that really matter" (2001: 163).

Example 3.19. Mozart, String Quintet in D major, K. 593/iv, mm. 14–21.

Example 3.20. Mozart, String Quintet in E-flat major, K. 614/iv, mm. 301–6.

In fact, Mozart's entire oeuvre of string chamber music includes only few general pauses. Most of them occur in his latest works, which suggests Haydn's direct influence. This influence is particularly evident in the case of general pauses from the finales of the String Quintets K. 593 and 614 (Examples 3.19 and 3.20), which represent stops after surprising dissonant harmonies. In K. 593 the eighth notes continue until the end of the measure so that, by the criteria presented above, the following pause is all the more startling. In K. 614 the pause takes place after a deceptive cadence followed immediately by a first-inversion dominant seventh. The same harmonic progression of vi and V^6_5 was observed in Example 3.16 from Haydn's Op. 64 No. 6. The fact that both examples occur in finales of works written in the same key (E-flat major) whose dates of composition are separated by not more than a few months—Haydn's Op. 64 was written in the autumn of 1790, Mozart's K. 614 is dated 12 April 1791—and that they occur in analogous formal positions just before the codas allows one to suspect that Mozart took the model of his trick directly from Haydn. A connection between the two finales is otherwise confirmed by the similarity of their themes: As was observed by Rosen (1971: 286), Mozart's theme is an inversion of Haydn's.[22]

One more interesting example occurs in the opening movement of the first "Prussian" quartet in D major, K. 575 (Example 3.21). Although surely inspired by Haydn, this metric manipulation nevertheless finds no equivalent in Haydn's quartets. Its particularly drastic effect is conditioned by the fact that the two pauses occur in the course of the cadential preparation immediately before the *Kadenz* closing the subordinate key area of the exposition. At the analogous moment of the recapitulation (mm. 175–76), they disturb the arrival of the final structural cadence of the movement. Both of them occur after the diminished seventh—the strongest and most dissonant precadential harmony of Viennese Classicism—and interrupt its resolution to the cadential six-four chord. After the first pause, the six-four is further postponed by the passing secondary dominant seventh to the minor subdominant, followed by a second precadential diminished seventh. The resolution of this chord, delayed by the second pause, is finally achieved at the downbeat of m. 61.

Example 3.21. Mozart, String Quartet in D major, K. 575/i, mm. 57–62.

Note that the size of the pauses in ¢ meter does not exceed one *Taktteil*. (Because the *Metrum* in this passage is based on the level of *Taktglieder* represented by quarters, two attacks are nevertheless missing during the second pause.) On the basis of Koch's definition in *Musikalisches Lexikon* quoted earlier, they are thus not to be classified under general pauses. Instead, one ought to classify them with the interruptions of *Metrum* illustrated by Example 3.6 from Koch, and the Haydn Examples 3.8 and 3.9. Yet in reality these phenomena are clearly not of the

22. Without this further evidence, the harmonic progression vi–V^6_5 would not suffice to claim Haydn's influence on Mozart in Example 3.20. In fact, one could rather suspect Mozart's influence on Haydn, because the same progression occurs in the slow movement of Mozart's String Quintet in G minor, K. 516, dated 16 May 1787. There (mm. 9–10) this progression is extended by one more chord—V^6_5/IV—forming an echo (*piano*) of the preceding V^6_5 transposed up a fourth. The following pause, taking half of the compound 4/4 measure, is one measure long from the point of view of the simple 2/4 meter and hence is to be classified as a general pause. In Haydn, the only other two instances of vi–V^6_5 progression after a deceptive cadence are in his Viennese quartets: Op. 76 No. 3/i (mm. 103–4) and Op. 77 No. 2/iv (mm. 161–62). In the former, the chords forming the progression are followed by pauses under fermatas.

same sort. The reason is that in the earlier examples, pauses fall during natural caesuras in the melody between phrases or incises so that the course of the melody as such is not affected by them, whereas the pauses in Mozart's K. 575 create drastic interruptions of the melody. From this point of view, although smaller in size, they are much more similar to the general pauses of the first type of the foregoing classification. As this example demonstrates, Koch's definition of general pauses based merely on their size may be inadequate in certain less typical cases.

3.4. Fermatas

The difference between general pauses and fermatas consists in that fermatas cause an interruption not only of *Metrum* but also of meter (*Takt*). This is what Koch emphasizes in the definition at the beginning of his entry from *Musikalisches Lexikon*: "Fermata. Such a resting point in the course of a musical composition at which the movement of the measure [*Bewegung des Taktes*] is for some time intentionally interrupted by sustaining the sound of a note or prolonging a little pause much longer than required by its [notated] duration."[23] Another difference indicated in this definition is that fermatas can be applied equally to notes and pauses, the former being in practice far more typical than the latter. Despite these differences, fermatas perform functions analogous to general pauses. This holds true for two out of three types of fermatas.

3.4.1. The Fermata as a "Question Mark"

Fermatas set at unexpected harmonic events are analogous to general pauses as "question marks." This function of fermatas is acknowledged by Koch further on in his entry, where he writes that one of their uses is to bring about "the expression of surprise or astonishment, a sensation during which the motion of the spirit itself seems to stand still a moment."[24] In the finale of the String Quartet in G major, Op. 54 No. 1, the fact that the harmonic surprise—created by the arrival on the secondary dominant of the dominant at the moment when the regular dominant is expected—is built into the rondo theme gives rise to the opportunity for several fermatas to occur in the course of the movement (Example 3.22). Repeatedly, the dominant harmony is set right by *staccato* chords and is followed by a general pause. This happens in a slightly different way each time, provoking, in addition to the original surprise, further secondary surprises caused by the changing continuations.

23. "Fermate. Ein solcher Ruhepunkt in dem Verfolge eines Tonstückes, bey welchem die Bewegung des Taktes dadurch auf einige Zeit mit Vorsatz unterbrochen wird, daß man den Ton auf einer Note viel länger aushält, oder bey einer kleinen Pause viel länger verweilt, als es die Dauer derselben erfordert" (Koch 1802: col. 562).

24. "Der Ausdruck der Verwunderung oder des Erstaunens, eine Empfindung, wobey die Bewegungen des Geistes selbst einen kurzen Stillstand zu machen scheinen, oder solche Stellen, wo die vorhandene Empfindung sich durch ihre völlige Ergiessung erschöpft zu haben scheint, sind hinreichend, das Daseyn solcher Fermaten zu begünstigen" (Koch 1802: col. 561–63).

Example 3.22. Haydn, String Quartet in G major, Op. 54 No. 1/iv, mm. 13–19 (a), 114–24 (b), and 148–57 (c).

3.4.2. *Fermatas at the Half Cadence (*Halbkadenz*)*

As general pauses, fermatas often occur at the half cadence after some period of standing on the dominant and immediately before the thematic return. Koch may have had this type in mind when he pointed out, as another possible reason for introducing fermatas, "such spots where the current sentiment seems to have exhausted itself through its complete outflow."[25] It can be related

25. "Solche Stellen, wo die vorhandene Empfindung sich durch ihre völlige Ergießung erschöpft zu haben scheint" (Koch 1802: cols. 562–63). In *Versuch*, Koch demonstrates a fermata at the end of an overhang after a *Quintabsatz* (1983: 35 ex. 107 [1787: 413]). Although this was normally prohibited, in this case he allows the overhang to extend until the downbeat of the next measure: "This can be done without harm or without violating the nature of the measure, because the measured metrical movement [*Tactbewegung*] is momentarily discontinued (35 [413])."

to the previous category, if the half cadence is achieved in a wrong key, as in the finale of Op. 64 No. 2 (m. 124), where it is in C-sharp minor instead of B minor.

3.4.3. Embellished Fermatas

A special type, without equivalent among general pauses, is represented by fermatas that offer the soloist an opportunity for improvised embellishments. Such fermatas occur most typically in two formal contexts: at the half cadence (*Halbkadenz*) and at the six-four chord of the full cadence (*Kadenz*).[26] The latter location, inviting the soloist to introduce a cadenza, receives a longer discussion near the end of Koch's entry (1802: col. 566).[27]

In Haydn's string quartets embellished fermatas occur regularly in the slow movements of his collections Op. 9 and Op. 17, where they are related to the earlier concerto-like conception of the string quartet as a virtuoso piece for first violinist with the accompaniment of the three other instruments. Although this conception remained influential in the later quartet cycles,[28] the tradition of playing solo cadenzas in string quartets gradually decayed. One embellished fermata can be found in the slow movement of Op. 33 No. 6. In Op. 50 No. 2/ii (mm. 35–36) a fermata at the half cadence occurs, provided with a remark *a suo piacere*, encouraging the soloist to provide embellishments at his own discretion. (The fact that the soloist needed such an encouragement shows the change of habits that had taken place among players since the earlier quartet groups.) In certain other cases the embellishments of the fermata are written out by the composer. This happens in the trio of the minuet of Op. 55 No. 2 (mm. 83–84), in the finale of Op. 55 No. 3 (mm. 76–77), and in the aforementioned finale of Op. 54 No. 1, where, apart from the fermatas assigned to the surprising secondary dominants (probably not intended to be embellished), Haydn playfully tests the listener's patience with one more fermata on a regular dominant chord (Example 3.23).

It might be observed that embellished fermatas are more effective in dissolving meter than nonembellished ones. This is because embellishments played ad libitum by the soloist betray from the outset that the set of projections characteristic of the metrical grid underlying the earlier musical passage is no longer valid. In fermatas performed without embellishments the listener may initially mistake the long-lasting note for a measured sound, so that the projections will continue for some time. Only after the fermata is excessively prolonged will the projections decay and the metrical grid be suspended.

26. These two types of fermatas are carefully distinguished in the eighteenth-century treatises on performing practice by Quantz (1752) and Türk (1789). For a concise discussion in the contemporary literature, see Whitmore (1991).
27. The former type is, in turn, shown in *Versuch* (1983: 35 ex.106 [1787: 413]).
28. For a discussion of concerto style in Haydn's quartets, see Grave (2001).

Example 3.23. Haydn, String Quartet in G major, Op. 54 No. 1/iv, mm. 60–65.

Projections characteristic of the earlier metrical grid will also continue during fermatas over pauses that, by definition, cannot be embellished. This sheds an interesting light on the relationship between fermatas over pauses and general pauses without fermatas. As indicated in the definitions in Koch's *Musikalisches Lexikon,* the difference between these two stems from their different effect on meter (*Takt*). Because the general pause does not interrupt meter, "it differs from a fermata that is made upon a little pause, and during which metrical progress [*Gang des Tactes*] itself is interrupted for some time."[29] This difference is relevant for the performer, who is thus supposed to "count" a general pause but not a fermata. For the listener the situation is different, because she may not know in advance which type of pause a given silence represents. From the instruction given by Koch to performers it follows that the way the performer approaches the fermata should not signal the interruption to come. This means that "the foregoing notes must not be sustained [beyond the proper time] but must be performed in the same way as every other note of equal [rhythmical] value followed by a pause."[30] If, as sometimes happens, the performed fermata is of such a length that the metrical grid is resumed after the pause, it is not possible for the listener to recognize the fermata and distinguish it from a general pause of an equivalent size. Koch admits this when he writes: "It has been suggested that the composers ought to determine the length of the standstill they demand at this opportunity [fermata] by pauses. One also finds here and there pieces in which this is the case; but heretofore very few composers seem to consider it necessary."[31] Those "very few composers" certainly

29. "Sie unterscheidet sich also von einer solchen Fermate, die auf einer kleinen Pause gemacht, und bey welcher der Gang des Tactes selbst auf einige Zeit unterbrochen wird" (Koch 1802: col. 660).

30. "Im letzten Falle ist bey der Ausführung derselben weiter nichts zu bemerken, als daß die vorhergehende Note nicht ausgehalten werden darf, sondern eben so vorgetragen werden muss, wie jede andere am Werthe ihr gleiche Note, auf welche eine Pause folgt" (Koch 1802: col. 563).

31. "Man hat darauf angetragen, dass die Tonsetzer die Zeit, wie lange sie bey dieser Gelegenheit den Stillstand der Taktbewegung verlangen, durch Pausen bezeichnen möchten. Man findet auch hin und wieder Tonstücke, in welchen es geschehen ist; bis jetzt noch scheinen es aber die wenigsten Tonsetzer für nötig zu halten" (Koch 1802: cols. 563–64).

include Haydn. In fact, several of the examples of his general pauses discussed earlier are written-out fermatas.

Only if the metrical grid is not resumed after the pause will the listener recognize the fermata. Note, however, that this recognition happens in retrospection. The fact that the listener can distinguish a fermata from a general pause in such cases testifies to the reality of automatic projection in an established meter, which apparently can be prolonged over several missing beats.[32] Nevertheless, it cannot be prolonged indefinitely. When the silence is particularly expanded, the projection will cease before the music resumes, so that the meter must be found again in the same way the listener usually does at the beginning of a piece. The same effect arises even if the silence is actually notated as a general pause of a precise duration counted by the performers. Because the metrical grid against which the listener would have measured the duration of the pause is no longer available in such cases, it is not possible for her to distinguish between these two phenomena. From these remarks it follows that the distinction between a general pause and a fermata over a pause, although theoretically clear-cut, is in practice much more equivocal. Whether counted by the performers or not, prolonged silence of either kind functions as a break that interrupts the metrical progress of music and hence does not properly "count" to it. Hasty dubs such a phenomenon a "hiatus" and defines it as "a break between the realization of projected potential and a new beginning" (1997: 88).

It is worth noting that the recognition of a fermata is always accompanied by an adjustment from the metrical grid established by the musical passage before the fermata to the pattern of phenomenal accents in the music after the fermata. This is possible due to the flexibility of mensural determinacy. As was pointed out by Hasty (1997: 86), the listener may accept a given duration as a reproduction of an earlier projective duration and hence as a realization of its projection, even if it is heard as not quite equal.[33] Flexibility of mensural determinacy can also cause an adjustment of the metrical grid after a much shorter pause. The effect of pauses—general or otherwise—lies thus not only in the surprise they arouse but, occasionally, in the consequences they have for metric perception after the pause. A unique example of a playful manipulation based on this effect is found in the opening Allegro of Haydn's Quartet in B-flat major, Op. 50 No. 1 (Example 3.24a).

As famously pointed out by Janet Levy (1981), this movement starts with a passage typical of codas, which then indeed returns as the coda at its end. The

32. Hasty questions the existence of automatic projection: "There do seem to be cases in which pulses may persist when not actually sounded, but these situations are, I think, better explained as products of active reproduction than as products of habit" (1997: 169). Hasty seems to allude in this passage to psychological experiments in synchronization that demonstrate that the listeners continue tapping after the stimulus is turned off. While the results of such experiments can be explained by reference to active reproduction, this explanation does not obtain for the ability to distinguish between general pauses and fermatas.

33. Flexibility is thus not the same as categorization. Categorization presupposes that the listener hears two durations as equal though they are not equal in absolute time values. An idea similar to Hasty's "durational flexibility" is formulated by Samarotto (1999b: 47).

Example 3.24. Haydn, String Quartet in B-flat major, Op. 50 No. 1/i, mm. 1–12 (a) and 34–37 (b).

metric manipulation arranged by the composer is related to this formal trick. It takes place after the rest in m. 6, which, in fact, constitutes its indispensable element. Because the metrical level constitutive for *Metrum* is here that of *Taktglieder*, two attacks represented by quarters are missing during the rest. As a consequence, the metric position of the following attack becomes uncertain for the listener. How the music after the rest will be heard metrically depends on its own characteristics rather than on the preceding metrical context. Yet these characteristics promote a misunderstanding because of the "improper" distribution of the tonic harmonies. Their harmonic stability determines that the tonics attract strong metrical beats, whereas the dominant between them is heard as falling on a weak beat. This metric perception is supported by the fact that the tonics implied by the sixths D–B♭ and then by the thirds B♭–D receive initial and terminal accents within their respective groups. Accordingly, the passage after the rest will naturally be heard with bar lines shifted by one quarter backward and the shorter rests in mm. 7 and 8 as falling on *Taktglieder* rather than *Taktteile* of ¢ meter. This analysis is more economical—in the sense of the "principle of economy" cited in chapter 1—than that indicated in the notation, where the pauses fall on *Taktteile.* It will be accepted by the listener all the more easily, since it is in line with her expectation concerning the point within the measure at which the music should resume. As follows from Kirnberger's remarks about *Rhythmus*, this expectation is guided by the point within the measure at which the preceding rhythmical group started. Since the movement started with the downbeat, the listener will be inclined to hear the music after the pause as starting at the same metrical position. To be sure, she will notice that the first event happens too soon—sooner than the expected downbeat—yet the flexibility of mensural determinacy helps to accommodate this imprecision to the established metrical structure. Hasty (1997: 86) estimates that this flexibility allows the listener to accept a duration that is at least three-quarters the length of the expected duration as its imprecise realization. This is exactly the duration in Haydn's example. In this particular case the extent of the flexibility might be even greater, since it concerns an interval between two rhythmic groups. As has been demonstrated in experimental studies, such "between-group intervals" are perceptually special and have hardly any reality for the subjects (Fitzgibbons, Pollatsek, and Thomas 1974). Also relevant to Haydn's manipulation are experiments (Fraisse 1980, 1987; Franěk and Mates 1997) showing that listeners have a tendency to anticipate events, that is to say, to expect or reproduce them too early rather than too late. Once again, Haydn seems well aware of psychological phenomena that have only quite recently become the object of experimental inquiry. A further clue that he exercised the metrical manipulation with full awareness of its consequences for the listener can be found later on in the movement, where a passage of figurations based on the triplet figure derived from mm. 7–8 is actually notated as starting with the downbeat, that is to say, in the way that it was at first erroneously perceived by the listener (Example 3.24b). The error Haydn induces in his listener in mm. 7–8 is corrected only by the powerful *tutti* chord in m. 9, which crashes in on the notated downbeat, throwing the listener back into the proper metrical track. The effect of startling surprise that this chord entrance brings is obviously the goal of the entire carefully planned manipulation.

3.5. Syncopations

Projection of a selected analysis determines expectations concerning not only the moments of future attacks but also their relative salience. Higher-level projections are expected to be articulated at the musical surface by more salient attacks than lower-level projections. This means that another way of challenging meter is through an attack that is articulated more strongly than is expected at a given point in the metrical grid. Such an "antimetrical attack" wakes up the processor and makes it elaborate new projections starting from the point within the measure at which the challenge occurred (Example 3.25). The set of projections initiated by the challenge depends on the ensuing pattern of attacks. If, however, the following antimetrical attacks are not strong enough, the projections generated by them in conjunction with the original attack will not be surfaced by the selection function, and so the single challenge will be accommodated to the old metrical grid.

Example 3.25. Projections initiated by an antimetrical attack.

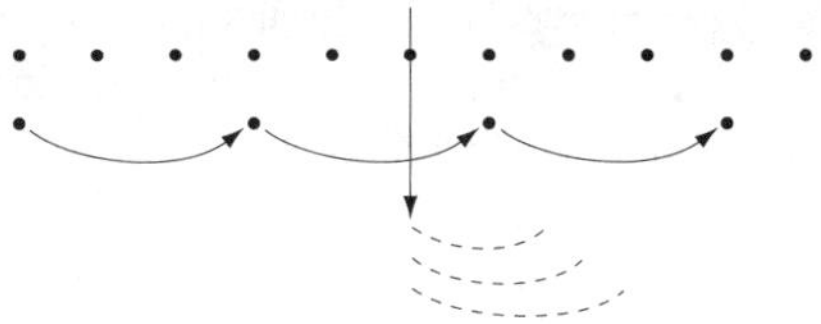

In eighteenth-century music theory, this kind of challenge to meter was known as *Rückung* (shift). In the entry "Rückung" in *Musikalisches Lexikon,* Koch explains that the meaning of this German term has long since been "completely synonymous with syncopation (*Syncope*),"[34] and he subsumes under it all phenomena resulting in disturbances of "grammatical accents" belonging to a given beat in virtue of its position in the measure. One type of such phenomena includes disturbances of the "grammatical accent" by phenomenal accents: stress or length. This type of *Rückung* is characterized by Koch as "a procedure through which the grammatical accent characteristic of the downbeat is obliterated by the fact that the note falling on the upbeat is performed with a greater force of sound than the one on the downbeat.... This also includes the case when the notes falling on the upbeat are greater in [rhythmical] value than the notes on the downbeat."[35] That Koch considers only stress and length able to obliterate "grammatical accents" must be related to the fact that in the eighteenth century these two parameters served to express the sense of subjective emphasis attached to the downbeat. In other words, syncopation arises when an "intrinsically short" (*innerlich kurze*) note is extrinsically long or an "unaccented" (*inaccentuierte*) note is accented.

If the extrinsic value of a note falling on the intrinsically weak last beat of the preceding measure is longer than the *Taktteil,* it reaches beyond the following

34. "Schon längst ist dieses Wort, als Kunstwort betrachtet, mit dem Ausdrucke Syncopation (*Syncope*) völlig gleichbedeutend" (Koch 1802: col. 1275).

35. "Dasjenige Verfahren, wobey der grammatische Accent, welcher den anschlagenden Noten eigen ist, dadurch verwischt wird, dass die im Nachschlage stehenden Noten mit mehr Stärke des Tones vorgetragen werden, als die anschlagenden.... Hierher gehört auch der Fall, wenn die im schlechten Tacttheile stehenden Noten größer am Werthe sind, als die Noten in dem guten Tacttheile" (Koch 1802: cols. 1280–82).

downbeat. This situation is represented in notation by a tie. For Koch, it forms a distinct type of syncopation, considered by him to be syncopation in the proper sense of the word: "Because all notes falling on the downbeat have the so-called grammatical accent, which is missing in those falling on the upbeat, the just-indicated tying of the note from the downbeat to the foregoing note from the upbeat will suppress this grammatical accent and in this way produce a seizure in the flow of the *Taktgewicht* [i.e., *Metrum*], thus making it necessary that another voice executes the downbeat instead of the tied note, in order that the *Metrum* may not be completely broken."[36] To be sure, an intervention of another voice is also necessary in the case of rhythmical values longer than the *Taktteil* that do not give rise to ties. This follows from Koch's remarks about continuity of *Metrum* summarized earlier in this chapter (see section 3.1). Indeed, the distinction drawn by Koch between ties on the one hand and other syncopations produced by durational accents on the other corresponds with their distinct presentation under points (2) and (3) of his discussion in *Versuch*. Whereas Koch concentrates there on the suppression of the following beat and its compensation by another voice, in the entry "Rückung" in *Musikalisches Lexikon* he pays more attention to the enhancement of the beat at which the longer rhythmical value starts. Obviously, in the case of durational accents these issues form two sides of the same coin.

The strongest challenge to meter arises when the compensation for the suppressed beat in another voice does not take place. Two syncopations of this sort occur in the second phrase of the principal theme from the opening movement of Haydn's Op. 55 No. 1 (Example 3.26). As a result, weak beats are missing in two consecutive measures. Note that the level of *Metrum* in the first phrase of the theme is that of *Taktglieder* represented in ¢ meter by quarters. These rhythmical values form the lowest level of projection continuously articulated by attacks in the accompaniment. At the beginning of the second phrase (m. 5) the articulation of quarters is interrupted and *Metrum* moved up to the level of *Taktteile* represented by half notes. The syncopations of mm. 6–7 bring a further interruption of *Metrum* on this higher metrical level.

In the opening movement of the String Quartet in F major, Op. 50 No. 5, syncopations are built into a more comprehensive compositional strategy. In its final occurrence in the coda (Example 3.27), the theme incorporates two uncompensated syncopations coming precisely at the moments when, in its original version shown in Example 3.8, the attacks missing in the melody were for the first time provided by the bass. While the final version of the theme normalizes the playful chromatic C♯—whose possible harmonic equivocation with D♭ Haydn has exploited throughout the movement—to the diatonic C set in the full context of the domi-

36. "Weil alle im Anschlage stehenden Noten den sogenannten grammatischen Accent haben, welcher den im Nachschlage stehenden mangelt, so wird durch das so eben angezeigte Zusammenbinden der anschlagenden Note an die vorhergehende nachschlagende dieser grammatische Accent unterdrückt, und dadurch eine Stockung im Flusse des Tactgewichtes erzeugt, zugleich aber auch dadurch nothwendig gemacht, daß eine andere Stimme statt der gebundenen Note den Anschlag verrichten muß, damit das Metrum nicht gänzlich unterbrochen werde" (Koch 1802: cols. 1275–76).

Example 3.26. Haydn, String Quartet in A major, Op. 55 No. 1/i, mm. 1–12.

Example 3.27. Haydn, String Quartet in F major, "The Dream," Op. 50 No. 5/i, mm. 159–66.

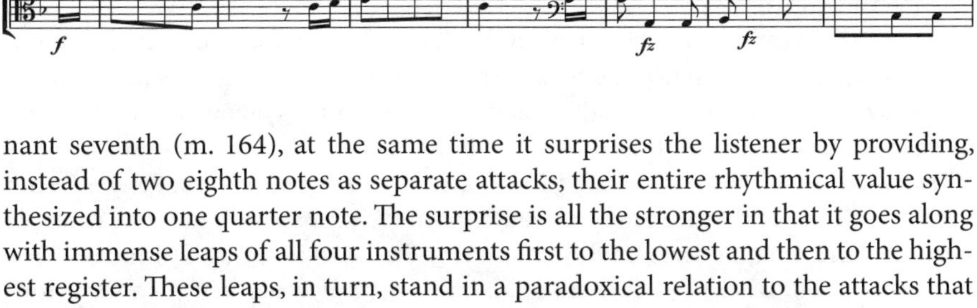

nant seventh (m. 164), at the same time it surprises the listener by providing, instead of two eighth notes as separate attacks, their entire rhythmical value synthesized into one quarter note. The surprise is all the stronger in that it goes along with immense leaps of all four instruments first to the lowest and then to the highest register. These leaps, in turn, stand in a paradoxical relation to the attacks that fill the gaps between the two earlier incises, which are provided not in the bass by viola and cello—as expected in the first presentation of the theme in the exposition and realized in its return at the beginning of the recapitulation (mm. 102–9)—but in the highest register by the two violins. The metrical effects of pauses and syncopations thus form one aspect of a far more complex transformation—involving harmony and texture—that the theme undergoes in the course of the movement.

Example 3.28. Haydn, String Quartet in F-sharp minor, Op. 50 No. 4/iii, mm. 60–68.

In both Examples 3.26 and 3.27, durational accents are combined with stress. Although these two can occur separately, they almost always occur together when a syncopation is not compensated in another voice. This aspect of compositional practice mirrors the performance practice of the time, in which phenomena straying from the norm were to be emphasized by dynamic accents. In chapter 2, I mentioned this practice in application to salient harmonic events dubbed "harmonic accents." Likewise, dynamic accents provided by the performer were supposed to enhance syncopations (Türk 1982: 326 [1789: 337]). To be sure, the most curious cases are those in which syncopation serves, in its turn, to enhance a harmonic surprise, so that harmonic, durational, and dynamic accents all converge on one and the same sound event. Crude effects that arise on such occasions act like negatives of general pauses. An intriguing example occurs in the trio of the minuet of Op. 50 No. 4 (Example 3.28). The syncopation comes in the course of the cadence on the startling diminished seventh chord after the cadential six-four. This event is completely gratuitous because it does not lead the harmonic process any further away from its original direction toward the tonic but immediately reverts it to the preceding chord. Consequently, it causes an insertion in the course of the phrase, which otherwise would proceed from m. 65 directly to m. 67.

As in this example, the connection of syncopations with unexpected harmonies always results in a syncopated harmonic rhythm. That Koch does not mention harmony as a factor of syncopations is probably because syncopated distribution of chords was considered faulty from the point of view of the eighteenth-century *Harmonielehre*. In fact, syncopated harmonic rhythm seriously challenges meter even if the surface rhythm does not contain syncopations. An interesting example occurs in the opening movement of Mozart's String Quintet in G minor, K. 516 (Example 3.29), where the chromatic alterations in the bass line turn local tonics into secondary dominants on the second quarters of mm. 15–16, one quarter earlier than the secondary dominant in m. 14, thus contributing to the sense of heightened emotional urgency of this passage. In other cases, syncopated harmonic rhythm adds a further dimension to the metrical disturbances on the surface. This concerns not only syncopations but also, occasionally, pauses. In the earlier examples from the finales of Mozart's quintets K. 593 and K. 614 (Examples 3.19 and 3.20), harmonic syncopations arise because the surprising harmonies falling on weak beats are conceptually sustained over the general pauses on the following downbeats. In K. 614 this detail bestows a particular sophistication on Mozart's elaboration of Haydn's trick from Op. 64 No. 6 (Example 3.16), where the dominant seventh enters on the downbeat of m. 176 and so the syncopated harmonic effect does not arise. Although Haydn's example contains two pauses, the challenge to meter is thus stronger in Mozart.

Example 3.29. Mozart, String Quintet in G minor, K. 516/i, mm. 12–17.

A similar phenomenon is involved in the combination of syncopations and pauses in the minuet of the G-minor quintet, K. 516 (Example 3.30). The syncopations in mm. 4 and 6 are called forth by dynamic accents attached to two diminished seventh chords (harmonic accents) played in multiple stops and hence characterized by extreme width of register. The dramatic effect of these jarring dissonances is even heightened by the fact that they are abruptly interrupted by the "loud pauses." Because, as a consequence of the pauses, no harmonic changes take place on the following downbeats, the harmonies from the preceding upbeats are mentally prolonged over the bar line, resulting in syncopated harmonic rhythm. It is worth observing that, after the opening phrase of the minuet has started with the upbeat, the listener does expect the second phrase, too, to start with an upbeat. Moreover, because the upbeat of the opening phrase was realized by a full chord, including the atypical upbeat entrance of the accompaniment, the listener expects that the upbeat of the second phrase will also be realized in this way. If followed by new chords on the downbeats, the powerful discords in mm. 4 and 6 would thus not produce any surprises. Yet the pauses create an impression that the diminished sevenths were not so much upbeats as rather the actual downbeats shifted back from their proper metrical positions. As a further consequence, the first events after the pauses receive initial accents. In this way they give support to the duple projections initiated by the processor at the preceding upbeats. Since the original triple projection, reflected in the notated meter, is suppressed at the same time, the single challenges brought by syncopations result in a momentary reorganization of metric perception. The phenomenon observed here is otherwise characteristic

Example 3.30. Mozart, String Quintet in G minor, K. 516/ii, mm. 1–13.

of syncopations in triple meter: When such syncopations, falling on the upbeat, occur along with a suppression of the following downbeat, they automatically yield hemiolas.[37]

The triple meter is restored in m. 8, but then challenged again in the last four measures of Example 3.30 following the deceptive cadence of m. 10. It is interesting to consider this passage in light of Koch's discussion of continuity of *Metrum*. From his discussion it follows that an intervention of the bass or the subsidiary parts is required only when a given beat of the metrical level constitutive for *Metrum*—*Taktteil* or *Taktglied*—is not articulated in the melody. But in his examples, the bass can be seen to articulate all downbeats, whether they are otherwise articulated by attacks in the melody or not. Exceptions from this rule take place only on the first downbeats of phrases and incises, if the melody has a clear attack (see Examples 3.2 and 3.6). Apparently, in the course of a phrase or incise, Koch considers a missing downbeat in the bass to be a metric disturbance. This sheds light on the disturbing effect of the missing downbeat in the accompaniment in m. 12. Note that the preceding upbeat is endowed with an accent in virtue of the correlation of attacks in melody and accompaniment, which happens here for the

37. Many "cadential hemiolas" observed in Baroque music by Channan Willner (1991) arise in this very way. See note 27 in chapter 4 here.

first time since the downbeat of m. 10. The upbeat also features harmonic syncopation (diminished seventh) because, due to the missing attack in the bass on the following downbeat, the articulation of the subsequent six-four harmony is shifted to the weak second beat of m. 12. This weak second beat, which brings the next bass attack after the pause, receives an initial accent in a way similar to the attacks after the pauses in mm. 5 and 7. The result is a hemiola emerging in mm. 11–12. Its location before the cadence corresponds with the usual formal function of hemiolas, which will be discussed in more detail in chapter 4. In another respect, however, this hemiola is quite unusual, in that it is not produced by long chords but by shorter attacks separated by pauses, which results in a peculiar effect of instability and hesitation. This effect is carried over to the following trio, which draws on the closing phrase of the minuet while changing its mode to the parallel major.

The model of metrical processor proposed in this study allows for certain generalizations about the surprising effect of syncopations. As in the case of pauses, the strength of this effect can be accounted for as a function of distance in the vertical and horizontal dimensions of metrical hierarchy. In both dimensions, however, the direction of this distance must be reverted. If in the vertical dimension the surprise elicited by pauses has increased with the skip *up* in the metrical hierarchy, in the case of syncopations this distance must be realized as a skip *down*. Clearly, the weaker the beat on which the syncopation falls, the stronger will be the surprise it causes. In the horizontal dimension, the smaller the distance by which the weak beat carrying the syncopation *follows*—rather than *precedes*—the downbeat, the greater will be the surprise. From this last observation it follows that the strengths of syncopations falling on different weak beats belonging to the same metrical level will be different. In triple meter, syncopations falling on the second *Taktteil* will be more surprising than those falling on the third *Taktteil*. Turning this statement around, one might say that the strength of beats in a measure depends not only on their metrical level but also on their distance from the downbeat. In triple measures this strength can be represented as 1–3–2 (Example 3.31a). In other words,

Example 3.31. Hierarchy of *Taktteile* in triple measure (a) and of *Taktglieder* arising from a duple (b) or triple (c) subdivision of *Taktteile* in duple measure.

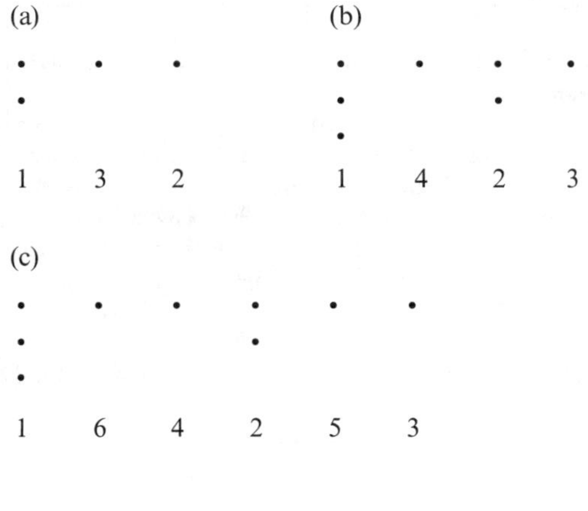

the third beat is stronger than the second beat. Interestingly, this corresponds with the gradation of stress between individual beats within a measure demonstrated by Türk in Example 2.6.[38] In duple meters, which have only one weak *Taktteil,* the differentiation goes down to lower levels of the metrical hierarchy represented by *Taktglieder* and *Taktnoten.* In 2/2 or 2/4 it yields gradation 1–4–2–3 (Example 3.31b).[39] *Taktglieder* arising from a triple division of *Taktteile* in mixed 6/8 meter form gradation 1–6–4–2–5–3 (Example 3.31c). Hierarchies of *Taktglieder* in triple meters (3/2, 3/4, 9/8) can be elaborated in the same way, as can also those of *Taktnoten* in each of these meters. It is noteworthy that the hierarchies shown in Example 3.31 correspond with the hierarchies of metrical attractors calculated by Lerdahl (2001: 291 fig. 6.44). This is because the strength of a given beat as a metrical attractor depends not only on its own stability but also on the stability of the preceding beat. The weaker the preceding beat, the more strongly it will be attracted by the later one. A weak beat after another weak beat is thus effectively stronger than a weak beat after the downbeat.

The formal similarity between tonal and metrical hierarchy, which allows Lerdahl to speak about metrical attractions as analogous to melodic attractions, invites one to compare the phenomenon of syncopation with that of dissonance. In the theory of tonal pitch space, Lerdahl defines dissonance in terms of depth in the tonal hierarchy: "Moving down in the space means increasing dissonance, to be relieved by moving up again" (1988: 322). Similarly, weak beats are achieved by a move down in the metrical hierarchy and can be said to "resolve" to strong beats by moving up. Note that, when so resolved, they are as little challenging to meter as resolved dissonances are to key. It is only unresolved dissonances that cause a challenge and for this reason were prohibited in the eighteenth-century harmony

38. The hierarchy of beats proposed here is elaborated only from the point of view of a surprise caused by a syncopation. When the theoretical interest is different, the evaluation of beats may differ as well. This is the case with Kirnberger, for whom the second beat in triple meter is stronger than the third because the former can occasionally carry a suspension or the caesura note of the cadence, whereas the latter cannot (1982: 397–98 [1776: 131]). His concept of strength is obviously based on the criterion of which of the weak beats is able to perform functions normally ascribed to the downbeat. That the suspension can enter on "two" in triple meter obviously has to do with the fact that the resolution of the dissonance can still follow on "three." Similarly, a strong syllable can be located on the second beat but not on the third (Kirnberger 1782: 8; Schulz 1794: 499). The problem of the second beat in triple meter was broadly discussed by theorists in the eighteenth century, as reported by Maurer Zenck (2001: 149–55).

39. At the beginning of the nineteenth century, the same gradation was adopted by Gottfried Wilhelm Fink (1808–9) for *Taktteile* of 4/4 meter. According to Fink, the first beat of 4/4 measure is stronger than the third, yet the second beat is weaker than the fourth because of the anacrustic function frequently performed by the latter in relation to the following downbeat (see Seidel 1975: 113; Grave 1985: 53; Schwindt-Gross 1989: 217–18). Since Fink writes about compound meter, with the first and third beats representing downbeats of simple 2/4 measures, the pattern of accentuation he describes transposes relationships between beats from metrical to hypermetrical level. In doing so, it forms further elaboration of the germinal idea of hypermeter included already in Kirnberger. As I indicated in chapter 1, the differentiation between the first and the third beat in compound 4/4 was adopted by Kirnberger in his "hierarchical" type of this meter. The same differentiation was accepted by Türk, as illustrated by the gradation of stress in 4/4 meter shown in Example 2.6.

handbooks. Their equivalents in the realm of meter are "unresolved rhythmical dissonances" represented by syncopations.

Because resolved rhythmical dissonances do not receive any discussion in this study, in what follows I will shorten the term "unresolved rhythmical dissonance" to "rhythmical dissonance," and will use it to refer to dynamic and harmonic syncopations, as well as syncopations arising from durational accents—thus including all types of events capable of challenging meter with their single occurrence. This sense of the word differs from that of Yeston's "rhythmic dissonances" (1976). Drawing on his definition of meter as "interaction of levels" (66), Yeston uses the term "rhythmic dissonance" to refer to conflicts between noncongruent levels of motion. But since such conflicts (which I will discuss in the course of the following two chapters) have more recently been given the name "metrical dissonance" in American music theory, "rhythmical dissonance" can now be used in the new way I propose here. Notably, although metrical dissonances challenge an established meter by means of a new regularity, they need not consist of events that would challenge meter if they occur singly. Whereas certain types of metrical dissonances actually arise as chains of rhythmical dissonances, metrical dissonances can be generated by other means as well. The connection between these two terms will prove useful in clarifying the connection of the phenomena they denote.

CHAPTER Four

Changing Meter I

Change of Period

In the eighteenth century, the constancy of notated meter was taken for granted equally by composers and listeners. Virtually every piece or movement was written with one time signature maintained from the beginning to the end. Exceptions to this rule occur only in movements preceded by a slow introduction, which normally differs from the following main part of a movement not only in tempo but in meter as well. However, within the same notated meter, the composed meter could change. One type of such a change was known in eighteenth-century music theory by the Italian terms *imbroglio* or *la confusione*, translated into German as *Verwirrung*, "confusion." In the entry devoted to *imbroglio* in his *Musikalisches Lexikon* (1802), Koch defines it as "those phrases of pieces in which a contrary meter is inserted."[1] He illustrates this phenomenon with the opening passage from the trio of the minuet of Haydn's String Quartet Op. 9 No. 3 (Example 4.1).

Floyd Grave (1995) quotes Koch's definition and example of *imbroglio* as a proof of an early theoretical awareness of "metrical dissonance." The theory of metrical dissonance, originating in Yeston's idea of "rhythmic dissonance," was expounded by Harald Krebs in his article "Some Extensions of the Concepts of Metrical Consonance and Dissonance" (1987) and further developed in his *Fantasy Pieces* (1999), a brilliant book devoted to metrical dissonances in the music of Robert Schumann. According to Krebs, metrical dissonance arises between two or more levels of metrical hierarchy (*interpretive levels*) that are based on a common lower level (*pulse level*) but group its beats in different ways. One of the higher levels usually does this in a manner corresponding with the metric notation. The hierarchical interconnection of this level with the pulse level is the "primary metrical consonance" of a given piece. The other interpretive level or levels are "antimetrical" in that they conflict with the notated meter. This conflict may originate either in different noninclusive periods (cardinalities) or in different phases. The former type of metrical dissonance is called by Krebs *grouping dissonance*, the

1. "*Imbroglio*, die Verwirrung. So benennet man zuweilen diejenigen Sätze eines Tonstückes, in welchen eine entgegengesetzte Taktart eingemischt ist" (Koch 1802: col. 776).

Example 4.1. Koch, *Musikalisches Lexikon*, cols. 775–78.

latter *displacement dissonance*.[2] In either case, the relation of interpretive levels to each other is nonhierarchical and results in a nonalignment of their beats—a state of affairs that justifies the term "dissonance" in its etymological sense of "non-sounding together."

The relation between interpretive levels, expressed as their ratio or index of displacement, forms the criterion for classification of metrical dissonances. This concerns dissonances not only of the same metrical level but also of different levels. Because, according to Krebs, all metrical levels arise through the grouping of beats of lower levels, the role of pulse level and interpretive levels can be played by any two levels of the metrical hierarchy. Although Krebs distinguishes among low-, mid-, and high-level metrical dissonances, dissonances of different levels that represent the same numerical relationship are basically equivalent for him: they differ only as regards the temporal scale in which this relationship is realized. However illuminating this view may be in certain individual cases, on the whole it is at variance with the way metrical conflicts were conceptualized in the eighteenth century. Because the concept of meter in the music theory of the time was based on the interconnection of *Taktteile* and *Takte*, these two levels of the metrical hierarchy form the pulse level and interpretive level in the primary sense of these words. Metrical dissonances based on other metrical levels are in principle *not* equivalent to those based on *Taktteile*. Even on the same level, metrical dissonances representing the same numerical relationship may differ in their historical origins and formal functions, as well as methods of generation in musical compositions. Historically sensitive application of the theory of metrical dissonance in the repertory of Classic music must take these differences into account.

2. These designations come from Peter Kaminsky (1989) and are adopted by Krebs in *Fantasy Pieces*. In the 1987 article, Krebs terms these types of metrical dissonances, respectively, "type A" and "type B."

4.1. *Imbroglio*

Assignment to the metrical level of *Taktteile* is evident from eighteenth-century definitions of *imbroglio*. Koch's definition, referred to by Grave, is rather late and unspecific in comparison with the much earlier and more informative descriptions of this phenomenon offered by Riepel and Türk. Already half a century earlier Riepel wrote in *De Rhythmopoeia* (1752): "*La confusione* as well as *imbroglio* means in German 'confusion' [*Verwirrung*]. It can result from a twofold [kind of] time [*Tempo*], namely from a triple and quadruple meter, as seen for instance [in Example 4.2a]. You will hopefully notice that at the sign + the 2/4 meter is inserted [Example 4.2b]. Or when the music begins with the quadruple meter, as for instance [in Example 4.3a]. Here at + the 3/4 meter begins [Example 4.3b]."[3] Later than Riepel's description of *imbroglio* but earlier than Koch's is Türk's discussion in his *Klavierschule* (1789), illustrated with an example from the final chorus of the oratorio *I pellegrini* (The Pilgrims) by Johann Adolf Hasse: "The metric confusion [*Verwirrung*] (*la confusione, imbroglio*)

Example 4.2. Riepel, *De Rhythmopoeia*, 59.

Example 4.3. Riepel, *De Rhythmopoeia*, 60.

3. "*La confusione* gleichwie auch *Imbroglio* heißt zu teutsch Verwirrung; welche aus zweyerley *Tempo,* nähmlich aus einem Trippel und gevierten Tacte entspringen kann, z. E. [Example 4.2a]. Du wirst hoffentlich merken, dass bey dem Zeichen + der 2/4 Tact eingeflochten ist, z. E. [Example 4.2b]. Oder wenn der gevierte Tact den Anfang hat, z. Ex. [Example 4.3a]. Bey + fängt hier der 3/4 Tact an, z. E. [Example 4.3b]" (Riepel 1752: 59–60).

is among those liberties of which composers have availed themselves for the contradiction of the established meter. The metric confusion occurs when a different meter is introduced in a composition, for example, where in 3/4, certain places are in 2/4, etc. Here is an example of this: [Example 4.4a]. At *a,* 2/4 is introduced and only further below, 3/4, although the composer has not indicated this with a signature. It should actually have been written as shown at *c*: [Example 4.4b]" (Türk 1982: 92, amended [1789: 93–94]).

Example 4.4. Türk, *Klavierschule*, 93 (a) and 94 (b).

(a)

(b)

From these discussions it follows that *imbroglio* is a grouping dissonance that consists in regrouping *Taktteile* into new *Takte.* The examples shown by Riepel and Türk demonstrate, further, that the privileged method of generating *imbroglio* is parallelism. This remains valid in the entire repertory of Haydn's and Mozart's string chamber music under consideration in this study. Examples of *imbroglio* without parallelism, such as those in Haydn's Op. 9 No. 3 or in the Menuet alla Zingarese from Op. 20 No. 4, are isolated experiments that are not repeated in his later quartets. Thus Koch's example, taken from Haydn's Op. 9 No. 3, is uncharacteristic. Koch might have been aware of this fact, for when discussing *imbroglio* again in the entry "Rückung" in the *Musikalisches Lexikon,* he supplements the excerpt shown in Example 4.1 with another anonymous example that does contain parallelism (Example 4.5).[4]

Example 4.5. Koch, *Musikalisches Lexikon*, cols. 1279–80.

4. In this entry, Koch does not write the term *imbroglio* but instead *tempo rubato,* a term that is synonymous with *imbroglio,* as he himself acknowledges in the entry devoted to *imbroglio* (1802: col. 776).

In today's music theory the notion of parallelism refers to the repetition of a group or segment at the musical surface. This includes literal repetition as well as sequential repetition that either preserves the precise size of intervals while changing the key or preserves the key while changing the intervals. The former type of sequence is commonly known as transposition. The latter type, which consists in shifting a given pattern along a diatonic scale up or down, does not have a proper name in musical terminology. In the eighteenth century it was called displacement (*Versetzung*).[5] To avoid confusion with metrical displacements, I will call it *translation*, by analogy to the operation of shifting a figure in a geometrical space.[6] Parallelism may further embrace ornamentation or simplification of a pattern as well as other types of its variation.

The importance of parallelism for metric perception lies in the fact that parallelism of patterns presupposes their metrical parallelism. In other words, to perceive patterns as parallel means to perceive them as having parallel metrical structure. This is why parallelism is included by Lerdahl and Jackendoff in the set of MPRs (MPR 1). Substantial work concerning the relationship between parallelism and meter along the lines drafted by Lerdahl and Jackendoff has been carried out more recently by David Temperley (1995, 2001), and a computational model of metrical induction based on parallelism has been elaborated by him and Christopher Bartlette (2002).[7] In the phase of metrical induction at the beginning of a piece, parallel patterns establish a metrical structure whose period is equal to the patterns' period or is related to it by an integral factor. This is because in such a structure parallel patterns, immediately repeated, will have analogous metrical position. In the course of a piece, when meter is already established, analogous position in measures in turn fosters recognition of patterns as parallel (Temperley 1995: 144). Patterns may still be recognized as parallel if they go against the established metrical structure, but in such cases they generate a metrical structure that conflicts with that of the notated meter (145, 161). This is precisely how *imbroglio* arises. It presupposes parallelism between patterns whose period is shorter or longer than one measure and is not related to the measure by any integral factor. As can be seen in the above examples offered by Riepel, Türk, and Koch, the most popular *imbroglios* by far were those arising from literal repetition, translation, or transposition of a pattern. These types of repetition, which secure an unmistakable recognition of parallelism, also prevail in further examples of *imbroglio* by Haydn

5. The term *Versetzung*, translated as "displacement" by Elaine Sisman (1993), occurs in Koch's *Musikalisches Lexikon* (1802: cols. 1676–79) and in the third volume of his *Versuch* (1793). In the second volume Koch writes about "repetition on other degrees of the same key which require another underlying harmony" (1983: 43 [1787: 430]). Other types of repetition distinguished by Koch include literal repetition (*Wiederholung*), transposition (*Transposition*), and variation (*Variation*). A special type of repetition he mentions is inversion (*Umkehrung*), which consists in a voice exchange on the same underlying harmony (1983: 42 [1787: 428]).
6. "Translation" can be applied not only to shifts on the diatonic but also on the triadic level of the tonal pitch space (Lerdahl 1988, 2001). Translation on the chromatic level is tantamount to transposition.
7. An earlier computational model taking parallelism into consideration was proposed by Steedman (1977).

and Mozart that I will discuss in this chapter. Variation, which could render this recognition more difficult, was used less frequently for *imbroglio*. It occurs in rare cases where the composer intends to veil parallelism for some strategic reason.

From the assumption that recognition of parallelism is tantamount to recognizing patterns as having parallel metrical structure, it follows that the "false" meter is established as soon as the parallelism is recognized. This happens, at the latest, with the completion of the second segment in a given chain of repetitions (Example 4.6). One may suspect that here lies the reason why parallelism was used in the eighteenth century as the almost exclusive means of generating *imbroglio*. Whereas establishing a false meter by means of "rhythmical dissonances" requires a minimum of three downbeats (as will be demonstrated in chapter 5, it is only at the third downbeat where the hypothesis of a new regularity, represented by the projection on the level of *Takte*, is confirmed), in the case of parallelism, the third downbeat already comes as an expected event. The change of meter elicited by parallelism is thus immediately recognizable, and its effect all the more striking. Parallelism may be recognized even earlier, if the pattern features a characteristic opening chunk. It is not by chance that many examples of *imbroglio* feature patterns that start with a quick turn, either carefully written out or indicated with a special sign (Example 4.7; see also Examples 4.8b and 4.11). Rather than a purely conventional embellishment, such a turn is designed to facilitate the recognition of the parallelism at the very beginning of the second segment. If this turn has an upbeat position in the pattern, its recognition by the listener renders the following downbeat—the second downbeat of the "false" meter—already expected.

Example 4.6. "False" meter established by parallelism.

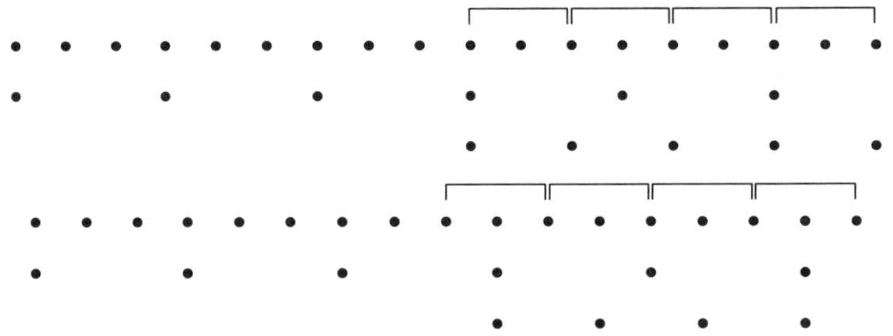

Example 4.7. Mozart, String Quartet in B-flat major, K. 589/i, mm. 62–66.

While parallelism determines the period of the false meter, it does not decide its phase. This means that the period of the pattern and the period of the metrical structure generated by it, while equal, may be either in phase or out of phase with each other, depending on where the perceived downbeat of the pattern is located. As proposed by Temperley and Bartlette (2002), this location is decided by phenomenal accents. This is certainly true for metrical induction at the beginning of a piece. In the course of a piece, however, the location of the perceived downbeat is decided, as a rule, by the immediately preceding metrical grid. It is in terms of this grid, normally identical with the notated meter, that the first segment in the chain of repetitions is heard. From the assumption that perception of parallelism goes along with perception of parallel metrical structure, it follows logically that the metrical structure assigned to the first segment is transferred onto the subsequent segments parallel to it.[8] Sometimes, however, the phase of the false meter in *imbroglio* is intentionally obliterated by the composer. Grave refers to such cases as metrically dissonant "free falls." As he points out, the technical means through which they arise is "imitation in virtual duple meter at the time interval of one beat, giving each beat the status of a downbeat in one part or another" (1995: 193 n. 31). This can be seen in Türk's example of *imbroglio* quoted from Hasse (Example 4.4a). Because imitation is a kind of parallelism, with parallel patterns divided between different voices, it presupposes a parallel metrical structure of those patterns. If the interval of imitation is different from the period of this metrical structure or its integer multiple, imitation causes a metrical displacement of voices in relation to each other. As a result, each of them proceeds in a different phase. This effect of imitation will be discussed in more detail in chapter 5 as one means of producing displacement dissonance. "Free fall" constitutes a particular case of imitation insofar as the displacement dissonance is combined here with grouping dissonance.

A representative example, analyzed also by Grave, comes from the minuet of Haydn's Op. 50 No. 5 (Example 4.8a). *Imbroglio* arises here in mm. 34–37 from parallel two-tone patterns descending stepwise as a melodic sequence. This sequence forms an imitation between two violins in the interval of one quarter, so that the downbeats collide with each other. Nevertheless, the downbeats in the first violin part take slight precedence because they coincide with the resolutions of secondary dominants to local tonics in the harmonic sequence that results from the cooperation of both instrumental parts. In m. 38 the downbeat of the first violin comes along with the notated downbeat of 3/4 meter. Interestingly, this happens after two full metric cycles and one harmonic cycle of transpositions leading from F major at the beginning of the *imbroglio* back to F major at its end.[9] Yet the greatest peculiarity of this *imbroglio* is that the notated 3/4 meter is never reestablished. Instead,

8. Of course, it is possible to have phenomenal accents override the metrical structure of the first segment inherited from the preceding grid, yet such cases are exceptional in *imbroglio*. They represent peculiar combinations of metrical dissonances with rhythmical dissonances. One example occurs in the minuet of Haydn's Op. 76 No. 5 (mm. 9–11, 25–27), shown by Grave (1995: 187 ex. 13a).
9. A metric cycle is an interval between points of alignment occurring at certain beats of interpretive levels in grouping dissonances. Krebs (1999: 32) introduces this term after Yeston (1976) and Horlacher (1992).

it is even more distorted by the chords of mm. 38–40. As Grave correctly observes, these chords make up a typical cadence in "a brisk-march *topos* of common-time allegros" (1995: 194). What he does not realize, however, is that they bring a further change of meter from 2/4 to 2/2. This is evident from the fact that the chords enter not every quarter, as is the case in other cadences of this sort demonstrated by Grave,[10] but every second quarter. As a result, quarters as *Taktteile* of 2/4 cease being consistently articulated. In the light of Koch's discussion concerning the continuity of *Metrum* and his assumption that *Metrum* is based at least on *Taktteile*, if not on *Taktglieder*, this situation must be interpreted as a shift of the metrical level of *Taktteile* from quarter notes to half notes. Such a shift and an attendant change of meter from 2/4, notated as compound 4/4, to alla breve was observed earlier in Example 2.36 from the opening movement of Op. 64 No. 2. Further similar examples will be analyzed in chapter 6. The uniqueness of Example 4.8a lies in the fact that the shift does not happen here in the framework of the notated meter but is applied to the false 2/4 meter introduced by the *imbroglio*.

Example 4.8. Haydn, String Quartet in F major, "The Dream," Op. 50 No. 5/iii, mm. 33–41 (a) and 1–4 (b).

(a)

(b)

10. These cadences stem from the first movements of Haydn's Trumpet Concerto, mm. 35–36 (Grave 1995: 195 ex.19c), and String Quartet Op. 77 No. 2, mm. 170–72 (ex.19d).

Particularly curious, because devoid of imitation, is the "free fall" in the String Quartet in D major, "The Lark," Op. 64 No. 5 (Example 4.9). Although the pattern of the second violin is independent of that of the first violin, it clearly proceeds in a different phase, so that every pair of tones forming the melodic sequence F♯–G, E–F♯, D♯–E, C♯–D is heard as an upbeat motive. The reason the second violin does not accommodate to the phase of the first violin has to do with the fact that the *imbroglio* in the first violin actually starts later. The first motive, derived from the beginning of the minuet, is presented in its original form corresponding with the notated triple meter. In the framework of this meter, both the F♯ and the G in the part of the second violin fall on weak beats. Consequently, the location of the downbeat in the passage of false duple meter that is initiated by them is not inherited from the old metrical grid but is determined by phenomenal accents that are attached to the higher tones of every pair. These melodic accents coincide with the local tonics in the harmonic sequence that arises from the superposition of both violin parts. The harmonic stability of the tonics clearly favors them as metrical downbeats. Because, in addition, the resolution to the local tonic G major in m. 27 marks the first harmonic change from the beginning of this section, the sense of perceptual downbeat on the G in the second violin is unmistakable and will be transferred onto the further repetitions of the pattern. Why, then, does the first violin not accommodate its phase to the second violin? This is determined by the melodic accents falling on the higher tones in this part and by the upbeat role of the lower tones established from the beginning of the piece in all presentations of this motive, including the one at the beginning of the section discussed. The conflict between the phases of the two violins in this example thus boils down to the incongruity between harmony and melody, each of them guiding the metric perception of one but not the other instrumental part.

Example 4.9. Haydn, String Quartet in D major, "The Lark," Op. 64 No. 5/iii, mm. 27–31.

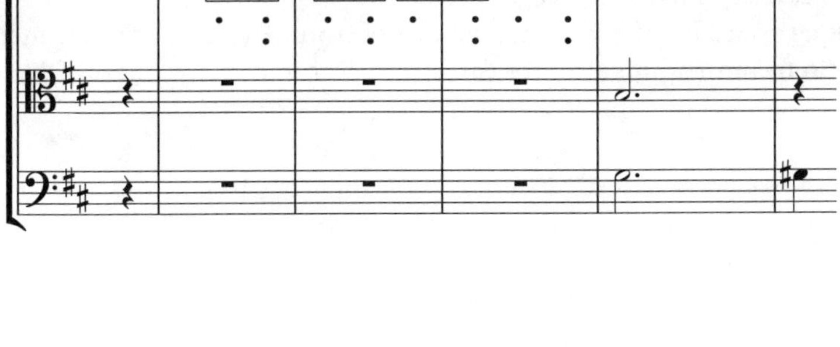

The connection between parallelism and meter works both ways, though. As noted by Temperley and Bartlette, "parallelism can often influence metrical analysis; but once a metrical framework is established, this can affect the parallelisms that are heard. In some cases parallelisms that go against an already established metrical framework will go by almost unnoticed" (2002: 147). This happens when the parallel patterns are uncharacteristic or when their similarity is attenuated by variation. Yet a parallelism that at first passed unnoticed can be recognized later. This makes compositional strategies possible in which an *imbroglio* reveals a potentially conflicting metrical structure contained earlier in the same piece. In Op. 50 No. 5 the parallelism of the two-tone patterns that produces the *imbroglio* in Example 4.8a is not recognized by the listener when it occurs in the theme at the beginning of the minuet (see Example 4.8b). Apart from the different position of the patterns relative to the notated 3/4 meter and to the slur articulating this meter at the musical surface, the feature that prevents the listener from recognizing parallelism in the first place is the embellishment assigned to the opening note in the first but not in the second pattern. Although this feature is subsequently preserved in the *imbroglio*, parallelism comes to the fore there, owing to the considerably longer continuation of the pattern and its imitation in the second voice. Given the two-way relationship between parallelism and meter, the question arises, when will parallelism prevail over meter, changing it, and when will meter prevail over parallelism, rendering it imperceptible? This question boils down to another, more fundamental one: How much similarity between patterns is needed in order that they may be perceived as parallel? This issue has not yet been theoretically explicated. Parallelism must thus be dealt with intuitively, in the same way it was dealt with by eighteenth-century composers.[11]

Examples from eighteenth-century treatises show the *imbroglio* as a juxtaposition of conflicting meters. Such a phenomenon is termed by Krebs "indirect dissonance." The *imbroglio* as a "direct dissonance," forming superposition of meters in different layers of motion, is not discussed in the treatises of the time. It is also of marginal importance in the eighteenth-century musical repertory. This indicates one more difference—in addition to those pointed out at the beginning of this chapter—between eighteenth-century music theory's understanding of metrical conflicts and the theory of metrical dissonance. In the latter, direct dissonances present the paradigmatic case of metrical dissonance because conflicting meters are simultaneously articulated at the musical surface. For the same reason, direct dissonances are considered stronger than indirect dissonances. By contrast, in the eighteenth century, departing from the assumed constancy of meter, the shock characteristic of indirect dissonances is apparently considered harsher than the effect of direct dissonances, in which the notated meter—although challenged—is nevertheless preserved in one layer of motion.

Unique examples of direct dissonances occur in Haydn. In the second reprise of the trio from the minuet of the String Quartet in F-sharp minor, Op. 50 No. 4

11. Some remarks about recognition of parallelism going in the direction of a preference rule approach are offered by Lerdahl and Jackendoff (1983: 52–53).

(Example 4.10), different meters are implied by two different parallel patterns running simultaneously in the melody and in the bass. The pattern of the melody, played by two violins, is three beats long and so corresponds with the notated meter of the piece. The two-beat cello pattern, on the other hand, goes against the notated meter. (Both patterns feature the characteristic upbeat turn that makes the parallelisms particularly obvious.) The fact that the antimetrical layer is located in the bass is significant: It bespeaks Haydn's intention to enhance the false duple meter by placing it in the more prominent auditory stream. The false meter is further reinforced by harmony. The bass pattern, forming a melodic sequence of falling fifths, F♯–B–E–A–D (interrupted only near the end when B follows instead of G♯), results in a harmonic sequence along the circle of fifths that also involves the upper stream. As it turns out, the parallelism that maintains the triple meter in the part of the two violins concerns only their rhythmic pattern: The melody forms, instead, a chain of two-beat patterns descending stepwise and cooperating with the bass: C♯/A–D/B, B/G♯–C♯/A, A/F♯–B/G♯.

Example 4.10. Haydn, String Quartet in F-sharp minor, Op. 50 No. 4/iii, mm. 50–56.

The kind of direct dissonance represented in Example 4.10 can be called *split dissonance*. Because, as proposed in chapter 2, the processor elaborates its analyses at first separately in auditory streams, the conflict of meters hosted in different streams is represented by the conflict of two analyses that, although different, are quite univocal. Another situation arises when the conflicting meters are hosted in the same auditory stream or in streams operating jointly. In such a situation, which I will call *merged dissonance,* no metrical structure is clearly exposed. Rather, the cues in favor of the conflicting meters hinder each other and blur the corresponding analyses, producing the effect of equivocation. This is illustrated in the trio from the minuet of the String Quartet in G major, Op. 54 No. 1 (Example 4.11). The false duple meter in mm. 53–56 arises from the parallelism between melodic patterns in the cello, each of them embracing four eighth notes. This relatively weak parallelism, based merely on the similarity of contour, is reinforced by the interventions of the first violin in a contrary motion to that of the cello. The original triple meter is, instead, continued by harmony, which forms a sequence tonicizing ii and then I. (This sequence, located at the beginning of the second reprise, forms a typical eighteenth-century gambit known as "Fonte.")[12] Yet at closer inspection, the harmonic rhythm of this sequence appears more complicated. The harmony of m. 53 starts already with the upbeat D–B in m. 52. The fact that it is prolonged over the bar line is typical of upbeats to large formal sections. In the first reprise of the trio, the tonic triad is prolonged in this way, in accordance with Kirnberger's instruction discussed in chapter 2. In the second reprise, the prolonged harmony is the secondary dominant seventh to A minor introducing the "Fonte." The same situation happens again with the last two tones C–A of m. 54, which belong already to the dominant seventh in G major, although they are heard as members of the local tonic A minor in the context of the preceding chord. In either case the harmonic change on the notated upbeat is coordinated with the downbeat of the false duple meter. By ingeniously taking advantage of the harmonic conventions concerning upbeats, Haydn is able to shape a Janus-faced harmonic progression that can support either of the superimposed metrical structures.

The move from direct to indirect metrical dissonance in the further course of this example is interpreted by Grave (1995: 180) as a resolution of an "uneasiness" of mm. 53–56 by a univocal duple meter of mm. 57–59. In keeping with the view assumed in the theory of metrical dissonance, this interpretation implies that the dissonance is weakened. It would be more historically appropriate to view this entire passage instead as a gradation of the dissonant effect, because the notated meter, first blurred, is then completely erased from the musical surface. It is interesting how the direct dissonance complicates the perception of downbeats in the indirect dissonance. This complication results from the fact that the conflicting meters are not only of different periods but also start out of phase: The virtual downbeat of the duple meter at the beginning of this section falls one quarter before the notated downbeat of m. 53. Consequently, at the beginning of m. 57 these two downbeats do not meet. From the point of view of the triple meter, the parallel pattern of the *imbroglio* is an upbeat motive. This interpretation is supported by the factor of harmonic stability: In the sequence, the local tonics tend to be heard as downbeats.[13] As a continuation of the antimetrical duple layer, however, the *imbroglio* pattern starts with the downbeat. In light of this interpretation, every measure of the false duple meter would embrace the entire secondary V–I progression, and this meter would be heard by the listener until the dominant marking the half cadence in m. 60.

12. "Fonte" is a model of transposition leading down from the second degree to the tonic, with both of these chords being preceded by their dominants. It is discussed along with two other gambits, "Monte" and "Ponte," by Riepel (1755: 44–48). For a concise summary of Riepel's discussion, see Ratner (1980: 213–14). A thorough discussion of "Fonte," including typical features of the melody and the bass inferred from Riepel's examples and their comparison with similar patterns from the repertory of Italian *partimenti,* is offered by Robert Gjerdingen (2007: 61–71).

13. Upbeat location of the characteristic opening turns is therefore most typical. It follows from the association of these turns with dominants, harmonically less stable than tonics in an underlying harmonic sequence and hence perceived as upbeats of the false meter established by the *imbroglio.* For the connection of *imbroglio* with sequence, see my further discussion below.

Example 4.11. Haydn, String Quartet in G major, Op. 54 No. 1/iii, mm. 53–60.

In the above examples of *imbroglio,* as well as those still to come, this phenomenon is represented by a change of meter from triple to duple. The same direction of change characterizes the examples in the eighteenth-century theoretical treatises by Koch and Türk. Only Riepel demonstrates *imbroglio* as a change possible in both directions between duple and triple meter. The tendency toward triple-to-duple metrical changes was noted already by Grave (1995: 186–88) and explained by him as a result of the "natural simplicity" of duple meter. This expression implies that it is easier to introduce the listener to duple meter after triple meter than vice versa. Grave's opinion can be substantiated by reference to the mechanism of projection.[14] As already indicated in chapter 2, triple projection is complicated by "deferral," with the result that, other things being equal, it will be less preferred than duple projection. The preference for the change from triple to duple meter is thus revealed as a corollary to the preference for "binary regularity" (MPR 10) in the process of metrical induction.

But if the preference for binary regularity were the whole explanation of the observed tendency, then the change from triple to duple could be occasioned equally by parallel patterns of two and four beats. Every four-beat pattern features binary regularity on two hierarchical levels, in that it comprises two measures of duple meter. In Riepel's example of *imbroglio* (Example 4.2b), parallel patterns of four beats are actually notated in 2/4. In reality, however, this example is not at all representative, because an *imbroglio* produced by four-beat patterns in triple meter occurs as seldom as an *imbroglio* produced by three-beat patterns in duple meter.[15] The explanation for this phenomenon has to do with the difference between processing events coming too early or too late. In the metrical change occasioned by two-beat patterns, the new downbeat comes too early (Example 4.12a). The effect is shocking and immediately perceivable because the triple projection, continued from the earlier metrical grid, is disturbed. At the same time, the recognition of parallelism, which is responsible for this shock, immediately clarifies the new metrical structure. By contrast, in the metrical change occasioned by four-beat patterns, the new downbeat arrives too late (Example 4.12b). Thus, projection on

14. Grave himself refers to Victor Zuckerkandl, who writes about "an interval of hesitation and suspense" in the flow of metric waves in triple meters (1956: 168).

15. One such example, shown by Wheelock (1992: 84) and Grave (1995: 194 ex. 18), occurs in Haydn's Symphony No. 65/iii, mm. 7–10.

the level of measure is first realized and only afterward put into question. As a result, the metrical structure is clarified only in retrospect. This means that such manipulation is less effective and at the same time cognitively more difficult. It is worth noting that the cognitive difficulty involved in the late arrival of the downbeat is essentially equivalent to the phenomenon of deferral.[16] Whereas deferral that is characteristic of triple meter can be called *structural*, the deferral shown schematically in Example 4.12b is *contextual,* as it depends on the context of the projection that is constitutive for the earlier established meter. If this projection is triple, deferral will be caused by a parallelism of four-beat patterns implying duple (quadruple) meter, which otherwise does not feature structural deferral. In the case of parallel three-beat patterns in duple meter, the effects of structural and contextual deferral combine, making this metrical change particularly rare.

Example 4.12. Downbeat of the false meter arriving "too early" (a) and "too late" (b).

(a)
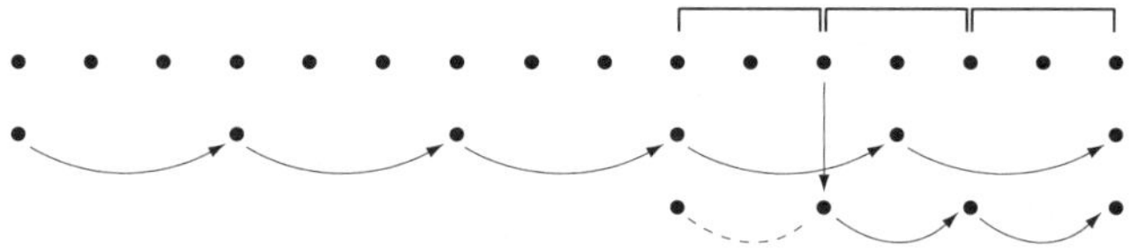

(b)
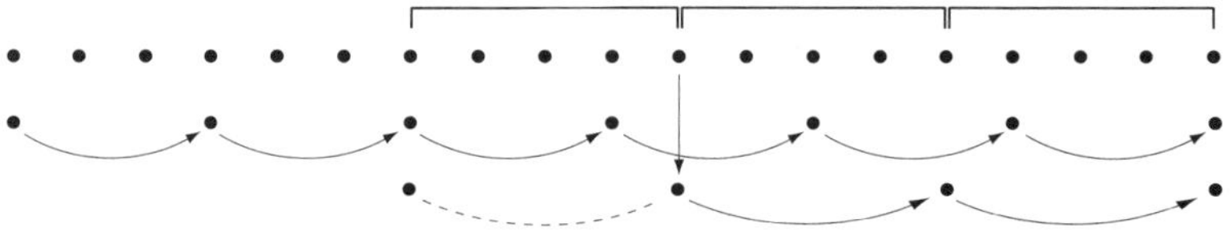

The fact that *imbroglio* is normally represented by the change from triple to duple meter explains why this phenomenon is found mostly in minuets. Among the types of movements entering into the composition of string quartets and quintets, only minuets are invariably in triple meter. An additional attraction of *imbroglio* in minuets lies in its pantomimic effect, vividly characterized by Wheelock as "falling out of step but continuing to run in place" (1992: 82). In slow movements *imbroglio* is scarcely ever introduced by the composers. Haydn does so in Op. 33 No. 3 (mm. 14–18, 43–47, 75–79) but not in his later quartet collections. Mozart composes *imbroglio* only in the slow movement of his String Quintet in C major, K. 515 (see Example 4.16) yet this example is at the same time the most elaborate one in his entire oeuvre. The only two examples of *imbroglio* in opening movements come from Haydn's Op. 50 No. 3 (Example 4.15) and Mozart's K. 589 (Example 4.7). It is noteworthy that in most cases *imbroglio* occurs in 3/4 meter. Although eighteenth-century music theorists do not state this explicitly, from their examples it follows that *imbroglio* as a regrouping

16. Hasty uses the labels "too early" and "too late" only in application to basic projections (1997: 86–91; see esp. exs. 7.3b and 7.4c), yet the complex feelings of realization and denial involved in "too late" are analogous to those mentioned by him as characteristic of deferral (138).

of *Taktteile* is most typically attached to the rhythmical values of quarters. In 3/8, normally notated as compound 6/8, *imbroglio* is relatively rare. This is the reason for its limited popularity in finales. Among few examples of this sort are those in Op. 50 No. 5 (Example 7.1) and Op. 55 No. 2 (mm. 60–62, 87–89).[17]

An interesting question about the *imbroglio* is whether there are any formal locations at which it typically occurs. At first glance, it seems that it can appear anywhere in the course of a movement. In minuets it is found equally in the theme (Op. 33 No. 5, K. 563/iii), at the beginning of the second reprise (Op. 54 No. 1, Example 4.11) and at its end (Op. 50 No. 5, Example 4.8a). However, a closer examination reveals the composers' tendency to place the *imbroglio* in the context of the cadence (*Kadenz*) or half cadence (*Halbkadenz*). In all the examples analyzed so far, the *imbroglio* immediately precedes one of these chief formal caesuras and endows the drive toward them with a particular momentum, due to the combined effect of metric and harmonic acceleration: the former resulting from the compression of measures from 3/4 to 2/4 and the latter from a sequence using secondary dominants or moving along the circle of fifths. The metric and harmonic instability is subsequently settled by the cadential formula. Such is the case in Haydn's Op. 54 No. 1 (Example 4.11), where the *imbroglio* occurs before the *Halbkadenz,* and in Mozart's String Quartet K. 589 (Example 4.7), where it is found before the *Kadenz*. The exceptionality of the *imbroglio* in Haydn's Op. 50 No. 5 (Example 4.8a) consists in the fact that the cadence does not restore the notated meter but rather continues the process of its corruption. In Op. 64 No. 5 (Example 4.9) the cadence, announced already in m. 30, is avoided and finally reached in m. 40 after a long parenthesis (see Example 5.16a).

In certain other cases, some of them shown in Examples 4.13, 4.14, and 4.15, the *imbroglio* before the cadence takes place on a single harmony represented by ii^6 or IV. Because this harmony is greatly prolonged, the *imbroglio* is here a purely melodic phenomenon performed by the first violin. The peculiar combination of metric acceleration with deceleration of the harmonic rhythm that arises in such cases will be addressed later in this chapter.

Example 4.13. Mozart, Divertimento for String Trio in E-flat major, K. 563/v, mm. 76–82.

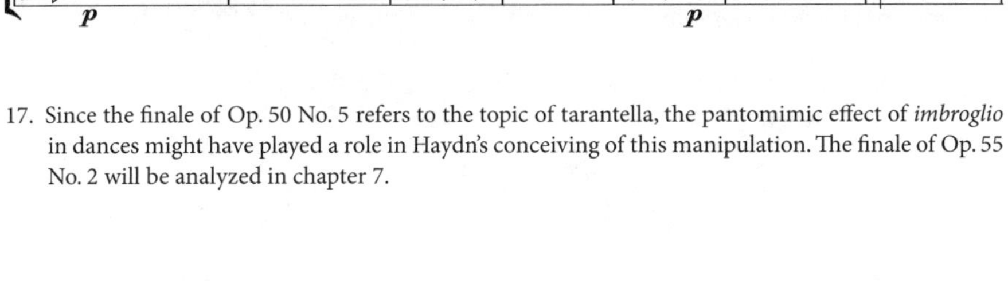

17. Since the finale of Op. 50 No. 5 refers to the topic of tarantella, the pantomimic effect of *imbroglio* in dances might have played a role in Haydn's conceiving of this manipulation. The finale of Op. 55 No. 2 will be analyzed in chapter 7.

Example 4.14. Mozart, String Quartet in D major, K. 575/iii, 56–60.

Example 4.15. Haydn, String Quartet in E-flat major, Op. 50 No. 3/i, mm. 31–33.

Imbroglio has an even stronger effect within the cadence. The only example of this sort, which is also the only *imbroglio* in a slow movement, comes from Mozart's String Quintet in C major, K. 515. It occurs during the cadence introduced by the first viola after the earlier attempt of the first violin has ended in a deceptive cadence at m. 51 (Example 4.16a). The *imbroglio* in mm. 53–54 is elicited by a highly decorative dialogue between these two instruments based on the prolonged six-four chord. Note that the assignment of the *imbroglio* to the cadential six-four is the only one possible, because the proper metric relations can still be clarified by the subsequent move from the dominant to the tonic. In the recapitulation (Example 4.16b) the *imbroglio* is even more expanded (mm. 113–16), and the following cadence crashes unexpectedly into another deceptive resolution in m. 118.[18]

18. Yet another deceptive cadence occurs in m. 121. After this almost painful postponement, the tonal goal of the recapitulation is finally reached in m. 124.

Example 4.16. Mozart, String Quintet in C major, K. 515/ii, mm. 51–58 (a) and 111–20 (b).

(a)

(b)

(*continued*)

Example 4.16. cont.

A reverse effect is achieved when *imbroglio* takes place, as it often does, after the cadence (*Kadenz*). Examples occur in the opening movement of Op. 55 No. 3 (mm. 155–57) and in the minuet of Op. 64 No. 6 (mm. 33–35). Mozart uses *imbroglio* in this way in the first minuet of his Divertimento for String Trio, K. 563 (mm. 16–23, 51–59). The consolidation of the notated meter achieved by the cadence is then shattered, and another cadence is required to restore it. Most curious in this respect is the *imbroglio* in the minuet of Haydn's String Quartet in B-flat major, Op. 64 No. 3, shown in Example 4.17. Because this *imbroglio* arises from the repetitions of the cadential V–I progression, the notated triple meter is not restored before the end of the first reprise. This leads to a curious effect at the beginning of the second reprise, which starts with the continuation of the *imbroglio* in the lower octave—a trick calculated by Haydn as both a metric and a formal manipulation referring to the topic of horn calls (Agawu 1991: 40–41).

Example 4.17. Haydn, String Quartet in B-flat major, Op. 64 No. 3/iii, mm. 9–17.

After an *imbroglio* following the half cadence (*Halbkadenz*), it is the thematic return that sets the metric relations right again. The *imbroglio* at this spot occurs during standing on the dominant, either over a bass pedal or without bass. Typical examples can be found in Op. 64 No. 1/ii (mm. 66–68) and Mozart's K. 593/iii (mm. 18–22; see Example 5.19). In the String Quintet in C major, K. 515 (Example 4.18), the *imbroglio* is one element of an interesting formal manipulation, which consists in starting the trio from a retransition over a dominant harmony obtained by adding the seventh to the final tonic of the minuet. Whereas the *imbroglio* is generated by the parallel melodic patterns in the first violin (mm. 5–6), the other instruments repeat the dominant harmony on the consecutive downbeats of the notated meter. The result is a direct grouping dissonance, albeit much simpler than those devised by Haydn in Examples 4.10 and 4.11.

Example 4.18. Mozart, String Quintet in C major, K. 515/iii, Trio, mm. 1–8.

4.2. Submetrical Dissonance

Destabilization of meter after the half cadence marking the formal caesura before the thematic return may be occasioned by regrouping not only *Taktteile* but also *Taktglieder* or *Taktnoten*. Characteristic examples of such a phenomenon occur in Mozart's String Quartet in B-flat major, K. 589, and String Quintet in G minor, K. 516 (Examples 4.19 and 4.20).

While generated through parallelism and hence strikingly similar to several examples discussed in the preceding section (see Examples 4.13 and 4.18), submetrical grouping dissonances are not to be subsumed under the concept of *imbroglio*. In the definitions of *imbroglio* and its examples offered by eighteenth-century authors, it is tacitly assumed that the size of *Taktteile* and *Taktglieder* remains

Example 4.19. Mozart, String Quartet in B-flat major, K. 589/ii, mm. 38–41.

Example 4.20. Mozart, String Quintet in G minor, K. 516/iv, mm. 50–55.

constant. This means that, despite the change of meter (*Takt*), the continuity of *Metrum* in Koch's sense of the word is not affected. By contrast, in Example 4.19 the parallel groups of three sixteenth notes yield dotted eighths rather than quarters as *Taktglieder,* which in turn combine into dotted quarters rather then half notes as *Taktteile* in alla breve meter. To throw the meter even more out of gear, these new rhythmical values of *Taktteile* and *Taktglieder* do not line up with the metrical downbeat but start with the second sixteenth note in m. 38. In the finale of K. 516 (Example 4.20), similar groups of sixteenths yield dotted eighths instead of eighths as *Taktglieder* of the mixed 6/8 meter. Because in this movement *Metrum* is based on *Taktglieder* (eighths), it is affected by the submetrical dissonance, even though the size of *Taktteile* (dotted quarters) does not change. It might be observed that the change in the size of *Taktglieder* and *Taktteile* in the above examples cannot be accounted for in terms of shorter projections. In most tempi sixteenth notes are under the level of durational determinacy and hence do not form projections. As a consequence, their regrouping resembles acceleration or deceleration of the beat in ad libitum sections, but more perfidious, since the constancy of some lower metrical level is nevertheless scented by the listener.[19] In the finale of K. 516 this irrational effect is used by Mozart in connection with the parody of the folk band already inaugurated by the theme (see Example 2.40). The solo flourish of mm. 50–53 jokingly imitates the leader of such a band who is eager to show off in front of the audience and his fellow musicians but gets lost in the course of his enterprise. The consequence of the loss of control is the written-out *rallentando* (mm. 51–53) that switches the rhythmical values of his figurations from *Taktnoten* (sixteenths) to a hierarchically higher metrical level of *Taktglieder* (eighths), ending up in a general pause. While this pause has a pantomimic effect—the band needs time to synchronize again after the irresponsible gambado of the leader—at the same

19. In light of Brower's (1993) remarks about perception of rhythm in different temporal scales, one might suppose that this level, lower than the lowest level of projection, is perceived not as a series of equal durations but as an underlying rhythmic pattern resulting from equal subdivisions of unequal durations. See note 4 in chapter 2 here.

time it allows the composer to win the half a measure that is necessary before the return of the theme. The notation of the theme, shifted by half a measure on the score, is of consequence at every thematic return.

The comparison of the effect produced by submetrical dissonance with that of ad libitum sections is not fortuitous. In fact, many submetrical dissonances occur at formal spots typically occupied by fermatas that are meant to be embellished by the soloist with a metrically free improvisation. As was observed in chapter 3, such typical locations for embellished fermatas are the dominant chord concluding the half cadence and the cadential six-four chord. The above examples of submetrical dissonances can be viewed as written-out embellishments of dominant fermatas. Examples of submetrical dissonances in two elaborated cadenzas over the six-four chord are found in the slow movement of Haydn's String Quartet in A major, Op. 55 No. 1. In the cadenza of the exposition, started by the solo violin and then joined in unison by the remaining instruments (Example 4.21a), the parallelism of melodic patterns embracing three thirty-second notes conflicts not only with the earlier metrical grid but also with the grouping indicated by slurs. The inconsistency in carrying on the three-note patterns, which are eventually abandoned and replaced by two-note patterns in m. 31, contributes to the impression of ad libitum improvisation. In the cadenza of the recapitulation (Example 4.21b), which is much more elaborated due to the fact that the individual instruments play independent polyphonic lines, the three-note patterns occur only in the initial section and from m. 63 are replaced by four-note patterns. A few examples

Example 4.21. Haydn, String Quartet in A major, Op. 55 No. 1/ii, mm. 27–32 (a) and 61–67 (b).

(*continued*)

Example 4.21. cont.

of submetrical dissonances in other formal contexts occur nevertheless in virtuoso passages entrusted to the soloist—the first violinist or, in Mozart's "Prussian" Quartets, the cellist—where they clearly allude to the improvised ornamentation of melodic line commonly practiced in the eighteenth century.[20] In so doing, they provide interesting information about the style of such improvisation and the role metric manipulations played in it.

An exceptionally elaborated example of submetrical dissonance occurs in the finale of Mozart's String Quartet in F major, K. 590. As noted by Hartmut Schick (1994), the theme of this finale is derived from the finale of Haydn's String Quartet in D major, Op. 64 No. 5, "The Lark" (Example 4.22). Mozart quotes the incipit of Haydn's theme in inversion, at the same time transforming it so as to obtain a parallelism of four-note patterns forming a descending melodic sequence (Example 4.23a). In the closing section of the exposition (Example 4.23b) this melodic idea is cut after its sixth note and spins around the central pitch G as in a child's spinning game, thus revealing a new parallelism of three-note patterns that had originally passed unnoticed. Observe that this parallelism is discovered by the listener only at the beginning of the third pattern when, expecting the continuation of the figuration down to E, she is turned back to A. Curiously, the parallelism of three-note patterns is contradicted by the articulation alternating between *legato* and *staccato*, corresponding to the notated meter. The combination of these two

20. See, for instance, Haydn's Op. 50 No. 2/ii (mm. 48–52), Op. 55 No. 1/i (mm. 44–46 [Example 6.5], 89–94, 164–67), and Mozart's K. 589/ii (m. 20–23).

Example 4.22. Haydn, String Quartet in D major, "The Lark," Op. 64 No. 5/iv, mm. 1–5.

Example 4.23. Mozart, String Quartet in F major, K. 590/iv, mm. 1–5 (a), 121–29 (b), and 297–305 (c).

(a)

(b)

(*continued*)

Example 4.23. cont.

(c)

factors in the first violin part produces a merged grouping dissonance on submetrical level. In addition, it is countered by the syncopations in the accompaniment, which yield a split displacement dissonance. The syncopated accompaniment and the chromatic auxiliary D♯ notes in the second violin, which jokingly obliterate the tonic triad, are clearly meant here as a commentary by the band on the exhilarating jest of the leader. That it is again a folk band is indicated by the viola's rustic drone fifths.[21] This particularly playful moment receives an intertextual dimension at its return in the recapitulation (Example 4.23c), where Mozart weaves in a quotation from the first movement of Haydn's String Quartet in C major, Op. 33 No. 3, in the part of the second violin. The grace notes, characteristic of Haydn's theme (mm. 1–6), contribute to the ironic mood of this brilliant conclusion.

The type of submetrical dissonance discussed so far fits the conceptual framework of Krebs's theory of metrical dissonance well. Curiously, however, Krebs himself does not mention it in his *Fantasy Pieces* (1999), even though he actually observes it in several examples. In discussing submetrical—or, as he calls them, low-level—grouping dissonances, he explains that they are "formed by the association of noncongruent subdivisions of metrical beats" (1999: 53). This definition does not apply to the above examples of submetrical dissonances. Instead, it accounts for a different type of submetrical dissonance, which, in a metrical hierarchy based

21. Jonathan Bellman suggests that the folk band consists of Hungarian Gypsies. He mentions this passage as an example of Mozart's stylized *ongherese* (1993: 55).

on duple subdivision of beats, is represented by triplets. In the eighteenth century, triplets were discussed as a means of metric confusion (*Verwirrung*) by Riepel (1752: 65–67). This view results from the fact that Riepel considers different divisions of beat in relation to one another. Koch takes a different approach to this issue, relating triplets to *Metrum*. His argument is analogous to the one he makes about the effect of syncopations, reported in chapter 3. According to him, triplets arising from irregular divisions of *Taktteile* are offensive only if *Metrum* is based on the level of *Taktglieder*, as in Example 4.24a. Because in such cases "our feeling bristles up" against them, triplets are prohibited.[22] If *Metrum* is based on the level of *Taktteile*, as in Example 4.24b, triplets do not affect it. Consequently, they are permitted because they have no unpleasant effect on the listener. Koch states expressly that the reason for the "unpleasant effect which these triplets cause [in Example 4.24a] consists not in that they are mixed with sixteenths, or else they would have had this unpleasant effect in the company of sixteenths under all circumstances."[23]

Example 4.24. Koch, *Musikalisches Lexikon*, cols. 959–60.

Krebs's definition of submetrical grouping dissonances as noncongruent divisions of the beat noticeably departs from his own concept of grouping dissonance discussed at the beginning of this chapter. Strictly speaking, Krebs's submetrical grouping dissonances are not grouping dissonances at all, because they do not arise from different ways of grouping beats of some lower metrical level common to them. Instead, they arise from different subdivisions of time spans between beats of a higher level. Henceforth I will call this type of submetrical dissonance *division dissonance*, reserving the term *grouping dissonance* for the type of submetrical dissonance instantiated in the examples at the beginning of this section. This terminological distinction sheds light on the difference between two traditions in the study of metrical dissonances, each of which construes these phenomena in an opposite direction, as either ascending or descending in the metrical hierarchy.

22. "Gesetzt aber, man wollte nun diesen Satz nachfolgen lassen [Example 4.24a], so ist es fühlbar genug, daß sich unser Gefühl dawider sträubt" (Koch 1802: cols. 959–60).

23. "Hier bestehet die unangenehme Wirkung, welche diese Triolen verursachen, nicht darinne, daß sie mit Sechzehntheilen vermischt sind, sonst würden sie diese unangenehme Wirkung in der Gesellschaft der Sechzehntheile unter allen Umständen äußern" (Koch 1802: cols. 959–60).

The former tradition, relying on grouping, is represented by Krebs; the foundation for the other tradition was laid down by Yeston in his definition of hemiola as "a bipartite and tripartite division of the same time span" (1976: 89).[24] Recently this tradition has been continued by Richard Cohn in his theoretical writings on "double," "generalized," or "complex" hemiolas (1992a, 1992b, 2001), consistently construed as divisions of "metric complexes" of ever larger size.

The reason that the difference between division and grouping dissonances has been virtually overlooked so far by the exponents of these different traditions is that, theoretically, either of them may be converted into the other. Mathematically speaking, cardinalities making up the ratio characteristic of a given dissonance can be treated either as factors or as dividers. This means that a given dissonance arising through different groupings of lower-level pulses may be construed alternatively as different subdivisions of some higher-level time span, and vice versa. For instance, a dotted eighth and a quarter may arise not only as two different groupings of sixteenths (3:4) but also as two different subdivisions of a dotted half note in the same ratio. Conversely, four sixteenths and an eighth-note triplet may be construed not only as different subdivisions (4:3) of a quarter but also as different groupings of micropulses whose length equals one-twelfth of a quarter. This possibility of converting every division dissonance into a grouping dissonance is exactly what allows Krebs to include division dissonances in his theory of metrical dissonance. At the same time, however, Krebs admits that "the 'micropulse' underlying such dissonances is not articulated within any single voice but is merely the resultant of the pulses of different voices" (1999: 53). This last statement is crucial. Although both ways of construing the aforementioned division dissonances are theoretically equivalent, they are not equivalent in the reality of metric perception. Conversion of a division dissonance into a grouping dissonance presupposes a pulse level of a fantastic rate far under 100 milliseconds, which is the shortest interval we can hear as an element of a rhythmic figure (London 2004: 27). Neither is the result of converting the aforementioned grouping dissonance into division dissonance perceptually more realistic. Obviously, there is no possibility for a listener to conceive of a dotted eighth and a quarter as different divisions of a dotted half note in a piece written, say, in 2/2 meter, where a dotted half note does not occur as projection on any metrical level.

The construal of metrical dissonances consistently in only one direction—either by grouping or by division—is closely related to the "flat" metrical hierarchies underlying the study of metrical dissonances in both the traditions delineated above. Because these hierarchies have no central level, all levels are equivalent to each other and arise through the same type of operation, recursively repeated either upward or downward. Eighteenth-century metrical hierarchy requires, instead, that metrical dissonances are construed in two directions departing from

24. At the beginning of his discussion (1976: 78), Yeston speaks about what he calls "rhythmic dissonances" in terms of both grouping (multiplication) and division. From this point of view, he is to be considered the founder of both traditions. Nevertheless, in his graphical representation (79 ex. 4.2) he demonstrates only division dissonances. Division subsequently forms the conceptual basis for his definition of hemiola and other, more speculative cases of metrical dissonances (122–39).

the level of *Taktteile*. Below this central level, they represent different subdivisions of *Taktteile* into *Taktglieder* and *Taktnoten,* yielding submetrical division dissonances. Above the level of *Taktteile,* metrical dissonances arise through a different grouping of *Taktteile* into *Takte,* as is typical for an *imbroglio*. Yet, as I observed earlier in this section, eighteenth-century compositional practice includes submetrical dissonances that are construed by applying the principle of grouping to beats below the level of *Taktteile,* which can thus be aptly described in the framework of Krebs's theory. It is by curiously contradicting the logic of the eighteenth-century metrical hierarchy that such dissonances affect the size of *Taktteile,* which—as the primitive beats—can never change if this logic is observed. Might there be any equivalent for this phenomenon operating in the opposite direction, by applying the principle of division to time spans above the level of *Taktteile,* which would correspond with Yeston's and Cohn's understanding of hemiolas? This question leads to the topic of the last section.

4.3. Hemiola

Whereas the term "hemiola" was not known in the late eighteenth century,[25] the authors of the time make mention of a phenomenon that corresponds to the traditional sense ascribed to the term today. They do not endow it with any special name, but in every case they clearly distinguish it from *imbroglio*. Türk (1789: 93), describing compositional licenses (*Freiheiten*) concerning meter, cites—apart from *imbroglio*—an example from Carl Heinrich Graun's oratorio *Der Tod Jesu,* in which one measure, notated in double metrical values, is inserted before the cadence. The same example—this time rendered in a full scoring and in a more complete form, including the preceding passage—is cited by Koch in *Musikalisches Lexikon* as yet another type of *Rückung*. In his commentary Koch describes it as "this procedure during which, in the course of a phrase, the value of *Taktteile* in one measure is doubled for the sake of a graver and more emphatic expression"(Example 4.25).[26]

This description makes clear the fundamental structural difference between the *imbroglio* and the hemiola in the light of eighteenth-century music theory. Whereas the *imbroglio* consists in regrouping beats (*Taktteile*) into new *Takte* (Example 4.26a), which results in a change of meter from 3/4 to 2/4, in the hemiola

25. In *Musikalisches Lexikon*, Koch includes the entry "Hemiolisch," but he refers with this term to a peculiar type of meter that arises from regular alternation of three and two equal rhythmical values and results in 5/4 or 5/8 (1802: col. 753). An earlier mention of "hemiolisch" in the same sense and in application to 5/1, 5/2, 5/4, 5/8 occurs in Marpurg (1760–63: 1:122). Koch relates this phenomenon to ancient Greek music.

26. "Man braucht das Wort *Rückung* auch in einem weitern Sinne, und bezeichnet damit, 1) dasjenige Verfahren, bey welchem, um den Ausdruck schwerfälliger und nachdrücklicher zu machen, mitten im Verfolge des Satzes der Werth der Taktheile eines Taktes verdoppelt wird" (Koch 1802: col. 1278).

Example 4.25. Graun, *Tod Jesu*, reproduced in Koch, *Musikalisches Lexikon*, cols. 1278–79.

the size of *Taktteile* changes: it is doubled. As a consequence, the size of the measure is also doubled, and thus the meter changes from 3/4 to 3/2 (Example 4.26b). Graun's example reflects this doubled measure directly in notation, in this way curiously breaking the tacit rule of a constant notated meter, otherwise obligatory for eighteenth-century composers. In virtually all other cases of the hemiola, where this rule is observed, the measure of 3/2 is notated as two measures of the original 3/4 meter.[27]

Example 4.26. Change of metrical hierarchy in *imbroglio* (a) and hemiola (b).

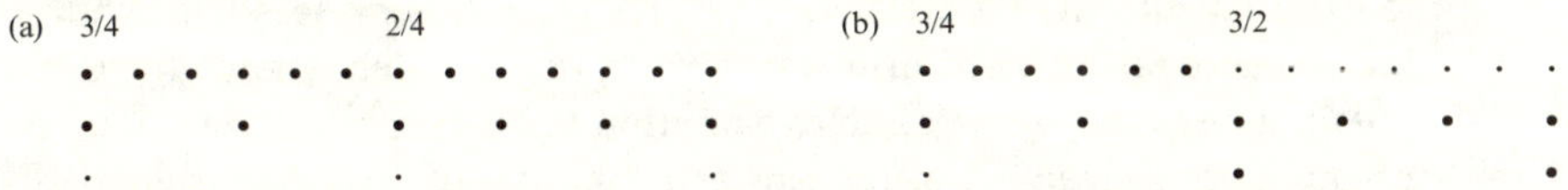

Although the resulting reorganization of the metrical structure is the same as in the *imbroglio,* the hemiola cannot be construed in the framework of Krebs's theory as a regrouping of pulses in a 2:3 ratio, because such regrouping does not account for the change of the level of *Taktteile* from quarter notes to half notes. But neither can it be construed in terms of division, since there is no higher-level unit whose division into the 2:3 ratio would yield the quarter note and half note as *Taktteile* of 3/4 and 3/2, respectively. Ironic as it may appear, the phenomenon of the hemiola in eighteenth-century music cannot be correctly accounted for by either of the two subtraditions of the theory of metrical dissonance, although it is treated as paradigmatic by representatives of both. This is because in the flat metrical hierarchies assumed in both of these subtraditions, no such thing as a shift of metrical level can sensibly be conceived of. Yet it is precisely this shift that occasions the effect of slowing down that is characteristic of the hemiola and is related to its formal function as a composed-out *allargando* before the cadence. In this respect the hemiola departs even further from the *imbroglio,* which normally features an effect of acceleration due to the contraction of the measure from 3/4 to 2/4. Finally, *imbroglio* and hemiola differ in that they are generated in different ways: While the former arises from parallelism, the deceleration of beat in the latter is occasioned by slowing down the harmonic or the surface rhythm, or both, in the precadential area. In Graun's example, where the harmonic rhythm of minims is identical with the surface rhythm, this results in interrupting the articulation of the quarters representing rhythmical values of *Taktteile* in 3/4 meter and in this way disturbing the continuity of *Metrum.*

Apart from the metrical level of *Taktteile,* formal function, and methods of generation, the *imbroglio* and the hemiola differ in their historical origins. By contrast to the modern *imbroglio,* which is emblematic of the galant style, the hemiola was a common feature of Baroque music.[28] In the Classic period, the hemiola was

27. Hemiola is also defined as a double measure by many contemporary authors (Cooper and Meyer 1960; Bernet-Kempers 1961; LaRue 1970; Cone 1985). At the same time, these authors are often inconsistent in their accounts of hemiola, mixing it up with *imbroglio.* The distinction between these two phenomena that I propose in this study corresponds to the distinction drawn between "contraction hemiolas" and "expansion hemiolas" by Willner (1991). "Cadential hemiola," which is the third type listed by Willner, is a side effect of harmony: In triple meter, cadential harmonic progressions frequently result in the cadential six-four falling on the weak second beat, although this chord arises from a double appoggiatura or suspension within the dominant harmony and—like any other suspension—should properly fall on the strong beat. This situation impels Kirnberger to assign a double—weak or strong—status to the second beat in triple meters. See note 38 in chapter 3 here.

28. About Baroque hemiolas, see Corrigan (1992) and Willner (1991, 1996, 2007b).

thus already well established, if not out of date, and was cultivated mostly in the strict style of church music. In this respect, the fact that Graun's hemiola demonstrated by Türk and Koch comes from an oratorio is very characteristic. The affiliation with church music is probably responsible for the absence of hemiolas in Haydn's string quartets. Mozart's early experiences with church music and his general inclination toward incorporating elements of the strict style in galant genres may serve as an explanation for his slightly greater interest in this phenomenon. Even so, in his earlier collection of string quartets dedicated to Haydn, hemiolas can be found only in the slow movement (mm. 28, 88–89) and the minuet of K. 428 (mm. 46–47), and in the opening movement of K. 464 (mm. 148–49). In Mozart's later string quartets and quintets, hemiolas occur by way of exception. One, in the minuet of the String Quintet in G minor, K. 516, has been shown earlier (Example 3.30, mm. 11–12); the other, from the String Quartet in F major, K. 590, will be discussed below. Otherwise, the old-style hemiola has been abandoned and its place taken by the type of *imbroglio* before the cadence that was presented in Examples 4.13–4.15. Despite the contraction of measure from 3/4 to 2/4, the *allargando* effect characteristic of hemiola arises in all these examples due to the prolongation of one harmony. These examples may thus be considered a particular fusion of the hemiola and the *imbroglio,* in the immediate context of a cadence, made possible by their identical metrical layout.[29] An interesting clue that the *imbroglio* functionally stands for the hemiola in precadential contexts can be found in the trio from the minuet of Mozart's String Quartet in B-flat major, K. 589 (Example 4.27), where both phenomena—instead of being fused—follow one another during one prolonged harmony of the cadential six-four. Because there is only one more chord—the dominant seventh—that follows before the resolution to the

Example 4.27. Mozart, String Quartet in B-flat major, K. 589/iii, Trio, mm. 14–17.

29. A possibility of such fusion is noted by Willner, who writes that in some cases, contraction hemiolas "may simply extend and embellish a single harmony and represent a special case of the expansion hemiola" (1991: 224).

tonic, this chord is introduced on the second antimetrical beat of the hemiola in m. 17. The first antimetrical beat, which should fall on the third quarter of m. 16, is not articulated by any harmonic change, but is suggested by the melodic accent (contour pivot) and otherwise carried over from the preceding *imbroglio*.

The only example of an old-fashioned precadential hemiola in Mozart's "Prussian" Quartets occurs not in 3/4 but in 6/8 meter. It comes from the slow movement of the String Quartet in F major, K. 590 (Example 4.28), which is a stylized siciliano. An interesting feature of this hemiola (m. 23) is that—in contrast to most other hemiolas, which constitute indirect dissonances—it forms a direct metrical dissonance with the second violin part, which sustains the notated meter through parallel melodic patterns. In addition, the alternation between *legato* and *staccato* articulation within these patterns implies triple grouping of sixteenth notes, and thus generates a submetrical grouping dissonance relative both to the notated 6/8 meter and to the 3/4 meter of the hemiola.

Example 4.28. Mozart, String Quartet in F major, K. 590/ii, mm. 21–24.

Hemiolas in 6/8 deserve closer consideration, because the change of meter occasioned by them can be represented in two different ways, depending on whether 6/8 is a simple or compound meter. If it is compound, with each notated measure comprising two real measures of 3/8, the conceptual structure of the situation does not vary in comparison with that illustrated in Example 4.26b. The size of *Taktteile* is doubled from eighths to quarters, and so doubled is also the size of the measures, resulting in metrical change from 3/8 to 3/4. If, however, 6/8 is a simple (mixed) meter, that is, tripled 2/4, this way of construing hemiola is not valid. This is exactly the case in Example 4.28. Although the size of *Taktteile* changes here as well, this change does not consist in doubling, but rather must be represented by the ratio 3:2 between the dotted quarter as *Taktteil* of 6/8 and the quarter as *Taktteil* of 3/4. By contrast to the *imbroglio*, the ratio 3:2 stands this time not for factors but for dividers. It seems that the hemiola in simple 6/8 meter represents the only type of metrical dissonance in which the principle of division, inherent in Yeston's and Cohn's notion of the hemiola, is implied by the music theory of the eighteenth century in reference to a time span longer than the *Taktteil*. Such a hemiola arises from the division of one notated measure (*Takt*) into two and three equal parts (*Taktteile*).[30] The representation of this metrical change in Example 4.29 preserves the layout of metrical structure from Examples 4.26a and b yet, once again, changes the location of *Taktteile* and *Takte*.

While old-fashioned when occurring before the cadence, hemiolas seem to have occasionally gained a certain favor with progressive composers, if used at less usual formal spots. The most famous example in the symphonic repertory is unquestionably the beginning of the Menuetto of Mozart's Symphony in G minor, K. 550, where the melody in 3/2 is set against the accompaniment in 3/4.[31] An analogous example occurs in the minuet of Haydn's String Quartet Op. 50 No. 6. Both of them form direct metrical dissonances. Whether they can be properly called hemiolas can be debated, however. In point of fact, they come close to certain more speculative combinations of conflicting meters known to eighteenth-century music theorists. One of them, described by Riepel, is particularly curious, since it concerns an early (fictive) composition for string quartet. In the course of the didactic dialogue between Praeceptor and Discantista, it is described by Discantista as follows: "The choirmaster in Vallenthal has [composed] an *Allegro,* where the first violin is in 3/4, the second violin in 2/4, the viola in *Allabreve* [2/2], and the bass in the common time [4/4]. Recently the four have rehearsed it but could in no way bring it together because no meter [*Tact*] can be beaten to it."[32] This description brings to mind the famous ballroom scene in the finale of act 1 of *Don Giovanni,* where Mozart makes three orchestras play simultaneously a minuet in 3/4, a contredanse in 2/4, and a German peasant dance or *Teitsch* in 3/8 (Allanbrook 1983: 281–85). In the repertory of chamber string music by Haydn and Mozart, however, such extreme experiments do not take place. The plausible reason for this is that in string quartets and quintets the individual layers of motion would need to be articulated by single instrumental parts and hence very difficult to perceive. At least, this seems to have been the opinion of the Viennese masters, if not of "the choirmaster in Vallenthal" mentioned in Riepel's dialogue.

Example 4.29. Hemiola in simple 6/8 meter.

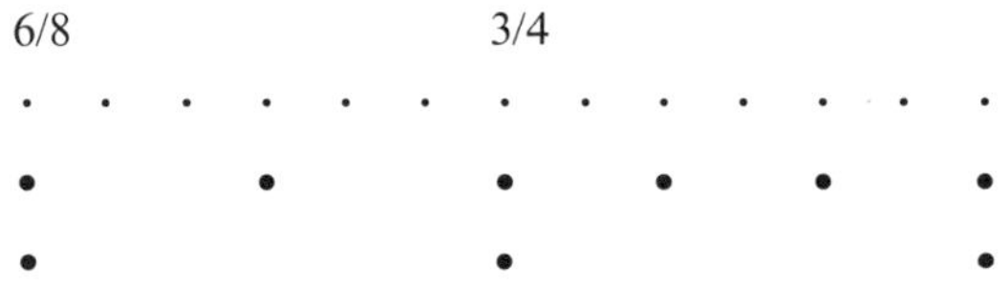

30. Although the size of notated measures is of structural importance only for hemiolas in simple 6/8 meter, it might have provoked composers to use hemiolas in both simple and compound 6/8 meter. This remark resonates with Willner's (2005: 235–36) observation that hemiolas are much more common in 6/8 meter than in 3/8, although both meters offer equally favorable conditions for hemiolas, and two measures of 3/8 meter are actually encompassed by one measure of compound 6/8. A detailed discussion of hemiolic 6/8 is included in Corrigan (1992).
31. Metric peculiarity of the theme of the minuet from K. 550 is analyzed in detail by Maurer Zenck (2001: 98–101). It is interesting to observe how, by taking into account the change in the size of *Taktteile,* her analysis departs from Cohn's interpretation of the same theme (1992b: 14–17).
32. "Der Herr Chorregent in Vallenthal hat ein *Allegro,* wo die erste Violine in 3/4, die zweyte Violine in 2/4, die Bratsche in *Allabreve* [2/2], und der Baß in allgemeinem *Tempo* [4/4] bestehet. Neulich haben selbes ihrer vier probirt, aber keineswegs zusammen bringen können, aus Ursache, weil sich kein Tact dazu schlagen läßt" (Riepel 1752: 64).

CHAPTER Five

Changing Meter II

Change of Phase

5.1. Chains of Rhythmical Dissonances

The other type of metrical dissonance distinguished by Krebs is displacement dissonance. It arises between interpretive levels having the same period but different phase. The structure of the metrical grid is not altered in such cases but only displaced to the left or right in relation to the notated meter. Accordingly, the perceptual effect is not one of changed time signature but of shifted bar lines. In eighteenth-century music theory, displacement dissonances were subsumed under the term *Rückung*, the German equivalent of syncopation. As noted in chapter 3, Koch's entry "Rückung" in the *Musikalisches Lexikon* includes a discussion of syncopations caused by stress and duration. Although such syncopations often occur singly as rhythmical dissonances, they can also form longer chains. Koch's examples of *Rückungen* show precisely such chains of rhythmical dissonances yielding metrical displacement dissonance (Example 5.1). One other type of rhythmical dissonances mentioned in chapter 3 is harmonic syncopation. In generating metrical dissonances, however, harmony seldom acts alone. Usually it cooperates with either stress or duration, or it articulates the notated meter that is challenged by them.

Example 5.1. Koch, *Musikalisches Lexikon*, cols. 1281–82.

The perceptual process involved in chains of rhythmical dissonances forming displacement dissonance is illustrated in Example 5.2. This example is to be read in connection with Example 3.25 in chapter 3. As was explained in the commentary to Example 3.25, each time a rhythmical dissonance presents a challenge to the established meter, it initiates a set of projections depending on the pattern of the following attacks. If one of these attacks presents another challenge to meter, the projection staked out by the two rhythmical dissonances will be surfaced by the selection function as a hypothesis of a new regularity. The third challenge confirms this hypothesis and establishes an analysis of a given passage as shifted in relation to the old metrical grid. By playing with two senses of the German word "verrückt," which means "shifted" as well as "crazy," authors of eighteenth-century treatises alluded to the eccentric perceptual effect of this manipulation.[1]

Example 5.2. Metrical displacement dissonance generated by a chain of rhythmical dissonances.

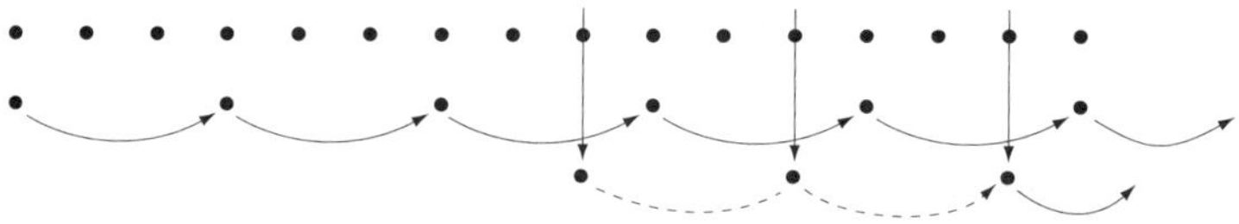

If the notated meter is no longer articulated at the musical surface, an indirect displacement dissonance arises. Such is the case in Example 5.3 from Haydn's String Quartet in G major, Op. 54 No. 1, where the notated downbeats cease even being articulated by attacks. If the notated meter is articulated side by side with the false meter, the displacement dissonance is direct. It can take the form of either split or merged dissonance, depending on whether the conflicting layers of motion are hosted in two auditory streams or in the same stream. A striking example of direct displacement dissonance can be seen in the trio of the String Quartet in B-flat major, Op. 64 No. 3 (see Example 3.14). The chain of rhythmical dissonances included in the coda (mm. 96–100) is one of the foot-stomping syncopations that so frequently subvert the courtly decorum of Haydn's minuets and turn them into peasant *Ländler*. Whereas the notated meter is articulated in the melody, the bass challenges this meter by heavily accented second beats. Note how this metrical conflict jokingly plays out the state of metrical non-alignment between the melody and the bass at the beginning of the trio (Example 2.20). If the bass strokes were perceived then on "two" yet notated regularly on "one," now they affirm themselves as blatantly antimetrical phenomena in both perception and notation. For further illustrations of direct displacement dissonances, see Examples 5.4 and 5.5. In Example 5.4, from Haydn's String Quartet in E major, Op. 54 No. 3, *fz* accents contradict the durational accents of the bass— accompanied in the upper

1. This particularly concerns Türk (1982: 364 [1789: 374]).

voices by slurs—assigned to the notated downbeats. In Mozart's String Quintet in C major, K. 515 (Example 5.5) stress and duration cooperate in generating the dissonant layer of motion, whereas the notated downbeats are articulated by harmonic changes. In contrast to grouping dissonances, in the case of displacement dissonances, direct dissonances are much more common than indirect ones. The intensity of displacement dissonances depends on the strength of the individual rhythmical dissonances contained in them, and can be evaluated in terms of horizontal and vertical distance from the preceding metrical downbeats along the lines proposed in chapter 3.[2]

Example 5.3. Haydn, String Quartet in G major, Op. 54 No. 1/i, mm. 66–72.

Example 5.4. Haydn, String Quartet in E major, Op. 54 No. 3/i, mm. 95–98.

2. Note that this way of evaluating the intensity of displacement dissonances differs somewhat from Krebs's criterion of "inherent" intensity, which is based exclusively on the proximity of a given displacement dissonance to consonance (1999: 57). For Krebs, the direction of the displacement to the left or right is of no significance for the intensity of the dissonant effect. This reflects his inherently atemporal approach to metrical dissonances, contrasting with my own approach, informed by the dynamic model of meter I adopt in this study. Importantly, Krebs distinguishes the "inherent" intensity of metrical dissonances from their "contextual" intensity, which depends on the number and kind of accents creating an antimetrical layer. "Contextual" intensity thus relates to the perceivability of metrical dissonances, a problem to be addressed in the following section.

Example 5.5. Mozart, String Quintet in C major, K. 515/i, mm. 115–23.

It can be observed that the account of metrical dissonances—both grouping and displacement—is possible only within the framework of the parallel multiple-analysis model of processor. Serial processors by definition cannot elaborate two analyses of the same passage at the same time. However, elaboration of two analyses does not yet mean that they are both perceived. Experimental work in perception of polyrhythms suggests that listeners are not able to hear two metric frameworks at the same time.[3] This can be explained by reference to the selection function, which always tends to choose one of the analyses as the frame of reference for the other. As in the phase of looking for meter, its choice depends on the number and kind of preference factors that articulate a given analysis at the musical surface and, in the case of split dissonances, on the assignment of these factors to a more or less prominent auditory stream. A preference factor that is not available in the phase of looking for meter but is decisive in the phase of monitoring meter is the preceding metrical grid. In most cases, the layer of motion that continues the preceding grid will be selected, even if it is more weakly articulated at the surface. Because the preceding metrical grid is normally that of the notated meter, this meter remains the frame of reference in direct metrical dissonances. The antimetrical layer of motion is perceived as its embellishment or "shadow," in the sense originating with Frank Samarotto (1999a).[4] But the projection of the grid characteristic of the notated meter is continued by the processor even if this meter is completely erased from the musical surface. This means that the notated meter can also form the frame of reference in indirect metrical dissonances. Only if such dissonances continue for a longer time can one properly speak of a change of meter. I will return to this issue in section 5.6, which is devoted to the notion of subliminal dissonance.

3. Most relevant in this respect are experiments conducted by Handel and Oshinsky (1981) and Handel and Lawson (1983). For a more general discussion see London (2001: 284, 2004: 50).
4. As Samarotto puts it, "the main meter, the meter as written, casts a shadow, as it were, on a subsidiary, displaced meter, which we are drawn to hear as real until it dissolves" (1999a: 235). The idea of "shadow meter" is further developed by Rothstein (1995).

Yet the fact that the listener hears the antimetrical layer of motion not merely as a series of single challenges but as a secondary regularity superimposed on the notated meter proves that the analysis determined by the antimetrical layer is actually accessible to consciousness. This suggests that, if two analyses exceed some threshold of perceivability, they are both surfaced to consciousness by the selection function, even if one of them is preferred over the other. Although such a possibility is not foreseen by Jackendoff in his parallel multiple-analysis model, it fits the preference rule approach adopted by Lerdahl and Jackendoff and is explored by Temperley (2001: 219–20) in the context of the computational model of metric perception drawing on the GTTM. For Temperley, two analyses of the same musical passage characterized by very high and almost equal scorings result in ambiguity. *Ambiguity* is thus to be considered a third possible kind of metric sensation, in addition to *clear* meter, in which only one analysis is surfaced to consciousness, and *vague* meter, in which no analysis is surfaced.

It is noticeable that in Examples 5.3, 5.4, and 5.5, displacement dissonances go along with *parallelism*. But, unlike grouping dissonances, in which parallelism creates the metrical effect, displacement dissonances are not created by parallelism. Because parallelism determines only the period of the secondary metrical structure, it cannot be effective as a method of generating metrical dissonances in which the same period is preserved. Nonetheless, parallelism is indicative of the way displacement dissonances usually arise. In most cases they are produced by repeating a motive derived from some earlier musical passage. If this motive contains a rhythmical dissonance, its repetitions yield metrical dissonance. In such cases the connection between rhythmical and metrical dissonances is particularly obvious. In Example 5.3 the original rhythmical dissonance occurs two measures earlier in the immediately preceding phrase (m. 67). The metrical dissonance in Example 5.4 refers back to a single syncopation that is contained in the principal theme of the movement, shown earlier in Example 2.16 (m. 3). Significant motivic connection with the principal theme characterizes many other displacement dissonances as well. One of them is worth analyzing in detail as it forms part of a metrical strategy that permeates a whole movement.

In the trio of Haydn's String Quartet in D major, Op. 50 No. 6, "The Frog" (Example 5.6a) the chain of syncopations arises from the continuation of two syncopations contained in the third phrase of the first reprise shown earlier in Example 2.17, which, in turn, form an echo of metrical perturbations in two preceding phrases. As was explained in connection with Example 3.13, in the second reprise the third phrase returns twice, both times delayed by parentheses and general pauses. These manipulations serve to postpone the final cadence. The strategy of postponing the cadence is continued in the last phrase of the trio by means of a peculiar harmonic loop that departs from and then returns to the cadential six-four chord. Structurally, this loop originates in the equivocation between the enharmonically equivalent pitches B♭ and A♯ in the bass. The B♭ in m. 80 serves as the chromatically lowered sixth degree in D major leading to the dominant in m. 81. Yet, when the suspensions G–E in the two upper voices fail to resolve to the cadential six-four on the second beat—the second violin moves to D♯ instead of D—the very same pitch, renamed as A♯, pulls away from the dominant and back to the submediant from which it descended in m. 80. The chromatic ascent in the bass, initiated by A♯–B, continues through B♯ in

m. 82 to C♯ and D in m. 83, the last step forcing the second violin to finally provide the D expected in m. 81. The subsequent skip of the bass up to G (m. 83) ultimately breaks the pendulum motion of the upper voices and approaches the dominant via the fourth degree harmonized as ii^6. The two dynamic accents *fz*, plaited into this process, look back to similar accents at the beginning of the trio.

Interestingly enough, the enharmonic equivocation A♯/B♭, so ingeniously exploited by Haydn before the final cadence, has already been planted by him earlier, in the developmental X section (Example 5.6b). This section, based on the dominant pedal A, forms an exceptionally long chain of syncopations played by the first violin against the middle voices articulating the notated meter. When, after the series of repeated Gs in the upper voice and chromatic adjustments in the middle voices, the dominant seventh is finally reached in m. 54, the listener expects a caesura followed by the thematic return, starting with the tonic. Instead, the bass unexpectedly moves up a semitone, creating a diminished seventh with the three upper voices. In this harmonic setting, the pitch played by the cello in m. 55 sounds like A♯ to be resolved further up to B, thus creating a deceptive cadence. What course will the music take after that cadence? When and how will the half cadence before the thematic return be reached? Having provoked the listener to ask these questions, the composer renders them null by moving the bass back to A and explaining the preceding pitch as B♭: a gratuitous neighbor-note postponing—but not thwarting—the dominant arrival. From this discussion it follows that the final episode of the metrical strategy in the trio from Op. 50 No. 6 (Example 5.6a) not only refers to the earlier episodes included in the theme (Example 2.17) and the thematic return (Example 3.13) but also links them to the X section reproduced in Example 5.6b. This metrical strategy goes hand in hand with the formal strategy of postponing structural cadential arrivals.

Example 5.6. Haydn, String Quartet in D major, "The Frog," Op. 50 No. 6/iii, mm. 78–86 (a) and 45–56 (b).

Example 5.6. cont.

Whereas in one sense the metrical dissonances in Examples 5.3, 5.4, and 5.6 are *derived* from "rhythmical dissonances," in another sense they can be said to have been *prepared* by them. In Krebs's theory, *preparation* of metrical dissonance is possible by means of one or two antimetrical attacks. While such attacks do not suffice to establish a metrical level—to this end at least three attacks are necessary—they can be used to foreshadow a later metrical dissonance within an earlier, consonant context.[5] As follows from the earlier examples, preparation of metrical dissonance

Example 5.7. Mozart, String Quartet in B-flat major, K. 589/i, mm. 23–26 (a) and 154–60 (b).

5. In his earlier article, Krebs speaks of preparation only in reference to two antimetrical attacks (1987: 110). In *Fantasy Pieces* he admits, however, that it can be accomplished by either one or two attacks (1999: 87).

occurs mostly in Haydn. In Mozart the only clear example of it is in the opening movement of the String Quartet in B-flat major, K. 589, where the single syncopation of m. 24 enhances the salient harmony of the diminished seventh chord—extremely surprising in the harmonically unproblematic context of the preceding section (Example 5.7a). This moment is elaborated in the recapitulation into the fancy polyphonic passage in mm. 154–57, in which displacement dissonance is combined with a harmonic sequence of utmost complexity (Example 5.7b).

Example 5.8. Mozart, Serenade *Eine kleine Nachtmusik*, K. 525/iii, mm. 1–8, reproduced in Krebs, "Some Extensions of the Concepts of Metrical Consonance and Dissonance," 109, ex. 11, with additions.

Although Krebs relates the concept of preparation to both grouping and displacement dissonances,[6] it should be clear from the foregoing discussion that, in practice, preparation by means of rhythmical dissonances applies exclusively to displacement dissonances. Grouping dissonances are not prepared in this way because they are not generated by chains of rhythmical dissonances but rather by parallelism. (To be sure, in some cases parallel patterns may include rhythmical dissonances, but even if these dissonances were removed, the effect of grouping dissonance would arise, provided the parallelism were perceived.) It is thus possible to foreshadow a grouping dissonance only with a hidden parallelism that was originally "overlooked" by the listener. This is precisely what happens in the minuet of Mozart's *Eine kleine Nachtmusik*, K. 525, offered by Krebs in his early article as an example of preparation (Example 5.8). The *imbroglio* of mm. 6–8 is foreshadowed in mm. 2–3 not by the antimetrical attacks in the form of melodic accents B and A (as Krebs indicated with the brackets above the stave) but rather by the parallelism between the two ascending steps A–B and G–A, marked by brackets under the stave. This parallelism goes unnoticed in the first phrase, in which the steps take different metrical positions. Only by shifting them by one quarter in the second phrase, and thereby connecting them with the preceding step B–C into a longer chain of three steps, prolonged by the fourth step of the melodic cadence, does Mozart bring the parallelism into prominence. In addition, he facilitates its recognition by means of the characteristic turns observed in several of the examples of *imbroglio* in chapter 4.

To conclude the discussion of preparation, it might be observed that grouping dissonances can also be prepared by displacement dissonances. Krebs does not sub-

6. In fact, in "Some Extensions" (1987) Krebs applies the concept of preparation only to grouping dissonances, as follows from this remark: "A dissonant level can be prepared during the preceding consonant collection by the statement of two attacks that create the *time span* about to be featured within an actual dissonant level" (1987: 110; emphasis added). A time span (period) conflicting with that of primary metrical consonance is characteristic of grouping dissonances and not of displacement dissonances.

Example 5.9. Haydn, String Quartet in B-flat major, Op. 50 No. 1/iii, mm. 1–8.

sume successions of different metrical dissonances under his concept of preparation.[7] Yet it seems that such preparation is possible if two metrical dissonances are brought into an appropriate structural relation. In triple meter including displacement dissonance whose downbeats are shifted by one beat "to the left" from the notated meter, the original triple projection is disturbed after only two beats. This is also what happens at the beginning of a grouping dissonance consisting in a metrical change from triple to duple meter. Consequently, the metrical position of the downbeat in the displacement dissonance corresponds to the metrical position of the first downbeat colliding with the notated meter in the grouping dissonance. This structural relation is ingeniously exploited by Haydn in the minuet of the String Quartet in B-flat major, Op. 50 No. 1 (Example 5.9). The first motive of the minuet contains a slurred semitone step in the first violin part, accompanied in parallel sixths by the second violin and in contrary motion by the cello (m. 2). At the second occurrence of this motive in m. 4, the cello part is modified in such a way that the first note under the slur expands to two quarters tied across the bar line. The resulting syncopation in the bass has a strongly antimetrical effect. In the next measure, ties occur both in the cello and in the second violin parts. If one more syncopation followed, the chain of rhythmical dissonances would yield metrical displacement dissonance. But in mm. 5–6 the three-beat patterns shrink to two beats: The first notes of the descending semitone steps played by the second violin and the cello are tightened back to quarters. At the same time, the ascending semitones in the first violin part are deprived of their upbeats and decorated with the characteristic sixteenth-note turns. The chain of semitones in the three instrumental parts forms an *imbroglio* combined with a harmonic sequence leading toward the *Halbkadenz* in m. 8.[8] Since the two syncopations in mm. 3/4 and 4/5 do not suffice to establish a displacement dissonance, the

7. In *Fantasy Pieces,* Krebs does not at all discuss metrical processes in which displacement and grouping metrical dissonances follow one another, but he does discuss dissonance-to-dissonance successions of this sort in "Some Extensions." He illustrates them with an excerpt from Ravel's *Valses nobles et sentimentales* (1987: 111 ex. 13), which displays the same structural relation of metrical dissonances as does my Example 5.9.

8. In sequences, harmonic stability of tonics usually prevails over dominants and hence determines the location of perceived downbeats. Yet the dominant at the beginning of the sequence shown in Example 5.9 falls on the metrical downbeat of m. 5. Parallelism consolidates this metrical position and, along with the harmonic salience of the dominants, outweighs the harmonic stability of the tonics.

grouping dissonance of mm. 5–6 is prepared by rhythmical dissonances. As a result, the type of preparation described by Krebs arises by way of exception.[9]

5.2. Other Parameters in Displacement Dissonances

Still, some displacement dissonances found in Haydn's string quartets are generated not by rhythmical dissonances but by other factors, including, in particular, melodic accents and grouping. Because in the eighteenth century these factors were not considered relevant for metric perception, Koch does not mention them in his discussion of *Rückungen*. It is by elucidating the metrically dissonant effect elicited by them that the twentieth-century theory of metrical dissonance can further aid the theoretical insights of the eighteenth century.

According to Krebs, factors that can articulate a layer of motion are all types of phenomenal accents in the general sense ascribed to this term by Lerdahl and Jackendoff (Krebs 1999: 23). This results in a great proliferation of such layers at the musical surface. As acknowledged by Krebs, "layers of motion are ubiquitous in pieces of music" (28). Yet not all of them are perceived: "We inevitably filter out those that are relatively hard to hear" (28). An obvious question that arises in this connection is which layers will be filtered out and which will not. That Krebs does not answer this question is because no clear theoretical answer can be given. Analytic description in terms of preference rules, proposed by Lerdahl and Jackendoff, determines only which and how many factors of metric perception articulate a given layer of motion, but not whether the strength of this articulation suffices for its being surfaced to consciousness. In the framework of this approach, it is just as impossible to make an unequivocal distinction between the state of ambiguity characteristic of metrical dissonances on the one hand and clear meter on the other hand as it is to make a sharp distinction between clear and vague metric sensation (see section 1.3). Metrical dissonance is a matter of continuous gradation. Consequently, no clear borderline can be drawn between metrical dissonances and no dissonances.

Although in this respect the preference rule approach aptly represents perceptual reality, it has one disadvantage from the point of view of the task undertaken in this study: It blurs the issue of the composer's intention. What an overeager analyst might wish to consider a weak metrical dissonance generated by contour or grouping may be only a by-product of melodic profile, neither intended by the composer as a metric effect nor perceived as such by the listeners.[10] Whether a given dissonant layer of motion is created intentionally or not in such cases can only be determined

9. In the further course of the minuet, the *imbroglio* occurs two more times: first during the varied repeat of the first reprise (mm. 13–14), with the melody played by the cello and accompanied by the two violins in parallel sixths, and then in the thematic return of the second reprise (mm. 29–30). In this last passage the roles of individual instruments are reshuffled yet again. While the ascending semitone steps are included in the second violin part, the first violin and the viola play the descending semitones, and the cello skips up and down by fifths and fourths, adding roots to the individual harmonies of the circle-of-fifths progression.

10. This remark applies to many instances of metrical displacements observed by Channan Willner (2005). Drawing on Krebs's notion of displacement dissonance, Willner finds that "metrical displacement…

by reference to the further course of metrical strategy. If the composer intended to introduce an antimetrical layer as a latent metrical dissonance, he will sooner or later activate it by means of other factors. Krebs describes analogous procedures under the term *intensification* of metrical dissonance, but this term implies that the dissonance is already perceived in the first place. To be sure, sometimes intensification may occur independently of activation or follow it as a further step of metrical strategy. Basically, however, I assume that in the case of *activation* no dissonance is at first perceived. The point of this strategy is to reveal metrically dissonant potential in material in which the listener did not originally suspect it. This point would be spoiled if the listener noticed the dissonance at once.

An ingenious example of activation occurs in the finale of Haydn's String Quartet in E-flat major, Op. 50 No. 3. The first phrase of the theme (mm. 1–12; Example 5.10a) is metrically straightforward, yet in the course of its immediate repetition the accompaniment is varied so as to activate the potentially dissonant layer of motion represented in mm. 5–8 by the melodic accents (highest pitches) falling on metrically weak eighths. The activation of this layer in mm. 17–20 is occasioned by the inner parts, due to the slurred motives going across metrical divisions. Although slurs can in principle take different positions relative to meter without eliciting metrical disturbances, in these motives no factors of metric perception are operative, apart from the initial accents at the beginning of slurs. In addition, the obstinacy of these motives, uninterruptedly alternating between the second violin and viola, and their location in the same register, result in their being perceived as one auditory stream distinct from both the cello part and from the melody. An additional support to the latent metrical dissonance of the melody comes from the single *staccato* tones in the second violin part. Because they are achieved by larger skips up, they are heard separately from the stream of the slurred motives and along with the stream of the first violin, in which they thus form density accents of two pitches against the notated downbeats articulated by only one pitch.

While it serves to activate the metrical dissonance in the melody in mm. 5–8, at the same time the transformation of the accompaniment in mm. 17–20 activates the dissonant potential contained in the accompaniment in mm. 13–16, where the slurred motives occur for the first time. Each of them starts with playful auxiliary tones that cause harmonic surprises by creating harmonies different than those expected on the basis of the theme's original harmonization (mm. 1–4). In addition, the auxiliary tones differ between consecutive measures based on the same harmony, thus creating secondary surprises in the context of each other. The

---

is a normative rather than an exceptional feature of Baroque style" (139) and identifies various metrical displacements characteristic of individual meters. All these displacements are generated by grouping. They arise whenever successive segments or phrases start with an upbeat of the same size. Willner calls such a shift of group boundaries relative to notated bar lines "thematic meter" (165–66); yet this terminology blurs the distinction between meter and grouping carefully drawn by Lerdahl and Jackendoff (1983). As a matter of fact, situations Willner discusses as "metrical displacements" are classical cases of meter and grouping being out of phase. Such situations do not automatically yield metrical conflicts to be classified as displacement dissonances. Historically, they have their origin in the theory of *Metrum* based on musical feet and in the derivative requirement formulated by Kirnberger: that successive *Rhythmen* begin on the same beat throughout the piece. See my discussion of this last point in chapter 3.

resulting harmonic accents cooperate with initial accents in bringing into relief the initial tone of each individual motive. In spite of this, the inner parts of the second violin and viola in mm. 13–16 do not yet create metrical dissonance, because they are perceived along with the bass as one stream embracing the entire accompaniment. The accompaniment's split into two streams in mm. 17–20 is effectuated by the rhythmic change of the bass part, which no longer consists of single attacks separated by pauses but instead forms a continuous line. By fostering horizontal connections of notes within this line, the composer at the same time detaches it from the middle parts. An analogous process takes place in the second violin and viola parts, whose motives, originally superimposed, now start alternating, thus bridging the pauses and joining in perception into one continuous stream.

From the preceding remarks it follows that, apart from metrical accent and grouping, one of the factors participating in the activation of latent metrical dissonance in the above example is streaming. As emphasized in chapter 2, an auditory stream is not always a single line but often a larger textural complex arising from cooperation among several instrumental parts. The "default" metrical properties of such individual parts in isolation may differ from the metrical properties of the entire stream. To activate them, it is enough to split one auditory stream into two. In mm. 17–20 this is done by manipulating the rhythmic and melodic connectedness of the parts. Another method of splitting one stream into two is to eliminate some other auditory stream. Haydn applies this method to the standard "oom-pah-oom-pah" accompaniment occurring in mm. 9–10 and 21–22. By itself, this and other related types of accompaniment are metrically unequivocal. At the same time, however, they contain latent metrical dissonance between the bass and the middle voices.[11] While it does not disturb the straightforward metrical character of the theme in mm. 9–10, the latent dissonance becomes slightly more palpable in mm. 21–22 in light of the direct metrical dissonance in the preceding four measures. Activation of the latent dissonance is eventually accomplished during the return of the theme in the recapitulation (mm. 163–64; Example 5.10b). Because the first violin takes over the metrically shifted line of the second violin from mm. 9–10, the original melody of this passage is eliminated, and the entire quartet plays a multiplied "oom-pah-oom-pah" whose component parts, separated from each other in register, turn into independent auditory streams. A glance at the immediately preceding passage reveals that the stream represented by the first violin activates the potentially dissonant layer of motion in this instrument's part in mm. 159–62. This layer is articulated by the initial accents attached to upbeats by virtue of slurs that, in their turn, refer to two similar slurs in mm. 155–58. At the same time, the strokes in mm. 163–64 betray their connection to the *staccato* strokes that close the first violin's little motives in mm. 159–62. These two latent dissonances contained in the melody supplement the direct displacement dissonance elicited in mm. 155–62 with a new syncopated accompaniment, added to the theme in its last presentation.

11. Krebs (1999: 92, 112) makes a similar point yet assumes that metrical dissonances arising from "oom-pah-oom-pah" or "oom-pah-pah" accompaniment, though weak, are nevertheless perceived by the listener. For Lerdahl and Jackendoff (1983: 337 n. 6), these types of accompaniment are entirely straightforward because of the metrically stable bass (MPR 6).

Example 5.10. Haydn, String Quartet in E-flat major, Op. 50 No. 3/iv, mm. 1–24 (a), 155–66 (b), and 48–66 (c).

(a)

(b)

(*continued*)

Example 5.10. cont.

While the passage in mm. 155–64 constitutes the final stage of a strategy of progressive metric variation or decomposition of the theme, it is not the climax of this strategy. The climax comes earlier, in mm. 48–60, where, as is typical of Haydn's monothematic sonata forms, the same theme launches the second group of the exposition (Example 5.10c). The accompaniment—with the playful auxiliary notes in the middle voices—corresponds to that of mm. 13–16 in Example 5.10a, yet the attacks in the bass are eliminated, leaving the slurred motives alone. After four measures, the theme departs from its original course, and the slurred motives gradually take possession of all instrumental parts, including the first violin and the cello. Although one might argue that in this passage (mm. 52–55) the notated meter continues to be articulated by the greater harmonic stability of the second notes under the slurs, this factor of preference is unlikely to stop the cumulative impact of the harmonic and melodic accents falling on the first notes. The default properties of the slurred motives thus cause a shift in metric perception. The change of perceived meter is followed in the subsequent measures by its complete dissolution. In m. 56 the switch to *staccato* articulation annihilates any sort of grouping, and in the following chromatic line of mm. 59–60 the listener loses the tonal orientation that could help her to regain the sense of meter by reference to harmonic stability. After this momentary breakdown in both syntactic dimensions of the piece, key and meter are restored in m. 61 by the cadential six-four chord launching the structural cadence (*Kadenz*) of the exposition.

The dissolution of meter in the finale of Op. 50 No. 3 represents the most spectacular of all the metric manipulations exercised by Haydn in his string quartet collections under consideration in this study. Its eccentric effect is exceeded only by passages found in the opening movements of Op. 17 No. 5 (mm. 59–68) and Op. 20 No. 3 (mm. 214–34) and in the finale of Op. 76 No. 6 (mm. 71–94); however, in those earlier and later quartets the dissolution of meter is achieved by different means having to do with irregular bass attacks. Also unique in its genesis is the displacement dissonance disturbing the notated meter in mm. 51–55 of Example 5.10c. This displacement dissonance stands out in relief from other metrical dissonances observed in the finale of Op. 50 No. 3 because its activation is not achieved by some external factor coming into play in either the same or a different auditory stream; rather, the dissonant potential of the slurred motive activates itself, as it were, in the chain of obstinate repetitions. This method of activating metrical dissonance is used in a handful of other examples in Haydn's string quartets of the same period.

In the finale of the String Quartet in D major, Op. 50 No. 6, the displacement dissonance is produced by a similar little motive made up of two eighths as *Taktglieder* slurred across the metrical division of *Taktteile*. In the theme it occurs in the accompaniment (mm. 9–12; Example 5.11a); in the coda it is played by all four instruments and multiplied in a chain of reiterations (mm. 225–29; Example 5.11b). It is worth noting how the resulting shift of the perceived meter by one eighth relates to the transitory metric perception that arises in the phase of metrical induction at the beginning of the piece (see Example 2.3). This shifted meter is contradicted in m. 229 by the powerful chord emphasized by the *fz* dynamic accent. At the same time, however, this chord is syncopated within the framework of the notated meter. As was observed by Sutcliffe (1992: 103), it initiates a curious "inter-movement quotation" of the cadential gesture that starts the first movement (see Example 2.1). In fact, the syncopation, while departing from the original version of this gesture, helps to bring it to the listener's attention. As in Example 5.10c, metric relations are set right again only by the six-four chord in m. 231 that initiates the final cadence. Most curiously, this cadence is never carried through. Instead, it is interrupted by a pause after which no new attempt at cadential closure is ever made. What follows is a collection of codettas that closes with a sheer *Grundabsatz* containing the third of the tonic in the uppermost voice.

Example 5.11. Haydn, String Quartet in D major, "The Frog," Op. 50 No. 6/iv, mm. 9–12 (a) and 221–31 (b).

(*continued*)

Example 5.11. cont.

(b)

In the opening movement of the String Quartet in F major, Op. 50 No. 5, the motive Haydn uses to produce displacement dissonance is not slurred but consists of two *staccato* tones. It refers back to the amusing moment in the theme (see Example 3.8) when the accompaniment enters for the first time, filling in the rests between the melody's incises. The result is an alternation of the motive between the upper and lower pairs of instruments. In the coda, when Haydn starts chaining the alternating motives in a longer series of reiterations (Example 5.12), the initial accents falling on their first notes acquire ever greater perceptual weight. Their effect is further reinforced by harmony, because the first note of each motive initiates a new chord. Note that the apparent durational accent of the second note, which is notated as a quarter, plays no role in perception because the *staccato* articulation makes the duration of both notes equal in practice. The ultimate consolidation of the false meter is achieved in m. 155–56, where the switch to *forte* happens on the first tones in every pair of instruments in line with the shifted metric perception. Immediately after, the false meter is deconstructed. The dynamic drops back to *piano,* and the following measure brings an alternation of single strokes, restoring the notated meter.

In the Op. 64 collection, a similar example of displacement dissonance occurs in the opening movement of the String Quartet in B-flat major, No. 3 (Example 5.13). Here, the segment isolated from its original context is the three-note upbeat of the theme. In mm. 122–23 it alternates between two pairs of instruments, yet the alternation forms a peculiar "stretto," arranged so that the segments overlap on their first and third notes falling on weak *Taktglieder* in 3/4 meter. Accents elicited by the correlation of streams are combined with initial accents naturally attached to the first tone of every motive and result in a shift of the perceived meter by one eighth. Displacement dissonance is, however, not the only effect of this manipulation. Because in every auditory stream the pattern of three eighth notes returns in

Example 5.12. Haydn, String Quartet in F major, "The Dream," Op. 50 No. 5/i, mm. 142–58.

cycles whose periods equal four eighths, the meter is twisted in perception from triple to duple—a curious case of grouping dissonance combined with displacement dissonance. What is more, the phase of the duple meter is further displaced by one quarter between auditory streams represented by the two instrumental pairs, thus forming a second-order displacement against the already displaced metrical grid. The grouping dissonance disappears in m. 124, where the viola and cello switch off and leave the two violins alone. From this point on, alternation of three-note patterns is replaced by their sheer repetition, elided so as to yield an oscillating pattern of two parallel thirds. However, the effect of displacement dissonance continues in perception until the middle of m. 125. It is only the thematic return at the beginning of the recapitulation that, while colliding with the twisted metric perception, puts the listener back on the right track. Interestingly, this collision does not interrupt the regular oscillation of the parallel thirds bridging over from the false meter back to the notated meter. The point of Haydn's joke lies exactly in the combination of smoothness and roughness: The same element that previously produced the false meter now restores the right metric perception, and does so by being constantly repeated. What makes this metric manipulation even more curious is the fact that it goes along with a harmonic manipulation: The series of oscillating thirds in mm. 122–25 makes a bridge not only between the false and the true meter but also between the key of G minor, achieved after the false retransition at m. 120, and the key of B-flat major, to be reached at the beginning of the recapitulation. This trick consists in the gradual change of the harmonic meaning assigned to the third B♭–D, which belongs to the former key when combined with the G–B♭ at the beginning of the passage but takes on the meaning of the latter when left alone from m. 124.

Example 5.13. Haydn, String Quartet in B-flat major, Op. 64 No. 3/i, mm. 117–27.

The common characteristic of Examples 5.10c, 5.11, 5.12, and 5.13 is that the process of metrical change accomplished in them is gradual. Its point of departure is always the notated meter, which determines the metrical structure of a given motive at the beginning of the chain of repetitions. Because the default metrical properties of this motive differ from the metrical structure assigned to it in the framework of the notated meter, in the course of further repetitions the notated meter gradually fades away in the face of the immediate acoustic cues provided at the musical surface. In the end, the default metrical properties of the motive take the upper hand, yielding a new metrical structure. Such smooth transition from one metric perception to another may be aptly called *metrical modulation*.[12] By contrast to chains of rhythmical dissonances, the parallel multiple-analysis processor is "waked up" not by a single challenge but rather in consequence of a longer stimulation by sound events that, taken singly, would be too weak to challenge the established meter. Because the projection of the notated meter is not articulated by any factor of preference, it grows ever weaker. The effect of the weak but prolonged stimulation of the antimetrical structure

12. In this context, the term "metrical modulation" has a different sense than it had in chapter 2. There it denoted recognition of a change of the metrical level of *Taktteile* by a knowledgeable listener; here it refers to perception of a metrical change by the metric processor vested in every listener. In the latter sense, the idea of metrical modulation has been used previously by other authors (Lewin 1981; Cohn 1992a). My usage is more specific, in that I limit it to changes of meter resulting from default metrical properties of motives activated by repetition.

grows stronger in relation to the decaying projection of the notated meter, and ultimately overrides it.[13]

In Examples 5.11, 5.12, and 5.13 metrical modulations cause only fleeting changes in the perceived meter, after which the notated meter is quickly restored. This determines their relatively modest effect in comparison with Example 5.10c, where metrical modulation immediately precedes dissolution of meter. One more example in which Haydn avails himself of metrical modulation as a point of departure for a much more radical disruption of the notated meter occurs in the first movement of "The Lark" quartet, Op. 64 No. 5. In mm. 32–35 (Example 5.14a) slurred motives, similar to those in Example 5.10c, are uninterruptedly repeated in all instruments. It is worth noting how the initial accent, falling on the first note in every motive, is enhanced by the *staccato* articulation of the second note, which results in its lighter and shorter performance. In contrast to Example 5.10c, however, the next step of Haydn's metrical strategy in Example 5.14a is not dissolution of meter but a further consolidation of the shifted metric perception by means of rhythmical dissonances. This happens at the beginning of the subsequent section (mm. 35–39), where slurs are replaced by ties, thus turning chains of motives into chains of syncopations. Only in m. 40, when the ties are "cut" and the notated downbeats start being articulated again by attacks and new harmonies, is the notated meter restored. The two rhythmical dissonances contained in mm. 40–41 function as an echo of the preceding metrical dissonance. The section in mm. 42–50 starts again with ties, suggesting repetition of mm. 35–41, but then takes a different course leading to the cadence, which brings the metric perception back on the right track. Haydn takes the metrical strategy he initiated in the exposition one step further in the development section (Example 5.14b), where the metrical modulation is eliminated and the displacement dissonance is introduced immediately as a chain of syncopations. In the absence of any interventions restoring the articulation of the notated meter, the old metrical grid is ultimately erased not only from the musical surface but also from the listener's memory, and the false meter establishes itself as the frame of reference in metric perception. This process culminates in mm. 92–95, when only the downbeats of the false meter are articulated by attacks. As a result, the impetuous beginning of the unison passage in m. 96 brings a startling surprise, entering one quarter earlier than the listener expects on the basis of the perceived meter.

In all the examples discussed so far, metrical modulation is effectuated by elementary melodic motives repeating the same pitch or consisting of neighboring pitches. In the latter case, the notes of such motives are typically joined by slurs. Although in

13. When the notated meter will be ultimately overridden is not easily determined, as it depends on the listener's ability to sustain metric projection in spite of conflicting evidence from the musical surface. In this regard, one can refer to the distinction between "radical" and "conservative" hearing drawn by Andrew Imbrie (1973) and adopted by Lerdahl and Jackendoff (1983: 23–25) in relation to hypermeter. For ultraconservative listeners, the antimetrical structure in some of my examples may not at all arise. I will discuss the question of mentally sustaining projection of the notated meter in section 5.6.

Example 5.14. Haydn, String Quartet in D major, "The Lark," Op. 64 No. 5/i, mm. 31–51 (a) and 88–97 (b).

most examples such motives originate in a theme—its melody or accompaniment—repetitions activating metrically dissonant potential of a given motive do not normally take place inside a theme: Either they destroy the theme, as in the finale of Op. 50 No. 3 (Example 5.10c), or they are extracted from a theme and transferred to a nonthematic section such as a retransition (Example 5.13) or coda (Examples 5.11 and 5.12). In this way they shape metrical strategies that are closely correlated with motivic-thematic processes in a given movement. Two exceptionally elaborated examples of such strategies will be analyzed in chapter 7. All the more curious is Haydn's metrical strategy in the first movement of the String Quartet in C major, Op. 54 No. 2, which starts from a chain of slurred motives yielding metrical displacement dissonance inside the subsidiary theme (Example 5.15a). Default metrical properties of these motives, played by the first violin and the viola (mm. 57–58), not only are enhanced by *staccato* articulation of the second notes but are further supported by single strokes of the second violin and by the harmonic rhythm. Because the slurred motives form intervals of thirds, rather than seconds, each motive is based on one harmony. Harmonic changes are thus shifted by one quarter "to the left" from the notated bar lines. At the upbeat to m. 59, the chain of slurred motives is interrupted by a new motive based on the harmonic progression from the pre-dominant to the dominant. The arrival on the dominant harmony and the initial accent attached to the first D in the series of its threefold repetition set the meter right again, yet, during the restatement of the theme from m. 64, this motive is playfully undercut. This has to do with a mock competition between the two violinists staged by Haydn. While the melody of the theme is taken over by the second violinist, the first violinist steps back and sustains the high D in a manner suggestive of an instrumental *mezza di voce*; but soon he recalls his role of quartet leader and, along with the so-far-silent cello, intrudes on the course of the theme by replaying it from the second measure. As a result, the expected pitch repetition at the end of the last motive played by the second violinist does not come about, and the notated meter is articulated only by the harmonic change to the dominant on the downbeat of m. 67. Preceded and followed by slurred motives, this last motive—itself containing a slur in the lower voice—can easily pass unnoticed, all the more so because Haydn cuts down the second note of the second violin to an eighth and marks *staccato* in the viola. In retrospect the chain of slurred motives, carried further by the first violin and the cello, seems uninterrupted, continues longer, and disturbs the notated meter more strongly than before. In mm. 67–69 the metrical dissonance is intensified through the leaps of the second violin—instead of single strokes played by this instrument in mm. 57–59—which expand the size of the slurred motives to octaves.

It is these octave leaps that play a particularly important role in the further course of the metrical strategy and lead to its climax during the return of the subsidiary theme in the recapitulation (Example 5.15b).[14] At first faithfully retraced, the theme is then interrupted by a pause two measures before the cadence and

14. In the codetta of the exposition (mm. 81–87) and the recapitulation (mm. 222–25), the slurred octave leaps migrate to the bass, thus undermining the sense of harmonic changes suggested by the upper voices. Single octave slurs in the bass occur also in the retransition (mm. 121–25), where, however, their antimetrical effect is negligibly small.

departs from its original course (m. 178). After two slurred motives *piano,* separated by further pauses, Haydn takes up these motives again *forte* and rolls them down in a cascade of octave leaps played by all four instruments. Texturally amplified and greatly multiplied, these leaps affect metric perception not only by means of their initial and melodic accents falling on the higher tones but also through the influence of harmony. Whereas the descent D–A–F–D at the beginning of the cascade prolongs the pre-dominant ii^6 from m. 181, the B♮ occurring on the upbeat to m. 183 implies a change to the dominant. When the last slurred leap shrinks from the octave to the major seventh and hits the A♭ in m. 185, the notated downbeat clashes with the perceived meter. After that, slurred motives resurface in the first violin part but do not disturb the notated meter as strongly as before, thanks to the lower parts marking the downbeats of the following measures with tones of the F-minor triad. Interestingly, at the same time that the meter aligns with the notation, the harmony pulls furthest away from the home key, starting a long journey toward the cadence, which was already close at hand.

From the discussion so far one can draw conclusions not only about typical formal functions of metrical modulations but also about their assignments to types

Example 5.15. Haydn, String Quartet in C major, Op. 54 No. 2/i, mm. 56–73 (a), 171–89 (b).

(a)

(continued)

Example 5.15. cont.

of quartet movements. All the foregoing examples come from opening movements and finales. Clearly, those movements can accommodate more involved motivic-thematic processes and longer metrical strategies than slow movements and minuets. Furthermore, they are usually in even meters, which makes possible uninterrupted repetitions of two-note motives, and in moderate to fast tempos, which apparently makes these repetitions more effective. One can hypothesize that in slow movements projection of the notated meter would less easily yield to default metrical properties of such motives. If metrical modulations are not frequently encountered in minuets, this may be not only because motivic-thematic processes in minuets are less elaborated but also because of their triple meter, in which two-note motives cannot form continuous chains but must be separated by other notes or pauses. In the repertory under consideration in this study metrical modulation occurs in the minuet of "The Lark" quartet (Example 5.16a). This example is very peculiar, though, in that it combines both elementary motives most frequently used by Haydn: Slurred motives are played by the first violin and the cello, whereas the second violin fills the harmonies with repetitions of the tonic pitch D. Whether the manifold reiteration of this motivic complex in mm. 31–36 is long enough for its default metrical properties to override the notated meter is open to debate. One argument that could be raised in this debate is that the slurred motives are derived from an emphatic semitone step in mm. 6–7 played by all four instruments in parallel octaves (Example 5.16b). In that original motive the first note under the slur, falling on the metrically weak beat, receives dynamic accent *fz*. This accent may well be imprinted on the listener's memory. Given that Haydn does not provide any dynamic markings in mm. 31–36, it may as well be recreated by the performers when the motive returns. As a result, a new metrical structure shifted by a quarter "to the left" from the notated meter can easily be established. Even so, this structure is continuously challenged by the series of single strokes played by the viola and falling in the pauses between the slurs. The metrical dissonance in this passage consists of two displacement dissonances split between two auditory streams. Incidentally, it occurs in the course of a phrase that began with a metrically dissonant "free fall" made up of two grouping dissonances (see Example 4.9). The passage shown in Example 5.16a starts immediately after the pre-dominant ii$^6_5$ in m. 30, included in Example 4.9, and ends with a functionally equivalent ii^6 chord in m. 37. It thus forms a harmonic loop postponing the minuet's final cadence.

Example 5.16. Haydn, String Quartet in D major, "The Lark," Op. 64 No. 5/iii, mm. 31–42 (a) and 1–8 (b).

(a)

(b)

Yet the argument referring to the listener's memory cuts both ways. If the dynamic accent *fz*, attached to the slurred motive in m. 6, is imprinted on the listener's memory and influences her perception of slurred motives in mm. 31–36, would the original metrical structure of this motive not be so imprinted? And, if it is, would it not sustain the projection of the notated meter in the absence of any other factors of preference articulating this meter at the musical surface and even in spite of factors contradictory to it? Obviously, these questions are pertinent not only to Example 5.16 but to all the examples of metrical modulation discussed in this section. Yet they cannot be answered on purely theoretical grounds. As has been observed, the preference rule approach allows one only to specify factors that influence metric perception of a given passage but not to determine the outcome of this perception. Weighting factors of metric perception against each other is difficult enough for factors occurring at the musical surface; it becomes much more difficult for factors coming from the listener's memory.[15] To establish which group of factors will take the upper hand in any given context requires experimental testing. What such testing is likely to reveal is that, even in the same context, the balance between them can be easily affected by performance nuance and differently perceived by different listeners on different listening occasions. This, however, need not cast doubt on the composer's intentions in the foregoing examples. As was pointed out earlier, his intention can be inferred from the further course of a metrical strategy in a given movement. I can now add that it can also be inferred from metrical strategies in other movements. If the ties shifting the perceived meter in the opening movement of Op. 64 No. 5 leave no doubts as to the intended metrical effect of the earlier slurs, one can assume that this effect was also intended by Haydn in other cases, even if not always pushed to the extreme.

It is worth noting that, except for the last one, all the displacement dissonances presented in this section result in shifts of the metrical grid by one *Taktglied*. This is also the case in the first movements of Op. 64 No. 5 (Example 5.14) and Op. 54 No. 2 (Example 5.15), where quarters represent *Taktglieder* of alla breve meter slurred across the metrical division of *Taktteile*. In light of eighteenth-century music theory such displacement dissonances are to be considered submetrical. Although it is perfectly possible to generate submetrical displacement dissonances by means of chains of rhythmical dissonances, as illustrated by Koch in Example 5.1, this method was seldom employed in the compositional practice of the time. More often, submetrical displacement dissonances were generated by grouping and melodic contour. An even more popular method of generating submetrical displacement dissonances will be discussed in section 5.4 under the rubric of retardation and anticipation.

5.3. Imitation

Although parallelism serves first and foremost to generate grouping dissonances, the principle that parallel patterns receive parallel metrical structures in perception has

15. This kind of memory is known as "episodic" and belongs to "long-term musical memory" (see Brower 1993).

consequences for displacement dissonances as well. This is so because parallel patterns arise every time in imitation. By contrast to the parallelism characteristic of the *imbroglio*, which occurs in the same voice, imitation presupposes parallelism between different voices. If the time interval of such imitation is different from one measure or its integer multiple, one of these patterns—normally the succeeding (*comes*)—will establish metrical structure of an identical period yet of a different phase than the notated meter. Along with the preceding pattern (*dux*), it will thus create a direct displacement dissonance. In the eighteenth century this type of imitation was known as *imitatio per thesin et arsin*. Koch refers to it in *Musikalisches Lexikon* as "imitation in mixed beats"[16] and illustrates it with the following example (Example 5.17):

Example 5.17. Koch, *Musikalisches Lexikon*, cols. 1039–40.

Because displacement dissonance arises in every case of *imitatio per thesin et arsin*, it may often be unclear whether the composer intended this effect as metric manipulation or the effect is instead a by-product of his polyphonic thinking. The latter seems characteristic particularly of Mozart, for whom complex polyphonic combinations had been an essential part of his personal style long before he developed more interest in meter. Mozart began exploring the metric potential of imitation on a larger scale only in his latest works. This includes in particular the last movement of the String Quartet in D major, K. 575, and the minuet of the String Quintet in D major, K. 593. In the former, the seed of metrical disturbance is contained in the theme as a syncopation caused by durational and dynamic accents falling on the half note in the middle of the second measure. In the polyphonic entanglements that follow in the course of the movement, this rhythmical dissonance turns into a metrical dissonance. Two ingenious stratifications of the theme in all four instrumental parts (mm. 46–49 and, reproduced in Example 5.18, mm. 142–45), are not only tours de force of polyphonic writing but also climaxes of metric complexity. In the minuet of K. 593, reproduced in its entirety in Example 5.19, displacement dissonance results from the canon between the first violin and the first viola, which stands for the thematic return (mm. 24–29). Another canon, played by

16. "In diesem Falle hebt die nachahmende Stimme im Aufschlage des Taktes an, wenn die nachgeahmte denselben im Niederschlage angefangen, und der Satz wird alsdenn eine Nachahmung im vermischten Taktheile, *imitatio per thesin et arsin* genannt" (Koch 1802: col. 1039–40).

all the instruments, occurs in the coda (mm. 40–45).[17] These two polyphonic passages form episodes of an intricate metrical strategy that is worth tracing in more detail.

Example 5.18. Mozart, String Quartet in D major, K. 575/iv, mm. 140–45.

Again, this strategy originates in the theme. In this case, however, it departs not from a rhythmical dissonance but from a latent metrical dissonance contained in the melody (mm. 1–4). Taken separately from the accompaniment, the theme's melody would be heard as starting with the downbeat. This is due to its contour, which consists of broken triads outlining a cadential harmonic progression I–IV–V–I. Each triad would fall most naturally within the confines of one measure. Because the first note of each triad is at once its highest pitch, it receives a melodic accent, which thus strengthens the initial accent assigned to the beginning of a three-note group. This hearing of the melody is particularly plausible in view of the slurs joining together two triads across bar lines. The notated meter is articulated in the accompaniment. Yet the downbeat motives of the cello and the second viola are answered by similar motives of the first viola and the second violin starting on upbeats. This causes minute imitations *per thesin at arsin* between these pairs of instruments. Note also that, even if the motives of the accompaniment consist of only two notes, they, too, outline triads and so can be heard by the listener as excerpted from the triadic motives of the melody. If this hearing comes about, the motivic imitations in the accompaniment may be perceived as imitating the melody of the first violin in inversion. Consequently, the accompaniment—rather than "correcting" the default metrical structure of the melody—may submit to it.

To be sure, this default metrical structure will be perceived very weakly—if at all. The latent metrical dissonance of mm. 1–4 is activated only in mm. 5–6 by dynamic accents placed on the motives' first notes. These motives refer back to the third motive of the theme (m. 3), whose triadic structure is filled in with passing notes. The descent from the sixth to the fifth scale degree forms a sequence modulating to the secondary key. Whereas in the course of this sequence the dynamic accents *forte* coincide with harmonic accents attached to the dominants, their

17. At the same time, they refer to the tradition of canonic minuets, popular in the eighteenth century. One of its most conspicuous instantiations is found in Mozart's earlier String Quintet in C minor, K. 406; another occurs in Haydn's late D-minor quartet Op. 76 No. 2.

resolutions to the tonics, rendered *piano,* receive durational accents due to longer rhythmical values. Since two rhythmical dissonances do not suffice to make up metrical dissonance, these challenges to the notated meter are, for the time being, left without further consequences. The cadence in mm. 7–8 restores metrical relationships reflected in the notation.

The default metrical structure of the theme becomes more perceivable at the beginning of the second reprise, when the melody is carried in the bass (mm. 9–12). At the same time, the web of motivic imitations between the upper voices, which now play the role of the accompaniment, becomes much more complex. The original two-note motives occur in the second violin and the second viola, while the first violin and the first viola introduce new motives with dotted rhythms. This process of intensification reaches its culmination in mm. 12–17, which refer back to mm. 5–6. This time the motives create an ascending sequence. It is much longer than in mm. 5–6 and hence produces a genuine metrical dissonance as a chain of rhythmical dissonances caused by dynamic accents. This metrical dissonance can thus be said to have been prepared by the earlier rhythmical dissonances. In comparison with mm. 5–6 the metrically dissonant effect of mm. 12–15 is further strengthened by delaying the resolutions of the harmonic dissonances in the cello part beyond the downbeats. Common tones between the dominants and the tonics, repeated in mm. 5–6 by the first viola, are now tied by the second violin and the second viola. Only the first violin and the first viola resolve to the tonics on the metrical downbeats and thus articulate the notated meter. Slight deintensification of the metrical dissonance happens again in mm. 16–17, when the melodic motives switch back to the first violin and the bass starts resolving regularly on the metrical downbeats. With these resolutions the sequence reaches the dominant of the home key. The harmonic progression V^4_3/V–V is stated three times. At the third time (m. 18), it marks the *Halbkadenz* before the thematic return, and the dominant bass pedal sets up the stage for the *imbroglio,* which Mozart generates by omitting the first quarters of the preceding motives.

The thematic return, which starts with the upbeat to m. 24, synthesizes both characteristics of the theme: the default metrical structure of the melody and the imitative accompaniment. Imitation *per thesin et arsin* is now applied directly to the melody played in canon by the first violin and the first viola—the pair of instruments that already collaborated earlier in the motivic imitations of the accompaniment at the beginning of the second reprise (mm. 9–12). In the canonic texture without accompaniment the default metrical structure of the melody comes more to the fore. After the *imbroglio* has blurred the notated meter, this structure is the only clue available for the listener in the process of deriving the meter again from the musical surface. Yet the default metrical structures in the two canonic voices contradict one another. Which of them will take the upper hand? Because the first violin starts the canon, one might think that its default meter would dominate the first viola. The issue is more complicated, though, owing to a subtle harmonic detail: the resolution of the dominant to the tonic at m. 24. Even if this resolution is playfully undermined—the part of the second viola is unexpectedly cut off and no tonic root reached on the following downbeat—the harmonic change gives precedence to the default metrical structure of the viola, which, as it happens, perfectly aligns with the notation, each broken triad falling into a slot staked out by one measure. If harmonic rhythm continues to support the default metrical structure of the viola, and with it the notated meter in the further course of the canon, this is because of the peculiar intervallic relation between the two voices. The canon is constructed in such a way that the first note of a new triad in the upper voice accommodates itself to the previous triad in the lower voice. As a result, harmonic changes take place on the notated downbeats. Yet in the polyphonic texture these changes are only implied and hence relatively unremarkable. All in all, it seems that metric perception of the canon—much like the "rabbit–duck" phenomenon in Gestalt psychology—can follow either of the two voices, and the choice between them will depend on subjective proclivities of individual listeners.

The uniform stepwise descent in mm. 28–29, melodically expanding the earlier two motives, makes metrical clues vanish from the musical surface. The notated meter is restored only at m. 30, and the music takes a course toward the structural cadence (*Kadenz*) of the second reprise. Yet it crashes into a deceptive cadence emphasized by two powerful rhythmical dissonances played by all five instruments *sf* and by most of them with double stops. Interestingly enough, the harmonic progression IV^6–V^6_5 in mm. 37–38 corresponds to vi–V^6_5 encountered in K. 614 (see Example 3.20), which was derived by Mozart from Haydn's Op. 64 No. 6 (Example 3.16). While the inceptions of harmonies take place on metrical downbeats and hence articulate the notated meter, this articulation cannot equal the startling effect of the dynamic and textural accents falling on the second beats. Note that this metrical position departs not only from the notated meter but also from the earlier displacement dissonances, which emphasized third beats in 3/4 meter. From the point of view of the metrical strategy carried out in the minuet, the rhythmical dissonances in mm. 37–38 form "foreign bodies" that neither prepare nor are prepared by any other metrical phenomenon: colossal stumbling blocks on the way to the cadence.

The pause under fermata in m. 39 blurs the listener's sense of meter before the coda as effectively as the *imbroglio* did before the thematic return, and the second canon highlights the default metrical structure of the theme much more than the first canon did. Not only is it played consistently *forte* by all five instruments in mighty parallel octaves, each of the triadic motives is delineated by a separate slur. Yet the most important novelty concerns harmony. Because the motives climb up by steps, the first tone of a new triad in the upper voice does not accommodate to the preceding triad continued in the lower voice, as it did in the first canon, but implies a new triad outlined by the interval of a sixth. As a result, harmonic rhythm follows the default metrical structure of the upper rather than the lower voice and acts against the notated meter. Apart from this metrical effect, the new intervallic relation of the canonic voices has a harmonic effect of masking the stepwise progression of the root-position triads. Such a progression was prohibited in the eighteenth century (see Kirnberger 1982: 292–93 [1776: 14]). While it lurks in the background as the underlying structure of *each* voice, the foreground displays first-inversion triads arising *between* the voices. This combination of mocked bungling with genuine smartness is what produces the witty effect of the canonic passage, which is reserved for *Kenner*. The effect of metrical dissonance is audible for *Kenner* and *Liebhaber* alike. In this ingenious way Mozart crowns a compositional

Example 5.19. Mozart, String Quintet in D major, K. 593/iii, mm. 1–47.

(*continued*)

Example 5.19. cont.

strategy in which metric manipulations are closely related to the thematic process and harmony.[18]

In Haydn, displacement dissonances occasioned by imitation involve, as a rule, not entire themes but only their individual motives or even smaller bits. Two examples are particularly interesting, as they relate to other episodes of metrical strategies discussed in this study. One of them occurs in the String Quartet in B-flat major, Op. 64 No. 3. In the opening movement of this quartet, imitations of the upbeat motive detached from the theme generate displacement dissonance in mm. 42–47 of the exposition (Example 5.20). Incidentally, the fact that this displacement dissonance occurs during standing on the dominant determines that its formal function is similar to the type of *imbroglio* represented by Example 4.18. Reminiscence of the same passage occurs again in the retransition during standing on the dominant

18. This strategy continues into the trio. The default metrical structure of the ascending arpeggiation played by the first violin at the beginning of the trio features the same displacement by one quarter "to the left" from the notated meter that the descending triads featured at the beginning of the minuet. Since this opening also has interesting consequences for hypermeter, I postpone its detailed analysis to another occasion.

before the beginning of the recapitulation in mm. 117–18 (see Example 5.13). Because the interval of imitation is reduced from half note to quarter, this displacement dissonance is stronger and leads to an even stronger metrical disturbance in mm. 122–25, which combines effects of displacement and grouping dissonance. As was explained in the preceding section, this is accomplished in the course of progressive liquidation of the motive during which imitation is replaced by alternation and, finally, by an uninterrupted repetition of its germ in the two violin parts.

Example 5.20. Haydn, String Quartet in B-flat major, Op. 64 No. 3/i, mm. 42–47.

The other example occurs in the String Quartet in E-flat major, Op. 64 No. 6 (Example 5.21), and relates back to the metric manipulation included in the theme of the opening movement, shown in Example 2.35. During the thematic return at the beginning of the recapitulation, the second phrase of the theme, instead of repeating the first phrase in its original homophonic texture, twists it into a polyphonic setting and uses its melodic idea as material for imitation, realized successively by two pairs of instruments. In mm. 102–4 the imitation takes place between viola and cello. Interestingly, the interval of imitation between them, which is at first a half note, changes in the next measure to a quarter. This change is clearly related to the switch from 2/2 to 4/4 that takes place in the course of the theme, as was pointed out in the commentary to Example 2.35. In addition to the displacement resulting from the imitation, melodic accents falling on the highest tones of every instrumental part cause secondary displacements by one quarter. The entrance of the second pair of instruments makes things even more complicated, because the leading instrument—the second violin—enters with the theme already displaced *per thesin et arsin* in comparison to its original form. Because in the first pair the leading instrument was coordinated with the notated meter, the listener, confused by the preceding two measures, will follow the second violin in good faith that she is again on the right metrical track. The subsequent change to quarters is this time even more puzzling because the descending pattern, reduced from four to three quarters, yields an *imbroglio*. This *imbroglio* is unique not only because it results in a change from duple to triple meter—thus going in the direction opposite to all other examples of *imbroglio* analyzed in chapter 4—but also because it features a metrically dissonant "free fall" produced by imitation, which further blurs the location of the already dislocated downbeats. The jest of this multilayered metric manipulation is enhanced by grace notes, which arouse associations with (the composer's?) chuckling.

Example 5.21. Haydn, String Quartet in E-flat major, Op. 64 No. 6/i, mm. 98–109.

One more example deserving closer attention occurs in the trio of the minuet of the String Quartet in B-flat major, Op. 50 No. 1 (Example 5.22). Its peculiarity resides in the fact that the displacement dissonance arising from imitation is directly followed by a metrical modulation similar to those discussed near the end of the preceding section. In the second reprise of the trio, the first violin's imitation of the two inner voices causes a displacement of the putative downbeats in the first violin by two quarters in relation to the notated meter (mm. 45–48). In the following passage (mm. 49–56) the original metrical position of the motive is completely eliminated from the musical surface. Only its displaced position, represented so far by the violin, is carried on, in a chain of repetitions, and is texturally amplified in the parts of all instruments. These repetitions activate the default metrical properties of the motive, which, like the slurred motives in Examples 5.10, 5.14, 5.15, and 5.16, features the initial accent falling on the first note under the slur. Starting in m. 51 (m. 50 in the cello), these initial accents are emphasized by *fz* dynamic accents. The resulting "false meter" is supported further by durational accents in the viola (m. 51) and cello (mm. 53–54). At the same time, the original meter is completely erased from the listener's memory, due to the fact that it is not articulated by any factor of preference.

As a result, the listener will be surprised by the number of repetitions of the *staccato* chord in mm. 55–56. According to the most recent metric perception, arising in the course of metrical modulation and marked by *fz*, one would expect only two *staccato* chords after the slur, the last of them falling on the false downbeat. This expectation will likely characterize a naïve listener who immediately yields to the cues provided by the composer. A more sophisticated listener, who has noticed the metric manipulation executed in the course of the passage and is aware of the fact that the metric perception in the preceding measures does not correspond with notation, might fight against these cues and try to keep track of the notated meter by referring back to the original metrical position of the motive at the beginning of the second reprise, which in turn refers to its two occurrences in the first reprise (not shown). In mm. 50–54 this metrical interpretation of the motive, in which the supposed downbeat falls on the second note under the slur, is supported every time by the harmonic change and the subjective accent falling on the new chord, which is followed by its repetition. Following this interpretation, the listener will expect three *staccato* chords after the last slur, by analogy to mm. 38–40 and 42–44. But also in this case she will be surprised by the fourth chord, which is needed to bring the mistuned meter in line with notation. Naïve or not, the listener is doomed to lose in this game arranged by the composer.

Example 5.22. Haydn, String Quartet in B-flat major, Op. 50 No. 1/iii, mm. 45–56.

5.4. *Ligaturae*, Retardation, Anticipation

Another contrapuntal device resulting in displacement dissonances is that of *ligaturae* or ties. Since Johann Joseph Fux's *Gradus ad parnassum* (1725), counterpoint based on tied notes has been traditionally classified as fourth-species or syncopated counterpoint. Fux distinguished between *ligatura consonantiae* and *ligatura dissonantiae*. In the former, the tied note forms consonance with the *cantus firmus* both at the moment of its inception on the weak metrical beat and on the subsequent strong beat. The latter arises in the process of preparing and resolving a dissonance. In the course of this process, the consonance forming the preparation must fall on a weak beat and is tied over the bar line to the strong beat, where it is turned into a dissonance in relation to the *cantus firmus*, before it resolves down by step on the weak beat. It is interesting to note that in *ligatura dissonantiae*, harmonic and metrical dissonances go hand in hand and have their common root in displacement.

Although *ligaturae* belong properly to the strict style (*strenge Schreibart, gebundener Stil*), longer chains of *ligaturae dissonantiae* in the form of characteristic stepwise descents occur also in the galant style of the late eighteenth century, where they serve to invoke the topic of learnedness. In certain cases, however, their learnedness is tinged with irony. This is clearly the case in the minuet of "The Frog" quartet, Op. 50 No. 6 (Example 5.6), where *ligaturae* comically contrast with the character of the dance and threaten to disturb the dancers' steps. A tint of irony behind *ligaturae* is also palpable in other types of movements. After the impish theme of the finale of Op. 50 No. 3 and its playful metric manipulations, discussed in section 5.2 (Example 5.10), the chain of *ligaturae* appearing first in mm. 41–45 and then again in mm. 175–82 (Example 5.23) is clearly a parody of the learned style. Whether it also forms an element of Haydn's metrical strategy, otherwise played out mostly by means of the slurred motives, cannot be stated with certainty. Because syncopation arises as a by-product of *ligaturae* in every case, the question of the composer's intention must remain open.

Example 5.23. Haydn, String Quartet in E-flat major, Op. 50 No. 3/iv, mm. 174–82.

That syncopations are to be treated in most cases as mere by-products of *ligaturae* is apparent from the description of this phenomenon by Koch. In *Musikalisches Lexikon* (1802) Koch discusses *ligaturae* using the term *Bindung*—a German equivalent of the older Latin term—as a type of *Rückungen* (cols. 1275–78). As he indicates, their proper purpose is to create suspensions or "nonessential dissonances," which distinguishes them from other syncopations caused by stress and length. This harmonic motivation is emphasized even more by Koch in his separate entry devoted to *Bindungen*: "The proper aim of such a tie [*Bindung*], which one calls also shift [*Rückung*] or syncopation, is that the part of the prolonged tone falling on the downbeat may turn into a dissonance due to the progress of another voice; since experience teaches us that dissonances are less harsh when they have immediately earlier been heard as consonances."[19]

19. "Der eigentliche Zweck einer solchen Bindung, die man auch *Rückung*, oder *Syncopation* nennet, ist, daß der in die gute Taktzeit fallende Theil des fortklingend erhaltenen Tones, durch den Fortschritt einer andern Stimme, als Dissonanz aufgeführt werde, weil die Erfahrung lehret, daß die Dissonanzen weniger härte äußern, wenn sie unmittelbar vorher als Consonanzen gehört worden sind" (Koch 1802: col. 254).

Whereas the terms *ligatura* or *Bindung* apply properly on the level of *Taktteile*, Koch refers to ties on lower metrical levels represented by *Taktglieder* and *Taktnoten* as retardation (*Retardation*, *Zurückhaltung*, *Aufhaltung*) or anticipation (*Anticipation*, *Vorausnahme*).[20] In retardation, as in suspension, the proper tone of a new harmony is delayed by a tone prolonged from the preceding chord (Example 5.24a). In this respect, closely related to retardation are little rests or *Sospiren* (sighs).[21] In anticipation, by contrast, the note of a new harmony is introduced earlier than the harmony itself (Example 5.24b). Yet retardation and anticipation may also result in a shift of a nonharmonic tone such as a passing note (*durchgehende Note*) or appoggiatura (*Wechselnote*). Finally, they can occur between different tones of the same underlying harmony, in which case they can easily be mixed in the same musical passage, as is shown by Koch in Example 5.24c.

Example 5.24. Koch, *Musikalisches Lexikon*, cols. 1275–76 (a), 1703–4 (b), and 1705–6 (c).

20. These terms, mentioned by Koch in the entry "Rückung," are discussed in more detail under the separate entries "Vorausnahme" and "Retardation" (1802: cols. 1249–50, 1703–6). In distinguishing them from *ligaturae*, Koch follows Mattheson (1722). Fux (1725) treats *retardatio* as synonym of *ligaturae*. Kirnberger does not use the last term at all and discusses all examples of syncopated counterpoint in terms of either *retardatio* or *anticipatio* (1982: 208–9, 228–31 [1771: 192–94, 217–20]).
21. Koch discusses the phenomenon of little pauses in the first volume of his *Versuch* (1782: 215–16). The term *Sospiren* occurs in his *Musikalisches Lexikon* (1802: col. 1421).

In the eighteenth century, anticipation and retardation were employed predominantly as techniques of melodic ornamentation. In accordance with the performing practice of the time, they were expected to be improvised by the soloist on the basis of some simpler prototype provided in the score. How this improvisation should be accomplished is illustrated by Türk with Example 5.25 in his *Klavierschule*. The connection of anticipation and retardation—representing submetrical displacement dissonances—with improvisation is remarkable, in that it corresponds with the role of quasi-improvised embellishments played by submetrical grouping dissonances discussed in section 4.3. If written out by the composer, anticipation and retardation were meant as an imitation of improvised embellishments, and such notations were employed almost exclusively in slow movements or sets of variations, where they were associated with the topic of sensibility (*Empfindsamkeit*). In keeping with their quasi-improvised character, supposedly resulting from the performer's initiative rather than the composer's, these phenomena do not normally participate in a compositional strategy related to meter, even if such a strategy is otherwise realized in the same movement. This accords with the view of eighteenth-century music theorists, who did not ascribe any remarkable metrical effect to anticipation and retardation. Türk's commentary to Example 5.25 is characteristic in this respect:

Example 5.25. Türk, *Klavierschule*, 374.

> From this one can see that through this kind of execution, the *Zeitmass* [i.e., *Taktteil*], or even more, the measure [*Takt*] as a whole is not displaced. Consequently, the customary but somewhat ambiguous German term *verrücktes Zeitmass* [i.e., displaced *Taktteil*] is not very fitting, for the bass voice goes its way according to the meter (without displacement), and only the notes of the melody are moved out of place, as it were. For this reason the expression *Versetzen* or *Verziehen* [changing the place of or dragging out] the *[Takt]noten* or the *Taktglieder* would be more correct. Even when more notes are added to the melody,... both voices must nevertheless correctly coincide each time at the beginning of the measure. In this case, then, no actual displacement of the *Zeitmass* [i.e., *Taktteil*] results. (Türk 1982: 363–64; amended)[22]

22. "Man sieht hieraus, daß durch diesen Vortrag das Zeitmaß oder vielmehr der Takt im Ganzen nicht verrücket wird. Folglich ist der gewöhnliche, aber etwas zweydeutige deutsche Ausdruck: 'verrücktes Zeitmaß,' nicht passend; denn die Grundstimme geht ihren Gang taktmäßig (unverrückt) weiter, nur die Noten der Melodie werden gleichsam aus der ihnen zukommenden Stelle verschoben. Daher wäre vielleicht der Ausdruck: das Versetzen (oder Verziehen) der Noten oder Taktglieder ec. richtiger. Sogar wenn in der Melodie mehrere Noten hinzu gesetzt werden,...müssen doch jederzeit beym Anfange des Taktes beyde Stimmen wieder richtig zusammen treffen. Es entsteht also auch in diesem Falle kein wirkliches Verrücken des Zeitmaßes" (Türk 1789: 374–75).

That Türk refuses to acknowledge the shift of measures (*Takte*) and *Taktteile* in the melodic lines of his example follows from the centrality of *Taktteile* in the eighteenth-century metrical hierarchy. Because *Taktteile* were conceptualized as a series of primitive isochronous beats continuing ideally throughout the entire composition, it was as impossible for an eighteenth-century music theorist to conceive of shifts of *Taktteile* in submetrical displacement dissonances as to conceive of a change in their size in submetrical grouping dissonances. As a consequence, however, it was equally impossible to satisfactorily account for such compositional strategies that, while derived from the phenomena of retardation and anticipation, at the same time went intentionally against the logic of the eighteenth-century metrical hierarchy, using them as tools of genuinely metric manipulations.

One such manipulation, in the opening movement of Haydn's String Quartet in E-flat major, Op. 64 No. 6, is shown in Example 5.26. It occurs in the coda, as the last stage of the metrical strategy whose earlier episode was shown in Example 5.21. Two features make for the strong metrical effect of this manipulation. First, the dissonant layer of motion is located in the lower voice. Although permissible, retardations and anticipations in the lower voice are extremely rare, due to its privileged role in metric perception. In the above quotation Türk actually uses the regular progress of the lower voice as one argument in his refutation of the metrical effect of retardation and anticipation. In the Haydn example, the shift of this voice starts already with the syncopated chords of the accompaniment in mm. 123–24 and then continues in the following passage played by the first and second violin. The change of roles between these two parts in the middle of the passage has the witty effect of a "stutter" or "slip." Second, the attacks of the shifted voice are separated by pauses. These pauses have little to do with *Sospiren*. Rather, they form counterparts of the *staccato* markings in the other voice. As a result, both voices constitute not lines, as in the otherwise similar example from Koch (Example 5.24c), but rather series of alternating strokes whose confusing effect on metric perception is considerably stronger. The change of the index of displacement from quarter note to eighth note between mm. 124/125 relates, again, to the change of the level of *Taktteile* from halves to quarters in the first presentation of

Example 5.26. Haydn, String Quartet in E-flat major, Op. 64 No. 6/i, mm. 123–27.

the theme at the beginning of the piece (Example 2.35). If one takes this last change into account, the index of displacement in either case equals one *Taktglied.*

Another interesting example of metric manipulation derived from retardation occurs in the String Quartet in E major, Op. 54 No. 3. In mm. 20–22 of the opening movement (Example 5.27a) Haydn inserts a chain of ties between the second violin and cello that, in alla breve meter, represent retardation of the upper voice by one *Taktglied.* A remarkable feature of this passage is the series of *staccato* strokes in the viola that coincide with and thus reinforce the attacks of the syncopated second violin part. Another *staccato* series occurs in the first violin. Because its tones are relatively distant from the following slurred motives, they form a separate auditory stream that is further displaced by one eighth (*Taktnote*) relative to the already displaced second violin. The significance of this secondary displacement is revealed by the composer in the recapitulation (Example 5.27b), where the same passage is directly followed by a new displacement dissonance between the first violin and the lower instruments. In the first violin the connection between the two displacement dissonances is enhanced by the melodic connection between the ascending melodic progression G♯–A–B–C♯ made up of the *staccato* strokes in mm. 126–27 and the following descent D–C♯–B–A. In m. 129 the first violin momentarily switches back to eighth notes. Both this and the *staccato* articulation in the second violin and viola affect the continuity of their melodic lines and turn them into series of alternating strokes similar to those observed in Example 5.26. Here, too, metrical confusion is further fostered by the fact that the voices do not come together on downbeats. The coinciding of voices on downbeats is another feature Türk points to in contesting the metrical effect of retardation and anticipation.

Not only do the eccentric retardations in Examples 5.26 and 5.27 have metrical effect, their effect is actually intensified by the diminution of the displacement dissonances. This process of intensification is properly accounted for in today's theory of metrical dissonance on the basis of the criterion that the inherent intensity of displacement dissonances grows with their proximity to consonance

Example 5.27. Haydn, String Quartet in E major, Op. 54 No. 3/i, mm. 19–22 (a) and 125–32 (b).

(*continued*)

Example 5.27. cont.

(b)

(Krebs 1999: 57). This criterion is further refined in the present study by taking into account vertical distance in the metrical hierarchy between layers of motion representing metrical dissonance and consonance and the direction of their displacement to the left or right of each other (see sections 5.1 and 3.3). By contrast, in light of eighteenth-century music theory, a smaller index of displacement in relation to the metrical consonance would have to be interpreted as a weakening of the dissonant effect, in patent disagreement with the composer's intention.

5.5. Syncopated Accompaniment

Syncopations can also occur in the accompaniment as longer chains of repetitions based on the same harmony. In such cases, a higher layer of motion is shifted by one *Taktglied* or *Taktnote* in relation to the proper metrical grid, articulated by the bass. Although the metrically dissonant character of such an accompaniment is plain, Koch does not discuss it as any separate category in his entry "Rückung," and he does not even point it out when it occurs in his example of hemiola borrowed from Graun (see Example 4.25).

In the eighteenth century, syncopated accompaniment gained popularity in connection with the *Sturm und Drang* topic. The most famous examples occur at the beginning of Mozart's Piano Concerto in D minor, K. 466, and in Haydn's "Farewell" Symphony. Increased rhythmic activity and metrical dissonance along with minor mode and chromatic harmonies serve to intensify the expressive effect of anxiety or agitation. As an emblem of *Sturm und Drang*, syncopated accompaniment occurs in Haydn's Op. 50 No. 1/iv (mm. 144–55, 206–15) and

Op. 50 No. 6/i (mm. 11–13, 65–67, 124–26) as well as in Mozart's K. 590/iv (mm. 223–37) and K. 593/ii (mm. 89–91). Otherwise, increased rhythmic activity makes syncopated accompaniment proper for certain formal contexts, independent of any reference to *Sturm und Drang*. These contexts include the drive toward the cadence and the development section. In conjunction with the major mode and syncopations in the highest register, this type of accompaniment occurs also in the exhilarating *tutti* after an achieved structural cadence (*Kadenz*) or half cadence (*Halbkadenz*). In more modest settings it is common as an accompaniment of principal themes in early symphonies. Syncopated accompaniment in some of these formal contexts occurs in Haydn's quartets Op. 50 No. 1/iv (mm. 206–15) and Op. 64 No. 6/iv (mm. 25–31) and in Mozart's K. 575 (i, mm. 72–75, 90–93; iv, mm. 125–26, 190–98), K. 589/i (mm. 27–38), and K. 614/iv (mm. 43–46, 226–29). As a rule, syncopated accompaniment does not enter into any significant relationships with other metrical dissonances in the framework of overarching compositional strategies.

5.6. A Remark on Subliminal Dissonances

According to Krebs, "primary metrical consonance" represented by the notated meter remains present even in sections where it is not articulated at the musical surface. "It acts as a constant frame of reference for metrical perception, just as the background tonic triad in the pitch domain acts as an omnipresent subliminal reference point for the hearing of the harmonic events of a given tonal work" (1987: 105). The result is *subliminal metrical dissonance* with the actually articulated antimetrical layer. As Krebs notes, however, for the subliminal dissonance to arise, it is necessary that the metrical layer be maintained by the performer: "Because they involve only one obvious interpretive layer, subliminally dissonant passages can easily take on the semblance of consonances. It is the performer's duty to ensure that this does not occur. In many cases, the performer can subtly stress a heavily contradicted and otherwise unarticulated primary metrical layer.... The longer the subliminal dissonance lasts, the harder the performer must work to convey to the listener a sense of conflict and tension" (1999: 47).

Eighteenth-century performers were, however, of a different opinion as to what their duty actually was. Treatises of the time explicitly require the performer to enhance the metrical disturbance introduced by the composer, rather than stifling it by stressing the regular beats of the notated meter. The way of performing Krebs suggests is considered a mistake by Türk in his commentary to the syncopations reproduced in Example 5.28: "At this point it should be noted that it is, after all, *incorrect* to perform the syncopated notes as shown in *e*, for the strong part of the beat should not be emphasized by a reinforcement of the tone" (1982: 102 [1789: 105]; emphasis added). Clearly, this remark is made not in reference to pianists, to whom Türk's treatise was primarily addressed, but to "various instrumentalists" mentioned in its further context, in particular players of string and wind instruments, who can control intensity during a sustained tone. In his note, Türk supports his opinion by pointing out that the performer, by artificially maintaining the notated meter, would in fact "work directly contrary to the intentions of the composer" (449 n. 19 [105]). Türk develops this observation still further when he returns at another point in his treatise to the performance of syncopations: "This species of note is employed, among other reasons, to interrupt for a while an all too great uniformity, and to effect, as it were, a shifting of the normal placement of beats [*Verrückung der Taktteile*]. This goal would not be reached if the first half of the notes we have been discussing were played weakly and the second half given emphasis" (327 [337–38]). Koch addresses a similar warning to performers in reference to the execution of *Bindungen* or *ligaturae*: "As concerns the execution of ties [*Bindungen*], it should be noted that the note falling on the downbeat, which is tied to the foregoing note, must not be marked, that is, receive any particular stress or accent; or else a large part of the peculiar effect of such a tie is lost."[23]

Example 5.28. Türk, *Klavierschule*, 105.

Suppression of the notated meter was required not only in passages containing displacement dissonances but also in grouping dissonances. When Türk discusses the *imbroglio* shown in Example 4.4a and then provides a rewritten version of it in 2/4 (Example 4.4b), he does so in order to instruct the performer that, to play this and similar passages correctly, he should first "normalize" the metrically deviant notation to the visual form it would receive in the composed meter. The rewritten version must be read, again, in connection with Türk's remarks about the gradation of stress in a measure, illustrated in Example 2.6. Clearly, this gradation should be rendered by the performer in accordance with the rewritten version of the passage and not with its actual notation on the score.[24]

The above evidence from eighteenth-century performing practice suggests that Krebs's idea of subliminal dissonance does not apply in this repertory. The only type of conflict between an unarticulated notated meter and an articulated false meter arises in the form of indirect dissonance due to the listener's mentally maintaining the metrical grid by means of projection. Basically, this is possible

23. "In Rücksicht auf den Vortrag der Bindungen ist noch anzumerken, daß dabey die Note auf dem guten Takttheile, die an die vorhergehende gebunden ist, nicht markirt werden, das ist, keinen besondern Druck oder Accent bekommen darf, wenn nicht ein großer Theil von der eigenthümlichen Wirkung einer solchen Bindung verloren gehen soll" (Koch 1802: col. 257).

24. This conclusion receives an interesting confirmation in the finale of Haydn's Piano Trio in E-flat major, Hob. XV:29, where the composer assigns numbers to consecutive measures of the false duple meter arising in the course of two short *imbroglio* passages (mm. 32–34 and 162–65), thereby

only in brief passages: "It is a listener's tendency to maintain an abandoned layer for only a few pulses, and then to be captured by whatever new interpretive layer the composer has offered. It is unlikely that a listener would indefinitely maintain a layer—even the primary layer—if it remained unarticulated for an extended period" (Krebs 1999: 46–47). To be sure, when the passage of false meter is brief enough, projection of the original meter may survive until its end. In such cases, the conceptual difference between subliminal and indirect dissonance practically disappears.[25] When the dissonant layer steps back, making room for the previously overshadowed consonant layer, the perceptual effect is one of release, similar to what Krebs calls "resolution" of a direct metrical dissonance (1987: 114, 1999: 109). After indirect grouping dissonances, composers usually take pains to foster this effect by shaping a smooth transition in which the first downbeat of the notated meter is aligned with the last downbeat of the false meter.

However, in longer passages of false meter, indirect dissonance will arise spontaneously only at the beginning. To keep track of the notated meter longer, it is the listener, not the performer, who must "work hard." But even in doing so, she is not infrequently doomed by the composer to fail. If the cues sustaining the notated meter on the musical surface are insufficient and the passage long enough, sooner or later this meter will be lost from the listener's memory. On the basis of the analogy drawn by Krebs between the "primary metrical consonance" and the tonic, such situations can be compared to the loss of the sense of the tonic, which can be intentionally effectuated in harmonic strategies and which actually does happen, in spite of Krebs's suggestion to the contrary.[26] After the original meter returns, it thus causes a clash: a new indirect metrical dissonance with the false meter, which in the meantime has taken on the semblance of metrical consonance.[27] As can be seen in some of the examples already discussed, predominantly from Haydn (see Examples 3.24a, 5.14b, and 5.22), the effect of such a clash is carefully arranged by the composer. Due to the modular character of metric perception, the clash will be perceived even if the listener is aware of the metric manipulation performed by the composer and consciously expects the restoration of the original meter.

clearly inviting the performers to reinforce the antimetrical layer of motion rather than to sustain the notated meter. As he writes in a remark at the beginning of the piece, "the Performer will find great facility by reckoning the Numbers in mind while playing the passages thus mark'd" (Haydn 1986: 253). This peculiar notational device is also noticed by Grave (1995: 191 n. 29).

25. Krebs implies as much when he remarks: "Furthermore, whereas indirect dissonance arises from the listener's brief maintaining of an abandoned interpretive layer, subliminal dissonance cannot, *except in brief cases*, be assumed to result from such mental maintaining" (1999: 46; emphasis added).
26. See the experimental results obtained by Nicolas Cook (1987) in relation to the perception of large-scale tonal closure, as well as Lerdahl's discussion of them (2001: 227–29).
27. Krebs calls this clash "corrective accent" (1999: 110). Unlike Krebs, who takes it to characterize every resolution of metrical dissonance into the primary metrical consonance, I contend that such "corrective accent" takes place only when the notated meter has been erased from the listener's memory. It does not occur when the notated meter is mentally maintained by the listener throughout a metrically dissonant passage.

How long the listener will mentally continue the notated meter cannot be precisely determined. Still, one can point to certain factors that influence continuation of its projection. One of these factors has to do with the relationship of the antimetrical layer of motion with the notated meter. On the whole, displacement dissonances are accommodated by the listener with greater ease then grouping dissonances. Consequently, in displacement dissonances the old meter will be forgotten sooner than in grouping dissonances. As Krebs observes, "the horizontal confrontation of a given layer of motion with a differently aligned but equivalent layer results in a brief effect of stammering or interruption, but the new layer, a mere repositioning of the earlier one, quickly effaces the memory of the original placement" (1999: 45).

The other factor is the degree to which the old meter is articulated in the passage dominated by the new meter. While Krebs contends that, in the state of subliminal dissonance, the "primary metrical layer" is "unarticulated" on the musical surface, strictly speaking, this applies only to passages in which the notated meter ceases being articulated even by attacks. Such cases, which occur in Op. 50 No. 5 (Example 4.8a) and in Op. 64 No. 5 (Example 5.14), are, however, least frequent among indirect dissonances. (In practice, they give the performer no possibility of maintaining the old meter, as Krebs otherwise requires.) Much more frequent are cases in which the primary metrical layer is articulated by attacks but is supported not at all or only very weakly by factors of metrical preference. Note that these factors cannot include stress, length, or harmonic changes. When the notated meter is supported by one or more of these privileged factors of preference, what arises is a direct metrical dissonance rather than an indirect one. In indirect metrical dissonances, however, the notated meter may be supported by other factors of preference, predominantly melodic accents and grouping. Because the strength of articulation elicited by these factors may vary, indirect and direct metrical dissonances form a continuous gradation and cannot be neatly distinguished. Transitions between them, called *surfacing* and *submerging* by Krebs, can be completely smooth.[28] Whereas Krebs is inclined to consider most metrical dissonances in which the notated meter is supported by melodic contour or grouping to be direct, the study of eighteenth-century music-theoretical writings suggests that it might be more appropriate to interpret the effect of these factors in the metrical strategies elaborated by Haydn and Mozart as subliminal, in the proper sense of the word, different from that used by Krebs. Although these factors are too weak to create a perceivable layer of motion when contradicted by other factors, composers employ them to help the listener mentally sustain the notated meter during the section of false meter, thereby prolonging the state of indirect metrical dissonance.

28. These terms are applied by Krebs to transitions between surface and subliminal dissonances (1999: 97). That they can be equally used for transitions between direct and indirect dissonances is because surface dissonances are tantamount to direct dissonances and subliminal dissonances automatically arise at the beginning of indirect dissonances (see note 25).

CHAPTER Six

Changing Meter III

Change of Tactus

The third and last type of metrical change consists in changing the metrical level of *Taktteile*. Whereas in the case of displacement dissonance the metrical grid is shifted horizontally to the left or right, the changes of meter to be discussed in this chapter constitute shifts up or down the metrical hierarchy. Because the metrical hierarchy itself does not change, no effect of metrical dissonance arises. The reason I call this type of change "change of tactus," in spite of the distinction I drew in chapter 1 between *Taktteile* in eighteenth-century music theory and tactus in the theory of Lerdahl and Jackendoff, will become clear near the end of this chapter.

6.1. Changes of *Taktteile* in Compound Meters

Changes of the metrical level of *Taktteile* have already been observed in chapter 2. As noted there, they take place typically in compound meters represented by 4/4 (c) and 6/8. In the former, shifting the level of *Taktteile* from quarters to half notes results in a change of meter to simple 2/2 (¢). In the latter, shifting *Taktteile* from eighths to dotted quarters causes a change to simple (mixed) 6/8 as tripled 2/4. The size of the notated measure in every pair of meters is identical; therefore, switches from one of them to the other do not change the location of bar lines. Metric notation is correct in either case.

Whereas such switches are unique at the very beginning of a piece, they occur frequently in the further courses of eighteenth-century compositions and are acknowledged by authors of composition handbooks. The earliest example of this sort is shown by Riepel (Example 6.1). What he illustrates by means of small and large numerals is that the shift of *Taktteile* from quarters to half notes has consequences for counting measures. At the beginning of the example, small numerals occur twice per notated measure, indicating measures of 2/4 meter contained in each measure of the compound 4/4 meter. In mm. 5–11, large numerals occurring once per measure indicate a change to simple ¢ meter (*Allabreve-Art*). Starting from m. 12 (*NB.*) the music turns back to the compound meter.[1]

Example 6.1. Riepel, *De Rhythmopoeia*, 52.

Koch discusses changes of meter occasioned by changes of the metrical level of *Taktteile* as one type of interpolation (*Parenthese*), consisting in "the insertion of melodic sections of a simple meter in a piece composed in a compound meter" (1983: 162–63 [1793: 223]). As does Riepel, Koch takes pains to instruct the beginning composer in how to properly count the measures of such sections. Commenting on the example reproduced in Example 6.2, he observes: "Feeling convinces us that the phrase beginning with the seventh measure consists of segments of an even number of measures and affects us as a phrase of four measures. It occurs, however, in the middle of a piece that is composed in compound meter. Now, if every measure is counted twice, as before, then the perfect incise [*der vollkommene Einschnitt*] in the eight measure would appear to be imperfect, and the entire phrase [*Satz*] until its ending would be regarded as a seven-measure phrase and thus as a melodic section of an uneven number of measures" (1983: 162–63; amended).[2] The criterion, pro-

1. A longer example of a similar sort follows in Riepel (1752: 53–54) and is quoted in part by London (2004: 54) as an illustration of a change of tactus. London supposes (53–54) that the small and large numerals are meant to indicate the most salient level of metrical hierarchy. This interpretation is incorrect, though. If Riepel uses numerals in order to indicate measures (*Takte*) rather than beats (*Taktteile*), this is not because he considers measures more salient but because he deals with proportions of melodic units, which—then as now—have been customarily accounted for in the number of measures. Whether or not a change of tactus does take place in his example is a question logically independent from the change of *Taktteile*. This point will be explained in section 6.4. In any case, Riepel deals only with the latter question, not with the former.
2. "Unser Gefühl überzeugt uns, daß der mit dem sechsten [*recto* siebenten] Tacte eintretende Satz ein solcher ist, der aus geradzähligen Gliedern bestehet, und der als ein Satz von vier Tacten auf uns würkt. Wollte man aber nun, weil er mitten in einem Tonstücke vorkommt, welches in einer

vided by Koch earlier in his handbook, that a beginner must follow in order to distinguish compound meters from simple ones is the location of *Einschnitte, Absätze,* and *Kadenze.* As was explained in chapter 2, caesura notes of these ending formulas must fall on strong *Taktteile.*[3] In simple meter they thus fall exclusively at the beginnings of notated measures. Instead, in compound meter they can occur equally at the beginning or in the middle of a notated measure, the latter location being much more common in practice.[4] This can be ascertained in Example 6.2. In mm. 1–6 *Absätze,* indicated by Koch with squares, fall in the middle of measures. In the phrase beginning at m. 7, however, *Einschnitte* (triangles) and *Absätze* (squares) occur at the beginnings of mm. 8, 10, and 12, with their caesura notes apparently shifted to weak positions by appoggiaturas. In m. 14 the caesura note of the *Kadenz,* falling similarly on the first beat, is elided with the beginning of the subsequent phrase. This means that the example demonstrates a switch from 4/4, indicated by the time signature c, to 2/2.[5] At a different point in his treatise Koch admits that a piece can also start in a simple meter and change to a compound meter (1983: 19 [1787: 384]).

Example 6.2. Koch, *Versuch einer Anleitung zur Composition*, vol. 3, 224–25.

(continued)

zusammen gesetzten Tactart gesetzt ist, so wie vorher jeden Tact doppelt zählen; so würde man den vollkommenen Einschnitt im siebenten [*recto* achten] Tacte für einen ungeraden Einschnitt, und den ganzen Satz bis zum Absatze für einen Siebener, und also für einen ungeradzähligen melodischen Theil halten" (Koch 1793: 224).

3. That my discussion in chapter 2 is limited to *Absätze* and *Kadenze* reflects the course of Koch's discussion in *Versuch*. There, he does not discuss *Einschnitte* as a separate type of ending formulas. See note 62 in chapter 2.
4. In a note (1787: 333), Koch indicates that the location of caesuras in compound meter relates to phrase structure. Marpurg, whose argument Koch retraces in this part of his discussion, is more specific (1760–63: 1:108): "The reason that in many pieces composed, for instance, in 4/4 meter caesuras fall neither consistently on the third nor on the first quarter lies partly in mixing three- and four-measure phrases, partly in suppression or stifling of a beat." ("Die Ursache, warum selbige öfters, z. E. in einem im 4/4 Tact componirten Stücke, weder allezeit auf das dritte noch das erste Viertheil fällt, rühret bald aus der Vermischung des drey- und vierfachen Rhythmus bald aus der Suppression oder Erstickung eines Tacttheils her.") To put it more precisely, caesuras falling at the beginning of a notated measure occur either in irregular phrases spanning an odd number of composed measures or in regular phrases started in the middle of a notated measure. This last situation results mostly from an elision with a preceding phrase, described by Marpurg as "stifling of a beat" and by Koch (1983: 54–56 [1787: 453–56]) as "stifling of a measure" (*Takterstickung*), but may also happen without elision, as Example 6.5 will show.
5. The criterion of caesura applies equally to Riepel's example (Example 6.1). The *Absatz* of the first melodic section falls in the middle of m. 4, indicating that the meter is compound 4/4 (c). The *Kadenz* falling at the beginning of measure 12 and elided with the subsequent section (*NB.*) testifies to the change from 4/4 to 2/2 meter (¢). The last *Absatz* falls again in the middle of the notated measure.

Example 6.2. cont.

Recently, this type of metrical change has been investigated by Claudia Maurer Zenck. In her insightful book *Vom Takt* (2001), which is the first extensive study of metrical phenomena of the late eighteenth and early nineteenth century from the perspective of the music theory of their own time, she analyzes many examples of switches between compound and simple meter in compositions by Mozart, Beethoven, and Schubert. Analogous examples occur in Haydn's string quartets. The slow movement of String Quartet in D major, "The Frog," Op. 50 No. 6, starts in compound 6/8 (Example 6.3). In the two regular four-measure phrases that make up its theme, the *Absätze—Quintabsatz* and *Grundabsatz*—fall clearly in the middle of notated mm. 2 and 4. The phrase starting in m. 5, which seems at first to be a repetition of the theme in the higher octave, then takes a different course and reaches the *Quintabsatz* on the downbeat of the notated m. 8, after four measures in the simple 6/8 meter. A reversed succession of meters takes place in the theme of the slow movement of the String Quartet in B-flat major, Op. 50 No. 1

(Example 6.4). Here, the 6/8 meter occurs at first in its simple (mixed) version as tripled 2/4, with *Einschnitt* and *Absatz* falling, respectively, at the beginning of notated mm. 2 and 4. In either case the caesura note is followed by an overhang (*Überhang*), which reaches to the subsequent weak beat. In mm. 5–6 the meter changes to compound 6/8 so that, as a result, the *Quintabsatz* at the end of the first reprise arrives in the middle of m. 6 after four measures of the composed 3/8 meter. Although both phrases are regular *Vierer*, the change of meter causes the theme to be curiously asymmetrical.[6] It is interesting to observe, parenthetically, how Haydn subtly disturbs the smooth metrical flow in the first halves of these examples by *fz* dynamic accents. The difference between the composed meters determines that in both examples the accents fall on the metrical level of *Taktteile*.

Example 6.3. Haydn, String Quartet in D major, "The Frog," Op. 50 No. 6/ii, mm. 1–10.

6. Caplin interprets it as an example of what he calls "compression of the continuation phrase" (1998: 48). More properly, one should speak here about compression of *measures in* the continuation phrase.

Example 6.4. Haydn, String Quartet in B-flat major, Op. 50 No. 1/ii, mm. 1–6.

In Example 6.4 they prepare the listener for a metrical dissonance materializing after the double bar.[7]

But the notation of metrical changes is quite easy to handle only in pieces where such changes proceed from compound to simple meter. This might be why only this direction of change is shown by Riepel and Koch in their examples. In pieces including a change from simple to compound meter, the beginning composer must be careful that the simple meter does not return shifted by half a measure relative to the notated meter. Problems that may arise for him in this regard are not discussed by Koch, but they receive a witty musical commentary from Haydn in the first movement of his A-major quartet Op. 55 No. 1 (Example 6.5).

In this movement, the simple alla breve meter indicated by time signature ¢ reigns from the beginning until m. 48. This is attested to by a number of caesuras, including those at mm. 4, 12 (see Example 3.26), and 48.[8] After the *Kadenz* in the dominant, which marks the structural end of the exposition, the closing theme switches from simple to compound meter. Note that this theme starts half a measure too early, cutting off the second half of the last ¢ measure. In this way it helps to avoid a long pause after the cadence that otherwise would last until the end of the measure. Such cadences, intervening in the course of a movement and interrupting its smooth flow, were criticized by Riepel (1752: 45) as "dead and rusty" (*todten und verrosten Cadenzen*).[9] Since the downbeats of the two 2/4 measures

7. In Artaria—and therefore also in Doblinger (Haydn 1985)—the dynamic accents in mm. 1 and 3 fall not on the fourth but on the sixth eighth notes (see Haydn 2003: 101). They thus form "preparation" of the metrical dissonance in mm. 8–9 in the technical sense of the word defined by Krebs.

8. The half cadence in m. 30 also falls on the first half of this measure but is curiously elided with the beginning of the second group. As for the *Absatz* falling in the middle of m. 8 (see Example 3.26), it results from twisting the cadence (*Kadenz*) that is expected on the downbeat of m. 8. A similar case of a twisted *Kadenz* occurs in the first movement of Mozart's String Quintet in C major, K. 515, m. 19.

9. In a series of examples (1752: 45–46), Riepel demonstrates how to avoid such cadences. In all examples, the means he recommends is an elision with the following section, achieved either through an expansion of the preceding section by an internal repetition or appendix or through an earlier entrance of the following section. The means used by Haydn is not shown. It cannot be precluded that, after all, the cadence in m. 48 remains "dead" by Riepel's lights.

Example 6.5. Haydn, String Quartet in A major, Op. 55 No. 1/i, mm. 44–60.

contained in every 4/4 measure are of equal weight, starting the theme on the second rather than the first downbeat is not objectionable[10]—only that caesuras of regular four-measure phrases fall in such cases on the beginnings of notated measures, as they otherwise would in ¢. Consequently, the location of caesuras cannot be used as a criterion in distinguishing simple 2/2 from compound 4/4 meter. That the closing theme is in compound meter can be inferred from other cues. As was observed in chapter 2, bass entrances take place typically on downbeats. The fact that the bass enters in the middle of m. 48 suggests that this beat is the downbeat of a 2/4 measure rather than the upbeat of a ¢ measure. The aural impression of the metrical downbeat is strengthened by the dynamic accent (*fz*). One more cue that speaks in favor of compound meter is the acceleration of the harmonic rhythm.

10. This point is elaborated at greater length by Grave (1985).

In mm. 48–52, harmonies change every half or quarter note, which contrasts with the whole- or half-note rhythm of such changes earlier in the movement. The caesura in m. 50 falls, then, in the fourth measure of 2/4 meter and marks the end of the first phrase. The second phrase ends with the caesura in m. 52.[11] In this last phrase, dynamic accents *fz* are placed at the beginning of every 2/4 measure.[12]

Consequences of the early entrance of the closing theme in m. 48 come to light after the caesura in m. 52. Since Haydn, or rather the beginning composer imitated by him, did not think about making up for the loss of half a measure, the subsequent phrase, returning to ¢, is shifted relative to notated measures. This is evident from the harmonic changes that fall in the middle of notated measures, each harmony filling the size of one composed measure. As a result, strong beats and weak beats exchange their metrical positions. This type of notation is, of course, incorrect. Kirnberger (1982: 389 [1776: 121]) calls it "the most blatant error that can be committed" and illustrates it with Example 6.6b, which similarly shifts the melody of Example 6.6a. Note that, as a consequence of this shift, the caesura in Example 6.6b falls on the upbeat. The same fatal error is about to happen in Example 6.5. To avoid it, Haydn's imaginary beginner inserts half a measure of triplets in m. 54, thus garbling the regular shape of the phrase. This ad hoc solution allows him to reach an *Absatz* correctly on the downbeat of m. 56. Alas, when the phrase is repeated with triplet figurations in mm. 56–60, he falls again in the same error and has to correct it once again.

Example 6.6. Kirnberger, *Die Kunst des reinen Satzes*, vol. 2, sec. 1 (1776), 121.

11. This phrase is left incomplete because the tonic triad underlying the caesura is in first inversion. Consequently, the *Grundabsatz* does not come into being, as this type of caesura should be properly made on a triad in root position (Koch 1983: 37 [1787: 417]). It might be observed that the phrase would close in a far more natural way with a *Quintabsatz* represented by a root-position dominant with the melodic appoggiatura G♯–F♯. The first-inversion tonic with its "improperly" harmonized appoggiatura occurs in place of this dominant. If this observation has merit, the manipulation performed by Haydn in the course of the closing theme concerns not only meter but harmony as well.
12. Peters edition, following Longman and Broderip (London 1789–90), includes no dynamic markings in mm. 51–52, but such markings are provided or editorially added in the Doblinger edition (1987a) on the basis of the prints by Sieber (Paris 1789–90) and Artaria (Vienna 1789–90). See the critical commentary in the Peters edition (Haydn 2004: 111).

Apart from the metrical shift, the remarkable feature of the two last phrases of the exposition is their syncopated accompaniment. The strokes of the viola and the cello in mm. 52–54 and 56–58 form direct displacement dissonance with the melody on the level of *Taktglieder*. This feature is employed by Haydn in the development to bring the metrical play with the listener one step further. When the phrase shown in Example 6.5 reoccurs in mm. 105–9 (Example 6.7), the listener hears it initially on the analogy to mm. 52–56 as metrically dislocated, with syncopations of the accompaniment switched from the metrical level of quarters (*Taktglieder*) to half notes (*Taktteile*). She thus waits for the "corrective" triplets before the cadence, yet, surprisingly, the cadence arrives perfectly on time at the beginning of m. 109 without any bungled adjustment.[13] This proves that the analogy to mm. 52–56 was wrong. Although similar to mm. 52–56, the phrase of mm. 105–9 has a completely different metrical structure, which is correctly reflected in the notation. The bass strokes are not at all syncopated but located on metrical downbeats. At this moment of metrical epiphany, the master steps out from the shadow of the beginner and the rationale behind the earlier incorrect notation is revealed.

Example 6.7. Haydn, String Quartet in A major, Op. 55 No. 1/i, mm. 105–9.

6.2. Changes of *Taktteile* in Double Measures

One might observe that the incorrect notation so ingeniously exploited by Haydn in the first movement of Op. 55 No. 1 to imitate the musical bungling of a beginning composer could be avoided by writing the piece in 2/4. In such a case, the shift of 2/2 by half a measure would not arise, because each measure of 2/2 would be notated as two measures of 2/4. This type of notation, labeled *Doppeltakte* (double measures) by Maurer Zenck, was frequently used by eighteenth-century

13. This cadence is "evaded," in the sense ascribed to this term by Janet Schmalfeldt (1992), due to the pause occurring in the bass on the downbeat of m. 109.

composers. It occurs in another example of metrical change shown by Riepel (Example 6.8). But it, too, was considered incorrect by the theorists of the time.[14]

Example 6.8. Riepel, *De Rhythmopoeia*, 66.

At a different place, Riepel points out that it is a mistake to notate 2/2 as 2/4 or 6/8 as 3/8 (1765: 77–78). Koch subjects double measures to an extended critique in many passages of his treatise. The primary reason for his critique is that this notation misrepresents the relationship of strong and weak beats (*gute und schlechte Taktteile*). It does so because "both main parts of each measure, thesis and arsis, are separated from each other by the bar line and occur in the outer form of two measures."[15] What can be seen between two bar lines on the score of such incorrectly notated pieces is not a measure (*Takt*) but only a *Taktteil* of the composed meter. Yet when every *Taktteil* is notated as *Takt*, all beats are downbeats, and the differences between them are leveled. As a further consequence, the notation in double measures misrepresents the phrase structure. Because the caesura note of *Kadenz* or *Absatz* indicates the last measure of the phrase, a regular four-measure phrase, such as that in Example 6.9a, appears irregular in this notation, its length being expressed in an uneven number of bars. Koch illustrates this in Example 6.9b. To complement the phrase to four composed measures, it is necessary to notate the weak beat of the fourth measure as an eighth bar following the caesura. While not to be counted in the preceding phrase, this bar does not yet start a new phrase. In the melody it is thus either "empty" or, as in Example 6.9a, filled with an incorrect overhang (*Überhang*) exceeding the length of one bar. (That Koch considered such an overhang incorrect was explained in chapter 2. See Example 2.39 and its commentary.)

14. Without any critical comment, double measures are shown by Kirnberger and Schulz (1794). Discussing the different "feel" of even and uneven meters, the authors speak about meter "that is made up of both (der aus beyden Arten zusammengesetzt ist)" (93) and that, logically, should be simple 6/8. However, they illustrate this meter with an example in which bar lines occur after every third eighth note. It cannot be absolutely precluded that this notation is a printing error. Maurer Zenck's reproduction of the example features another printing error: it shows quarters instead of eighths (2001: 43).

15. "Der zweyte Abweg bey der in den Tact einzukleidenden Darstellung der Melodie, wenn man nemlich die Tactglieder als Tacttheile dastellt, ist noch fehlerhafter als jener, denn in diesem Falle bekommt man eigentlich gar keine Tactart, sondern die beyden Haupttheile eines jeden Tactes, Thesis und Arsis sind durch den Tactstrich von einander getrennt, und erscheinen in der äusserlichen Gestalt zweyer Tacte" (Koch 1787: 302).

Example 6.9. Koch, *Versuch einer Anleitung zur Composition*, vol. 2, 398, fig. 13 (a) and fig. 14 (b).

(a)

(b)

The phenomena of the "empty bar" and incorrect overhang can serve as indicators of double measures in eighteenth-century compositions. They are related to the criterion of caesura, because an "empty bar" or incorrect overhang always arises as a result of the location of the caesura note of the *Kadenz, Absatz,* or *Einschnitt* in the preceding notated measure. Referring to this criterion, Maurer Zenck finds double measures in numerous pieces by Mozart and Beethoven, predominantly in their minuets and scherzos, which are often composed in 6/4, though notated in 3/4. Double measures occur also in the repertory under consideration in this study. In the minuet of Haydn's String Quartet in E major, Op. 54 No. 3 (Example 6.10), the caesura of the first melodic section falls in m. 4 and is followed by an incorrect overhang in the bass reaching to m. 5. The Scotch snaps in the melody form what can be called an "incorrect upbeat" leading to m. 6. Although m. 5 is filled with melodic activity in the melody and the bass, it is thus structurally "empty." It introduces no new harmony but only prolongs the dominant of m. 4. That the second melodic section starts in m. 6 is particularly evident from the non sequitur between the dominant harmony of mm. 4–5 and the subdominant introduced in this measure. The composed meter of the minuet is thus not 3/4 but 6/4. Consequently, the caesura in m. 4 does not close a phrase of four measures but a perfect incise of two measures. This explains why it is made on the dissonant harmony of dominant seventh in the second inversion, which could not close a complete phrase. The second perfect incise is closed by the caesura at m. 8.[16] This time the bass overhang does not cross the bar line but, at the repeat, the incorrect upbeat in the melody leads to the first incise started at m. 2. Note that this upbeat is not "elongated" in the sense ascribed to this term by William Rothstein, since in

16. It follows that the first reprise comprises only one phrase. Haydn plays here with the norm, acknowledged by Koch (1983: 118 [1793: 130]), according to which the first reprise of a minuet should contain two phrases.

6/4 it is shorter than one measure.[17] Although elongated upbeats do exist, in many cases what looks like an elongated upbeat is an upbeat in double measures.[18]

Example 6.10. Haydn, String Quartet in E major, Op. 54 No. 3/iii, mm. 1–8.

Two further examples of notation in double measures occur in the minuets of Mozart's String Quintet in C major, K. 515, and String Quintet in E-flat major, K. 614. In the minuet of K. 515 (Example 6.11) the caesura arrives with the dominant at the beginning of m. 3. Its peculiarity, indicated in the course of the earlier analysis in chapter 2 (see Example 2.21), is that the entrance of the accompaniment happens only one quarter later. The tonic occurring on the last beat of m. 3, which arises from an "improper" harmonization of the melodic tone E in the overhang, forms an auxiliary chord within the prolongation of the dominant. The incorrect size of the overhang, reaching over the bar line to m. 4, betrays that the composed meter is 6/4. An analogous situation can be observed in the minuet of K. 614 (Example 6.12). There, too, the caesura arrives in m. 3 and is followed by an overhang reaching to m. 4. The prolongation of the dominant is even more evident due to the ties in the middle voices. Because these voices do not move, the E♭ played by the second viovla—corresponding with the C of the cello in Example 6.11—does not result in an improper harmonization but merely constitutes an auxiliary note in the bass. In both examples the 6/4 meter subsequently changes to 3/4. In Example 6.11 this is evidenced by the *Kadenz* in m. 10, closing the regular four-measure phrase initiated in m. 7. (If the 6/4 meter continued until the end of the first reprise, the caesura note of this *Kadenz* would fall incorrectly in the middle of a composed measure.) Similarly, in Example 6.12 the 3/4 meter is confirmed by the *Kadenz* in m. 12.

17. "Elongated upbeat" is defined by Rothstein "an upbeat lasting a full measure or more" (1989: 39).
18. The reason I nevertheless call the upbeat in Example 6.10 "incorrect" is that it starts before the weak beat of the composed 6/4 measure. According to Koch (1983: 11–13 [1787: 366–71]), an upbeat can start only on or after the weak beat (*schlechter Taktteil*). If it starts before the weak beat, the entire measure is counted to the phrase length, and thus there is no upbeat.

As a result of the metrical change, the listener's understanding of the phrase structure becomes a highly complicated process. In both examples the first four notated measures are to be understood as a perfect incise of two measures in the composed 6/4 meter. However, in both of them this understanding is achieved by the listener in retrospect. On the one hand, the 6/4 meter is explained only at the end of the incise by its caesura. In this way the caesura determines the size of the composed measures to be counted by the listener. On the other hand, it determines the moment when to start counting. Because it arrives at the end of the incise as its second measure, it renders the foregoing chain of parallel thirds as the first measure, even if the listener would have originally been inclined to hear the unaccompanied melody in two violins as an "elongated upbeat" or anacrusis, which does not count in the length of the phrase.[19] Note that this time the upbeat would be really elongated because it is longer than one measure of 6/4 meter. One will fully appreciate the complexity of these two examples when one recalls that, as explained in chapter 2 (see Examples 2.21 and 2.22), the unaccompanied melody in parallel thirds in mm. 1–2 offers no perceptual cues that would allow the listener to infer the grouping of quarter notes. Consequently, both the period (2/4 or 3/4) and phase of the measure are at first ambiguous and can be inferred by the listener only in retrospect on the basis of the caesura in m. 3.[20]

The understanding of the first melodic section, achieved at the caesura, guides the listener's interpretation of the melodic section after the caesura. Since in both examples this section begins in an analogous way, the listener will count it analogically by taking mm. 5–6 for the first measure of a new incise. Yet this interpretation must be revised in the light of the different continuation containing the change of meter. The revision concerns not only the size of measures but also the identification of measures to be counted as first. In K. 515 the notated measures 5–6, containing the unaccompanied melody, turn out to be an elongated upbeat to a regular four-measure phrase (*Vierer*) in 3/4, started at m. 7, and hence not to be counted as part of its length. The introductory function of this melody, belied in the first instance, is thus confirmed in the second. In this way Mozart dupes his listener twice by means of one and the same musical device. He plays out this trick once again in K. 614, with the sole difference that the structure of the following phrase (mm. 7–12) is more complicated, due to the varied repetition of mm. 7–8 in mm. 9–10. Although the phrase is six measures long, the repetition determines that it is not a *Sechser* but an expanded *Vierer*. Repetitions were a standard means of phrase expansion (*Erweiterung*) in the eighteenth-century *Satzbau*, and expanded phrases (*erweiterte Sätze*) starting with

19. In the trio of the minuet of Mozart's String Quartet in D major, K. 575, analyzed by Rothstein (1989: 40 ex. 2.17), the elongated upbeat is similarly represented by an unaccompanied melody played by two violins.

20. The difference between these inferences and the inference concerning the metrical level of *Taktteile* is that whereas the period and phase of the metrical hierarchy are found by the metric processor operating unconsciously, the metrical level of *Taktteile* must be consciously recognized by the listener on the basis of her theoretical knowledge. Such recognition is possible only for a knowledgeable listener (*Kenner*) informed about the rules governing the location of caesuras in the eighteenth century.

repeated perfect incises of two measures were most common of all. Koch's statement that "such a four-measure phrase, which has been extended to six measures by the repetition of two, is always considered a four-measure unit with respect to the rhythmic relations of phrases" (1983: 43 [1787: 429]) implies that the repeated measures are supposed to be counted by the listener with repeated numerals. This is why, in Example 6.12, mm. 9–10 are numbered once again as the first and the second.

Example 6.11. Mozart, String Quintet in C major, K. 515/iii, mm. 1–10.

Even if, for Koch, notation in double measures is always a mistake—a "mistake that one encounters almost daily in modern compositions, and that is promoted by the tyranny of habit, but that remains a mistake, whether committed by a beginner or by an already trained composer"[21]—this notation certainly does not occur by mistake in pieces by Haydn, Mozart, or Beethoven. These masters' occasional use of double measures serves two purposes, logically independent from one another and hence operating either separately or together. The first relates to irregularities of composed meter resulting either from changes of its phase or period. One exceptional case where change of phase did *not* motivate the composer to take recourse to double measures, instead leading him to a different kind of incorrect notation, was seen earlier in Example 6.5. The shift of 2/2 meter by half a measure happened there after an intervening passage in 4/4 meter. But such a shift can also happen directly. If the notation were to reflect the composed meter, it would display an extra beat or beats inserted between complete measures. In principle, this was not precluded. Türk demonstrates an insertion of an incomplete measure in excerpts "(*a*) from a Bach sonata and

21. "Ein Fehler den man baynahe täglich in den modernen Tonstücken antrifft, und den die Tyranney der Gewohnheit zu begünstigen scheint, der aber bey alle dem ein Fehler bleibt, es mag ihn der Anfänger oder der schon geübtere Tonsetzer begehen" (Koch 1787: 319).

Example 6.12. Mozart, String Quintet in E-flat major, K. 614/iii, mm. 1–12.

(*b*) from Reichardt's *Ariadne auf Naxos*" (1982: 91[1789: 92]; Example 6.13), implying that further similar cases can be found in the musical repertory. Even so, in the eighteenth century such cases were exceptional.[22] Because at that time the constancy of notated meter was commonly taken for granted, changes of composed meter were usually concealed under the guise of smaller time signatures in which the *Taktteile* of the composed meter were notated as *Takte*. These changes also involve changes of period. The most celebrated example comes from the Scherzo of Beethoven's Ninth Symphony, in which verbal designations used by the composer—"ritmo di tre battute" and "ritmo di quattro battute"—indicate different groupings of notated 3/4 measures. The result is alternation of the composed meter between 6/4, 9/4, and 12/4. As has been pointed out by Maurer Zenck (2001: 47), Beethoven does not use any verbal designation

22. Presumably, they became more common in the nineteenth century. Rothstein (1989: 41) quotes examples from Beethoven's Piano Sonata in E Major, Op. 109/i, m. 15, and Brahms's Intermezzo in A Minor, Op. 76 No. 7, m. 23.

for passages composed in 6/4 meter since this meter, notated in 3/4, represented the standard case of double measures. If he does so for 9/4 and 12/4, it is because these meters exemplify less usual cases of what could be called "threefold" and "fourfold" measures.[23]

Example 6.13. Türk, *Klavierschule*, 93.

The second purpose served by the use of double measures has to do with the old time signatures. Observe that Koch's examples of double measures concern exclusively an improper use of time signatures 2/4 for alla breve and 3/8 for simple 6/8 meter. In either case, the time signature of the composed meter was available and could be used in the properly rewritten versions of such examples.[24] Instead, double measures in the minuets of Haydn's Op. 54 No. 3 and Mozart's K. 515 and 614, as well as other instances of this notation identified by Maurer Zenck, result from the use of old meters—preeminently 6/4 and 2/1 or 4/2[25]—whose time signatures had already been dropped from the notational conventions of the late eighteenth century. That composers nevertheless continued to use these meters under the guise of modern time signatures was because these meters were bearers of different affects. This explanation, proposed by Wye J. Allanbrook (1983), is seminal for her discussion of musical *topoi.* As Allanbrook indicates (13–27), in the

23. Lester considers changes of period of the composed meter to be the main reason for the notation in double measures (1986: 107–8). In this connection, he also refers to the Scherzo of Beethoven's Ninth. In contrast, Rothstein (1989: 38–39) and Cohn (1992a) interpret Beethoven's annotations in this Scherzo as referring not to composed meter but to hypermeter.
24. For the example in 2/4 and its rewritten version in 2/2 see, respectively, Koch (1787: 305 and 307); for the example in 3/8 and its rewritten version in 6/8 see, respectively, 320 and 324.
25. Koch (1787: 334, 1802: cols. 1481–82) knows 4/2 only as compound meter. For Kirnberger, this meter can be either compound or simple. In the latter case, it is included in the category of simple quadruple meters (see Table 1.1). Since caesuras fall in it only at the beginning of measures, it is virtually indistinguishable from 2/1. As 2/1, however, it is "no longer in use" (1982: 386, 390 [1776: 118, 122]).

Affektenlehre of the early part of the century, every meter was ascribed a unique *topos* or affect that belonged to its very nature and defined its expressive quality by association with a specific musical style or genre. To evoke this affect, it was thus indispensable to use its proper meter. This tradition was continued in the later part of the eighteenth century by Kirnberger and Schulz. For Kirnberger it is still essential that "the spirit or character of each meter be specified as precisely as possible" (1982: 383 [1776: 114]; quoted in Allanbrook 1983: 15). In his discussion of individual meters he points to styles (church, theatrical, chamber) and genres (fugues, choruses, types of dances) in which they are used. The large number of meters he discusses reflects the wealth of passions conveyed by music. A correlate to expression was the manner of execution. According to Kirnberger, different meters imply different weight of individual notes and different tempo: the so-called *tempo giusto*. "Thus the *tempo giusto* is determined by the meter and by the longer and shorter note values of a composition" (377 [107]).[26]

The higher or lower status of a given meter was determined above all by the rhythmical values of *Taktteile*. Meters with the half note as the *Taktteil*, as well as their tripled versions, such as 6/4, were emblems of the church style. Smaller values of *Taktteile* indicated more mundane affects.[27] Consequently, changes of the metrical level of *Taktteile* resulted in changes of *Affekte*. Such changes start occurring in the latter half of the eighteenth century. As Allanbrook indicates, "since Baroque composers generally allowed one spun-out affect to dominate an entire movement, they could choose a time signature which would notate that affect with precision" (1983: 24). Classic composers' practice of shaping each movement around several affects is motivated by the new structural demands of the sonata form. In this form changes of affects serve to dramatize the polarity of tonic and dominant key areas and contribute to establishing the thematic contrast between them. "The practice necessitated the choice of a flexible, chameleonlike time signature, harmonious not just with one affect but with a particular handful of them" (24). According to Allanbrook, this was the very reason older time signatures disappeared. "Composers preferred to choose a metrical 'lowest common denominator' for a time signature, avoiding the radical metrical extremes" (24).

Allanbrook demonstrates this occurrence in the finale of Mozart's String Quartet in G major, K. 387, in which the meter 4/2 should properly be assigned to the opening fugal section, and 2/4 to the swift contredanse. The closing idea, identified by her as a bourrée, in ordinary circumstances would be written in 4/4. The time signature ¢ (2/2), which Mozart actually uses on the score, falls halfway between these extremes. As Allanbrook observes, the notated meter "suits all three topics at once by not quite suiting any of them" (1983: 25).[28] Another example of how change of meter and topic

26. For more information about the history of *tempo giusto*, see Seidel (1975: 117–19), Houle (1987: 35–61), and Maurer Zenck (2001: 14–16).

27. The other factor determining the status of a given meter was duple or triple grouping of *Taktteile*. It will be addressed briefly in the next chapter.

28. In Allanbrook's example 1-1 (1983: 20), the notated meter is indicated erroneously as c (4/4). Incidentally, her analysis demonstrates that what she calls a metrical "lowest common denominator" is not to be misunderstood as the "smallest" meter of a given collection.

brings into relief thematic contrast in sonata form comes from the opening movement of Mozart's D-minor Quartet K. 421. The analysis carried out by Maurer Zenck (2001: 251–54) reveals that the principal theme of this movement (mm. 1–8) is set in 2/2 (¢) and the subsidiary theme (mm. 24–32) in 2/4. Although Maurer Zenck does not attempt to identify their topics, the former theme represents what Allanbrook would call "exalted march," and the latter is an example of "singing style." As Maurer Zenck convincingly demonstrates, sophisticated decorations obliterate the location of *Absätze* and *Einschnitte* in the course of the transition section, thereby allowing Mozart to shape a sort of metrical modulation parallel to the harmonic modulation between the themes. While in this case both meters comfortably fit the notation of the compound meter, in certain other cases changes of the level of *Taktteile* result in double measures. In the opening movement of the String Quartet in D major, K. 575, the principal theme is in 2/1, as attested by the structurally "empty" bars following the caesuras in mm. 7 and 15, but appears under the time signature ¢ (Example 6.14). Alla breve meter is introduced only from m. 17 by the gavotte, and from m. 64 the principal theme adapts to this meter, its segments being presented in halved rhythmical values. In the finale of the String Quintet in D major, K. 593, the principal theme is a tarantella

Example 6.14. Mozart, String Quartet in D major, K. 575/i, mm. 1–17.

in 12/8 notated in 6/8 (Example 6.15). The "empty bar" characteristic of double measures occurs here not immediately after the *Kadenz*, falling in m. 8, but only after the appendix (*Anhang*) prolonging its final tonic. The repeated A of m. 10 joins directly to the chromatic descent of m. 1, leading back to the theme's structural beginning at m. 2. Note that, as in Example 6.10, this lead-in does not form an elongated upbeat because in 12/8 it is shorter than one composed measure. Later, from m. 54, the fugato brings in 6/8 meter. Since the fugato theme is three measures long, in 12/8 each entrance of this theme would be notated differently in relation to the bar lines.[29] Otherwise, 12/8 meter, though not very common, was not quite out of date by the end of the eighteenth century and could be used by Mozart in his finale.[30]

Example 6.15. Mozart, String Quintet in D major, K. 593/iv, mm. 1–10.

The view that old meters were used under the guise of modern time signatures for the sake of their expressive qualities, advocated by Allanbrook, seems to be contradicted by the gradual dissolution of *tempo giusto* in the course of the eighteenth century. As a result of this process, observed with disapproval by some theorists, with sympathy by others, toward the end of that century, meter emerged

29. This reason for the notation in double measures is related to irregularity caused by the change of period—except that, in this case, the irregularity concerns not meter but hypermeter.
30. It is famously used by Beethoven in the Piano Sonata Op. 57, the "Appassionata." On the internal structure of the 12/8 meter in the "Appassionata" as well as Example 6.15, see note 49 below.

as an independent dimension of musical compositions, orthogonal to tempo and expression. To the second group of theorists, opposing the views of Kirnberger and Schulz, belonged Riepel and Koch. As early as 1752 Riepel declared that every piece of music "from Jubal's time" could be written either in 2/4 or in 3/4 (1752: 68). At that date his assertion must have sounded provocative.[31] More than three decades later Koch states already as a matter of course that no difference exists between meters whose time signatures have same numerators yet different denominators, such as 2/2 and 2/4 (1787: 290) or 3/2, 3/4, and 3/8 (311–12). He does so while being well aware of the idea of *tempo giusto* and granting it in theory. Yet, as he emphasizes, this idea is no longer alive in practice. The relevant passage from his handbook is worth quoting in its entirety:

> Now, this difference [between 2/4 and 2/2] ought to be used according to the nature of things. A phrase [*Satz*] in slow tempo should be set in 2/2 meter and a phrase in fast tempo in 2/4 meter so that tones in slow tempo can be designated with corresponding rhythmical values and thus the sign and the signified brought into closer relation. If this rule were accepted, then the following phrase, if set out [*eingekleidet*] in 2/2 [Example 6.16a], would thus necessarily have to be executed slowly, and in the following example [Example 6.16b], set out in 2/4, always fast. The rhythmical values would thus, even if not quite precisely, to some extent still determine the tempo of a phrase, and all the more precisely determined would be the expressions one attached to each phrase in order to designate its tempo. Only that one does not follow the hint offered us by the nature of things. If it sometimes happens, it is more by chance than on purpose, because the use of both meters regarding tempo is treated completely at will. In most cases one proceeds the other way around and, availing himself of a simple even meter, uses 2/4 for phrases in slow tempo and 2/2 for those that should be performed in fast tempo.[32]

31. Yet it is not completely unprecedented. Among earlier music theorists who acknowledged—in more reticent ways and to a more limited extent—the increasing independence of tempo from time signatures were Johann Peter Sperling and Mattheson (see Houle 1987: 45–47).
32. "Dieser Unterschied sollte nun aber auch der Natur der Sache gemäs benuzt [*sic*], und ein Saz [*sic*] von langsamer Bewegung in den Zweyzweyteltact, ein Saz aber von geschwinder Bewegung in den Zweyvierteltact gesezt [*sic*] werden, damit Töne von langsamer Bewegung auch mit einer ihrer Bewegung entsprechenden Notengattung bezeichnet, und also das Zeichen und die zu bezeichnende Sache in ein engeres Verhältniß gebracht würden. Wäre dieses als Regel angenommen, so müßte alsdenn nothwendig folgender Saz, wenn er in den Zweyzweyteltact eingekleidet wäre, z. E. [Example 6.16a] jederzeit in einer langsamen Bewegung, in folgender Einkleidung in den Zweyvierteltact hingegen [Example 6.16b] jederzeit in einer geschwindern Bewegung vorgetragen werden; und alsdenn würde die gebrauchte Notengattung, obschon nicht auf das genaueste, dennoch einigermaßen die Bewegung des Satzes bestimmen, und um desto bestimmter würden alsdenn die Ausdrücke seyn, die man, um die Bewegung zu bezeichnen, jedem Satze beyzufügen gewohnt ist. Allein man folgt in diesem Stücke dem Winke nicht, den uns die Natur der Sache giebt; geschieht es ja zuweilen, so ist es mehr Zufall als Vorsaz [*sic*], weil der Gebrauch dieser beyden Tactgattungen in Absicht auf die Geschwindigkeit der Bewegung als ganz willkührlich angenommen ist. Im Gegentheil verfährt man in den mehresten Fällen ganz umgekehrt, und braucht zu Sätzen von langsamer Bewegung den Zweyvierteltact, und zu Sätzen, die in geschwinder Bewegung vorgetragen werden sollen, den Zweyzweyteltact, im Falle man sich der einfachen geraden Tactart bedient" (Koch 1789: 291–93).

If tempo, and hence expression, are no longer determined by meter, they must be indicated in some other way. This leads to the increasing role of tempo markings and expressive designations near the end of the eighteenth century.[33]

Example 6.16. Koch, *Versuch einer Anleitung zur Composition*, vol. 2, 292.

Yet, paradoxically, the dissolution of *tempo giusto* not only did not invalidate the assignments between affects and meters originating earlier in the century but contributed even further to the possibility of including several affects in one piece. If it is possible to write the same musical passage with different rhythmical values in different meters, as demonstrated by Koch,[34] then an affect requiring a slower tempo can be notated with larger rhythmical values in a fast piece and an affect requiring a swift tempo can be notated with smaller rhythmical values in a slow piece. It follows that changes of rhythmical values of *Taktteile* may represent not changes of meter but changes of tempo. This point is not explicitly corroborated by Allanbrook, but it is implied in her analysis of K. 387. Note that the fugue theme, as it stands on the score, is in 4/1 meter. When Allanbrook writes that it is in 4/2, she means that the theme would normally be notated in half notes in tempo Andante rather than with whole notes in Molto Allegro (1983: 24 ex.1–3). The same is true for the closing idea. In Molto Allegro it is in 4/2, but it would be notated in 4/4—or, more properly, 2/2—in a more moderate tempo (25 ex. 1–5).[35] Incidentally, although Allanbrook suggests that this closing idea is a bourrée, no clear traits of the bourrée occur in it. The moderate tempo and the half-measure upbeat speak rather for a gavotte, and the dotted rhythmic gesture used by Mozart

33. Tempo markings are also mentioned by Kirnberger but the role he attributes to them is quite different. They are not independent designations of the absolute speed but only modifications of *tempo giusto* indicated by the time signature. For more details concerning the changing roles of tempo markings in the eighteenth century, see Maurer Zenck (2001: 15).
34. Apart from the examples reproduced above, further examples of alternative metric notation of the same musical passage are shown by Koch (1787: 297 and 335).
35. If the closing idea were in 4/4 (c), as Allanbrook has it, this meter would be not compound but simple, representing the category of simple quadruple meters discussed by Kirnberger (see Table 1.1). Simple 4/4 cannot be distinguished from 2/2 on the basis of the criterion of caesura, since in either meter, caesuras fall at the beginnings of measures only. Compare note 25 here.

actually resembles an example of the gavotte shown by Allanbrook.[36] Another example of metrical change acting as a change of tempo occurs in the String Quartet in D major, K. 575 (see Example 6.14). The principal theme occurs in 2/1 in tempo Allegretto but is meant as 2/2 in a slow tempo. According to Kirnberger and Schulz, 2/1 was reserved for the church style, whereas the theme clearly represents singing style. Later, from m. 64, the singing style comes even more to the fore, when segments of the theme return in 2/2 meter, turned into "singing allegro." The rationale behind this unusual opening could be to mislead the listener by suggesting that the quartet starts with a slow movement. Though rare, instances of such quartet cycles did exist,[37] and might have prompted Mozart to undertake this manipulation with an eye to his knowledgeable listeners. One more illustration of the ability to change tempo by changing the rhythmical level of *Taktteile* occurs in the minuet of Op. 50 No. 5, discussed in chapter 4 (see Example 4.8a). The shift of *Taktteile* in the course of the *imbroglio* from quarter notes to half notes, seemingly resulting in a metrical change from 2/4 to 2/2 and twisting the minuet into march, is better explained as a change from brisk 2/4 to 4/4 (c) in a slower tempo. This interpretation is actually adopted by Grave, as follows from his temporal reduction of mm. 38–41 with halved rhythmical values and time signature c (1995: 195 ex. 19b). This last time signature was more typical of marches than 2/2 (¢) and occurs in two other examples of martial cadences offered for comparison by Grave (195 ex.19cd). On the other hand, a nonnotated change of tempo can take place without changing the rhythmical values of *Taktteile*. In Example 3.16, from the finale of Op. 64 No. 6, a change of this sort is brought about by augmentation of the melodic motives and combined with a change of topic from contredanse to march. This time the march is written in 2/4, the same meter that has been previously used for the contredanse.[38]

The line of reasoning drawn above may lead an attentive reader to the following objection. If in the late eighteenth century time signatures and rhythmical values could be freely chosen by composers to notate their melodic ideas, why did they not avoid the objectionable notation in double measures by using smaller rhythmical values? For instance, if the rhythmical values in the first movement of K. 575 were halved, the principal theme would be in 2/2, and all the rest, including the diminished segments of the theme—would be in 2/4 notated as compound 4/4 meter. Yet

36. Allanbrook describes the gavotte as a dance in 4/4 meter but shows exclusively examples in 2/2 (1983: 49–51). One of them (ex. 2–24a) is similar to the closing idea of K. 387 and shares its key of D major.

37. For instance, Haydn's Op. 17 No. 3 and Op. 55 No. 2.

38. Even if 4/4 meter is more typical of stylized marches, many eighteenth-century popular and military marches were written in 2/4 and alla breve (Monelle 2006: 120). The meter of the march in mm. 178–82 of Example 3.16 could be interpreted as alla breve notated in double measures, in which case the *Taktteile* would actually change from quarter notes to half notes. The location of caesuras, which in most cases provides an unequivocal criterion in identifying *Taktteile*, is unclear in this example, since no harmonic changes take place within incises. A similar case, from the finale of Haydn's F-major string quartet "The Dream," Op. 50 No. 5, will be discussed below (Example 6.21).

in this case the composer would have had to take recourse to thirty-second notes or even smaller rhythmical values at a few points of the movement. Although Koch writes that the rhythmical value selected for *Taktteile* does not matter, he warns a beginning composer "not to unnecessarily overload the eye of the performer with too many hooks and beams attached to notes" and does recommend selecting a larger rhythmical value of *Taktteile* in order to avoid this.[39] Furthermore, had the composer halved the rhythmical values in K. 575, the gavotte in mm. 17–34 would have been written in 2/4 (compound 4/4) rather than 2/2. Despite the dissolution of *tempo giusto*, in the late eighteenth century there is a tendency to retain the traditional meters and rhythmical values of dances. Exceptions occur when different dances collide with one another. This is what happens in the finale of K. 387 between the contredanse and the gavotte. The reason the gavotte is written in 2/1 rather than 2/2 is that, at this occasion, Mozart chose to retain the rhythmical values and meter of the contredanse. As indicated by Allanbrook (1983: 24), if notated in sixteenth notes, the contredanse would look like an instrumental figuration rather than a dance. The tendency turns into a strict rule in minuets. As a type—not just style—this dance must be notated in 3/4.[40]

But changes of topics do not accompany changes of meter in all the examples discussed thus far. Clearly, topics are determined not only by meter but, above all, by characteristics of musical material. If these characteristics do not change, one cannot plausibly refer to a change of topic as an explanation of a metrical change. This is true of the quick metrical changes that occur in the course of the themes from the slow movements of Haydn's Op. 50 No. 6 (Example 6.3) and No. 1 (Example 6.4) and in the course of the minuets of Mozart's K. 515 (Example 6.11) and K. 614 (Example 6.12). The first two examples represent the topic of siciliano. While this topic may be less pronounced when its characteristic accompaniment and rhythm disappear, it does not seem to be replaced by any other topic.[41] In the two minuets the introduction of the church style, customarily associated with 6/4 as tripled alla breve, is not only not observed but would even be improper. In all these examples the intention of the composers seems to consist not in varying the affect but simply in playing with meter by shifting the gear of the *Taktteile*. To be sure, this effect cannot be achieved merely by manipulating the metrical position of the caesuras. As

39. "Ohne Noth das Auge des Ausführers mit zu viel an die Noten gehängten Abtheilungsstrichen zu überhäufen" (Koch 1787: 290). For this reason, Koch excludes 2/8 from the range of available even meters.

40. The distinction between *types* and *styles* stems from Leonard Ratner. He defines the former as topics that "appear as fully worked-out pieces," the latter as "figures and progressions within a piece" (1980: 9).

41. Apparently, a siciliano could be either in simple or in compound 6/8 meter. In the late eighteenth century, one can find examples with caesuras falling at the beginnings of measures, as in the second movement of Mozart's Sonata for Piano and Violin, K. 377 (Variation VI "Siciliana"), and with caesuras located in the middle of notated measures, as in the celebrated theme of first-movement variations from the Piano Sonata K. 331. Comparison with the latter example suggests that the dynamic accents I observed earlier in Examples 6.3 and 6.4 may be characteristic of the siciliano topic. Allanbrook (2008) offers a more specific explanation of the function performed by the two *sf* in mm. 4 and 7 of K. 331/i.

emphasized in chapter 2, the criterion of caesura is purely theoretical, referring to the knowledge of the listener and, thus, a matter of her conscious recognition rather than cognition. Moreover, this recognition is possible only in retrospect, because caesuras come at the ends of phrases (*Absätze*) or incises (*Einschnitte*) whose meter they determine. For the change of metrical gear to be perceived by the listener, it must be indicated by other cues. Some of them I have already mentioned in chapter 2. They include the lowest metrical level consistently articulated by attacks, harmonic rhythm, and phrase structure. A more systematic discussion of these perceptual factors in light of eighteenth-century music theory is now in order.

6.3. Perceptual Factors

The role of the lowest metrical level that is consistently articulated by attacks as a criterion for the identification of *Taktteile* can be derived from Koch's teaching about *Metrum*. As reported in chapter 3, Koch requires that *Metrum* be based on a certain metrical level—normally that of *Taktteile*. Continuity of *Metrum* presupposes, in turn, that *Taktteile* must be consistently articulated by attacks on the musical surface. If they stop being so articulated, this is a cue that the metrical level of *Taktteile* has shifted up the metrical hierarchy. Such a shift takes place in the aria by Christian Gotthelf Scheinpflug shown by Koch in Example 6.17.[42] In the first half of the example the lowest metrical level is that of quarter notes representing *Taktteile* of 2/4 meter. It changes in mm. 13–16, where only half notes are consistently articulated. The empty measure at the end of the phrase (m. 20) retrospectively confirms the metrical change from 2/4 to ¢ (2/2), which has already happened in m. 13, resulting in double measures.[43] Interestingly, however, Koch does not interpret it this way. Having previously criticized the notation in double measures as incorrect, he would now hardly recommend it to the adepts of composition as legitimate notation of a metrical change.[44] Instead, he uses the example to demonstrate how *Metrum* can occasionally be interrupted for reasons related to the meaning of the text. In the case given, articulation of the lowest metrical level is interrupted on the words "Langen, langen" (long, long). As Koch admits, interruption of *Metrum* can also take place in instrumental music, even if—without an accompanying text—justification for such exceptions is "for the most part easier felt then explained" (Koch 1983: 76 [1793: 38]). Striking examples of this sort occur in Haydn's quartets Op. 64 No. 2/i (mm. 28–29, 53–54) and Op. 64 No. 3/iv (mm. 47–52, 103–10, 174–81).[45]

42. Scheinpflug was Koch's teacher and Kapellmeister at the court of Rudolstadt.

43. Apparently, the reason Scheinpflug uses double measures is the series of three-bar segments in 2/4 at the beginning of the example. If written in compound 4/4, these segments would start in different metrical positions. This example is thus similar to that from the finale of K. 593 (Example 6.15; see note 29).

44. Maurer Zenck (2001: 40) seems to think that Koch actually acknowledges the change of meter in this example and that he prohibits double measures only as a notation of entire pieces; yet no proofs occur in Koch's treatise that would testify to this opinion.

45. Also in Op. 50 No. 6/iv (mm. 63–68, 192–97), despite the pulsating accompaniment in eighths.

Example 6.17. Koch, *Versuch einer Anleitung zur Composition*, vol. 3, 35–38.

(*continued*)

Example 6.17. cont.

But—even apart from the possibility of interrupting *Metrum*—changes of the lowest metrical level consistently articulated by attacks cannot serve as an absolute criterion in detecting changes of *Taktteile.* Since, as Koch remarks, *Metrum* may also be based on *Taktglieder,* shifting up the lowest metrical level may indicate not a change of meter but only a change of *Metrum* from *Taktglieder* to *Taktteile.* Conversely, shifting the lowest level down may indicate a change of *Metrum* from *Taktteile* to *Taktglieder.* Furthermore, since no constraints exist as to the lowest metrical level consistently articulated by attacks, shifting this level up or down by adding or subtracting metrical subdivisions under the level of *Taktteile* may result in making the metrical hierarchy deeper or shallower in the framework of the same meter.

Yet, even if *Metrum* is articulated by *Taktglieder*, the latter are not normally bearers of harmonic changes. Koch's examples demonstrate that in such cases harmonic rhythm remains on the level of *Taktteile* or *Takte* (1983: 72 ex. 214, 74 ex. 220 [1793: 25–26, 30]; see Example 3.5). Most typically, harmonies change on downbeats. This observation is endorsed by Koch in *Musikalisches Lexikon*, where he writes that "the downbeat receives invariably the metrical stress or accent and mostly also a change of harmony."[46] If, then, harmonic rhythm starts following rhythmical values shorter than the previously established beat (*Taktteil*), this likely indicates that the metrical level of *Taktteile* has shifted down the metrical hierarchy. Harmonic rhythm is often referred to by Maurer Zenck as an auxiliary criterion in distinguishing among simple, compound, and double measures. But, as she makes clear, this criterion is also not absolute. On the one hand, harmonic changes more frequent than every *Taktteil* are not prohibited. On the other hand, there is no upper limit to the rate of harmonic changes. Harmonies can be and often are longer than one measure.

Another criterion frequently referred to by Maurer Zenck is the size of melodic segments. Longer segments speak for larger rhythmical values of *Taktteile*; shorter segments for smaller values. In the light of eighteenth-century music theory this is justified, insofar as the shortest melodic segments—imperfect incises (*unvollkommene Einschnitte*)—are one measure long. Incises shorter than one measure of the earlier meter would thus suggest that the meter has changed. Again, however, this criterion is not absolutely reliable, as follows from Koch's remarks:

> There are phrases whose figures are combined with short rests which often have the appearance of an incise. For instance, when the phrase... is formed as in [Example 6.18], it seems that two incises are found in the first measure. Only in this and the following section, we are not concerned with such incises, if one even wishes to call them that. They arise merely through the different variations of the main notes of the melody. Here we shall only consider such incises which are perceptible resting points; the main notes of the melody can be varied with whatever figures are desired. (1983: 10 [1787: 364–65])

Where such perceptible resting points are located, however, is not always easily determined. We will return to this issue shortly.

Example 6.18. Koch, *Versuch einer Anleitung zur Composition*, vol. 2, 364–65.

46. "Auf den Anschlag fällt jederzeit das Taktgewicht oder Accent, gemeiniglich aber auch zugleich der Wechsel der Harmonie" (Koch 1802: col. 150).

One can add to these criteria the range of rhythmical values that occur in a given musical passage. In their discussion of meters, Kirnberger (1776) and Schulz (1794) routinely indicate the shortest rhythmical values available in each of them. This complies with the tradition of *tempo giusto* represented by these two authors. From their remarks certain useful hints can be derived particularly for the distinction between 2/2 and 2/4 as well as 6/4 and 3/4. In the former meter of every pair, representing alla breve in its basic (2/2) and tripled (6/4) form, the smallest rhythmical values available for composers are eighths, whereas the latter meters (2/4 and 3/4) tolerate all note values including sixteenths (Kirnberger 1982: 387, 396 [1776: 119, 129]). The lower limit of rhythmical values is less useful in distinguishing between 6/8 as simple and compound meter, because in either case sixteenths are available as the smallest note values. Yet the limits of rhythmical values determined by Kirnberger and Schulz are not observed by authors not committed to the tradition of *tempo giusto*. For instance, Riepel transgresses them in Example 6.1, and Koch shows several examples that include sixteenth notes in ¢.

Although, as indicated above, perceptual factors do not represent absolutely reliable criteria in the identification of *Taktteile*, and their changes often take place without any changes of meter, they are indispensable if metrical changes are to be perceived by the listener, rather than merely recognized. In fact, they accompany the changes of meter effectuated by shifts of *Taktteile* in the examples from Haydn and Mozart discussed earlier in this chapter. In all of them, changes of meter are accompanied by changes of the harmonic rhythm. In some, changes of meter are additionally enhanced by other factors, including the smallest rhythmical values, the size of melodic sections, and the lowest metrical level consistently articulated by attacks.[47] In these examples the perception of metrical changes is thus confirmed by caesuras, but not produced by them. It would arise even if not confirmed by any caesura or, for that matter, even if contradicted by it. From here it follows that perceptual factors can play a particularly important role in indicating changes of *Taktteile* in the course of phrases that do not display any subdivision into incises (*Einschnitte*) or in which such a subdivision is not unequivocal. The position of the *Absatz* at the end of a phrase does not necessarily determine the meter at the beginning, if this meter is not confirmed by an earlier *Einschnitt*.

That it is not always possible to unequivocally identify *Einschnitte* as resting points in the course of phrases has to do with two different problems inherent in the eighteenth-century *Satzbau*. The first of these is related to the decorations (*Verzierungen*) of ending formulas, which may obliterate the position of caesuras. While these deco-

47. Changes of some perceptual factors can also be observed in the examples taken from composition handbooks by Riepel and Koch. Changes in harmonic rhythm between sections of simple and compound meter are clearly implied in Examples 6.1 and 6.2, whereas changes in the smallest rhythmical values take place in Examples 6.2 and 6.8. Note that changes in the lowest metrical level do not normally accompany changes of meter in minuets because in this dance the lowest level consistently articulated by attacks had to be that of quarters (Riepel 1752: 4–5). If at all, such changes take place between minuet and trio, the latter occasionally being based on eighths, as for instance in Op. 50 Nos. 2 and 3, Op. 54 No. 1, Op. 55 No. 1, and Op. 64 Nos. 5 and 6. In these examples, however, the meter does not change.

rations, divided by Koch into appoggiaturas, overhangs, and lead-ins (1983: 19–34 [1787: 392–412]), are unproblematic insofar as the harmonic goal is achieved in a straightforward way, they may cause problems when receiving an "improper" harmonization. Since Koch offers no criteria for distinguishing chords resulting from an improper harmonization and prolonging the harmonic goal of a given melodic section from structural chords preceding such a goal, in certain cases the position of the caesura is not easily determined. While this problem is less evident in Example 2.32, showing an improper harmonization of an overhang, because of its triple meter, it becomes critically important in another example, kept in duple meter, with which Koch illustrates an improper harmonization of an appoggiatura (Example 2.33). As has been observed by Maurer Zenck (2001: 187) and illustrated by her with an ingeniously retouched version of Koch's example (Example 6.19), if the size of measures and rhythmical values in this example were doubled, it would be difficult to decide whether it illustrates an improper harmonization of an appoggiatura in simple 2/2 or an undecorated caesura in compound 4/4 meter. The second problem concerning the identification of *Einschnitte* is that such caesuras, or "resting points of the spirit" (*Ruhepunkte des Geistes*), are marked by several different formulas that can otherwise occur in the course of melodic sections without any closing effect. As Koch remarks, "the ending formulas of these sections are so various and can be formed in such manifold ways that it would be very questionable to decide, by means of these figures, where resting points are present in the melody; not to mention that such figures in the melody also can be used where there is no resting point. In short, nothing concrete can determine the places where they are in the melody" (1983: 4 [1787: 350]).

Example 6.19. Maurer Zenck, *Vom Takt*, 187, ex. 82d, right col.

Both problems are illustrated in Example 6.20a from the minuet of Haydn's String Quartet in E-flat major, Op. 64 No. 6. The *Absatz*, falling in m. 6, indicates that the meter at the end of the first phrase is 3/4. But what is the meter at the beginning? If the answer to this question were to be given on the basis of a caesura occurring earlier in the course of the phrase, it would not be unequivocal. Is there any caesura here at all? And if so, does it fall in m. 3 or 4? Theoretically, both interpretations are possible. Provided the caesura is achieved with the subdominant in m. 4, the meter is 3/4 throughout the phrase, and the chord of m. 3 has the structural function of a secondary dominant. In this case, however, the caesura does not represent an *Einschnitt* but an *Absatz*. This is because, by arriving in the fourth measure, it closes a four-measure phrase (*Vierer*).[48] The two following measures (mm. 5–6) are to be taken for an appendix (*Anhang*) closed with another *Absatz* on the tonic. Although not quite common, appendices closing on a different harmony than that of the proper phrase are discussed by Koch as an available compositional option (1983: 47–48 [1787: 440–41]). Yet it is also possible to interpret the first four notated measures as a perfect incise in 6/4. In this interpretation the caesura falls in m. 3 and is decorated by an appoggiatura (*Vorschlag*) that delays the proper caesura note C to m. 4. The chord in m. 3 is auxiliary, resulting from an "improper harmonization" of the appoggiatura note B in the melody accompanied by another appoggiatura G in the bass. The evidence for the auxiliary status of this chord—arising from the superposition of two appoggiaturas within the underlying subdominant harmony—is the common tone E-flat in the middle voice (mm. 3–4). Of these two theoretically possible interpretations, only the latter is supported by perceptual factors. Between mm. 4 and 5 of the first phrase, the harmonic rhythm, the rate of bass attacks, and the shortest rhythmical values in the melody all shift downward in the metrical hierarchy. This clearly suggests a switch from 6/4, notated in double measures, to 3/4 meter. The same switch happens in the second phrase between mm. 10 and 11, even if not marked by any caesura. As a result, both phrases are asymmetrical (4 + 2) and have an irregular length of six bars. If the change of meter is taken into account, however, each of them counts as four measures long.

It may be interesting to observe that the answer to the question about the status of mm. 3–4 given in the first reprise is turned around in the second reprise (Example 6.20b). There, in the course of the thematic return, the first phrase is interrupted after the fourth notated measure (m. 24). What follows is a parenthesis made up of two varied repetitions of the phrase's two last measures. In the first repetition a slight harmonic adjustment determines that the chord in m. 25 cannot be interpreted as an appoggiatura within the subdominant but only as a secondary dominant (V^6_5/IV) resolving to the subdominant in m. 26. The meter is thus not 6/4 but 3/4, and mm. 21–24 form a complete phrase. Consequently, they do not need to be complemented by another incise. The parenthesis is followed by a four-measure phrase (mm. 29–32) and a codetta with a postcadential *imbroglio*.

Another example of a perceived metrical change not unequivocally endorsed by a caesura occurs in the finale of String Quartet in F major, Op. 50 No. 5 (Example 6.21). At the beginning of the theme every composed measure embraces two notated measures, each of them filled with a homogenous motivic substance. This suggests that the meter is 12/8 as a tripled version of alla breve.[49] Even in

48. In Koch's theory, the distinction between incises (*Einschnitte*) and phrases (*Sätze*) is based on length. A given melodic section is a phrase if it is at least four measures long. (But length alone does not suffice to determine a phrase's completeness. While most phrases are complete melodic sections, a phrase can be incomplete if, for instance, it closes with a dissonant sonority. I am grateful to William Rothstein for a thorough critical discussion of this aspect of Koch's theory.) Although caesuras of phrases (*Absätze*) are made usually on the dominant (*Quintabsatz*) or the tonic (*Grundabsatz*), phrases ending on the subdominant are not entirely uncommon (Koch 1983: 36 [1787: 415]).

49. Triple subdivision applies here not to *Taktteile* but to *Taktglieder* in alla breve meter. The resulting 12/8 meter was not known in eighteenth-century music theory. For Koch, 12/8 is always a compound meter derived from 4/4. Riepel speaks, likewise, about 12/8 as tripled *gemeiner Takt* (4/4). Nevertheless, simple 12/8 derived from 2/2 occurs frequently in eighteenth-century compositions. Compare the discussion of Beethoven's "Appassionata" by Maurer Zenck (2001: 47–48).

Example 6.20. Haydn, String Quartet in E-flat major, Op. 64 No. 6/iii, mm. 1–12 (a) and mm. 20–36 (b).

this composed meter, harmonic changes are very slow because they take place only every second measure. In the notation, one harmony covers four measures, which make up a perfect incise. Although this incise is clearly separated from the next one, the location of the caesura is not clear because no harmonic changes take place within the incises. The harmonic rhythm is drastically accelerated in mm. 9–12, where harmony changes with every notated measure. At the same time the size of melodic units is reduced to one measure. The unit of mm. 1–2, which formed half of the perfect incise in 12/8, corresponds to twice the shorter unit of m. 9 as an imperfect incise in 6/8. This last meter, reflected in notation, is ultimately confirmed by the caesura in m. 12. Again, the change of meter in the course of the phrase results in its irregular length of twelve bars and in an asymmetry of its component elements (8 + 4) that is apparent in the notation. If the change of meter is considered, the phrase turns out to be eight measures long and perfectly symmetrical, containing four measures of 12/8 and four measures of 6/8.

Example 6.21. Haydn, String Quartet in F major, "The Dream," Op. 50 No. 5/iv, mm. 1–12.

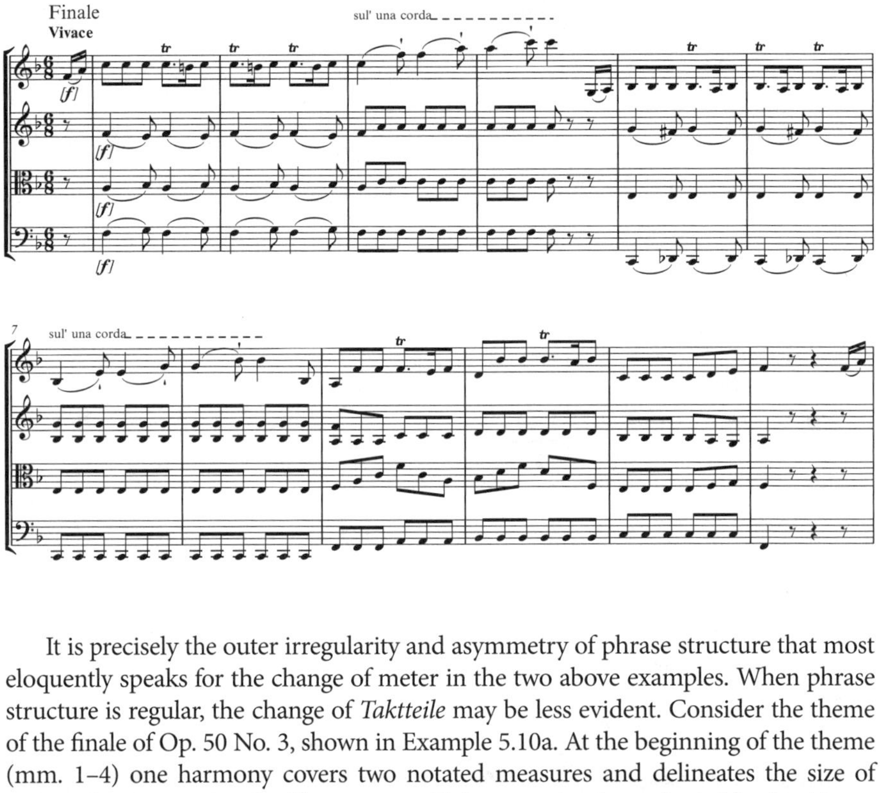

It is precisely the outer irregularity and asymmetry of phrase structure that most eloquently speaks for the change of meter in the two above examples. When phrase structure is regular, the change of *Taktteile* may be less evident. Consider the theme of the finale of Op. 50 No. 3, shown in Example 5.10a. At the beginning of the theme (mm. 1–4) one harmony covers two notated measures and delineates the size of incises, thus suggesting double measures. This suggestion is confirmed by the *Absatz,* which falls in m. 11 but reaches across the bar line to m. 12 containing the resolution of appoggiatura. This means that the phrase starts and ends in 2/2 meter. But does it stay in this meter the whole time? From m. 5 on, the harmony changes every notated measure, and the size of the incises, indicated by slurs, is contracted accordingly. This might suggest a switch to 2/4, the meter Haydn indicates in the time signature. Even so, this change does not cause any outer asymmetry. One perfect incise in 2/4 (mm. 5–6), made up of two imperfect incises, equals the length of one imperfect incise in 2/2 (mm. 1–2). Along with its repetition in mm. 7–8, it takes the same amount of time as the repetition of the imperfect incise of mm. 1–2 in mm. 3–4. But a reading of mm. 5–8 in 2/2 meter is possible as well, since the caesuras of imperfect incises in mm. 5 and 7 are not unequivocal. If the only caesuras fall in mm. 6 and 8, the melodic units of mm. 5–6 and 7–8 can be considered imperfect incises in 2/2.[50] The acceleration of harmonic rhythm is in itself no firm proof of a metrical change. It acquires greater weight from m. 9, where the harmonic rhythm is even more accelerated. Although one might not be inclined to think that the meter changes twice in the course of this phrase from 2/2 to 2/4 and from 2/4 to 2/8—in the late eighteenth century this last meter is "not in use" even according to the conservative Kirnberger (1982: 387 [1776: 119])—at least one change from 2/2 to 2/4 is likely to have taken place, because the harmonic rhythm in mm. 9–10 is uncharacteristically fast for alla breve.

6.4. *Taktteile* and the Tactus

Even if, in this and other similar examples, the change of the metrical level of *Taktteile* cannot be determined with certainty, one can securely speak of the change of tactus. Interestingly, the perceptual cues indicating changes of *Taktteile* on the grounds of eighteenth-century music theory correspond to factors influencing perception of tactus in the theory of Lerdahl and Jackendoff. Two of these factors are rhythmical values and harmonic rhythm (1983: 73–74). With regard to the former, Lerdahl and Jackendoff observe that "the tactus cannot be too far away from the smallest metrical level: a succession of notes of short duration is generally an indication of a relatively fast tactus."[51] With regard to the latter, "each beat of the tactus must have only a single functional harmony." That means that changes of harmony follow beats of the tactus or a slower—but not faster—metrical level.[52] These factors refer to what can be called "density of events" on the musical surface. The third factor is absolute speed.[53] It is subjective, in that it relates information from the musical surface to the speed of processing this information by the listener. According to Lerdahl and Jackendoff, the tactus is invariably between 40 and 160 beats per minute (1983: 73). More recent studies reveal that, within this range, the preferred rate for tactus is around 600 milliseconds, that is, 100 beats per minute (Parncutt 1994). This rate, known in psychology as *natural* or *human pace*, scores high

50. These caesuras are secured by repetition. As was observed independently by Yeston (1976: 15) and by Wolfgang Budday (1983: 37), repetitions unequivocally delineate the size of melodic units even in the absence of pauses or longer rhythmical values, which otherwise make caesuras more noticeable.
51. On the other hand, tactus cannot be the lowest level of the metrical hierarchy. It must have subdivisions (Temperley 2001: 53).
52. As an auxiliary factor, Lerdahl and Jackendoff mention "prevailing note values." From their example, taken from the finale of Mozart's "Jupiter" Symphony (1983: 73 ex. 4.8), it follows that they mean rhythmical values representing the smallest metrical level in one auditory stream: the melody.
53. My distinction between absolute speed and "density of events" corresponds to that drawn by Berry between *pulse-tempo* and *activity-tempo*, the latter defined by him as "the eventfulness" of music (1976: 305).

in various sorts of perception and memory tasks as well as motoric activities.[54] Although absolute speed was not mentioned in the preceding section among perceptual factors pertinent to the identification of *Taktteile*, in reality eighteenth-century music theorists were aware of this factor too. According to Riepel, 6/8 in tempo Presto is to be understood as tripled 2/4, that is, simple meter (1765: 77), and 4/4 in Presto is the same as alla breve (78). Consequently, shifts of *Taktteile* up the metrical hierarchy take place most naturally in rapid tempi. For instance, alla breve may arise transitorily in Allegro, Allegro assai, Presto, and Prestissimo (Riepel 1752: 47). In his example reproduced at the beginning of this chapter (Example 6.1) as well as Koch's example (Example 6.2) it takes place in Allegro.[55]

The reliance on the same perceptual factors explains why *Taktteile* and tactus are so closely related. Even so, as emphasized in chapter 1, they are independent. *Taktteile* may but need not represent the same metrical level as the tactus. An interesting clue that *Taktteile* may differ from the perceptually most salient level of meter can be found in Kirnberger and Schulz's entry "Rhythmus" in Sulzer's *Allgemeine Theorie*. Reflecting on the process of counting as it occurs in various situations of everyday life, the authors observe: "When the counting proceeds slowly, so that it is not possible to take more numbers to one group, then one tries to break the excessive uniformity in that one divides each numeral into two parts. Instead of counting one–two–three–, so that a longer time elapses between words, one soon takes it into one's head to count one–and–two–and–three–and etc."[56] Transferring this to music, counted beats (numerals) would correspond to the metrical level of *Taktteile*, whereas the tactus would be located on the level of their subdivisions represented by inserted syllables. The example thus illustrates the situation, considered by Koch, when—in slow tempo—*Metrum* is based on *Taktglieder*.[57]

The independence between the tactus and *Taktteile* extends itself onto their changes in the course of a musical composition. Whereas in some cases a change of tactus may happen along with a change of *Taktteile*—indeed, it must if the

54. For a useful summary of experimental data concerning natural pace, see Dowling and Harwood (1986: 181–82).

55. The tempo marking Allegro does not occur in Example 6.1 but is assigned by Riepel to the same musical passage earlier in his handbook (1752: 46–47).

56. "Geschiehet das Zählen langsam, so daß es nicht wohl mehr angeht, mehr Zahlen zu einem Glied zu nehmen: so sucht man die zu große Einförmigkeit dadurch zu unterbrechen, daß man eine Zahl in zwey Theile theilet. Anstatt so zu zählen: Eins–zwey–drey–, so daß zwischen zwey Wörtern eine merkliche Zeit verflösse, fällt man bald darauf, so zu zählen: Ei–nes; zwey–e, drey–e; u. s. f." (Kirnberger and Schulz 1794: 97).

57. On the basis of this example, one would be tempted to assume that the tactus is equivalent to *Metrum*. Since *Metrum* is based in most cases on *Taktteile*, this would, in turn, explain the close relationship between *Taktteile* and tactus. This would also explain why, in slow tempi, the tactus corresponds with *Taktglieder*. According to experimental findings reported by Dowling and Harwood, in such tempi "the subjective beat shifts to relatively shorter temporal units to stay within the range of preferred pace" (1986: 189). However, in fast tempi tactus often corresponds to *Takte* or even higher metrical levels, which is not permissible for *Metrum*.

latter change is to be perceived rather than merely recognized—in other cases tactus may change without any attendant change of *Taktteile* and vice versa. For instance, playing a given passage considerably faster or slower will cause a change of tactus but have no effect on the size of *Taktteile*. Changes of tactus can also be caused by accelerating or decelerating harmonic rhythm or introducing shorter or longer melodic segments or smaller or larger rhythmical values—while retaining the same *Taktteil*. Changes of *Taktteile* without changes of tactus result, in turn, from manipulations that affect the locations of caesuras but are not accompanied by changes of the absolute speed or of the "density of events" at the musical surface. The most glaring examples of such manipulations occur when, at the repetition of a given phrase, the caesura's location changes. This often happens in phrases that stand in antecedent–consequent relationship to each other. In Example 5.10a from the finale of Op. 50 No. 3 the half cadence (*Quintabsatz*) of the antecedent, falling in m. 11, attests to 2/2 meter notated in double measures, but in the consequent, the full cadence (*Kadenz*) in m. 24 indicates 2/4. The effect exerted on the metrical level of *Taktteile* by the manipulation of caesuras in Example 2.38 has already been discussed. Since the consequent includes invariably one more chord—the tonic—than the antecedent, different locations of caesuras in these phrases arise naturally, unless the composer intentionally counteracts this by accelerating the harmonic rhythm before the cadence. The question whether in every case these different locations are indicative of an intentional change of *Taktteile* remains open.

The discussion up to this point suggests that, by taking into account the relationship between tactus and *Taktteile*, one can elaborate much more complex analytic descriptions of metric processes in eighteenth-century music than has been customary until now. However, the difficulty with this sort of description lies in the fact that the assignment of the tactus to a given metrical level is not unequivocal. As was pointed out in chapter 1, different assignments are possible for different listeners and on different listening occasions. A way out of this difficulty would be, instead of more or less arbitrarily designating certain metrical level as the tactus, to account for the perceptual factors on which it depends. Two of these factors—harmonic rhythm and the lowest level consistently articulated by attacks—were mentioned above. Note that they belong to the set of MPRs listed by Lerdahl and Jackendoff. Whereas one can easily agree that these two factors are of greatest importance for the perception of tactus, it might be reasonable to assume that this perception is not completely unaffected by other factors, such as the bass activity or the rate of dynamic and textural changes. The final stage of sophistication in analytic description of meter would thus be achieved by taking into account complete distribution of all preference factors across all levels of metrical hierarchy. Such a distribution is actually shown by Lerdahl and Jackendoff in their analysis of the opening measures of Mozart's G-minor symphony, K. 550 (Example 6.22). What is remarkable about this example is the consistency with which individual preference factors are assigned to metrical levels. The lowest metrical level of eighth notes is consistently articulated by attacks in the accompaniment, not shown in the example. The level of quarters arises from the alternation between the slurs (*5c*) and the durational accents (*5a*) in the melody. Half notes are articulated by durational accents alone (*5a*), whereas whole notes—tantamount to measures—are marked by the bass. The level of two measures coincides with the bass strokes located in the lower octave.[58]

Example 6.22. Lerdahl and Jackendoff, *A Generative Theory of Tonal Music*, 86, ex. 4.35.

While Lerdahl and Jackendoff do not further theorize this aspect of their analysis, distribution of preference factors across levels of metrical hierarchy has been explored by other authors adopting methodological approaches different from the GTTM. In his *Structural Functions of Music*, Wallace Berry (1976: 315) shows distribution of "rhythms" created by various "elements and parameters of musical events" (313) in Variation XIV of Beethoven's *Diabelli Variations*. Berry's idea was systematically elaborated by Frank Samarotto (1999b) in the framework of his theory of temporal plasticity under the concept of *temporal plane*, which he defines as a relatively stable configuration of "temporal plastic-

58. Of course, a given preference factor does not need to consistently articulate all strong beats of a given metrical level. It may also occur inconsistently on strong and weak beats or act consistently against the metrical hierarchy by marking weak beats only. In this last case, it gives rise to a potentially or actually antimetrical layer of motion (see section 5.2) and thus yields metrical dissonance. In Example 6.22, an antimetrical layer is created by the beginnings of slurs (*5c*). For Krebs, "the extent to which the antimetrical layer is formed by a consistent event type" is a factor in determining the contextual intensity of a metrical dissonance. As he observes, "the more similar the type of recurring event, . . . the more perceptible is the layer of motion [because] similarity of event type invites the listener to perceive the events as a connected series" (1999: 59).

ity conditions." Changes in this configuration represent *temporal disjunctions* and, if a new configuration persists, result in changes between temporal planes. Samarotto traces such phenomena in the music of Haydn, Mozart, and, particularly, late Beethoven. Curiously enough, he finds the earliest proof of their theoretical recognition in Koch's commentary on the example from Scheinpflug's aria (Example 6.17). Several other examples of perceived changes of *Taktteile* that I have discussed in the course of this chapter exemplify what Samarotto calls changes of temporal planes.[59] As he emphasizes, such changes are much more complex than changes of tactus (141).[60] Obviously, one and the same change of tactus can result from many different changes of temporal planes.

Phenomena similar to those studied by Samarotto in the repertory of late eighteenth- and early nineteenth-century music are discussed by Channan Willner in his studies of Baroque rhythm and meter (1999, 2005, 2007a, 2007b). According to Willner, the temporality of Baroque music emerges from the configuration of different paces, determined, yet again, by different parameters. The central level of this configuration is occupied by the "basic pace," which is characterized by Willner in terms of Schenkerian analysis as the underlying pace of middleground tonal motion disclosed by prolongational reduction of surface activity.[61] Faster metrical levels are inhabited by "figural paces" that mediate between the basic pace and its foreground diminutions. Slower metrical levels are delineated by several "grouping paces."[62] Although Willner apparently

59. Changes of temporal planes between formal sections, as in Mozart's string quartets K. 387, 421, and 575 and the string quintet K. 593, are characterized by Samarotto as "unmarked" (1999: 148). "Marked" changes of temporal planes are those that happen in the course of a section or phrase. It is interesting to note that some changes of temporal planes are interpreted by Samarotto as nonnotated changes of tempo (129–33)—thus, much the same way I interpret the changes of *Taktteile* in the first movement of K. 575 (Example 6.14) and in the minuet of Haydn's Op. 50 No. 5 (Example 4.8a).

60. Samarotto does not refer directly to Lerdahl and Jackendoff's concept of tactus but to "primary rhythmic level" and "primary metric level" as equivalents of tactus in the theories of, respectively, Cooper and Meyer (1960) and Lester (1986).

61. Although the concept of "basic pace" resembles tactus, Willner distinguishes between these two. When "basic pace" expands or contracts, tactus can be taken over by a different kind of pace (2005: 7). Generally, for Willner, tactus is stable throughout a piece (12). Although he occasionally refers to Lerdahl and Jackendoff, his concept of tactus comes not from them but from the mensural theory, whose precepts are still alive in the repertory of Baroque music.

62. In his dissertation (2005) and several other publications (1999, 2007a, 2007b), Willner takes "basic pace" as the criterion in distinguishing between what Kirnberger calls "large," "simple," and "compound" 4/4 meters. Yet this criterion cannot be inferred from Kirnberger's descriptions of these meters. At the same time, Willner ignores the criterion clearly offered by Kirnberger, which is the metrical placement of caesuras. Some examples Willner claims are in simple 4/4 meter have caesuras consistently falling on the second halves of measures and hence, by Kirnberger's lights, represent compound 4/4 meter. As a matter of fact, phenomena Willner describes as changes between different species of 4/4 represent various fluctuations of the metrical hierarchy in the framework of one and the same meter. Incidentally, such phenomena could be better approached from the perspective of Mattheson's theory, in which, indeed, quick changes of metrical divisions are interpreted as changes of meter (Schwindt-Gross 1989: 207). Although Kirnberger's admiration for his teacher, J. S. Bach, is well known, it is still hard to see why Willner applies Kirnberger's theory—reflecting a new concept of meter characteristic of the late eighteenth century—in analyses of Bach's and Handel's music.

considers these assignments typical of Baroque music, they are actually similar to those observed earlier in this chapter as characteristic of the Classic style. This suggests that, rather than being style-specific, assignments of metrical preference factors to levels of metrical hierarchy are, at least to some extent, natural and conditioned by the mechanism of metric perception. Naturally enough, attacks articulate the lowest level of metrical hierarchy and constitute an indispensable condition for any other factor. Harmonic rhythm operates mostly on the levels of beats (*Taktteile*) and downbeats (*Takte*). The size of melodic segments marks the level of measures (*Takte*) or higher. These assignments presumably have to do with differing effectiveness of preference factors in different temporal scales.[63] While this issue requires experimental investigation, it seems reasonable to hypothesize that statistical factors represented by durational, dynamic, and melodic accents are effective preeminently on small temporal scales, whereas the metrical effect of harmony as the syntactical factor—which requires more processing—comes into play only on the middle scale. Melodic units typically articulate the level of measures and hypermetrical levels. This explains why, according to Lerdahl and Jackendoff (1983: 99), at the highest levels meter is superseded by grouping. Hierarchical factors, such as harmony and grouping, can for themselves articulate several levels of meter.

From the assignments of preference factors to metrical levels a set of further characteristics of metrical hierarchy can be derived. So far in the course of this discussion it has been taken for granted that metrical hierarchy is always continuous—in other words, that there are no gaps between metrical levels. If this were so, the only characteristic of metrical hierarchy—apart from numerical ratios between levels—would be its *depth*, determined by the lowest metrical level consistently articulated by attacks.[64] However, one of the most intriguing aspects of metrical hierarchies are the discontinuities or gaps contained in them. Such discontinuities arise when certain metrical levels are not articulated on the musical surface. Certainly, all levels are articulated by attacks. But the question is whether this articulation is additionally supported by other factors of preference. If a metrical level is not articulated by any factor of preference independently of those that articulate the lower level or levels, it can be said to be "empty" and considered a discontinuity in the metrical hierarchy of a given piece or section thereof. By identifying such "empty" levels, one can determine—in addition to depth—the *density* of the metrical hierarchy as its further characteristic. Most dense will be a hierarchy with no empty levels. With an increase in the number of such levels, several looser metrical hierarchies can be obtained. This issue, implicit in the theoretical approaches to rhythm and meter of Berry, Samarotto, and Willner, was explicitly raised for the first time by Joel Lester (1986: 75–77) in his analysis of the first movement of Beethoven's Fifth Symphony and further corroborated in London's analysis (2004:

63. Some experiments indicate that certain factors are effective only on certain levels of absolute tempo and not on others. For instance, durational (agogic) accents were shown by Parncutt (1994, experiment 1) to have perceptual effect only in fast tempi. The same can be assumed about melodic accents. See notes 23 and 30 in chapter 2.
64. This characteristic is called by London "depth of entrainment" (2004: 17–19).

89–99) of the same piece.[65] In reference to eighteenth-century compositions, an important question to ask concerns the articulation of *Taktteile* (beats) and *Takte* (downbeats). Particularly intriguing are cases when one or both of these levels are not articulated by any preference factor, that is to say, are empty.[66]

Yet another characteristic of metrical hierarchy, related to its depth and density, is the *strength of articulation* of individual levels. When several factors of preference are clustered on one level, this level is very strongly articulated, but, given the limited number of such factors, fewer factors are available for the articulation of other levels. The metrical hierarchy will thus be either very shallow or very loose. In the opposite case, when several levels are articulated by single factors, their articulation is weaker, but the hierarchy can be denser or wider. In terms of the cognitive model underlying this study, stronger or weaker articulation of individual metrical levels will result in stronger or weaker projections of these levels being elaborated by the metric processor.[67] The strongest level of projection will be perceived as the tactus. However, the strength of articulation depends not only on the number of factors assigned to a given level but also on the salience of these factors and of the auditory streams to which they belong. Since harmonic rhythm is the most salient factor of preference in metric perception, Lerdahl and Jackendoff are certainly right that it will determine tactus in most cases, yet tactus may also be determined by a higher level of tonal motion, represented by the "basic pace."[68]

The complex cluster of questions related to the articulation of metrical levels on the musical surface leads toward what can be called a "theory of metrical consonance." Interestingly, the possibility of such a theory is indicated by London in the conclusion to his analysis of Beethoven's Fifth Symphony: "Whereas Krebs (1999) has described the way that metrical dissonance can fluctuate over the course of a piece, here the fluctuations of metric 'consonance' have been described" (2004: 98). These fluctuations are tantamount to changes in the distribution of individual preference factors relative to metrical hierarchy and to attendant changes in the aforementioned characteristics of metrical hierarchy, including its depth, density, and strength of articulation. If limited to these interrelated perceptual

65. For instance, in reference to the passage starting at m. 26, London writes that "the cascading figures do not really articulate a two-beat level, so we hear just an undivided four-beat measure." Starting from m. 44, "four-beat measures continue, though again without a two-beat level, until measure 56" (2004: 92). Beethoven's Fifth seems to be a particularly tractable object for this kind of analysis. It is also discussed by Samarotto (1999b: 158–70) as an example of changing "temporal planes."

66. In the Fifth, this problem is complicated by the notation in double measures (Maurer Zenck 2001: 120–26). From the quotations included in the preceding note, it follows that the level of *Takte*, represented by "a two-beat level" and notated as two-measure units, is occasionally left empty. Another celebrated example in which *Takte* and *Taktteile* are not articulated at the musical surface is the beginning of the Ninth Symphony.

67. This idea has an equivalent in London's theory of meter, according to which "the degree of metrical accent is correlated with the relative strength and temporal focus of our entrained temporal expectancies" (2004: 26).

68. Strength of articulation is addressed by Willner in his discussion of the reconfiguration of grouping and figural paces in the first movement of Mozart's Piano Sonata K. 330 (1999: 214–15). In Willner's graphical representation (ex. 6), the "basic pace" is kept apart from these paces, which suggests that its salience is superior to any of them.

characteristics, a theory of metrical consonance may apply to any musical repertory. By including theoretical aspects concerning the metrical levels of *Taktteile* and *Takte*, it may be adjusted to the needs of a historically informed analysis of eighteenth-century music. In spite of many valuable efforts of the authors mentioned above, this theory has yet to be developed. The analogy between the hypothetical future "theory of metrical consonance" and the existing theory of metrical dissonance lies in that both of them can trace their origins back to the metric theory of the eighteenth century.[69] To be sure, their elements are not directly recorded in theoretical writings of the time. Yet, as I have attempted to demonstrate in this chapter, these writings do include hints about assignment of individual preference factors to metrical levels as well as changes of the metrical level that is perceived as the most salient. In this sense, a "theory of metrical consonance" is compatible with the metric theory of the eighteenth century and can be viewed as its organic outgrowth. Although many questions raised in the course of this chapter are not discussed in eighteenth-century handbooks of composition, addressed to beginners, they nevertheless logically follow from their authors' premises and play an important part in the metrical strategies elaborated by master composers.

69. These two theories can also be combined. "Surfacing" and "submerging" metrical dissonances (section 5.6) result from fluctuations of the "primary metrical consonance" of a given piece, through variation of the strength of articulation of the interpretive level contained in it. Activation of a metrical dissonance, as well as its intensification or deintensification (section 5.2), consists in varying the strength of articulation of the "antimetrical" interpretive level.

CHAPTER Seven

Analyses of Long-Range Metrical Strategies

So far in this study, musical examples have served to illustrate different types of metric manipulations occurring in late eighteenth-century music. To this end, they have been isolated from the contexts of their respective movements. This approach was not entirely inappropriate as regards the function performed by them in that context. Indeed, many metric manipulations are isolated phenomena whose effects originate in their singularity and consist in taking the listener by surprise. Yet this is not always the case. In other cases, metric manipulations may be connected into longer chains and form different episodes of metrical strategies that are carried out throughout entire movements. In the preceding chapters, it has only been possible to trace such metrical strategies to a limited extent, by drawing connections between two or three episodes. Moreover, analyses of those episodes that represent different types of metric manipulations have been presented in different chapters or sections. In chapter 5 I discussed one longer strategy, from the finale of Op. 50 No. 3, and included an analysis of the minuet of K. 593, but these are not the only metrical strategies of this scope and complexity that occur in the repertory under consideration, or even the most elaborate ones. In Haydn's chamber music for strings of 1787–91, one can find other long-range metrical strategies that deserve detailed analyses. The purpose of this chapter is to analyze two such strategies. One of them comes from the opening movement of the String Quartet Op. 50 No. 2, the other from the finale of Op. 55 No. 2.

Yet, although metrical strategies can be analyzed for their own sake, they are not normally unrelated to other aspects of eighteenth-century compositions. This is understandable in light of the metaphor of music as language, fundamental for eighteenth-century discourses about music. If meter is an aspect of musical grammar, as was pointed out in the introduction, metric manipulations bear some relation to broader compositional strategies on the level of musical rhetoric. Earlier in this study I sought, in particular, to indicate connections of metric manipulations to the musical form and its topical decorum. It will be helpful to summarize these observations before proceeding with analyses of the selected movements.

Connections between meters and topics—particularly those related to dances—have been explored in depth by Allanbrook (1983). As reported in the preceding chapter, changes of the metrical level of *Taktteile* are frequently correlated with changes of topics. This happens usually at boundaries between longer sections of musical forms, yet less usual examples are not unheard of. One such example was analyzed in chapter 2. In the first movement of Op. 64 No. 2 (Example 2.36), the change taking place in the course of the theme from 2/4 and D major to 2/2 and B minor results in a twist from contredanse to "exalted march." The change of meter and key in that example is thus not a purely intellectual exercise appealing to the listener's abstract sense of humor, as in other examples of quick metrical changes shown in chapter 6, but is semanticized, inviting the listener to develop expressive associations along the lines of eighteenth-century conventions. Somewhat less definite semanticization of a quick metrical change might be observed in the first movement of Op. 64 No. 6 (Example 2.35). The white-note rhythm and the chordal texture of the theme in 2/2 suggest a chorale, whereas short chords and dotted rhythms in 4/4 arouse associations with a march. In these examples, connections between meters and topics concern denominators of time signatures. Yet, according to Allanbrook, these connections extend to numerators. As she indicates (17–18), apart from rhythmical values of *Taktteile*, an important factor determining the status of a given meter in the eighteenth century was duple or triple grouping of *Taktteile*. Duple meters were associated mostly with sacred music, triple meters with the world of human passions. Within the latter domain, duple or triple meters distinguished further between individual dances. Following in Allanbrook's footsteps, one may thus look for changes of topics caused not only by changes of the metrical level of *Taktteile* but also by changes of period. In the minuet of Mozart's String Quintet K. 515 (Example 2.21) the fleeting sensation of duple meter brings a flavor of the singing style characteristic of a slow movement. In the minuet of K. 614 (Example 2.22) a similar sensation creates an allusion to march. Occasionally, a change of topic is also caused by an *imbroglio*. Two such cases occurring in Haydn's string quartets were identified by Grave (1995). In the fourth-movement trio of his early String Quartet Op. 2 No. 4 (mm. 9–14), an ingenious *imbroglio* turns the minuet into a bourrée. In the minuet of String Quartet Op. 50 No. 5, the *imbroglio* shown in Example 4.8a introduces the march topic. These cases are exceptional, however. In other examples analyzed in this study, the effect exerted by an *imbroglio* consists not in introducing another topic but in subverting the topic at hand. In reference to Haydn's minuets it is vividly characterized by Levy (1992) as "something mechanical encrusted on the living" and by Wheelock (1992: 82) as a series of "frozen gestures" disturbing the natural course of the dance. On the other hand, certain types of metrical disturbances are connected with specific topics. This observation, made several times in the course of this study, relates not so much to dances, investigated by Allanbrook, as to topics drawing on associations with other genres and types of music making, characterized by Leonard Ratner (1980) as styles. For instance, submetrical grouping dissonances, discussed in chapter 4, that yield an impression of being improvised ad libitum by the soloist have been found to be characteristic of the cadenza or brilliant style. Submetrical displacement dissonances represented by retardation, anticipation, and *Sospiren*, while also related to improvisation, suit the topic of sensibility (*Empfindsamkeit*). Syncopations such as those in Mozart's String Quintet in C major, K. 515 (Example 5.5), are emblematic of *alla zoppa* (Agawu 1991: 87), whereas syncopated accompaniment evokes associations with orchestral style and occurs frequently in connection with *Sturm und Drang*. General pauses evoke a rustic air, related to the "low comic" and contrasted with the stylized Arcadian atmosphere of pastorale or musette. Old-fashioned hemiolas refer on the one hand to Baroque dances and on the other to the church style. Also related to the church or learned style are displacement dissonances arising from *ligaturae* and imitations. Because connections with topics often motivate a given manipulation or strategy, analyses of metrical strategies cannot abstain from making them explicit.

Not less significant than their connections with topics are connections of metric manipulations with musical form. As was observed in chapter 6, changes of the metrical level of *Taktteile*, correlated with changes of topics, frequently mark boundaries of formal sections. Earlier, in chapter 3, I pointed to the role of general pauses as "question marks" commenting on formally surprising strokes or causing such surprises themselves. In chapters 3 and 4 several other manipulations were shown to occur at typical formal spots. Their particular concentration was observed in the context of the *Halbkadenz* or *Kadenz*. This reflects the prominent role played by cadential caesuras in articulating musical forms of the eighteenth century. The *Halbkadenz* separating the development from the recapitulation is often followed by a surprising general pause or fermata. The sense of acceleration in the passage immediately preceding this cadence can be achieved by an *imbroglio*. *Imbroglio* or submetrical grouping dissonance may also occur after the *Halbkadenz* during standing on the dominant. Similarly, the *Kadenz* marking the structural end of exposition or recapitulation can be preceded and followed by metrical dissonances. The contrast between the surrounding metric irregularity and the regularity of the cadential formula serves to dramatize the formal structure. Alternatively, metric irregularity can break into a cadential formula. This is illustrated by the interruptions of *Metrum* in the String Quartet in D major, K. 575 (Example 3.21). Finally, by means of metric manipulations, the composer can postpone a cadential arrival or even create the impression of losing his bearings in the course of approaching it. The most eccentric illustration of this last possibility that has been shown in this study is the dissolution of meter in the finale of Op. 50 No. 3 (Example 5.10c), happening immediately before the *Kadenz* of the exposition. A postponement of the final cadence resulting from a syncopation assigned to a surprising harmony and a postponement resulting from a chain of syncopations built into a longer harmonic loop were observed in the minuets of Op. 50 No. 4 (Example 3.28) and Op. 50 No. 6, respectively (Example 5.6a). At these and other similar moments, musical grammar becomes, as it were, independent from rhetoric and turns into a force impinging on the course of the musical argument.

A particular aspect of musical form is the thematic process. In recent decades the role of the theme in the eighteenth-century conception of form has been fiercely debated. After a strong emphasis had been placed on the arrangement and treatment of themes in the nineteenth century, the rediscovery of eighteenth-century music theory in the twentieth century led at first to a radical rejection of theme as a formal factor. This change of perspective—concerning mainly but not only the sonata form—is reflected in the writings of Ratner (1949, 1980), for whom the musical forms of the eighteenth century are defined primarily by tonal processes. But more recent research along the lines initiated by Ratner has revealed that musical forms of the time were conceived both tonally and thematically. As was observed by Bonds (1991b: 90–118), eighteenth-century writers on the form did pay attention to themes and their arrangement. Within the rhetorical conception of form adopted by them, the main theme of a musical composition (*Hauptsatz*) was equivalent to the subject matter of an oration. As might be expected, metrical disturbances are found mostly in nonthematic sections. In themes they are far more unusual. One such example occurs in the opening movement of Haydn's C-major quartet, Op. 54 No. 2 (Example 5.15), where metrical dissonance makes an appearance within the subsidiary theme. But, even when not hosting any metric manipulation, a theme may be involved in a metrical strategy. This happens, for instance, when a theme contains a latent potentiality of a displacement dissonance and that potentiality is activated in the further course of a piece, as in the finale of Haydn's String Quartet in E-flat major, Op. 50 No. 3 (Example 5.10). In other cases, metrical dissonances refer back to a theme in that they arise from a repetition of its single motive. If this motive contained a rhythmical dissonance, as in the first movement of Haydn's E-major quartet Op. 54 No. 3 (Example 2.16), its repetition yields a metrical displacement dissonance (Example 5.4). If not, repetition of its abridged version can nonetheless give rise to a grouping dissonance represented by an *imbroglio*, as in the minuet of Op. 64 No. 5 (Example 4.9) and in the first movement of Mozart's B-flat-major quartet K. 589 (Example 4.7). Both types of metrical dissonance thus play an important role in the thematic process.

In this connection it is worth noting that motivic-thematic similarity between metric manipulations occurring in a given movement is strong evidence for their forming a metrical strategy. In the absence of such a similarity this question must remain open. Metric manipulations may not be strategically related to each other. If a given movement does contain a metrical strategy, not all metric manipulations may be included in it. Finally, not all of them may be included in the same strand of a metrical strategy. A given strategy may consist of several strands carried out independently from each other or crossing at certain points of the movement.

One more question to consider concerns the scope of metrical strategies. In Haydn's and Mozart's string chamber music, metrical strategies fall normally within the scope of one movement. Analysis of rhythm and meter in this repertory does not support the idea of cyclic integration. This last idea was proposed in reference to Haydn's symphonies by James Webster (1991) and Ethan Haimo (1995) and received considerable attention in recent studies devoted to his string quartets (Sutcliffe 1992; Grave and Grave 2006). All these authors base their arguments on analysis of harmonic phenomena. They identify, early in a cycle, some destabilizing harmonic event—a salient pitch, sonority, harmonic progression, or key—and connect it with passages of later movements in which this event is readdressed and ultimately resolved. Intermovement connections between metric manipulations in Haydn's string quartets are exceptional, however. In the repertory under consideration in this study the only such connection occurs in the F-major quartet, Op. 50 No. 5. The *imbroglio* in mm. 34–38 of the minuet, shown earlier in Example 4.8a, finds an equivalent in mm. 42–43 of the finale (Example 7.1). The similarity between these two passages is so striking because each of them is based on a sequence leading to a cadence.[1] Strangely enough, this intermovement connection is missed by Webster, although he provides an illuminating analysis of the minuet and the trio (1991: 159–60). Another strategic connection between metric manipulations in different movements occurs in Mozart's String Quartet in B-flat major, K. 589. The rhythmical dissonance represented by the syncopation in m. 24 of the first movement and later elaborated into a metrical dissonance in mm. 154–57 (Example 5.7) is echoed in the trio of the third movement by three rhythmical dissonances in mm. 23, 25, and 27, followed by Mozart's most spectacular general pause (Example 7.2). Again, the harmonic context is strikingly similar, since all these rhythmical dissonances—except the last in Example 7.2—are set in a progression from the tonic to the dominant represented by a diminished triad. Without this similarity, the connection of the metric manipulations in the third movement to those heard previously in the first movement would have almost certainly been missed by the listener after the intervening second movement. This last remark helps to corroborate an earlier point: The larger the distance between metric manipulations, the more necessary is motivic-thematic similarity to secure strategic connections between them. To claim a strategic connection between any two syncopations across a quartet cycle would be very questionable, to say the least.[2]

Example 7.1. Haydn, String Quartet in F major, "The Dream," Op. 50 No. 5/iv, mm. 41–45.

1. In the minuet, this is the final cadence, in the finale—the *Kadenz* of the exposition. Later in the finale, *imbroglio* and sequence occur once again in mm. 73–74, during the standing on the dominant that follows the *Halbkadenz* and seems to prepare the recapitulation. Since this *Halbkadenz* is in A minor instead of F major, further tonal and metrical adventures are necessary to bring the music back to the main key.
2. The reliance of strategic connections between metric manipulations occurring in different movements on motivic-thematic connections explains why metrical strategies embracing more than one movement are unique. In eighteenth-century cyclic compositions, motivic connections between movements are hardly ever observed. According to Webster, "the intermovemental motivic links adduced for Haydn are so elementary and local as to fail to support any claim of unity" (1991: 266). Neither for Webster nor for Haimo do they play any significant role in cyclic integration. Haimo (1995: 69) classifies movements that share similarities in themes as having only "moderate" intermovemental relationship. For a critical discussion of the idea of cyclic integration in reference to the musical repertory of the late eighteenth century, see Hoyt (1997).

Example 7.2. Mozart, String Quartet in B-flat major, K. 589/iii, Trio, mm. 23–35.

7.1. Haydn, String Quartet in C Major, Op. 50 No. 2, First Movement

The first movement of Haydn's C-major quartet, Op. 50 No. 2, is a fascinating example of a metrical strategy carried out in two strands. One of them consists in preparation and gradual activation of metrical dissonance. The other is related to changes of the metrical level of *Taktteile*. While the former strand influences several details of motivic-thematic process, the latter brings out more general contrasts between formal sections. Together, they are at play uninterruptedly from the beginning to the end of the movement and cross at the movement's high point.

The strand of metrical strategy related to metrical dissonance originates in the principal theme. The adventures to come are announced by metrically disturbing features of the accompaniment and the melody (Example 7.3). The "oom-pah-pah" accompaniment evokes the waltz topic of the theme. As was observed by Krebs (1999: 92) and indicated in the discussion of the finale of Haydn's Op. 50 No. 3 in chapter 5, this and other related forms of accompaniment contain latent metrical dissonances between the bass and the middle voices. Initially, in Op. 50 No. 2 this metrically dissonant potential of the theme is not active because both components of the accompaniment are perceived within one auditory stream. Despite the rather large registral distance between them, this perception arises due to the

Example 7.3. Haydn, String Quartet in C major, Op. 50 No. 2/i, mm. 1–42.

(continued)

Example 7.3. cont.

complementary rhythm: the "pah-pah" repetitions in the middle voices fall within pauses between the "oom" strokes of the bass. This changes only in m. 5. The fact that this time the bass note is not interrupted by a pause but prolonged for two measures causes it to turn into an auditory stream in its own right. As a consequence, the middle voices are detached from the bass, and the initial accent falling on the first "pah" acquires greater weight. This moment is brought into prominence by two dynamic accents *forzando* assigned to the bass and the middle voices. The rhythmical dissonance between them momentarily reveals the metrical conflict inherent in the accompaniment. For the time being, however, this conflict is immediately calmed. The "oom-pah-pah" accompaniment disappears and the *fz* in m. 7 emphasizes the notated downbeat.

The other seed of corruption is planted in the theme's melody: the syncopation in m. 3. Interestingly, this metrical disturbance results from an earlier melodic surprise. After the simple diatonic turn of the first violin in mm. 1–2, played *sotto voce*—as if hummed—against the relaxed accompaniment based on the plain C-major triad, the chromatic step to C♯ at the beginning of m. 3 sounds like a "slip of the bow." The C♯ occurs in place of D as its lower neighbor and postpones the D to the weak second beat of the measure.[3] Note that this syncopation coincides with the reentrance of the middle voices after a pause, strengthening the metrically dissonant potential of the "oom-pah-pah" accompaniment on the way from its harmless occurrence in m. 1 to the striking rhythmical dissonance in m. 5. Another melodic surprise comes with the F, which occurs in place of E in m. 5. Without these two inflections, the melody would have formed a sequential pattern consisting of the structural pitches C, D, and E ($\hat{1}$–$\hat{2}$–$\hat{3}$) prolonged by means of their lower neighbors, as shown in Example 7.4. The F of m. 5 is surprising not only in comparison with this normative version of the melody but also with the first inflection contained in m. 3. If then the pitch taken by the first violinist was too low, now it is too high, reaching to the upper neighbor of the structural pitch E. This second surprise does not result in a metrical disturbance, however, since the appoggiatura represented by F is held for one measure and resolved to E only on the downbeat of m. 6. Through this durational accent in m. 5, combined with *fz* (dynamic accent), highest pitch (melodic accent), and dissonance (harmonic accent), the melody helps the bass to maintain the notated meter threatened by the middle voices.

Example 7.4. Normative version of the melody from Haydn, String Quartet in C major, Op. 50 No. 2/i, mm. 1–6.

The metrically dissonant potential of the accompaniment is activated during the varied repetition of the theme starting from m. 21. The bass strokes are now eliminated so that the accompaniment consists only of the "pah-pah" repetitions of the middle voices. Consequently, the default metrical properties of these voices, determined by initial accents, come to the fore. This, in turn, strengthens the antimetrical effect of the syncopation contained in the melody, which coincides with the entrance of the middle voices in m. 23. In m. 25 the juxtaposition of *forzandi* weights more in favor of the weak beat than it did in m. 5 owing not only to the absence of the bass but also to the reentrance of the cello. Having played the bass strokes in the original version of the theme and been silent so far in the course of the theme's varied repetition, the cello now joins the middle voices. It does so, however, not with C but with C♯. This surprise and the dissonant character of the resulting diminished triad cause a strong harmonic accent.

3. For the role played by this and other prominent occurrences of C♯ in the cyclic integration of Op. 50 No. 2, see Sutcliffe (1992: 81–83).

True, harmonic surprises caused by deviations from the original version of the theme have occurred already: Whereas in mm. 1–6 each harmony continued for two measures, the harmonies initiated in mm. 21 and 23 change to their respective dominants in mm. 22 and 24.[4] By m. 25 the listener has learned to expect such changes, but now it is the initial harmony that is varied. Again, as in the original version of the theme, the strongest exposition of the metrical conflict precedes its total liquidation. Starting from m. 26 the metrical dissonance disappears, and the strand of metrical strategy related to it will not be resumed for a long time.

The other strand of Haydn's metrical strategy can also be traced back to the beginning of the movement. The time signature 3/4 suggests that *Taktteile* are represented by quarters, but initially the notated meter does not correspond to the composed meter. Rather than in 3/4, the theme starts in 6/4 notated in double measures. *Taktteile* are thus represented by dotted half notes. Every *Taktteil* appears in the notation as one measure, and every *Takt* as two measures. Note how this qualifies the tempo marking Vivace on the score: This marking concerns the swift pace of quarters as *Taktteile* in 3/4 meter. In 6/4 meter, by contrast, the pace of the dotted half notes is rather lazy, corresponding to the soft dynamics *piano* and *sotto voce*.[5] In mm. 1–6 this slow pace is clearly enhanced by perceptual factors—bass strokes and harmonic changes—that mark the downbeats of the composed measures. If 6/4 was retained until the end of the theme, the theme would be five measures long (*Fünfer*). Yet, from m. 7, both the bass and the harmonic rhythm accelerate. Is this still 6/4 or does the meter change to 3/4? This question is not easily answered because the caesura in m. 9 does not clearly confirm either meter. The following measure is not empty, as it would have to be if the meter were 6/4, nor does it start a new phrase, as it should in 3/4. What follows is instead an enigmatic gesture made up of the two notes G–E (mm. 10–11). Sutcliffe (1992: 77) characterizes this gesture as a pantomimic reaction by the players to the oddity of the theme, as if to say "Did we really mean that?" This is an apt characterization, although the reasons for it may go beyond those listed by Sutcliffe. The theme is odd not merely because it is "asymmetrical and loosely presented," as he points out, but because it closes with a *Kadenz*. According to eighteenth-century authors, a *Kadenz* in the main key should occur only at the very end of a piece. Kirnberger expressly criticizes the bad style of the composers who "at the very beginning of a piece close again in the principal tonic after two or four measures, and hence stand again exactly where they began" (1982: 406 [1786: 139]).[6] In the light of this

4. Harmonic accents caused by these last changes fall on weak beats of 6/4 meter, which, as will be explained below, is the composed meter of the theme. As such, they pose weak challenges to this meter, which, however, remain without strategic consequences for the further course of the movement.
5. The importance of the metrical level of *Taktteile* for proper interpretation of tempo markings is emphasized by Maurer Zenck (2001: 85–92, 126–40).
6. Even though in the musical repertory of the time a *Kadenz* in the main key does occasionally occur at the end of a principal theme (see Budday 1983: 28), it is not normally used to close the first phrase.

remark the pantomimic gesture of mm. 10–11 is likely meant to express consternation on the part of the players about an unconventional move on the part the composer. Technically speaking, this gesture is a parenthesis (*Parenthese*). In the eighteenth-century, the parenthesis denoted "something foreign that attracts the attention in a special way" and distinguishes itself from the context of preceding and following music in regard of dynamics or texture (409 [143]). In mm. 10–11 texture is reduced to unison, and the dynamics drops to *piano*. If the composed meter were 3/4, the parenthesis would be two measures long. In 6/4 meter it would span one measure and form an upbeat motive: weak–strong. While either metrical interpretation is plausible, it is the 6/4 meter that will be confirmed when the same motive returns later in the movement (see below). In this meter, measure 12 is again metrically weak, despite the dynamic accent *fz*—which thus creates a rhythmical dissonance in 6/4—and measure 13, with the onset of the G-major harmony, is strong. The regular alternation of strong and weak beats of 6/4 meter, notated as measures of 3/4 meter, continues until the end of this section. There, 6/4 meter is ultimately confirmed by the caesura falling in m. 17 and the incorrect overhang reaching to m. 18. In mm. 19–20 the dominant triad of mm. 17–18 is repeated *piano* and turned into dominant seventh in first inversion.

Note, however, that the section started at m. 12, after the parenthesis, is not a new phrase. Rather, the virtuoso scales and broken triads over the prolonged dominant harmony form an appendix (*Anhang*) to the theme. From the point of view of eighteenth-century music theory this yields an eccentric phrase construction with an appendix detached from the preceding phrase by a parenthesis and a pause.[7] Making this construction even more eccentric is the harmonic relation between the caesuras closing the phrase and the appendix. Normally, an appendix serves to strengthen the closure achieved by a phrase. An appendix after a phrase that has closed with a *Kadenz* must thus close with another *Kadenz*.[8] Yet the secondary dominant in m. 12 causes a sudden harmonic twist from the tonic to the dominant so that the caesura reached at the end of the appendix is a *Quintabsatz*.[9] The appendix starting at m. 32, after the varied repetition of the theme, contains not one but two such twists, the second of which leads to the *Quintabsatz* in the dominant (m. 35). In this way, the secondary key of G major is reached without any proper modulation. The dominant harmony is then prolonged in mm. 35–42. In comparison with mm. 13–16, new materials of this section are the melodic motives in the second violin and the viola. It is worth noting that the upbeats of these motives are derived from the "pah-pah" repetitions of the accompaniment

7. A pause between a phrase and an appendix is customary after an *Absatz*. After a *Kadenz*, an appendix always starts in elision with the preceding phrase (Koch 1983: 45–51 [1787: 435–47]). In neither case is it to be detached from this phrase by a parenthesis.
8. Exceptions to this rule include deceptive cadence, as well as *Grundabsatz* used by way of an improper cadential formula (Koch 1983: 48–51 [1787: 441–47]).
9. According to Koch (1983: 49 [1787: 443]), a *Quintabsatz* after a *Kadenz* can occur only at the end of a piece. In such a case, it is usually marked with a fermata and "presupposes another piece immediately following upon it." In *Versuch*, Koch calls this special type of *Quintabsatz* a half cadence (*Halbkadenz*). See note 16 in chapter 3 here.

previously played by the same instruments. However, in the context of the virtuoso scales of the first violin and the cello, these repetitions lose their metrically dissonant character. The last motive is left incomplete and forms an incorrect overhang corresponding to that witnessed previously in mm. 17–18. In this way, the motivic connection of the overhang in mm. 17–18 to the "pah-pah" repetitions, at first not at all obvious, is now revealed.

The formal boundary between the first and the second group of the exposition is marked by the change of the metrical level of *Taktteile*. Against Haydn's habit of monothematicism, cultivated in all other sonata-form first movements of Opus 50 (Sutcliffe 1992: 77),[10] the second group of this movement is launched not with a restatement of the principal theme but with a new theme: an easygoing *Ländler* in 3/4 (Example 7.5). The change from 6/4 to 3/4 is clearly indicated by perceptual factors. Whereas at the beginning of the principal theme bass strokes and harmonic changes occurred once in two notated measures, thus marking downbeats of composed 6/4 measures, now they articulate every measure. At the same time, the lowest metrical level consistently articulated by attacks shifts down from quarters to eighths.[11] All these changes take place in the accompaniment. By contrast to the principal theme, however, the accompaniment of the subsidiary theme is completely regular. Metric irregularities are also eliminated from the melody. The upbeat repetitions (mm. 43, 47), taken over by the first violin from the melodic motives played by the second violin and the viola in mm. 35–42, are as harmless as before because of strong phenomenal accents falling on downbeats: The first upbeat is followed by a large intervallic skip and durational accent on the downbeat of m. 44; the second by a dynamic accent *fz* on the downbeat of m. 48. Metrical irregularities start occurring again from m. 51. First, the consistent articulation of eighths is terminated so that the lowest metrical level shifts back to quarters. Then a dynamic accent *fz* occurs. In m. 52 the *Metrum* based on the metrical level of *Taktteile*, represented by quarters, is interrupted by a half note and in m. 54 by a pause. Finally, just before the cadence, the upbeat to m. 57 brings another dynamic accent *fz*.

If the cadence was completed, its caesura would fall at the beginning of m. 58 and last only one measure, thus confirming 3/4 meter. Yet, instead, the cadence is "evaded" and another phrase follows, leading to another cadence.[12] During this

10. In Op. 50 No. 4, the sonata-form first movement is shifted to the second place in the cycle. The quartet starts with a set of variations.
11. This may be interpreted as a shift of the metrical level of *Metrum* from *Taktglieder* of 6/4 to *Taktglieder* of 3/4 meter. According to this interpretation, the termination of the consistent articulation of eighths in m. 51, discussed below, would cause an interruption of *Metrum*. However, Koch's remarks about *Metrum* based on the metrical level of *Taktglieder* concern only slow tempos. It is doubtful whether he would admit of this phenomenon in tempo Vivace.
12. The concept of "evaded cadence" was introduced by Caplin (1987) and further developed by Schmalfeldt (1992). It denotes a cadence whose ending is deleted and replaced by a new beginning. In Schmalfeldt's account, the rest in the bass, the substitution of first-inversion tonic for the expected root position, and the sudden leap in the melody—all of them observed in m. 58—are straightforward signals of cadential disruption represented by the evaded cadence.

Example 7.5. Haydn, String Quartet in C major, Op. 50 No. 2/i, mm. 43–84.

(continued)

Example 7.5. cont.

phrase the "pah-pah" repetitions return in the accompaniment. Note that they coincide with pitch repetitions in the melody that, however, acquire now a new function: rather then upbeats, they form central parts of melodic motives. That this metrically dissonant pattern of the melody and the accompaniment does not succeed in disturbing the listener's metric perception is because it takes only two measures. After the long chord filling in m. 60, which causes another interruption of *Metrum*, the cadence is evaded again in m. 63. It may be noted that the two evaded cadences in the secondary key correspond to the two premature cadences in the main key, closing the principal theme (mm. 8–9) and its varied repetition (mm. 28–29), respectively. Indeed, the cadential formulas in mm. 57 and 62 are identical to those in mm. 8 and 28 (see Example 7.3).[13] After the second evaded cadence, the phrase of mm. 58–62 starts "one more time" at m. 63,[14] but this time the metrically dissonant character of the "pah-pah" repetitions is countered by

13. One might be tempted to draw the conclusion that in either case these formulas confirm 3/4 meter; but this conclusion would be false. What indicates the metrical level of *Taktteile* is only the location of the caesura note, not the length and location of the "note of preparation" and the "cadential note," which can be augmented or diminished (Koch 1983: 39 [1787: 421]). It follows that the same cadential formula may be used in different meters.
14. As demonstrated by Schmalfeldt (1992: 6), the "one more time" (OMT) technique is closely related to evaded cadences and performs the role of extending the cadential function.

dynamic accents *fz* placed on downbeats. More significant, the strategy of postponing the structural cadence of the exposition now enters a new phase. In the notation this is already visible in mm. 64–65, where in the first violin part the pitch corresponding to the D♯ in mm. 59–60 is respelled as E♭.[15] Consequences of this enharmonic change become audible starting from m. 66, where the phrase departs from its original course and starts journeying into the flat side of the tonal pitch space. During this journey pitch repetitions occur again, but their function changes back to that of melodic upbeats. Actually, the motives played by the first violin in mm. 70–77 are analogous to those in mm. 35–42 (Example 7.3).[16] In mm. 79–80 they pass to the second violin and viola and in mm. 81–82 to the bass. In the end, however, the tonal journey does not lead back to the cadence (*Kadenz*) but to a *Quintabsatz* in the secondary key. This caesura has already been reached earlier in m. 41. By reaching it once again in m. 83, Haydn prepares the secondary key, as it were, for the second time. The listener's sense of "having been here before" is heightened by the melodic figure of the second violin in m. 84, which is identical to that of the cello in m. 42.[17]

Whereas at m. 43 the second group of the exposition was launched with a new—subsidiary—theme, at m. 85 Haydn proceeds in his habitual way by restating the principal theme of the movement in the dominant. As in its original presentation in the tonic, the theme is in 6/4 meter, but, as a matter of fact, the return to this meter has already taken place earlier. This is attested to by the "empty bar" following the caesura of m. 83. Screening the music back from the caesura, one discovers that the metrical change from 3/4 to 6/4 happens along with the enharmonic change that starts the tonal journey. More precisely, it coincides with the second interruption of the *Metrum* by the long dotted-half-note chord in m. 65. In the following measures the *Metrum* remains on the level of quarters, now representing *Taktglieder* of 6/4 meter, yet the shift of the metrical level of *Taktteile* is indicated by the deceleration of the rhythmical values of the accompaniment. Apart from occasional imitations of melodic motives, from m. 65 on the lower parts move consistently in dotted half notes. Incidentally, these melodic motives themselves have been previously associated with 6/4 meter.[18] Note, however, that, in comparison with mm. 35–42, the motives of mm. 70–83 shift their metrical position. In mm. 35–42 pitch repetitions occur *after* the downbeats of the

15. An illuminating characterization of this moment from the point of view of the roles played by individual performers is offered by Floyd and Margaret Grave (2006: 240), who also point to the harmonic consequences of respelling D♯ as E♭: In their words, the need for the former dissonance to resolve "has magically vanished in the process."
16. The motives in mm. 66–67 are derived directly from the "pah-pah" repetitions of the accompaniment. Accordingly, in m. 67 they are played by the middle voices.
17. Grave and Grave (2006: 242) consider this figure to be influenced by Mozart and compare it with m. 30 of Mozart's String Quartet in C major, K. 465/i.
18. The same applies to the "pah-pah" repetitions (mm. 66–67) derived from the accompaniment of the principal theme. See note 16.

composed measures, falling in notated mm. 35, 37, and 39. Although in 3/4 meter these repetitions looked like upbeats—and so they have been designated so far for the sake of convenience—in reality they still belonged to the downbeats of 6/4 meter.[19] By contrast, the pitch repetitions in mm. 70–77 in the first violin part are real upbeats, since they occur *before* the downbeats of the composed measures falling in notated mm. 71, 73, 75, and 77. The motives shift back to their original metrical position only in mm. 79–83, when they migrate to the lower parts. The last motive, played by the cello, receives an extra note that reaches the downbeat in m. 83. A similar extra note has occurred in m. 41. In both cases the extra note marks the arrival at the *Quintabsatz* in the secondary key.[20]

The metrically dissonant characteristics of the principal theme, brought into relief in its original presentation in the tonic, are concealed during its restatement in the dominant, started at m. 85 (Example 7.6). In the melody, played on this occasion by the second violin, the syncopation in m. 87 is countered by the dynamic accent *fz* placed on the downbeat. Another accent falls on the downbeat of m. 89. In the accompaniment the "pah-pah" repetition occurs only once, in m. 85, yet it is immediately twisted into a melodic motive equivalent to those heard in mm. 70–83 and earlier in mm. 35–42. The second measure of this motive (m. 86), then repeated (m. 88), is inverted and moves in parallel fourths and sixths with the melody. This reveals its pedigree. As it turns out, the melodic motives of mm. 35–42 and 70–83 are composed of two different elements of the principal theme: the "pah-pah" repetitions of the accompaniment and the bending neighbor-note figures of the melody played in inversion.

Undisturbed by metrical irregularities, the theme drives toward the cadence. Yet, as it was the case with the subsidiary theme, the cadence is postponed. In m. 93 the dominant seventh resolves deceptively to first-inversion tonic rather than to the expected root-position form.[21] The next approach toward the cadence is interrupted by a pause in m. 95 and, with it, the *Metrum* based on quarters is also interrupted. After the pause, what remains of the full four-part texture of the string quartet is only a curved chromatic line of the first violin, soaring and lonely

19. In his composition handbook (1782–93), Koch alternates between the view of downbeat (*guter Taktteil*) and upbeat (*schlechter Taktteil*) as points in time or time spans between such points. The former view is implied in his discussion of *Metrum*, summarized in chapter 3; the latter underlies his idea of meter (*Takt*). Here I refer to the latter view.

20. A shift in the metrical position of a phrase or motive that results in its last note falling on a downbeat is mentioned by Abbé Georg Joseph Vogler as a means of achieving closure (1778: 377–78; see Grave 1985: 41–42). Recently, this phenomenon was observed by Rothstein (2008: 139–41 ex. 5.23) in the finale of Haydn's String Quartet Op. 71 No. 3. But the examples shown by Vogler and Rothstein are notated in compound measures. The aim of such shifts is thus to reach not metrical but hypermetrical downbeat. Metrical downbeat—the second of the two downbeats contained in each compound measure—was already reached in the first place.

21. For Schmalfeldt, a cadential progression leading to first-inversion tonic forms the "evaded cadence (EC): deceptive type" (1992: 13). Because the first-inversion tonic in m. 93 starts a new section, this moment would be interpreted by her either as an elided form of such a cadence or as a genuine evaded cadence. As she observes (20), from the purely theoretic viewpoint, clear distinction between these two types of cadences is not always possible.

Example 7.6. Haydn, String Quartet in C major, Op. 50 No. 2/i, mm. 85–106.

in high register (mm. 96–97). This drastic reduction of texture makes mm. 96–97 sound like a parenthesis. Yet they are not a parenthesis, since the melodic descent from e^3 to a^2 forms a necessary link between the pre-dominant harmony of m. 95 and the dominant seventh of m. 98. Nonetheless, the normative version of this link would consist of only one measure, as shown in Example 7.7a. Its extension to two measures causes metrical irregularity (Example 7.7b): In 6/4 m. 95 is a strong beat; m. 97 should thus be strong again, yet it is weak. The next strong beat occurs only in m. 98, along with the harmonic change and the restoration of the full four-part texture. Note that m. 96, at first perceived as weak, becomes strong in the light of the following measure. This is because m. 96 starts a new type of texture. When the solo line of the first violin continues over the bar line into m. 97, the beginning of m. 96 receives an initial accent coinciding with the single stroke of the second violin. The retrospective change of metric perception is indicated in Example 7.7b with the backward arrow. The comparison of Example 7.7b with its recomposition in Example 7.7a suggests that the solo line in mm. 96–97 illustrates another slip of the first violinist—this time not of the bow but of a finger failing to reach directly from e^3 down to b^2 and then making it up in smaller chromatic steps.

Example 7.7. Recomposition (a) and metric analysis of the original version (b) of mm. 93–100 from Haydn, String Quartet in C major, Op. 50 No. 2/i.

(a)

(b)
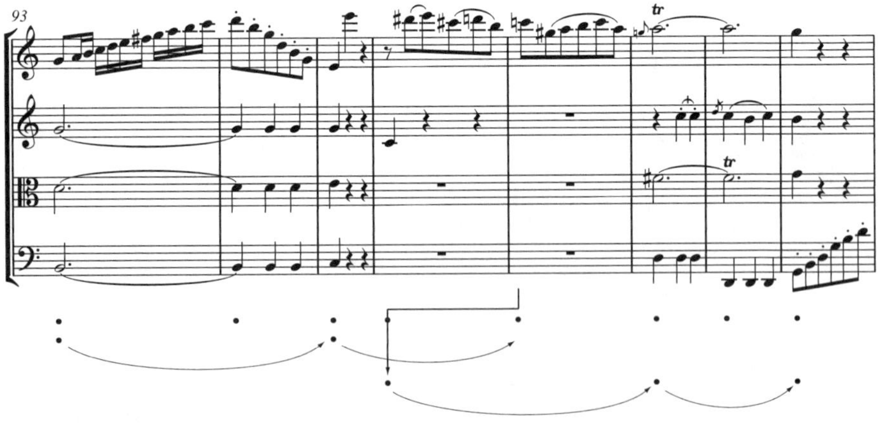

After that, the meter is again regular. Measure 99, prolonging the dominant of m. 98, is weak, and m. 100, with the resolution of the dominant to the tonic, is strong. As a result, starting from m. 98 the phase of 6/4 meter is shifted by half a measure, a shift that is masked by the notation in 3/4 meter. Against the shifted metrical grid, the melodic motive interwoven in the course of the cadence by the second violin occurs in the metrical position it had before the caesuras in mm. 83 and 41. As it did there, it receives an extra note that reaches the caesura in m. 100 representing the structural cadence (*Kadenz*) of the exposition, awaited by the listener since m. 58. The following measures bring back the motive of the parenthesis in mm. 10–11, presenting it now within the main stream of the music and providing it with an accompaniment. The metric profile of this motive is thus explained: it is an upbeat motive proceeding from a weak to a strong beat of 6/4 meter.[22] This follows not only from the phase of 6/4 meter that has been established during the cadence but also from greater harmonic stability of tonics over dominants in the course of the codetta. The last notated measure of the first reprise (m. 106) is strong. Since the movement starts with a strong beat, the repetition of the first reprise elicits another shift of 6/4 meter. The same phenomenon takes place after the repetition, when the music moves ahead to the second reprise.[23]

Having been suspended for a longer time, the strand of metrical strategy related to metrical dissonance is resumed in the development. The first phase of the development is a fugato based on the principal theme (Example 7.8). In application to the waltz-like melody of the theme, fugal procedure sounds like a paradox. At the same time, it sheds a new light on several characteristics of this melody that I pointed out earlier. The fact that the melody is based on a sequential pattern is typical of fugue. Inflections of this pattern, apparently accidental in the course of a diatonic dance tune, turn out to be essential aspects of a chromatic fugue subject. The soft dynamics is felt not so much as relaxed but rather as a sign of concentration related to the abstract and unexpressive character of fugue.[24] The aura of paradox enveloping the subject is heightened by the countersubject being played *staccato*. It is precisely the countersubject, featuring prominent second beats, that most significantly contributes to the progress of the metrical strategy. Not only does it start on the second beat (initial accent), it contains a syncopation (durational accent) falling on the second beat of the second measure and forming a suspension that is resolved on the second beat of the

22. In other words, it forms an end-accented group. Such groups were found typical of closing themes by Temperley (2003). Because the end-accented groups Temperley discusses are not one-measure motives but phrases spanning several measures, the final accent of such groups is not only metrical but hypermetrical.

23. The Peters edition has *fz* rather than *f* assigned to dotted half notes in all instrumental parts in mm. 101–6, but those dynamic markings appear in only a small minority of sources.

24. On chromatic and sequential fugue subjects, see Kirkendale (1979: 94, 109–16). As Kirkendale points out, uniform *piano* dynamics was particularly typical of eighteenth-century "galantry fugues" (76). Sutcliffe also has commented on the "whiff of a contrapuntist's tag" contained in the melody of the waltz theme (1992: 77) but he does not explain it in detail.

third measure.[25] The resolution receives an initial accent as the first note in this measure and starts a sequential repetition of the preceding incise one step higher. While the syncopation is not repeated, the second beat of the fourth measure retains the melodic accent, which then reappears in the fifth measure as a part of a descending sequence. After another suspension, the countersubject ends with a resolution on the second beat of the seventh measure. These features of the countersubject strengthen the metrically dissonant characteristics of the subject, including not only the syncopation in the third measure (m. 109) but also the first attacks in the second and fourth measures (mm. 108, 110) which have not been a noticeable source of metrical disturbance until now. When the subject enters in the cello (m. 113), the same effect is produced by its superposition on the countersubject in the first violin. After the pause, the second violin enters again on the second beat of m. 114. The list of antimetrical factors in this section is completed by pitch repetitions initiated on second beats in the viola (m. 113) and second violin (m. 115). These are discrete motivic allusions, respectively, to the "pah-pah" repetition in the accompaniment of the principal theme and to the melodic turn of the first violin in m. 69, itself derived from the "pah-pah" repetition. So as to restrain the antimetrical effect of all these factors, in the two first entries of the theme the composer places dynamic accents *fz* on the downbeats of mm. 109, 111, and 115, as he previously did in the course of the subsidiary theme in mm. 85–92. The third entry of the theme, starting at m. 117, is played by the first violin and the viola in parallel tenths without *fz*. Dynamic accents occur again in the fourth entry played by the second violin from m. 120. Note that this last entry starts in a different phase from the preceding ones. It is an instance of *imitatio per thesin et arsin* notated in double measures and thus brings about yet another shift of composed 6/4 meter by half a measure.[26]

At this point, however, the polyphonic texture is interrupted by the return of the "oom-pah-pah" waltz accompaniment (mm. 120–25). Starting from m. 126, the entrance of the theme in the first violin is accompanied by the arpeggiations originating in the coda (mm. 100–6). At m. 132 the "pah-pah" accompaniment returns without the bass strokes so that its metrically dissonant character becomes more palpable. Ironically, this accompaniment occurs along with one of the most sophisticated contrapuntal techniques: inversion (mm. 132–36). After the inverted theme has been played by the first violin, it is imitated by the viola (m. 136) and the cello (m. 140). In this way the polyphonic texture is restored. Since the imitative entries happen every fourth measure, they form a stretto. The inverted theme receives no countersubject but only free counterpoints. It is worth observing the correspondence between the pitch repetition in mm. 136–37 in the second violin,

25. As noted by Kirkendale (1979: 114–16), suspensions are typical of contrapuntal writing and represent a particularly characteristic feature of countersubjects.

26. Shifts of entries by half a measure are customary in contrapuntal texture (Grave 1985), but they usually occur in compound meters. Consequently, they have no metrical effect of *imitatio per thesin et arsin*, since strong and weak beats in such entries are not exchanged. Their effect is either hypermetrical or—nil.

Example 7.8. Haydn, String Quartet in C major, Op. 50 No. 2/i, mm. 107–58.

(continued)

Example 7.8. cont.

which is a continuation of the "pah-pah" accompaniment of the earlier section, and that played by the viola in mm. 113–14. At m. 144 the "pah-pah" accompaniment returns once again, along with the original version of the theme. The antimetrical effect of this accompaniment is particularly salient not only because it is played by as many as three instruments but also because it is aligned with two successive syncopations of the melody in mm. 146 and 148. One more syncopation, this time stressing the third beat of the melody, occurs in m. 149. This peculiar fugato, several times interrupted by homophonic passages, leads ultimately to a half cadence in the key of the sixth (m. 151). Whereas the arrival at this cadence causes one more shift of 6/4 meter—if the preceding phase of this meter continued, m. 151 would be weak, but it is strong due to the onset of the dominant harmony—it clears the air of metrical dissonances. The prolongation of the dominant in mm. 151–58 corresponds to that in mm. 35–42 (see Example 7.3).

The second phase of the development, starting at m. 159 (Example 7.9), is based on the subsidiary theme being presented in A minor (mm. 159–62) and then transposed to F major (mm. 163–67). Yet the accompaniment of the theme is terminated in m. 167, and the melody migrates to lower parts. At first (mm. 167–69) it is played in parallel thirds by the second violin and the viola (D minor), enhancing the connection of the upbeat repetition with the "pah-pah" repetition in the accompaniment of the principal theme, originally entrusted to these very instruments. It is then taken over by the viola and the cello in mm. 169–71 (C major) and further repeated in mm. 171–72 (G major). Since the upbeat repetitions occur every second measure, their antimetrical effect becomes palpable, all the more so because in m. 168 one more repetition occurs in the first violin as an echo-imitation of the second violin and the viola. This repetition refers back to m. 85: the first time where the first violin participated in the execution of the "pah-pah" accompaniment. After the arrival at the dominant of the main key in m. 173, the repeated chords in mm. 174–75 recall the incorrect overhang in mm. 17–18 and its echo in mm. 19–20. Would Haydn's intention have been to turn from 3/4 meter to 6/4 meter just one measure before the recapitulation? If yes, the succession of the strong and the weak *Taktteile* of this 6/4 measure nevertheless collides with the hypermeter established earlier by the alternation of strong and weak measures (*Takte*) of 3/4 meter. Consequently, it causes a (hyper)metrical irregularity not associated with the incorrect overhang at its first occurrence.[27]

It is only in the recapitulation that the metrical strategy of this movement achieves its culmination. In place of the varied repetition of the theme, which would have corresponded to mm. 21–29 of the exposition, in mm. 196–213 another polyphonic section occurs, based on the theme's melody (Example 7.10). In this section the metrical dissonance is brought into relief, however, not by a superposition of the subject and the countersubject, as in the polyphonic section of the development in mm. 107–19, but by the superposition of metrically dissonant characteristics of the subject alone in different instrumental parts. The

27. If not, hypermetrical irregularity would arise anyway, because the initial accent attached to the first of the repeated chords in mm. 174–75 makes of it a hypermetrical downbeat in 3/4.

Example 7.9. Haydn, String Quartet in C major, Op. 50 No. 2/i, mm. 159–75.

polyphonic section of mm. 196–213 is a series of canons played by two pairs of instruments. Since, in every pair, the second voice enters a measure after the first, the syncopation contained in the third measure of the theme in one part coincides with the first note after the tie in the second or fourth measure of the theme in the other part. After the first pair of instruments (cello–viola) has played the original version of the theme, further canons follow, in inversion (first violin–second violin, viola–cello) and back in the original (first violin–second violin).[28] This passage of learned polyphony unexpectedly crashes into a homophonic section in which stomping syncopations are chained together to create a harsh metrical dissonance (mm. 214–17). In the two violins the syncopations (durational accents),

28. Each of the canons is an instance of *imitatio per thesin et arsin* in 6/4 meter.

derived from the first violinist's "slip of the bow," are reinforced by *fz* (dynamic accents). In the viola and the cello the "pah-pah" repetitions of the accompaniment are multiplied by double stops. The metrical dissonance of mm. 214–17 thus forms a combination of two metrically disturbing features, contained in the melody and in the accompaniment of the principal theme, respectively, and used by the composer as two different methods of announcing a metrical dissonance in the course of the movement: preparation and activation. Note that this metrical dissonance is indirect. Harmonic changes, which often articulate the notated meter even if all other perceptual factors contradict it, are at this time determined by the accompaniment and so yield harmonic syncopations. Consequently, the notated meter is articulated by no preference factors but only by attacks. The fact that the goal of the process of activation and gradual intensification of the displacement dissonance is represented by an indirect dissonance supports the suggestion made earlier, in chapter 4, that in the eighteenth century indirect metrical dissonances were considered stronger than direct ones because they erased the notated meter more thoroughly from the musical surface. What is particularly interesting about mm. 214–17, however, is that this passage—which forms the goal of one strand of the metrical strategy—is at the same time the point of its crossing with the other strand. In this passage the displacement dissonance goes along with motivic parallelism: it arises from a varied repetition of a single motive derived from the principal theme and heard for the first time in m. 23. Whereas in 6/4—the composed meter of the theme—this motive spanned half a measure and represented only part of an incise, the very fact of repetition turns it into a one-measure-long imperfect incise in 3/4.[29] The resulting change of meter from 6/4 to 3/4 is correlated with the change of topic from learned style to a jovial *Ländler*. While in the most immediate context of the preceding canons this last topic brings a dramatic contrast between high and low style, in the broader perspective of the entire movement it completes the gradual descent in the affective and social hierarchy of dances from the noble waltz of the principal theme through the graceful *Ländler* of the subsidiary theme to a heavy-footed peasant dance.

The crux of the metrical strategy, falling in mm. 214–17, is also the formal and energetic climax of the movement. After the notated meter is restored in mm. 218–24, the rest of the recapitulation retraces the equivalent portion of the exposition and replays the metric adventures described earlier.[30] One last point worth mentioning occurs at the very end. Transposed to the main key of C major, the codetta starts with the melodic motive G–E (mm. 285–86) and so renders the pantomimic gesture of the parenthesis from mm. 10–11 on its original pitches.

29. I have mentioned the role played by repetition in delineation of incises in connection with the finale of Op. 50 No. 3. See note 50 in chapter 6.

30. The only slight deviation from the original course of the exposition happens in mm. 275–77 of the recapitulation. Because the tonic triad in m. 275 is in root position, it forms a perfect authentic cadence rather than a deceptive cadence, as was the case in m. 93. The ascending virtuoso scale, elided with the cadence, is played by the second violin and then in parallel octaves by the viola and the cello before it is taken over to the highest register by the first violin in m. 277.

Example 7.10. Haydn, String Quartet in C major, Op. 50 No. 2/i, mm. 196–224.

7.2. Haydn, String Quartet in F Minor, Op. 55 No. 2, Finale

Another example of a metrical strategy in two strands is the finale of Haydn's Op. 55 No. 2. As in the first movement of Op. 50 No. 2, one of these strands is related to metrical dissonance, whereas the other consists in changes of the metrical level of *Taktteile*. The mutual relationship of these strands to each other as well as their connections to the formal design of the movement and to its musical topics are quite different, however.

This time metrical dissonance is foreshadowed in the theme's melody only (mm. 1–6; Example 7.11). It has its origin in the slurs joining the eighth notes across metrical divisions established by dotted quarters. As was pointed out in chapter 5, the default metrical properties of such slurred motives differ from the metrical structure assigned to them in the framework of the notated meter: the first note is stronger than the second due to the initial accent falling on the beginning of the slur. In the present example, the second notes under the slurs are additionally weakened by the *staccato* articulation. At the same time, first notes are strengthened by harmonic accents because they form dissonances within their underlying harmonies: In mm. 1–4 each slur starts with an auxiliary tone resolving on the second note. Similar auxiliary tones were observed in the finale of Op. 50 No. 3 (Example 5.10a). In Op. 55 No. 2 they take the form of chromatic inflections slurred to the following diatonic tones, which could be easily played as slides on a single finger yielding small instrumental *portamenti*. Although this manner of playing is not indicated on the score and was actually criticized by eighteenth- and nineteenth-century writers (see Brown 1999: 560–65), the very zeal of their criticism betrays that it was frequently adopted by professional violinists, and was supposedly quite common among folk-band musicians.[31] This points to the musical topic of the theme. Its rustic flavor, corresponding to the expressive character commonly associated with 6/8, represents "low pastoral" (Monelle 2006). The topic can be identified even more precisely when one takes into account that during Haydn's years in Eszterháza folk bands in Hungary consisted almost exclusively of Gypsies and that chromatic inflections in diatonic Hungarian melodies were among most remarkable features of the "Gypsy" style of performance. The mix of Gypsy and Hungarian national elements was known in the late eighteenth century as *ongherese* or *style hongrois*.[32] Apparently, it is this style that stands behind the metrical dissonance in Haydn's theme.

Yet the metrical dissonance is not steadfast. Rather, it is pulled back and forth between the eighth-note slurred motives and more conventional sixteenth-note figures in mm. 2 and 4. Besides, this dissonance is quite weak because antimetrical characteristics of the melody are neutralized by the accompaniment

31. One of the eighteenth-century professional violinists who frequently used *portamenti* was Niccolò Mestrino, who worked at Eszterháza from 1780 to 1785. Further historical evolution of this manner in the nineteenth century is discussed by Raymond Monelle (2007). As he indicates, new Romantic aesthetics led ultimately to appreciation of instrumental *portamenti* in both solo and orchestral performances and to their deliberate exploitation by composers in the construction of melodic themes.
32. Characteristics of this style and its role in Western art music of the eighteenth and nineteenth centuries are discussed by Bellman (1993, 1998).

Example 7.11. Haydn, String Quartet in F minor, Op. 55 No. 2/iv, mm. 1–20.

clearly articulating the notated meter. At first glance, it may appear that the metrical dissonance is thus split between the melody and the accompaniment. Yet on closer inspection it turns out that it is a merged dissonance, since the notated meter is also sustained by certain preference factors contained in the melody. The second note under the slur is repeated so that it receives another type of initial accent embedded in a durational accent (pitch duration). This note is also preferred as metrically strong owing to its greater harmonic stability, which is due to the fact that it brings the resolution of the dissonance represented by the first note.[33] In mm. 5–6 the distribution of preference factors changes in favor of the notated meter. The first notes under the slurs are not strengthened by harmonic accents. Instead, they receive melodic accents (highest pitches), but the following skips down cause the second notes to be stronger than before. At the same time, the strokes of the accompaniment, articulating the notated meter, have longer rhythmical values (quarters). If in mm. 1–4 the metrical dissonance was only weakly perceived, in mm. 5–6 it becomes latent.

An activation and at once a considerable intensification of metrical dissonance takes place during the varied repetition of the theme in mm. 7–12. Yet this dissonance is more complex than that in mm. 1–6. This is because the rhythmical pattern of the accompaniment in mm. 7–10 shifts by one eighth "to the right" in comparison with mm. 1–4. Because the metrical dissonance of the melody, related to the slurred motives, causes a shift of the perceived meter by one eighth "to the left" from the notated meter, the superposition of the melody and the accompaniment yields direct metrical dissonance between two displacement dissonances. This time it is a split dissonance since the perceptual factors articulating the two antimetrical layers are neatly sorted out between the two auditory streams. The primary metrical consonance of the movement, represented by the notated meter, is not at all articulated at the musical surface and hence participates in the metrical dissonance only in an indirect way. It is erased not only from the accompaniment but also from the melody. Note that the pitch repetitions in mm. 7 and 9 are cancelled and replaced by pauses so that the second notes under the slurs receive no initial accents. The strokes of the accompaniment, falling in these very pauses, produce the characteristic stumbling effect of this passage. The complementary rhythm of the melody and the accompaniment is of further consequence for the perception of harmonic changes, in that the auxiliary tones can be easily heard as appoggiaturas wrongly located on weak rather than strong beats and thus implying harmonic changes not aligned with the notated meter. Under these circumstances, the only preference factor that can be said to support the notated meter is greater stability of the harmonic tones in the melody, but it is countered by greater salience of the nonharmonic ones.

As in mm. 2 and 4, the disappearance of the slurred motives from mm. 8 and 10 eliminates the antimetrical layer of the melody, yet this does not dissolve the

33. Harmonic stability and harmonic salience (harmonic accent) pull in different directions here because, in theoretical terms, they form a direct logical opposition. See the discussion at the end of section 2.2.

metrical dissonance. Rather, paradoxically, it makes it even more involved. This happens because the sixteenth-note figures enter now into new relationships with the shifted accompaniment. On the one hand, the initial accents falling on the first sixteenth notes D (m. 8) and C (m. 10) strengthen the initial accents attached to the first attacks of the accompaniment. On the other hand, the terminal accents of the melody, falling on the eighth notes G and F, respectively, collide with the terminal accents of the accompaniment occurring one eighth note later. As a result, they group the four eighth notes in the accompaniment into twos and so impose a touch of grouping dissonance on the displacement dissonance. This grouping dissonance extends backward on the two eighth notes contained in the preceding slurs. The notated meter is restored only in mm. 11–12. The accompaniment shifts back to its original position and aligns with the notated meter. In the melody the pitch repetitions return. The fact that they extend to the accompaniment may be an echo of the earlier displacement: Both the original and the shifted location of the accompaniment strokes now occur side by side.[34]

The course of the theme hitherto suggests a rondo-finale. In fact, it is a typical rondo-theme in both its character and structure. The first phrase (mm. 1–6) forms the first reprise of a small two-reprise form.[35] This explains why it modulates to the dominant and closes with a cadence (*Kadenz*). Only in a small two-reprise form can a modulation to the dominant happen at this early stage. Normally, the repetition of the first reprise would be indicated with a repetition sign and hence literal. That it is varied by Haydn and written out once again in its full length as the second phrase of the theme in mm. 7–12 may have to do with his purpose of imitating a band of incompetent musicians. Would it be going too far to suggest that the shift of the accompaniment in mm. 7–10 illustrates a mistake made by some of the musicians, entering too late by an eighth and then trying to catch up with the rest of the band? The second reprise starts with the quasi-developmental X section (mm. 13–20). The metrical dissonance again becomes more palpable because the slurred motives saturate all instrumental parts. The homogenous texture of the string quartet leaves no room for the accompaniment, and so the probability increases that the first notes under the slurs will be heard as metrically strong appoggiaturas notated on weak beats. This way of hearing is most natural in the bass. As a matter of fact, its chromatically descending line is an inversion of the ascending melody of the theme. Yet the harmonies that arise from the supposed appoggiaturas are not as long as those that result from their resolutions, and the longest of all are the harmonies started on the downbeats of mm. 14 and 16. As in the first reprise (mm. 2 and 4), the notated meter is retrieved near the caesuras.

The two segments closed by these caesuras (mm. 13–14 and 15–16) form a type of rising sequence called the "Monte" (Riepel 1755: 44–45).[36] While this

34. Alternatively, the accompaniment in m. 11 may be considered an echo of the two last eighths in m. 10.

35. For a discussion of the small two-reprise form, see Ratner (1980: 209–16). Apart from short compositions—such as dances, marches, or songs—this form occurs most typically in themes of rondos and variations.

36. A brief discussion of "Monte" is provided by Ratner (1980: 213–14). For a thorough exploration of this model in the light of eighteenth-century Italian *partimenti*, see Gjerdingen (2007: 89–106).

sequence was a typical gambit serving the purpose of modulation in the X section of a small two-reprise form, in the late eighteenth century it was already out of date and for this reason not recommended, unless the transposition of a segment was veiled by its variation. The literal transposition of a segment a tone higher is contemptuously called a "cobbler's patch" (*Schusterfleck*) by Riepel (1757: 81–82) and a *Rosalia* by Koch (1983: 101 [1793: 100]).[37] The fact that the segment of mm. 13–14 is transposed literally by Haydn in mm. 15–16 indicates that, apart from the incompetence of folk-band musicians, his aim in this finale is to imitate the bungling of an incompetent composer. In addition to using the "Monte" in its unveiled form, the bad composer chooses an improper starting point for this type of sequence. Instead of moving from the subdominant to the dominant in order to achieve the *Quintabsatz* of the main key (F major), he starts with the dominant and so arrives at the *Quintabsatz* in the key of the second degree (G minor). The bass pedal D, initiated in the middle of m. 16 and prolonged in m. 17, represents a standing on the dominant in this wrong key. As if noticing his mistake, at the last minute the composer abandons the bass pedal and closes with a cadence (*Kadenz*) in G minor. The way back to the main key is traced in the next two measures in the most unsophisticated way imaginable: The G-minor triad is repeated (m. 19) and then followed directly by F major (m. 20).[38] Embellished with chromatic auxiliary tones of the slurred motives, this harmonic progression sounds as if the musicians are retuning their instruments. Not only was it prohibited by the harmonic rules of the time (see Kirnberger 1982: 292–93 [1776: 14]), it does not lead to the obligatory dominant preparation before the thematic return (Koch 1983: 235 [1793: 399]). The tonic of the main key is reached prematurely in m. 20 and then simply repeated when the theme returns, whereby the entire tension of this moment as at once a thematic and a tonal return is lost.

The return of the theme (mm. 21–26; Example 7.12) takes the process of its deconstruction one step further in comparison with the varied repetition of the first reprise (mm. 7–12). In this process the stumbling effect of the metrical dissonance is intensified to the point of parodic exaggeration. This results from its textural transformation. In the first two segments of the theme (mm. 21–24) the quartet divides into two pairs of instruments—the violins against the viola and the cello—locked in octave doublings. The slurred motives, in mm. 7–10 played by the two violins in parallel thirds and sixths, are thus multiplied in all four instrumental parts and greatly expanded in register. The upper tones are transferred one octave up, the lower tones one and two octaves down. In this way, they come to cover an immense range of more than three octaves. In each pair of instruments the slurs are separated from the following single strokes by large leaps. In the violins the leaps are descending, in the viola and cello ascending. Consequently, the strokes—made up of two interlocked octaves—are more

37. Baker explains that this last term comes from an Italian song, "Rosalia, mia cara," which begins with such a transposition (Koch 1983: 101 n. 23).

38. Note that the progression from G minor to F major in mm. 19–20 is a reversal—in a more rudimentary form—of the progression from F major to G minor within the "Monte" in mm. 13–16.

constrained in register and are perceived as an auditory stream of their own corresponding to the accompaniment in mm. 7–10. The metrical dissonance is again split, but this time the auditory streams are not to be labelled as melody and accompaniment, nor are they assigned to specific instruments. Rather, all instruments participate in both streams.

While the octave doublings continue throughout mm. 21–24, the distinction between the melody and the accompaniment is reintroduced near the caesuras. As in mm. 8 and 10, the metrical displacement dissonance is not dissolved by the disappearance of the slurred motives in mm. 22 and 24 but is combined with grouping dissonance. The duple grouping of eighths, previously imposed by the melody, is now more audible, due to changes of implied harmonies and the harmonic-melodic parallelism in the accompaniment. Apparently, the series of four eighth notes in the viola and the cello, underlying the sixteenth-note figures of the violins, outline single harmonies of G minor (m. 22) and F major (m. 24).[39] Yet, because of the nonharmonic tones F♯ and E inserted in them, the first two eighths of each series (D–F♯, C–E) can be heard as representing the root and the third of the dominants ($\hat{1}$–$\hat{3}$), and the last two eighths (G–B♭, F–A) as the root and the third of their respective tonics ($\hat{1}$–$\hat{3}$).[40] Again, as in mm. 8 and 10, the grouping dissonance attaches to the preceding slurs consisting of two eighth notes. The metrical consonance returns along with the original texture of the theme in the last segment (mm. 25–26). Note that the single strokes of the accompaniment refer back to mm. 5–6 rather than 11–12. The cadence (*Kadenz*) in the main key marks the structural end of the second reprise.

After the music has reached the cadence, the listener expects that the second reprise (mm. 13–26) will be literally repeated or, perhaps, varied, as was the case with the first reprise. What follows instead is a codetta. The slurred motives, alternating in pairs of instruments, imitate horn calls (mm. 27–28). In this new topical guise, the antimetrical effect of these motives is strengthened due to the greater harmonic stability of the tonics over the dominants. By contrast to the last segments of the thematic return (mm. 25–26) and of the theme (mm. 5–6 and 11–12), the last segment of the codetta does not restore the notated meter, nor does it return to the original texture. Rather, the slurred motives continue in three instrumental parts and lead to a particularly strong metrical surprise: It is as if the composer replaced a slur with a tie and notated its cumulated duration as a quarter. The result is an outright syncopation in m. 29. Its surprising effect is all the stronger in that it coincides with a dynamic accent *fz*. The notated meter is restored only by the cadential formula in m. 30. But even this cadence does not yet bring the second

39. The first two segments of the theme thus retrace the progression from G minor to F major that has been exposed before the thematic return in mm. 19–20, which in turn forms a reversal of the "Monte" in mm. 13–16. This means that the theme of the finale is based on another typical eighteenth-century gambit: the "Fonte" (Riepel 1755: 46–47). See note 12 in chapter 4 here.

40. Other instances of melodic parallelism in the bass—which, however, accord with triple grouping of eighths—occur between A–B♭–D and F♯–G–B♭ in mm. 21/22 and between G♯–A–C and E–F–A in mm. 23/24. Within the intervallic structure of the second groups, the semitone steps F♯–G and E–F correspond to the slurred motives A–B♭ and G♯–A of the first groups, even though they are devoid of slurs.

Example 7.12. Haydn, String Quartet in F minor, Op. 55 No. 2/iv, mm. 21–40.

reprise to an end. A varied repetition of the codetta (m. 31–34) follows, during which sixteenth-note figures neutralize the hunting topic and the metrical dissonance associated with the slurred motives. The last segment (mm. 33–34) is not varied and hence it is again metrically dissonant. However, the repetition of the codetta in mm. 31–34 casts doubt on the formal scenario of the movement suggested by the small two-reprise form of its theme. If one codetta is common in a small two-reprise form, two codettas are not, so the listener may justifiably wonder whether this form will ever be completed. The doubt is finally cut short by the composer, when the cadence in m. 34 elides with the beginning of the transitory section. This makes clear that the repeat of the second reprise is not to be expected and, consequently, that the putative rondo-theme does not really imply a rondo-finale. From this point on, the formal scenario adopted by the listener is the sonata form.

The transition (mm. 34–40) eliminates the slurred motives that until now have almost uninterruptedly dominated the musical surface and relieves the listener of the metrical displacement dissonance that she has perceived with lesser or greater intensity from the beginning of the movement. But this section does not allow her to pass straight off to the state of metrical consonance. The first three measures contain submetrical grouping dissonance that arises from a triple grouping of sixteenth notes in the first violin part. This dissonance is mostly indirect. Only occasionally do the middle voices articulate the original duple grouping of sixteenths by eighths and so create a direct metrical dissonance. More important from the point of view of the metrical strategy, the beginning of the transition marks a change from compound to simple 6/8 meter and hence a change of the metrical level of *Taktteile* from eighths to dotted quarters. In point of fact, changes between compound and simple meter could already have been observed before. They form a regular pattern throughout mm. 1–26. The first such change takes place in the theme (see Example 7.11). In mm. 2 and 4 caesuras fall on the beginnings of notated measures, indicating simple 6/8 meter. This means that the sixteenth-note figures following the caesuras are overhangs. The segments of mm. 1–2 and 3–4 represent perfect incises. Because the second one is a repetition of the first a tone lower, together they form an incomplete phrase of four measures (*Vierer*),[41] which is to be completed by the third segment. In the following segment, however, the caesura of the cadence falls in the middle of m. 6. It thus closes a four-measure phrase (*Vierer*) in compound 6/8 meter, each notated measure embracing two measures of composed 3/8. In spite of its apparent asymmetry (4 + 2), the six-bar theme forms a compound eighth-measure phrase (4 + 4) that switches from 6/8 to 3/8. This switch is accompanied by acceleration of the harmonic rhythm. Analogous changes of meter indicated by the caesuras of incises and cadences take place in the course of the varied repetition of the theme (mm. 7–12) as well as

41. From Koch's discussion in the second volume of his *Versuch*, it follows that an incomplete phrase can arise from two incises "of which the second contains a repetition of the first on a different harmonic basis," that is, from a displacement of an incise to another scale degree, "when the ending formula of the second incise is the same as the ending formula of the first" (1983: 56 [1787: 457]). If such a phrase is followed by a complete phrase, the two phrases are compounded into one.

the X section (mm. 13–18) and the thematic return (mm. 21–26; Example 7.12) of the second reprise. Only the two codettas in mm. 27–34 have no clear incises. Their cadences, falling in the middle of notated measures, confirm the compound 6/8 meter established earlier by the structural cadence in m. 26.

The change to simple 6/8 meter at the beginning of the transition is easily perceivable due to a slower harmonic rhythm and longer rhythmical values of the accompaniment. Yet the elision with the cadence falling in the middle of m. 34 causes this meter to be shifted by half a measure relative to the notated meter. As was explained in chapter 6, this notation is incorrect, and it threatens to end in the even more grievous mistake of placing the caesura on the upbeat. Apparently, having ridiculed the imaginary composer's incompetence in the realm of musical form and harmony, Haydn demonstrates it now in the realm of meter. As in the first movement of Op. 55 No. 1 (Example 6.5), the incompetent composer avoids the mistake by garbling the phrase structure. Given the perceived meter, the first segment of the transition, spanning four measures from the middle of m. 34 to the middle of m. 38, is regular, yet the second segment is only two and half measures long and hence quite awkward. What the composer achieves through its irregular length is, however, that the caesura arrives correctly on the first half of m. 40 and its overhang extends to the second half of the measure. At this point, metric perception aligns with the notation, and simple 6/8 meter is confirmed.

The caesura at the end of the transition forms a half cadence in the dominant or, in eighteenth-century terms, a *Quintabsatz* in the key of the fifth. It is thus the medial caesura of the exposition. After that, the listener expects a theme in the secondary key (C major). Yet this expectation is frustrated. What follows in m. 41 is not a theme but an array of slurred motives that bring back the metrical dissonance associated with them (Example 7.13). Moreover, the first slurred motive is most naturally heard not in C major but in F major. Indeed, it is rendered on the very same pitches as the first motive of the theme in its original presentation (m. 1). The parallel thirds of the two violins refer back to the varied repetition of the theme (m. 7). Only in the light of the second motive is the tonic in F major reinterpreted as the subdominant in C major, followed by the dominant and the tonic. This trick illustrates another mistake of the incompetent composer. As one can guess, he intends to launch the second group with the recall of the principal theme in the dominant, but by mistake—perhaps glancing at the beginning of the movement—he starts it in the tonic and then tries to save the situation by quickly modulating to C major. The wit of this modulation consists in that it is accomplished merely by altering the second violin part and adding the viola. The melody of the first violin is left intact. In m. 42 the incompetent composer starts the theme once again in C major, but he does not continue—could it be because he has forgotten about the accompaniment? In m. 43 the slurred motives occur in three-part texture, with the first violin and the viola playing in parallel tenths and the second violin filling the harmony. The first motive of this measure corresponds to the motives of mm. 1/2 and 7/8, but it does not mark the caesura, as they did in the course of the theme. The second motive departs further from the theme, and then, with the entrance of the cello, the music suddenly approaches the cadence (*Kadenz*). The second group closes before it has properly started.

Example 7.13. Haydn, String Quartet in F minor, Op. 55 No. 2/iv, mm. 41–54.

Yet, although the cadence commences emphatically with an entire measure of the pre-dominant harmony (m. 44),[42] the cadential six-four and the dominant seventh follow each other too hastily, merely in half-measure intervals, thus weakening the cadential effect (m. 45). The resolution to the tonic is further weakened by the step up to the third in the melody. In terms of eighteenth-century music theory, this cadence is thus deceptive.[43] The second approach toward the cadence starts in elision with the tonic in m. 46. The slurred motives, eliminated in the course of the first cadence, return in unison in parts of the three lower instruments, decorated by sixteenth-note figuration in the first violin, but they do not cause any metrical dissonance because the notated meter is clearly articulated by harmonic rhythm. What also supports the notated meter is harmonic stability. The influence of this last preference factor increases in comparison with the theme, in that it relates not to different tones within the same underlying harmony but to different harmonies. The slurred motives form the bass line of a sequential progression made up of secondary dominants and their respective tonics. The first notes under the slurs are leading tones of the dominants. Their resolutions to tonic roots, represented by the second notes, are thus much stronger than the resolutions of nonharmonic to harmonic tones in the course of the theme. This is, in turn, of consequence for the articulation in that, for the first time, the second notes under the slurs occur without *staccato* markings. The long and vigorous ascent of all four instruments, started with the sequence, is crowned with a greatly expanded cadential formula. The six-four chord, previously compressed in half a measure, now takes one and a half measures. Note, however, that the metrical location of this chord in m. 48 is incorrect. The six-four chord, carrying the "note of preparation of the cadence," should fall on the metrical downbeat (Koch 1983: 38 [1787: 419–20]), but it falls on the upbeat. As a consequence, the dominant seventh with the "cadential note" falls on the downbeat and the tonic with the "caesura note" on the upbeat in m. 50. In this way, the grievous mistake avoided by the incompetent composer before the half cadence in m. 40 happens during the structural cadence of the exposition.

The shift by half a measure relative to the notated meter, initiated by the cadence, continues in the course of the codetta. The materials of the codetta stem from mm. 46–47, but their distribution is different. The sixteenth-note figurations are now in the cello, whereas the slurred motives are played by the two violins in parallel thirds ascending along the tonic triad. In the absence of any harmonic changes articulating the notated meter, the metrical dissonance associated with these motives is more palpable. In the notation the second notes under the slurs are again assigned *staccato* markings. At the same time, the first notes are strengthened by the melodic accents in the cello occasioned by the leaps to the low Cs between the stretches of *legato* and *staccato* articulation. Although similar leaps occurred in the first violin part in mm. 46–47, their antimetrical effect is stronger

42. The melodic descent of the first violin in broken octaves notated by means of grace notes is almost identical to that in Mozart's cadenza to the second movement of his Piano Concerto in B-flat major, K. 238.

43. According to Koch (1983: 50–51 [1787: 444–47]), a deceptive cadence could be produced either by the melody or by the bass.

in the bass because they form registral extreme accents.[44] The only instrumental part that finds no equivalent in mm. 46–47 is that of the viola. It consists of octave leaps between eighth-note strokes. Note that the two component strokes of each leap are preferred as metrically strong due to different perceptual factors: The first, higher stroke, which articulates the notated meter, receives an initial accent; the lower stroke is marked by a registral extreme accent (melodic accent). Due to the large size of the leaps, the lower strokes can easily be perceived as belonging to a separate stream. The fact that they fall in pauses between slurred motives of the two violins makes them analogous to the *staccato* strokes of the accompaniment in mm. 7–10 (see Example 7.11). The analogy is even closer to mm. 21–24 (Example 7.12). As a matter of fact, the leaps of the viola in mm. 50–54 are derived directly from the octave leaps included there in the two violin parts. It follows that the textural complex of the two violins and the viola in mm. 50–54 echoes the compound metrical dissonance of mm. 7–10 and mm. 21–24, made up of two displacement dissonances shifted by one eighth "to the left" and "to the right" from the notated meter. But this echo is weak. While the two displacement dissonances palpably scratch the musical surface, they only enrich the perception of the primary metrical consonance without overthrowing it. On the whole, the metrical course of the codetta is regular. This regularity is disturbed only at the last moment, when the violins add the seventh to the tonic triad of C major, turning it into the dominant of the main key. The slurred motive reaching the seventh (m. 53), and then being embellished by a sixteenth-note turn, occurs too many times. Consequently, the codetta is half a measure too long. This is how the composed meter is adjusted to the notated meter before the repeat of the exposition.

The development starts with a canonic imitation based on the melody of the theme (Example 7.14). Such a contrapuntal treatment of the unpretending rondo-theme is another example of Haydn's play with topics. As with the waltz theme in the first movement of Op. 50 No. 2, strict counterpoint makes structural characteristics of the theme appear in a new light. Chromaticism, originally serving to illustrate the blameworthy mannerism of uneducated musicians, now turns into an emblem of speculative learnedness. Accordingly, it becomes more rigorous: semitone steps, staked out by the slurred motives, are pulled together into uniform chromatic lines that saturate all the instrumental parts.[45] The fact that the theme is played in inversion, as a descending rather than ascending line, increases the impression of learnedness, but it also has another, more concealed sense related to the musical form. The melody of the theme in inversion occurred for the first time in the cello part at the beginning of the X section of the small two-reprise form embedded in the

44. The other leaps to the low Cs, occurring between the *staccato* and the *legato*, articulate the notated meter. This last articulation may be stronger than that of the antimetrical layer because the *legato* slurs are longer than the following *staccato* (durational accent). On the other hand, if the low Cs are heard as a separate stream—this way of hearing may easily arise due to high velocity of octave leaps—they will form groups of twos in which initial accents further strengthen the antimetrical layer.

45. Compare the discussion by Grave and Grave (2006: 261). While linking this moment primarily to the chromatic theme of the finale, the authors consider it from the perspective of the entire quartet cycle as "a subtle yet satisfying culmination to a cyclic process of modal transformation and accommodation."

sonata form of the finale (m. 13). By recalling it at the beginning of the development, Haydn establishes an explicit connection between these equivalent components of the small and the large two-reprise form. In m. 55 the descending chromatic line is likewise played by the cello and is actually rendered on the same pitches as it was in m. 13. Yet, if then it was combined with the ascending melodic lines of the two violins, now it is brought to the listener's attention by the cello entering alone. The viola joins it half a measure later. The canon of the lower pair of instruments is answered by the upper pair from m. 56.[46] Only starting from m. 58 does the homogenous texture made up of the slurred motives gradually spread to all instrumental parts. The uninterrupted repetition and multiplication of these motives, taking possession of the string quartet for no less than five measures (mm. 55–59), effectuates a change of perceived meter. While previously the displacement dissonance associated with them has more or less noticeably blurred the notated meter, now it totally erases the notated meter, not only from the musical surface but also from the listener's memory. This is an introduction to the greatest metrical *Verwirrung* of the finale.

In m. 60, in place of another slur, a quarter note marked by dynamic accent *fz* occurs. From the point of view of the notated meter, it forms a syncopation analogous to that encountered earlier in m. 29, but—given that by now the notated meter is no longer remembered—this syncopation is not perceived as such. Rather, the rhythmical dissonance created by it ultimately consolidates the displacement dissonance in the function of apparent metrical consonance. Immediately after that, the displacement dissonance is twisted into grouping dissonance: an *imbroglio*. As often happens, the *imbroglio* combines with a sequence. By contrast to the ascending sequence of mm. 46–47, this is a descending sequential progression consisting of major triads, each of them preceded by its secondary dominant in the form of a diminished triad. Consequently, the implied root progression travels down the circle of fifths: A–D–G–C–F–B♭–E♭. Note, however, that the sequence has already started before the *imbroglio*. In fact, it governs the harmonic course of the entire passage played by the two violins and the viola (mm. 60–63). The first two chunks of the sequence are three eighth notes long and belong to the displacement dissonance. The *imbroglio* arises from the compression of the second chunk to two eighth notes by shortening the quarter note to an eighth. If the perception of metrical accents in the course of the sequence were determined by harmonic stability, these accents would coincide with the local tonics. Yet at this time the influence of harmonic stability is outweighed by melodic contour. The large intervallic skips alternately a fourth up and a fifth down in the first violin part cause strong melodic accents that fall on the dominants. The same effect, albeit weaker, results from the viola skipping a third down. The influence of these melodic accents on the perception of metrical accents is amplified by other factors. In m. 60 the melodic accent is combined with the durational and dynamic accent brought by the syncopation, which, in its turn, coincides with the location of the metrical accent in

46. In the upper pair, the first two slurred motives are then transposed a tone higher. Would this be an allusion to the "Monte" in mm. 13–16? This is all the more likely in that the first four slurred motives in the first violin part correspond exactly to those in the part of the cello underlying that very sequence.

Example 7.14. Haydn, String Quartet in F minor, Op. 55 No. 2/iv, mm. 55–77.

Example 7.14. cont.

the course of the displacement dissonance. This last location is inherited by the *imbroglio* due to harmonic-melodic parallelism and subsequently confirmed by the dynamic and durational accent in m. 61. Clearly, the quarter note marked *fz* in m. 61 corresponds to the one in m. 60 and challenges the *imbroglio* by inserting a three-eighth-note-long chunk into a chain of two-eighth-note-long ones.[47] Yet it is not a syncopation from the point of view of the notated meter. Observe that its metrical position is different from that of the syncopation in m. 60: The quarter note falls not on the third but on the fourth eighth in 6/8 measure, that is to say, on its second *Taktteil*. Two further stops on quarters, this time not marked by *fz*, follow on the first and the second *Taktteil* in m. 63. In this way, the notated meter is restored by the same means that was originally used to destroy it. The sense of key, lost by the listener in the course of the sequence, is regained when the expected G-major triad is replaced by G minor (m. 63). This last triad, interpreted as subdominant, leads to the half cadence (*Halbkadenz*) in the key of the sixth (D minor).

The dominant, reached in m. 64, starts a new virtuoso section that looks back to mm. 34–40. The submetrical grouping dissonance in the first violin part is at

47. This metric irregularity in the course of the *imbroglio* is correlated with a harmonic irregularity that consists in substituting a minor triad (C minor) for a diminished triad in the course of the sequence. It would be tempting to interpret this correlation as meaningful. However, another harmonic irregularity, represented by the G-minor triad in m. 62, is not marked by any rhythmical dissonance. These two adjustments prevent the sequence from flying beyond the commonly accepted spectrum of keys.

first direct, since in mm. 64–65 the primary metrical consonance is articulated by the middle voices and only later dissolved. By contrast to mm. 34–40, however, the section of mm. 64–71 is correctly notated in measures. The manipulation carried out in its course concerns not meter but the musical form defined by the succession of cadential closures. Although the standing on the dominant in mm. 64–67 seems to consolidate the half-cadential arrival, this function is increasingly undermined by the dissonant seventh and ninth that are added to the dominant triad. In the end, the dominant prolongation following the half cadence becomes a point of departure for an emphatic full cadence (*Kadenz*). In the eighteenth-century theory of sonata form, such a cadence was a valid compositional option. According to Koch (1983: 200 [1793: 308]), a *Kadenz* in the key of the sixth, second, or third should close the second *Hauptperiode*—his designation for the development—and be followed by a retransition leading to a half cadence in the main key. After the dramatic ascent of the first violin in mm. 68–69, the easiest way to proceed toward the cadence would be by moving in m. 70 to the pre-dominant ii^6, the dominant seventh, and the tonic (see Example 7.15). But, as if overshooting himself, the first violinist climbs one more step up to G, in this way reaching the highest pitch of the movement and the greatest distance from the bass, which at the same time descends to the low C♯. The sonority in which both these tones are incorporated is the diminished triad on the raised seventh degree in D minor. The resolution of this diminished triad to the tonic involves a leap of the bass up by two octaves. The subsequent inversion of the tonic takes both the bass and the melody by one octave down, and only in m. 71 does the music finally proceed to ii^6–V^7, albeit reduced in register by one octave from above and from below in comparison with the earlier expected course of the cadence. Measure 70 thus forms a parenthesis. Significantly, it is in this measure that the slurred motives return. Not that they have been completely absent from the preceding measures—closer inspection of the first violin part reveals the semitone steps F♯–G, A–B♭, C♯–D camouflaged under the broken octaves in mm. 68–69. But it is only in m. 70 that the slurred motives are brought from the background into the foreground and occur again in their characteristic form in all instrumental parts.

Example 7.15. Recomposition of mm. 68–71 from Haydn, String Quartet in F minor, Op. 55 No. 2/iv.

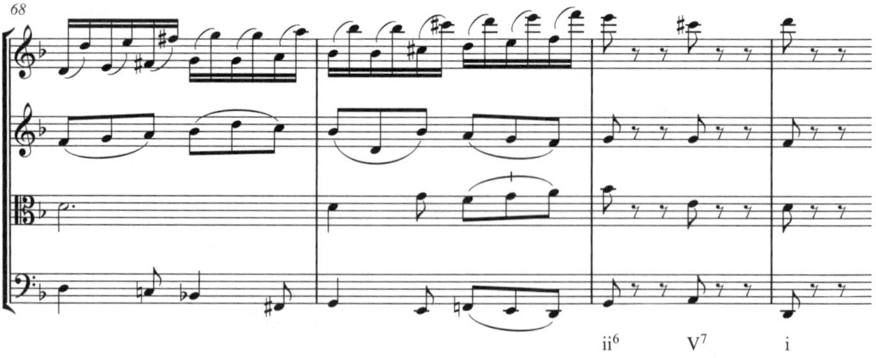

One more slurred motive at the turn of m. 71 twists the tonic into a secondary dominant of the subdominant and starts the retransition.[48] The materials of the retransition and their distribution across registers are analogous to those in the codetta of the exposition (mm. 50–54): the slurred motives in the upper voices; the sixteenth-note figuration in the bass. What is missing, however, are the octave leaps of the viola. Consequently, the compound metrical dissonance between two displacement dissonances does not arise. Besides, the displacement dissonance associated with the slurred motives is only latent. Accordingly, no *staccato* markings are assigned to the second notes under the slurs. The reason that the antimetrical effect of these motives is considerably weaker in comparison with the codetta has to do with the harmonic process taking place in the course of the retransition. Whereas the codetta prolonged the tonic harmony, the retransition forms a sequence of dominants moving along the circle of fifths. The harmonic changes falling on the metrical downbeats in mm. 72, 74, and 76 strongly articulate the notated meter. After the dominants in G major and C major, the dominant in F major is interrupted by a pause (m. 77). With this last dominant, the sequence has reached the main key. After the pause, the recapitulation follows, but it is unprepared. The dominant seventh in m. 77 marks no half cadence to be reached at the end of the retransition. It is actually shorter than the two earlier dominants in the course of the sequence, and the return of the main key is recognized by the listener only in retrospect in the light of the thematic return (mm. 78–83).

Given that the scenario of rondo-finale has long since been rejected by the listener, there is no reason to preserve the small two-reprise form of the theme in the course of the recapitulation. The section corresponding to the varied repetition of the first reprise in mm. 7–12 is thus omitted and the metrical dissonance of this section eliminated. Also eliminated is the further intensification of this dissonance that took place in the course of the thematic return in mm. 21–26. The section started at m. 84 (Example 7.16) corresponds to the beginning of the second reprise (m. 13), but from m. 86 the music departs from the course of the exposition and unexpectedly drives into a passage (mm. 87–90) equivalent to the great metrical *Verwirrung* of the development (Example 7.14, mm. 60–63). As there, so also here both meter and key are distorted by a harmonic sequence combined with an *imbroglio* and additionally challenged by rhythmical dissonances. Only in mm. 90–91 are meter and tonality restored. The double grace note played on the lowest string of the violin in m. 90—the only such embellishment in the course of the entire movement—is an unmistakable reference to the manner of Gypsy musicians. This time, however, the music does not reach a half cadence. Instead, it leads directly to the cadence (*Kadenz*) in the main key (m. 92), which corresponds with that in m. 34 and elides with the transition. Since the cadence falls at the beginning of the notated measure, rather than in the middle, there is no shift by half a measure and hence no need to garble the phrase structure in order to align the composed meter with the notated meter before the half cadence in m. 96. The transition included in the recapitulation (mm. 92–96) is shorter than in the exposition (mm. 34–40) because it does not modulate, but it consists of five full measures.

48. Grave and Grave (2006: 63) point out that the rhetorical power of the cadence is "deftly undercut" in m. 72, but they apparently notice nothing irregular about its earlier course.

Example 7.16. Haydn, String Quartet in F minor, Op. 55 No. 2/iv, mm. 84–96.

The following portion of the recapitulation (mm. 97–106) faithfully retraces mm. 41–50 of the exposition. This includes the shift of the composed meter by half a measure relative to the notated meter and the mistake of placing the caesura of the cadence on the upbeat. The mistake is all the more grievous as it now concerns the structural cadence of the entire movement—indeed, of the entire quartet cycle! To continue with the original codetta of the exposition would mean to consolidate this mistake and to preserve the shifted meter until the end. Probably this is why Haydn does not choose this option. Instead, he turns to the omitted section of mm. 27–34. This section formed the codetta of the second reprise of the supposed rondo-theme (see Example 7.12). The fact that it serves now as the coda of the sonata form establishes another connection between equivalent components of the

Example 7.17. Haydn, String Quartet in F minor, Op. 55 No. 2/iv, mm. 107–18.

small and large two-reprise form in addition to that observed at the beginning of the development. The coda does not elide with the cadence falling in the middle of m. 106 but starts in m. 107, thus adjusting to the notated meter (Example 7.17). This results in metrical irregularity, elicited by two successive downbeats following each other in the space of only half a measure.[49] But mm. 107–14 are varied in comparison with mm. 27–34. The first violin provides the viola and the cello

49. "Successive downbeats" are discussed in relation to hypermeter by Rothstein (1989: 58–63).

with a halo of flickering tremolandos and then continues in broken octaves. This virtuosic display recalls that of mm. 68–69, not only because of the broken octaves but also because they apply again to slurred motives. Another variation from mm. 27–34, more important from the point of view of the metrical strategy, is that in mm. 107–14 rhythmical dissonances are eliminated. Instead of turning into syncopations, the slurred motives continue throughout the coda. Apparently, the purpose of the composer is to clear the musical surface of these metrical surprises near the end of the movement. Yet, for the listener who has already learned to expect the surprises caused by the syncopations in the course of the exposition, their absence in the recapitulation causes a secondary surprise, all the greater as the *forte* dynamics, originally associated with the syncopations, arrive on time in mm. 109 and 113. While in and of themselves these dynamic accents do challenge the notated meter, as signals announcing the durational accents they remain void.[50]

With their increased dynamics and exhilarating virtuosity, mm. 107–14 would form an ideal conclusion of the finale for any other composer. But not for Haydn. After all, there is one more section of the exposition to be recycled in the recapitulation.[51] It is the varied repetition of the theme in mm. 7–12. While this section does not return in its literal form, Haydn avails himself of its materials in order to build up another coda, all in *piano* (mm. 115–18). The superposition of the slurred motives, played in parallel thirds and sixths in the upper voices, on the bass strokes falling between the slurs yields the compound metrical dissonance not heard since the end of the exposition. But the slurred motives are diatonic rather than chromatic, and they form descending rather than ascending lines. The coarse playing of folk-band musicians, mimicked by the instrumental *portamenti* designed to provoke laughter, is thus gone. What remains is the knowing smile of a connoisseur: The trill-like sixteenth-note motive, transferred from the melody to the bass in the last measure of the finale, can be heard as the connoisseur's suppressed chuckle at the adventures of the imaginary composer portrayed by Haydn.

50. That in this particular case the dynamic accents can function as signals announcing the durational accents is a consequence of the fact—indicated in chapter 2 (see note 45)—that durational accents are perceived only in retrospect. At the moments when the dynamic accents in mm. 109 and 113 set in, it is not yet clear that the durational accents will not come about. Incidentally, the Peters edition does not provide any dynamic markings in mm. 106–13, apparently following Longman and Broderip. The dynamic markings included in Example 7.17 are based on the editions by Sieber and Artaria, as specified in the critical commentary (Haydn 2004: 116), and correspond almost exactly with the edition by Doblinger (Haydn 1987b).

51. By this remark I do not mean to imply that in his compositional choices Haydn followed some sort of modified or amplified "sonata principle" (Cone 1968), which would constrain him to restate all sections of the exposition—whether originally in the tonic or in a key other than the tonic—in the course of the recapitulation. No such principle was included in the eighteenth-century theory of sonata form. If in the finale of Op. 55 No. 2 Haydn apparently strives to recycle all sections of the exposition in the recapitulation, he does so presumably not as a matter of principle but rather as a matter of strategy in this particular sonata-form movement.

CHAPTER Eight

Wit, Comedy, and Metric Manipulations in Haydn's and Mozart's Personal Styles

8.1. Haydn

The suppressed chuckle of the connoisseur at the end of the String Quartet Op. 55 No. 2 leads us straight into the discussion of the role played by metric manipulations in Haydn's personal style. Many, if not all, of these manipulations are musical techniques used by him to achieve the "humorous." This broad aesthetic category, ranging from wit to parody and artful imitation of musical bungling, was frequently discussed in the late eighteenth and early nineteenth century. The first mention of the subject was made in the entry "Comisch" in the fourth edition of Sulzer's *Allgemeine Theorie der schönen Künste* (1792–94). Although this entry concentrates on comical theater, a long final note includes a comment made by Johann Friedrich Reichardt in a review of a public concert given by an Italian violinist and composer, Antonio Lolli. In Reichardt's words, Lolli "was the first to show us that instrumental music by and for itself is capable of highest comical expression."[1] Friedrich August Weber (1800), Friedrich Rochlitz (1805–6), and Christian Friedrich Michaelis (1807) followed with articles published in the Leipzig *Allgemeine musikalische Zeitung*. Although Weber mentions Lolli among the performers who excel in "comical caricature," Rochlitz and Michaelis acknowledge Haydn as the founder of humorous music. Michaelis points to him as "the greatest master in this genre," who "set the tone in his original symphonies and quartets" and "awakened a large number of famous composers of the most recent times to write in this manner."[2] But Haydn's reputation as a musical humorist had

1. "Lolli ist hierin der erste gewesen, der uns gezeigt hat, daß die Instrumentalmusik an und für sich des höchsten komischen Ausdruckes fähig ist" (quoted in Sulzer 1792–94: 1:485).
2. "Hingegen ist unsere neueste Musik grossentheils humoristisch, besonders seitdem Joseph Haydn als der grösste Meister in dieser Gattung, vorzüglich in seinen originellen Sinfonieen und Quartetten, den Ton dazu gab.... Auch K. Ph. Eman. Bach komponirte nicht selten im launigen Stil: aber Haydn that es zuerst mit dem allgemeinen Effekt, und weckte eine Menge berühmter Tonkünstler der neuesten Zeit, in diesem Charakter zu schreiben" (Michaelis 1807: col. 729). This English translation combines bits from Maurer Zenck (2008: 55) and Paul (1981: 451).

been consolidated much earlier in musical criticism because of his characteristic mixture of "the serious" and "the comic," or of the high and the low styles. This feature of Haydn's music was not well received during the early stage of his career. In the controversy that broke out in the 1760s against the new style of South German symphonic compositions, Haydn—"a man who seems to be made for humor" (Junker 1776: 29)—was branded by North German critics as the chief corrupter of musical taste.[3] Although this evaluation of Haydn's music had considerably changed by the 1780s, his humor and bias for comedy remained among the most commonly recognized features of his musical personality. They are hailed, among others, in the review of his string quartets Op. 33 and six symphonies by Reichardt (1782) and in Charles Burney's *General History* (1782), feature prominently in Haydn's first biographies, by Griesinger (1810) and Dies (1810), and since then have permeated the history of Haydn's reception.[4]

It is not difficult to see how Haydn's metric manipulations are related to his humor. Almost all musical means of the "humorous" mentioned by eighteenth-century authors are departures from what is usual and hence expected.[5] While these authors concentrate on harmony, counterpoint, and treatment of themes or motives, the catalogue of humorous means compiled by Michaelis includes "the notes and accents [being] arranged against the beat."[6] Indeed, from the expectation of metrical regularity, conditioned by the mechanism of projection, it follows that irregularities resulting from metric manipulations are by definition unexpected. As startling surprises, they feature most prominently in Haydn's minuets, and it is in this genre that they have been most frequently observed by critics from the eighteenth century to this day. One particularly intriguing aspect of metric manipulations in minuets is their effect of physical disturbance. Insightfully described by Wheelock, this effect has been touched on several times in the course of this study. In her seminal account of Haydn's musical wit and humor (1992), Wheelock points out that "when expectations are grounded as habits and tendencies in patterned motions and gestures, discontinuities of motion and disturbances in metric and phrase patterns can have a visceral impact, taking the body

3. See Landon (1978) for historical documentation of this controversy and Wheelock (1992: 33–51) for its succinct summary. The translation of Junker comes from Wheelock (47).
4. Countless remarks about Haydn's comedy, wit, and humor can be found, among others, in Tovey (1935, 1949) and Rosen (1971). These characteristics are the subject of extensive studies by Paul (1980) and Wheelock (1992), as well as articles by Paul (1981), Poundie Burstein (1999), and Scott Burnham (2005) and a book chapter by Ludwig Finscher (2000: 452–62). Historical studies by Howard Irving (1985) and Bonds (1991a) concentrate on the comparison drawn in the eighteenth century between Haydn's music and the humorous novels of Laurence Sterne and Jean Paul.
5. The unexpected is also the most important source of musical humor for today's authors. It is particularly highlighted by Paul (1980, 1981) and Wheelock (1992), whose studies are strongly influenced by Leonard B. Meyer. Meyer himself makes numerous references to Haydn's wit and accounts for it in terms of his theory of musical expectation. See my further discussion in the main text and in note 20.
6. "Der Komponist... vertheilt die Nothen und Accente so wider den Takt" (Michaelis 1807: col. 726). The musical means of the humorous listed by Rochlitz and Michaelis are summarized by Maurer Zenck (2008).

by surprise" (89). To prove that patterns of steps and gestures guided expectations of eighteenth-century listeners not only in danced but also in heard minuets, she refers to Abbé Georg Joseph Vogler's discussion of the minuet of a piano sonata in terms of departures from "the regular movement of the feet" and "their prescribed steps" (56).[7] Whereas Vogler refers to irregular phrase structure, his discussion is of consequence for irregularities of meter. As Wheelock has observed, the irregularities most obviously incompatible with a dance are interruptions of regular motion by general pauses and fermatas. Both these phenomena were discussed at length in chapter 3. In the same chapter I described more subtle effects: interruptions of *Metrum* by means of short pauses, illustrated in Examples 3.8 and 3.9. From the point of view represented by Wheelock, particularly intriguing are pauses—whether general or other—that affect the size of an upbeat and hence the *Rhythmus* of a given composition (Examples 3.12 and 3.17). Because danced minuets start either with a quarter-note upbeat or without an upbeat and preserve their pattern of steps throughout,[8] changing it in minuets not designed for dancing results in confusion of the imaginary dancers about when to take the first step of the next figure. While continuity and uniformity of musical motion, related to the concepts of *Rhythmus* and *Metrum* by Kirnberger and Koch, were considered obligatory in all genres, they acquire special significance in dances, where musical motion sustains the motion of feet. A missing beat in a minuet feels like stepping into a hole.

The opposite effect is caused by syncopations. A surprisingly strong event falling on a weak beat feels like stumbling against a stone. As was further observed in chapter 3, such stumbling syncopations represent rhythmical dissonances and may yield metrical displacement dissonances if they are joined into chains. In the latter case, discussed in chapter 5, they have the power to bring the dancers out of step with the notated meter. By contrast, the effect of physical disturbance caused by metrical grouping dissonances, which were discussed under the rubric of *imbroglio* in chapter 4, is confusion in the etymological sense of the Italian word: Rather than being shifted against the notated meter, the pattern of steps is entangled and ultimately lost. In its basic form *imbroglio* was an unsophisticated effect common in the late eighteenth century, but Haydn gives it a special sophistication by experimenting with direct grouping dissonances (Examples 4.10 and 4.11) and by combining such dissonances with imitation, which results in metrically dissonant "free falls" (Examples 4.8 and 4.9). In both cases the melody and the bass go their separate ways. If one were to look for correlates of such effects in the actual experience

7. "Man merkt es auch am ersten Period, oder am ersten und zweiten zusammengerechnet, daß hier ein Rithmus von 5 Schlägen vorkomme, wobei die regelmäßige Bewegung der Füsen [*sic*] ihre vorgeschriebene Schritte nicht anbringen kann" (Vogler 1778: 380).

8. According to Allanbrook, minuets "habitually begin on the downbeat" (1983: 33). Wheelock points to cross-rhythms between the downbeat pattern of music and the upbeat pattern of dance steps, yet in the further course of her discussion she acknowledges that eighteenth-century sources describe various step patterns (1992: 59–60). As for music, the ratio between upbeat and downbeat patterns in the eighteenth-century repertory of both danced and heard minuets seems pretty much equal.

of dancing, they could be said to portray a pair of dancers trying to keep step with each other as their patterns of steps are falling apart.[9]

The effect of physical disturbance in the minuet is closely combined with an aesthetic provocation: In this aristocratic dance such disturbances break the rules of stylistic etiquette by portraying not only slips and stumbles of imaginary dancers but their generally indecorous manners. Wheelock speculates that they may have served as parody of how minuets were actually danced near the end of the eighteenth century: After Vienna's Redoutensaal and other ballrooms became open to the "mixed company" of nobility and bourgeoisie, the manner of dancing minuets may have rapidly deteriorated. Indeed, in 1801 an eyewitness reported with amusement how "many light-footed tailors wound through the grave minuet... entirely without propriety, without the proper step, without grace and dignity in their movements... without fulfilling a single one of the conditions of the dance" (quoted in Wheelock 1992: 61). While unable to properly perform the steps and gestures of the minuet, those inept dancers brought elements into it of other dances corresponding to their lower station. It is here that the mixture of "the high" and "the low" crops up. Competing with the minuet on its own terrain was the Austrian *Ländler*. As Wheelock has observed (71), this dance frequently featured duple grouping of beats in triple meter. It follows that the subversive effect of the *imbroglio* can be interpreted not merely as thwarting the steps of dancers but—at least in certain cases—as encroaching on the courtly decorum of the minuet with elements of a different topic.

If in minuets the mockery is of dancers, in other quartet movements it may be of players. The mixture of "the high" and "the low" manifests itself in such cases as a conflict between the noble character of the string quartet and the "indecorous manners" of folk-band musicians. Artful imitation of such musicians' bungling can have metrical consequences that, while less commonly recognized, are often more ingenious than those observed in minuets. Some of them are so peculiar as to occur in only one piece: the slips of the bow and finger in Op. 50 No. 2/i (Examples 7.3 and 7.6), the competition between two violinists in Op. 54 No. 2/i (Example 5.15), or the late entrance of the accompaniment in the finale of Op. 55 No. 2 (Example 7.11). Others occur in many pieces and consolidate into types of metric manipulations. For instance, as was suggested in chapter 4, an imaginary performer losing the sense of meter in a display of virtuosity can be evoked by submetrical grouping dissonances. Since such dissonances arise from repetition of a single figure taken from the stock repertory of eighteenth-century finger exercises, they give the impression that the fingers, once set in motion, continue to play by themselves, defying the ear. If in actual fact this was the composer's intention, the humorous character of such phenomena as mimicked mistakes would explain why they were not discussed by eighteenth-century music theorists. Another

9. This is how the metrical effect of imitation *per thesin et arsin* is interpreted by Lawrence Zbikowski (2008) in the finale of Op. 76 No. 4, which is based on the topic of bourrée. Although Zbikowski's view of dance topics as sonic analogues of bodily motion relies on the concept of construction grammar taken from cognitive linguistics, it comes close to the more informal way Wheelock accounts for the effect of bodily disturbances in Haydn's minuets.

aspect of musical bungling affecting meter is the blameworthy mannerism represented by finger slides, which are imitated by slurred motives in the finale of Op. 55 No. 2. My analysis of this finale in chapter 7 sheds light on other examples of metric manipulations caused by such motives, analyzed in chapter 5. Although I did not make this point explicit, all of them can be interpreted as virtuoso imitations of inept musicians losing themselves and their meter in obsessive exploration of motivic material. As already observed, motives slurred over the bar line represent Haydn's stylistic fingerprint. Not only are they the most popular among his elementary motives discussed in chapter 5, they belong to the most remarkable means of metric manipulation used by Haydn, in that they affect meter by melodic contour and grouping—factors of metric perception not recognized in music theory of the time. They also occasion some of the most elaborated metrical strategies analyzed in this study. In chapter 5 I speculated about the reasons for the prevalence of such strategies in opening movements and finales. One can now add that these movements have been traditionally devoted to virtuoso displays on the part of the quartet leader. Such displays can easily turn into a quasi-theatrical play in front of the audience. In the eighteenth century this sort of play was frequently enacted by soloists and featured unusual metrical effects. Reichardt, quoted in Sulzer, reports that children present among the audience during Lolli's concert "were laughing so whole-heartedly and uninterruptedly in a comical concert piece that one could not possibly have failed to recognize the strong effect of the frequent comical accents and leaps."[10] The comical style of performance, cultivated most notably by Lolli and another famous eighteenth-century violinist-virtuoso, Michael Ritter von Esser, is mentioned by Weber (1800: col. 141) as a subspecies of humorous music called by him "instrumental mimicry" (*Instrumentalmimik*). Interestingly enough, Weber discusses it along with "vocal mimicry" (*Singmimik*) in comic operas. Whereas the theatrical quality of Haydn's chamber music has frequently been acknowledged, it is typically related to aspects of nonmusical activity: Charles Rosen writes about the "pacing" of events "happening on the stage" in comic opera (1971: 119), Wheelock about a "comedy of errors" resulting from a "staged conversation" in the string quartets Op. 33 (1992: 133). But in some cases it is the very act of musical performance that turns into a comedy.[11] My remarks about metrical aspects of this comedy, scattered over preceding chapters and now summarized, are admittedly subjective in that they lack the authority of a final

10. "In einem öffentlichen Concerte, daß Lolli gab,... waren auch Kinder zugegen; diese lachten in einem komischen Concertsatze so herzlich und anhaltend, daß man die starke Wirkung der häufigen comischen Accente und Sprünge gar nicht verkennen konnte" (Sulzer 1792–94: 1:485).

11. Wheelock explores this purely musical sense of comedy in her insightful analysis of Haydn's Symphony No. 98 (1992: 183–92). Similar analytical exercises have been recently undertaken in reference to Mozart's String Quintet K. 614 by Cliff Eisen (2003), to Haydn's keyboard sonatas by Tom Beghin (2007) and James Webster (2007), and to Beethoven's Sonata Op. 31 No. 1 by Claudia Maurer Zenck (2008). In keyboard music, whose composers were frequently also its performers, these two sides of musical personality merge together into one complex persona of composer-performer. As a result, many observations made by Beghin, Webster, and Maurer Zenck come close to mine in the next paragraph.

proof and hence do not stand on equal footing with the supposedly objective analyses. Yet, without those subjective interpretations, analyses boil down to mere descriptions and fall short of explaining what is going on, which, not infrequently, is parody of a musical performance.

Both the inept dancers and players staged by Haydn are actors animated by the composer, but occasionally the composer himself climbs up onto the stage. According to Weber, the "artfully imitated bungling"[12] of an inept composer represents the most sophisticated species of the musically humorous. The mistakes of such a composer are slips not of the foot or the finger but of the pen: ineptitudes related to various aspects of compositional métier. With regard to meter, they can manifest themselves in an "incorrect" metrical notation—either suggested, as in the finale of Op. 55 No. 3 (Example 2.38), or actually committed, as in the first movement of Op. 55 No. 1 (Example 6.5) or the finale of Op. 55 No. 2 (Example 7.12). But metric manipulations can also be used to intrude on the formal plan of a given composition or to comment on unsuccessful attempts to carry it through. As Wheelock has observed, "the two events that Haydn most frequently manipulates . . . by prolonged delay and by avoidance of the anticipated goal are the return of the refrain or the moment of recapitulation, and the approach to the final cadence of the closing section" (1992: 147). In the preceding chapter I showed how the caesuras related to those two events—*Halbkadenz* and *Kadenz*—can be delayed or otherwise manipulated by metrical means. But mocked bungling can also occur in other formal contexts. In chapter 3 I indicated that general pauses at the beginning of the development may portray the hesitation of an imaginary composer starting and stopping in an apparent lack of purpose and direction. Within the metaphor of conversation, adopted to account for relations between players but then extended to the composer and the audience, Wheelock relates such musical phenomena to the psychological phenomenon of distraction. For instance, to follow a general pause after the *Kadenz* with some more music is like "saying something after you've finished—in seeming distraction saying the same thing over again" (81). She backs up her argument with references to Haydn's Symphony No. 60, "Per la Commedia intitolata il Distratto," but she could have consolidated it even further by including evidence from eighteenth-century music theory. In the second volume of his composition handbook Koch asks: "How, for example, does the composer represent an absent-minded person in an instrumental piece?" and answers: "He connects sections which properly do not belong together; he makes a triple rhythm [*Rhythmus*] where we expect a duple; without reason he alternates the minor mode with the major, and so on" (Baker and Christensen 1995: 155 [Koch 1787: 41]). This list can be easily continued. For instance, he starts a rondo but provides a sonata form.[13] Or he starts talking about one topic but slips into another. In relation to musical topics, this last phenom-

12. "Künstlich nachgemachte musikalische Stümperey" (Weber 1800: col. 143).

13. Wheelock (1992: 143–46) recognizes this type of formal manipulation as a means of strategic play with the listener's expectations in Haydn's symphonic finales, but she does not relate it to the phenomenon of distraction.

enon may result in a change of meter caused by change of the metrical level of *Taktteile*. Haydn's unorthodox use of such changes in the course of a phrase, discussed in chapters 2 and 6, can thus be viewed as yet another species of mocked mistake. Of course, to appreciate artful imitation of bungling—whether undertaken for its own sake or as a musical representation of distraction—requires theoretical knowledge of compositional rules. All such manipulations are thus addressed to *Kenner*.

8.2. Mozart

In Mozart, unsurprisingly perhaps, metric manipulations have been found to play a lesser role than in Haydn. The difference concerns not only the type and number of Mozart's metric manipulations but also their purpose. Even if in the eighteenth century Mozart's string quartets were considered "humorous" by many critics and offered Reichardt an opportunity to count Mozart—along with Haydn and Beethoven—among "the three true humorists,"[14] his humor was clearly different from Haydn's: less a matter of comedy than wit. Not that wit is in short supply in Haydn. But the happy marriage between Haydn's technical artifice and the popular air of his music—his "artful popularity [*kunstvolle Popularität*] or popular artfulness [*populäre Kunstfülle*]" (Triest 1801: col. 407)—made it appealing to all kinds of listeners.[15] In Mozart, instead, the "overwhelming art" was more clearly manifest.[16] This issued from the harmonic and polyphonic complexity of his music, which required greater intellectual involvement of listeners and called for a more exclusive audience.[17] Discussing

14. "Die drei echten Humoristen" (Reichardt 1810: 231).

15. For this aspect of Haydn's musical personality, see Sisman (2005) and Bonds (2006, 2007, 2008). A translation of Triest's essay by Susan Gillespie, as "Remarks on the Development of the Art of Music in Germany in the Eighteenth Century," is included in Sisman (1997: 321–94).

16. This phrase comes from Carl Dittersdorf—letter of 1788 to Artaria, quoted in Eva Badura-Skoda (1988: 47)—and refers to Mozart's "Haydn" Quartets, which, in Dittersdorf's words, are "not everyone's kind of purchase, because of the overwhelming art that predominates in them."

17. "Wit" as an intellectual and hence artificial feature was contrasted with the more natural "humor" by eighteenth-century English writers (Wheelock 1992: 19–25). In Germany this contrast was captured by the terms *Witz* and *Laune*. Wheelock discusses the aesthetic underpinnings of both terms in German philosophical tradition and their relations to the English terms (28–32). Yet—as follows from Wheelock's further discussion (197–201)—this terminology was not consistently applied in early German writings on musical wit and humor. Indeed, the musical writers mentioned at the beginning of this chapter treat "the humorous" (*Humoristisch*) and "the comic" (*Komisch*) as synonyms, referring to a superior category of which wit was a species. *Laune* is not always opposed to wit (*Witz*). For Weber (1800: col. 141–42), *musikalische Laune* is a subspecies and summit of wit. For Michaelis, *witzig* (witty) refers to humorous music "of merry and pleasant character" ("von heiterm, plaisantem Charakter") (1807: col. 727). In my own informal distinction between wit and comedy I do not follow any single eighteenth-century author, but I do hope to capture what all of them considered essential for the phenomenon of humorous music.

the finale of Mozart's String Quartet in A major, K. 464, Ernst Ludwig Gerber notes that, with its excessive saturation with chromaticism and dissonance, "such music can only succeed with musicians whose ears have become to a certain extent dulled and desensitized by constant study and playing...or with those educated in the art who listen merely with the intellect and seek no enjoyment other than that which springs from any gratification of the mind." For Gerber this complexity is justified in a genre designed "for the private music making of a quartet for musicians and educated friends of arts" and "praiseworthy as an exercise and wonderful effusion of humor" (quoted in Wheelock 1992: 115).[18] But many of his contemporaries found in it reason to criticize Mozart for writing excessively intellectual compositions from which "feeling and heart profit little" (Cramer 1787: col. 1274; quoted in Irving 1998: 75). Ironically, for later generations of listeners this very complexity became the source of the expressive power of Mozart's music. These two standpoints do not exclude each other. Complexity is a function of the unexpected and, as was pointed out by Leonard B. Meyer (1956), the unexpected can be the source of both meaning and emotion.[19] After everything that has been said so far in this book about the anticipation of twentieth-century ideas by eighteenth-century music theorists, it should not come as a surprise that this idea, too, was familiar in the eighteenth century. Whereas the aestheticians mentioned at the beginning of this chapter related the unexpected to the humorous, Koch mentions it as a means to arouse feelings (Baker and Christensen 1995: 147 [Koch 1787: 23]).

This leads to a dilemma: Given that metric manipulations, too, are unexpected, when do they serve the purpose of expression and when that of humor? Finding an answer to this question depends not on metric manipulations per se but on several contextual factors such as tempo, key, dynamics, and musical topics. An answer can therefore be given not generally but only case by case on the basis of careful consideration of the musical context. Complexity itself may be one of those factors. An unexpected event presented in an easygoing context is likely to be felt as humorous, whereas in a complex musical situation it will

18. "Eine solche Musik kann doch nur Musikern gefallen, deren Ohr durch unaufhörliches Studiren und Musiciren bis auf einen gewissen Grad abgestumpft und empfindungslos geworden ist, und deren Geschmack gleichsam nur noch durch musikalische *Asa foedita* gereizt werden kann; oder Kunstgelehrten, welche blos mit dem Verstande hören, blos mit dem Verstande folgen, und keinen Genuss suchen, als der aus jeder Befriedigung des Verstandes entspringt. Da indessen der ruhmwürdige Verfasser dies Finale nicht für ganze Orchester zum öffentlichen Gebrauche, sondern in ein Quartett zur Privatunterhaltung für Musiker und ausgebildete Kunstfreunde geschrieben hat: so ist dieses sein Kunststück, an der Stelle, welche es einnimmt, nicht nur tadellos, sondern als Aufgabe und wunderlicher Erguss der Laune, lobenswerth" (Gerber 1813: col. 461).

19. According to Meyer, "whether a piece of music gives rise to affective experience or to intellectual experience depends upon the disposition and training of the listener" (1956: 40). This squares with Gerber's remarks quoted earlier about the audience of Mozart's K. 464. The change in Mozart's reception that was taking place in the early nineteenth century can be explained by the change in the disposition of the Viennese concert audience under the influence of Beethoven. This last process is insightfully described by Bonds (2006).

be felt as awesome.[20] As has already been observed, Mozart's metric manipulations are frequently combined with his contrapuntal and harmonic complexities. One particularly striking example of this combination is the *imbroglio* in K. 515 (Example 4.16), whose scope and artful polyphonic elaboration cannot be compared to any instance of *imbroglio* ever composed by Haydn. Whereas in this case imitation forms an embellishment of metric manipulation caused by parallelism, in other cases imitation is the proper means of metric manipulations. This could be ascertained from the displacement dissonance based on *imitatio per thesin et arsin* in the finale of K. 575 (Example 5.18) and from the elaborated metrical strategy in the minuet of K. 593, including canonic imitation (Example 5.19). Metric manipulations combined with complex harmonic progressions occur in K. 589/i (mm. 154–57; Example 5.7b) and in the trio from K. 515/iii (mm. 25–32), among others.

Regarding the role of metric manipulations in Mozart's personal style, it is significant that similar examples occur in his earlier set of "Haydn" Quartets. Polyphonic entanglements in the finale of K. 575 and in the first movement of K. 589 (mm. 100–3) have precedents in the finale of K. 464 (mm. 25–39, 169–83), discussed by Gerber, and in the first movement of the same string quartet (mm. 100–3). Although they are presented in various formal contexts, all are based on an actual or implied bass pedal and prolong one underlying harmony. Consequently, they form harmonically static and metrically dissonant plateaus of utmost complexity, the most sophisticated of them being the earliest chronologically: The second variation of the finale from the D-minor quartet, K. 421 (mm. 49–72), contains a constellation of submetrical dissonances whose polymetric complexity reaches the level of experiment by "the choirmaster from Vallenthal," denounced by Riepel and reported near the end of chapter 4.

The combinations of harmonic and metric complexities in the "Haydn" Quartets seem to result from Mozart's use of dynamic markings. Even a cursory survey of this set reveals that the dynamic markings *f*, *fp*, *sf*, or *sfp* are often assigned by Mozart to salient harmonic events such as dissonant, chromatic, or otherwise unexpected harmonies or tones. This usage is in line with Türk's instructions regarding accentuation of salient events in performance. Apparently, Mozart was among those "various composers" mentioned by Türk (1982: 327 [1789: 338])

20. In *Sweet Anticipation: Music and the Psychology of Expectation* (2006), David Huron observes that violation of expectation may evoke three different emotional reactions to music: frisson, laughter, and awe. Huron raises the question "What it is about some thwarted expectations that leads to *laughter* rather than *frisson*" (287). In answer, he refers to factors involved in musical or extramusical context. Context suggestive of "playfulness and parody" will lead to laughter, "serious or solemn" context to frisson (288). All these expressive categories can be accounted for in terms of musical topics. Note that topics function as an umbrella category for many contextual factors of musical surface, in that they bear relations, among others, to keys, tempi, dynamics, and various levels of structural complexity. Huron's psychological theory of expectation, labeled ITPRA (Imagination–Tension–Prediction–Reaction–Appraisal), elaborates on Meyer's theory and recasts it in light of contemporary experimental and theoretical knowledge. Although Huron treats "laughter" as a category of emotion, it closely relates to Meyer's "meaning," because spontaneous "Ha-ha" frequently results from reflective "Aha."

who preferred to explicitly mark such accents rather than leaving them to the discretion of performers. If salient harmonies fall on metrically weak beats, the dynamic accents assigned to them cause rhythmical or metrical dissonances. Later this may have motivated Mozart to explore metrical effects for their own sake. But not all of Mozart's dynamic accents are motivated by salient harmonic events. In the "Haydn" Quartets one can also find purely gratuitous changes of dynamics between *f* and *p* following in quick succession. Sometimes such changes yield highly idiosyncratic effects. A curious example can be found at the beginning of the minuet of the G-major quartet, K. 387, where a solo chromatic line of the first violin with the dynamic changes *p–f–p–f* taking place at each note (mm. 3–6) creates a sense of 2/4 in spite of the notated 3/4 meter. A similar line is then played by the cello (mm. 7–8). In the further course of the minuet, imitation and superposition of such lines leads to collisions between *p* and *f* in different instrumental parts (mm. 13–16, 65–70). Interestingly enough, the source of this effect seems to be a chromatic line of the second violin plaited in a series of *p–f–p–f* chords in the first movement (mm. 37–38, 145–46). It occurs once again in the slow movement of K. 428 (m. 90).[21]

While this effect is not revisited by Mozart, his "Prussian" Quartets, as well as his last quintets, include several new effects that reveal the strong influence of Haydn's metric manipulations. This influence is particularly evident in interruptions caused by general pauses and fermatas. In his earlier "Haydn" Quartets, Mozart avails himself of these means most sparingly.[22] By contrast, in the repertory under consideration in this study, apart from the examples discussed earlier (Examples 3.19, 3.20, 3.21, 7.2), general pauses occur in K. 515/i (m. 321), K. 515/iv (mm. 211, 466, 476), K. 516/ii (m. 10, 47), K. 589/iv (m. 90, 92), K. 593/i (m. 101, 105, 144, 232), K. 593/iv (m. 103, 189), K. 614/i (m. 99), and K. 614/iv (mm. 86, 105, 108, 111, 269, 286). The finale of K. 590 contains as many as eleven fermatas over notes and pauses. Haydn's influence can be demonstrated not only generally but also quite specifically in connections between individual works. As was indicated previously in the course of the analysis, the general pause in K. 614 (Example 3.20) refers to that in Haydn's Op. 64 No. 6 (Example 3.16). Another example of a direct connection is the one between the finales of Op. 64 No. 5 (Example 4.22) and K. 590 (Example 4.23), even if in this case the metrical disturbance represented by submetrical dissonance is introduced by Mozart into Haydn's metrically straightforward theme. Haydn's influence on the finale of K. 590 is not only stylistic but also aesthetic: It manifests itself in parody of folk-band musicians. One more example of such parody is the finale of K. 516. Although Mozart elaborates no metrical strategies comparable in scope and radicalism to Haydn's and does not go

21. The curious beginning of the minuet of K. 387 is discussed by many authors (Keller 1956: 108–10; Steinbeck 1984: 221–25; Küster 1996: 191–92; Irving 1998: 28–29; Krummacher 2001: 152; Rushton 2006: 170) but none of them, except Irving (93 n. 5), has noted its connection to the first movement of the same quartet and to the slow movement of K. 428. Whereas the former connection contributes to cyclic integration of K. 387, the latter is an aspect—if tiny—of what can be viewed as the integration of this quartet set.

22. General pauses occur only in the finales of K. 428 and 465 as well as the minuet of K. 464.

so far as to dissolve the notated meter, in these and other pieces from Mozart's late period the spirit of comedy à la Haydn triumphs over Mozart's more intellectual wit. In K. 516, parody of inept musicians is combined with artful imitation of the bungling of an imaginary composer when Mozart suggests—if he does not actually commit—the mistake of an incorrect metric notation (Example 2.40). Two further examples of Haydn's specific influence, not discussed previously, are found in the finale of Mozart's String Quartet in B-flat major, K. 589, and in the opening movement of his String Quintet in D major, K. 593. The finale of K. 589 contains an extensive passage of metrical dissonances (mm. 29–44) whose motivic content and formal location at the beginning of the development are strikingly similar to those in Haydn's finale of Op. 55 No. 2 (mm. 55–63; Example 7.14). The D-major quintet K. 593, on the other hand, contains the only instance of metrical dissonance that Mozart includes in the theme of an opening movement (mm. 23–25). Slurred motives generating this metrical dissonance resemble those occurring in the subsidiary theme of the opening movement of Haydn's String Quartet in C major, Op. 54 No. 2 (mm. 56–73; Example 5.15a). The influence of Op. 54 No. 2 extends to the form of the opening movement of K. 593, closed with the material of the slow introduction. This construction was almost certainly inspired by the highly unusual finale of Op. 54 No. 2, starting with an enormous Adagio, followed by a brief Presto, and returning to Adagio.[23]

8.3. Haydn's Earlier and Later String Quartets

If Haydn's influence on Mozart in 1787–91 manifests itself so strongly in metric manipulations, this may be because in this period Haydn begins cultivating metric manipulations with particular intensity. To be sure, his interest in rhythm and meter reaches back to the beginning of his career. Among his earlier string quartet collections, the most spectacular manifestations of this interest include the minuet of Op. 9 No. 3—which Koch cites (Example 4.1) as an illustration of *imbroglio*—and the notorious Menuet alla Zingarese from Op. 20 No. 4. In those minuets, switches between 3/4 and 2/4 are effectuated not by parallelism but by more pedestrian means, including pattern of attacks as well as durational and dynamic accents. Such means occur again in the minuet of Op. 33 No. 5 (mm. 16–21), side by side with an *imbroglio* caused by parallelism and an excessive number of other metric manipulations, but are not used by Haydn in his later quartets. Two other notorious examples are the opening movements of Op. 17 No. 5 and Op. 20 No. 3. The dissolution of meter in those movements is far more daring than in the finale of Op. 50 No. 3 (Example 5.10c) yet, again, is caused by different means: the sheer pattern of attacks in the accompaniment. Since in both cases those attacks accompany virtuoso displays by the first violinist, they sound as if the other players are

23. A thorough discussion of this finale from the position of the listener's formal expectations, drawing on an earlier analysis by Edward T. Cone (1962), is offered by Webster (1991: 300–13).

pursuing their leader in a passage of less than successful improvisation—early instances of Haydn's musical comedy of errors!

Apart from these few excesses, however, Haydn's earlier quartet collections contain much more standard types of metric manipulations. Many of them are side effects of harmonic and contrapuntal techniques: suspensions (*ligaturae*), single and in chains—characteristic of the fourth species of counterpoint—as well as retardation, anticipation, and *Sospiren*. To be sure, chains of suspensions (*ligaturae*) belong to the rudiments of contrapuntal technique and hence occur—simple or decorated—in all genres throughout Haydn's oeuvre. Conspicuous, however, are their occurrences in minuets—especially in the trios in Op. 9 No. 5, Op. 17 No. 1, Op. 17 No. 4, and Op. 20 No. 1, a thread culminating in Op. 50 No. 6 (Example 5.6). Retardations and anticipations feature most prominently in the theme of the finale of Op. 9 No. 2, where syncopated repetitions of the first violin sound like an *agitato* accompaniment for an absent melody. More conventional use of retardations is made in the theme of the finale of Op. 9 No. 5 (mm. 7–10) and in the opening movement of Op. 9 No. 6, where chains of retardations (mm. 33–41, 115–22) lead to the structural cadences of the exposition and the recapitulation. In Op. 17 No. 2/iv a shorter chain of anticipations contained in the theme (mm. 5–6, 9–10) forms part of a compositional strategy as it develops into a longer chain during the thematic return (mm. 106–11). Whether this strategy is specifically metrical or only motivic-thematic is not yet quite clear, but the metrical effect of retardation and anticipation is clearly exploited by Haydn in the opening movement of Op. 17 No. 5, where retardations originally contained in the melody (mm. 13–14 and 16–17) are transferred to the bass (mm. 42–47) and form a much longer chain blurring the notated meter. In the finale of Op. 20 No. 1, chains of retardations not only are particularly long but combine with other metrically challenging phenomena such as *imitatio per thesin et arsin* (mm. 65–72), syncopated accompaniment, and pitch repetitions—a type of elementary motive that would be exploited by Haydn more extensively in his later quartets. Retardations and anticipations make a remarkable appearance once more in Op. 33 No. 5/i (mm. 61–64, 251–58), but they occur very rarely in Haydn's later quartets and for the most part without being clearly connected to any metrical strategy. In the repertory under consideration in this study the only example of their strategic use by Haydn occurs in the finale of Op. 64 No. 3, where the chain of anticipations included in mm. 7–8 refers back to the tie in mm. 2/3 that contributes to the perception of false meter at the beginning of the theme (see Example 2.4).

Conversely, many of the most original types of metric manipulations in Haydn's string quartets of 1787–91 are not yet in use in his earlier quartet collections. In Op. 9 No. 2/i slurred motives contained in the theme (mm. 1–5) remain without consequences. In Op. 9 No. 5/iv (mm. 100–9) long chains of such motives do not cause any metrical disturbance because the harmonic changes, falling on the motives' second notes, clearly articulate the notated meter. The same is true of the slurred motives in Op. 17 No. 6/i (mm. 19–20, 142–49) and in Op. 20 No. 4/iv (mm. 15–17). The antimetrical potential of these motives might have occurred to Haydn for the first time in the slow movement of Op. 20 No. 4 (mm. 110–15), where the first notes under the slurs receive dynamic accents *fz*. This does not lead to any spectacular effect, though, or to any elaborated metrical strategy comparable with those in Op. 50 No. 3/iv (Example 5.10), Op. 54 No. 2/i (Example 5.15), or Op. 55 No. 2/iv. Similarly, the pitch alternations in Op. 20 No. 6/i (mm. 27–28) and the repetitions in Op. 33 No. 5/i (mm. 89–95, 170–79) remain without any metrical consequences, although Haydn takes ample opportunity for metrical play with the same motives, respectively, in Op. 64 No. 3/i (Example 5.13) and Op. 50 No. 5/i (Example 5.12). Pitch repetitions are for the first time strategically exploited in Op. 33 No. 1/i (mm. 65–71). If Haydn's metric invention has its origin in his sensitivity to factors of metric perception going far beyond the views commonly accepted in the eighteenth century, he has apparently acquired this sensitivity over time through attentive listening to compositions by himself and others. By the late 1780s this process of attentive listening has brought him to a new stage of metric creativity and aroused in him a particular interest in the default metrical properties of his materials, which he now starts manipulating much more frequently and in more ingenious ways than ever before.

Once aroused, this interest remains with Haydn until the end of his career. In his later string quartets, slurred motives continue to occur as means of metric manipulations. In Op. 71 No. 1/i (mm. 119–21) and Op. 74 No. 1/ii (mm. 33–35) the default metrical properties of these motives are again reinforced by *fz*. In the finales of Op. 71 No. 1 and of Op. 74 No. 2—as in Op. 64 No. 5/i (Example 5.14)—slurred motives are combined with or replaced by ties. In the latter case the extremely elaborated metrical strategy of the finale begins with the first two notes of the theme joined by a slur across the bar line. Slurred motives combined with ties and pitch alternations play a significant role in the subsidiary theme of the finale from Op. 76 No. 4 (mm. 35–66). Haydn also plays with the metrical properties of other elementary motives. The antimetrical effect of pitch repetitions in the form of "pah-pah" accompaniment—similar to those in Op. 50 No. 2/i—is exploited by him in Op. 74 No. 3/i, especially in the main theme (mm. 11–20) and before the recapitulation (mm. 114–27). Threefold repetitions occur in Op. 71 No. 3/i (mm. 290–98), and fourfold repetitions yield momentary metrical modulations in Op. 76 No. 5/iv (mm. 166–74) and Op. 77 No. 1/i (mm. 75–76). In the opening movement of Op. 71 No. 2 an elaborated metrical strategy is derived from octave leaps: In mm. 53–56 the leaps change their sizes and are slurred, as in Op. 54 No. 2/i (Example 5.15). On the other hand, one of the most spectacular metrical strategies of Haydn's entire oeuvre—contained in the finale of Op. 76 No. 6—completely dispenses with elementary motives, instead exploiting series of uniform stepwise motion along a diatonic scale that combine into all sorts of metric manipulations and saturate the movement from the very beginning—famously analyzed by Lerdahl and Jackendoff (1983: 90–96)—until the end, culminating in the dissolution of meter (mm. 67–94). Yet in these quartet collections Haydn seems no longer as consistently given to metric playfulness as in Op. 50, Op. 54/55, and Op. 64. In Op. 71/74 the central problem for the composer seems to be a new style suitable for the large audiences of London public concerts (Somfai 1981). In the Viennese collections Op. 76 and Op. 77 Haydn generally moderates his eccentric habits. Although comedy is not absent from them, those collections bear accents of seriousness not encountered in his earlier string quartets.

8.4. Inconclusive Conclusion

However great the differences between the two composers, from the foregoing remarks it follows that 1787–91 was the period of the most intense metric experimentation in the string chamber music of both Haydn and Mozart. Obviously, this statement cannot be adequately substantiated within this study. It requires much more detailed analysis of earlier and later quartet collections. To understand the role of metric manipulations in Haydn's and Mozart's personal styles, it is further necessary to extend the radius of analysis to other genres cultivated by both composers. Do these genres display metric manipulations similar to those found in string quartets and quintets? Can other types of metric manipulations be observed in them? Is the intensity of such manipulations particularly high in compositions from the late 1780s and early 1790s? Or does it reach its peak in different periods? Finally, is the increased intensity of metric manipulations peculiar to string chamber music by Haydn and Mozart or can it be ascertained in string quartets by other composers active in Vienna in the same period, for instance Carl Ditters von Dittersdorf, who participated in a quartet soirée with Haydn and Mozart in 1784, playing the violin, and whose collection of string quartets appeared 1788? Or by Johann Baptist Vanhal, who played the cello during the same soirée and published two quartet collections in the 1780s?[24]

Clearly, I have more questions than answers. While readily acknowledging the preliminary character of this study and awaiting the results of further investigation, I would like to conclude with the observation that Haydn's and Mozart's chamber music for strings of 1787–91 has not achieved outstanding popularity among listeners. Haydn's Op. 50, Op. 54/55, and Op. 64 are far less popular than Op. 33 and the later quartets Op. 76 and Op. 77. The same is true of Mozart's "Prussian" Quartets, which are much less celebrated than the set dedicated to Haydn. Similarly, Mozart's string quintets K. 593 and 614 are commonly considered not as excellent as K. 515 and 516, if excellent at all. This criticism, which can be traced back to the nineteenth century, contrasts with opinions of eighteenth-century critics, who praised Mozart's late collections as standing on equal footing with or even surpassing his earlier achievements.[25] Surely, the reasons for their changed reception by today's audiences are not to be sought in metric playfulness alone. They may have to do with several aspects of these compositions such as play with topics and other musical conventions concerning form, texture, or stock harmonic models. A study of hypermeter and phrase structure is likely to bring further insights into this complicated matter. Yet metrical disturbances may contribute to unfavorable reception because they hinder the listeners' ability to make sense of a composition on the most elementary level of musical grammar. As Wheelock has observed, "to

24. An account of this soirée and its illustrious participants was recorded several years later by an eyewitness, Michael Kelly, in his *Reminiscences*, cited by Landon (1978: 491).

25. Reception of Mozart's late chamber music is discussed by Eisen (2003). Among the authors of the most depreciating opinions are Otto Jahn (1891), Eric Blom (1935), and Hans Keller (1956). See also Keefe (2007: 105–7).

experience disorder as an agreeable surprise requires a compensatory shock—of recognition that the seeming dysfunction is uniquely functional in context" (1992: 76).[26] This recognition requires, however, that the context be understood. For the twenty-first-century listener who has lost the knowledge of eighteenth-century conventions related to topics and form, to understand how they motivate metric manipulations in a given context may be very difficult, if not impossible. To delight in the play with meter, the listener of today has to regain at least part of the theoretical knowledge and listening habits characteristic of the "historical listener" of the eighteenth century.

26. In Huron's ITPRA theory of expectation (2006), mentioned in note 20, this recognition corresponds to the last A of the acronym, which stands for *appraisal response*. By contrast to the *reaction response*, which is quick and unconscious, appraisal consists in conscious assessment of the surprising event in its broader context. In Fodor's terms (1983), the reaction response thus takes place on the modular level of processing, whereas the appraisal response belongs to the central level. As has been pointed out by Huron, the negatively valenced reaction response to surprise may be usurped by an appraisal response leading "to a generally positive aura or feeling" (304). This phenomenon is called "contrastive valence."

BIBLIOGRAPHY

Agawu, V. Kofi. 1991. *Playing with Signs: A Semiotic Interpretation of Classic Music.* Princeton, NJ: Princeton University Press.

Allanbrook, Wye Jamison. 1983. *Rhythmic Gesture in Mozart:* Le Nozze di Figaro *and* Don Giovanni. Chicago: University of Chicago Press.

———. 2008. Mozart's K331, First Movement: Once More, with Feeling. In *Communication in Eighteenth-Century Music,* ed. Danuta Mirka and Kofi Agawu, 254–82. Cambridge: Cambridge University Press.

Badura-Skoda, Eva. 1988. Dittersdorf über Haydns und Mozarts Quartette. In *Collectanea Mozartiana,* ed. Cordula Roleff, 41–50. Tutzing, Germany: Schneider.

Baker, Nancy Kovaleff, and Thomas Christensen, eds. 1995. *Aesthetics and the Art of Musical Composition in the German Enlightenment: Selected Writings of Johann Georg Sulzer and Heinrich Christoph Koch.* Cambridge: Cambridge University Press.

Beghin, Tom. 2007. "Delivery, Delivery, Delivery!" Crowning the Rhetorical Process of Haydn's Keyboard Sonatas. In *Haydn and the Performance of Rhetoric,* ed. Tom Beghin and Sander M. Goldberg, 131–71. Chicago: University of Chicago Press.

Bellman, Jonathan. 1993. *The* Style Hongrois *in the Music of Western Europe.* Boston: Northeastern University Press.

———. 1998. The Hungarian Gypsies and the Poetics of Exclusion. In *The Exotic in Western Music,* ed. Jonathan Bellman, 74–103. Boston: Northeastern University Press.

Berger, Karol. 1992. Toward a History of Hearing: The Classic Concerto, a Sample Case. In *Convention in Eighteenth- and Nineteenth-Century Music: Essays in Honor of Leonard G. Ratner,* ed. Wye J. Allanbrook, Janet M. Levy, and William P. Mahrt, 405–29. Stuyvesant, NY: Pendragon.

———. 1996. The First Movement Punctuation Form in Mozart's Piano Concertos. In *Mozart's Piano Concertos: Text, Context, Interpretation,* ed. Neal Zaslaw, 239–59. Ann Arbor: University of Michigan Press.

Bernet-Kempers, Karel Philippus. 1961. Hemiolenrhythmik bei Mozart. In *Festschrift Helmuth Osthoff zum 65. Geburtstage,* ed. Lothar Hoffmann-Erbrecht and Helmut Hucke, 155–61. Tutzing, Germany: Schneider.

Berry, Wallace. 1976. *Structural Functions in Music.* Englewood Cliffs, NJ: Prentice-Hall.

Blom, Eric. 1935. *Mozart.* London: Dent.

Bonds, Mark Evan. 1991a. Haydn, Laurence Sterne, and the Origins of Musical Irony. *Journal of the American Musicological Society* 44/1: 57–91.

———. 1991b. *Wordless Rhetoric: Musical Form and the Metaphor of the Oration.* Cambridge, MA: Harvard University Press.

———. 1993. The Sincerest Form of Flattery? Mozart's "Haydn" Quartets and the Question of Influence. *Studi musicali* 22: 365–409.

———. 2006. *Music as Thought: Listening to the Symphony in the Age of Beethoven.* Princeton, NJ: Princeton University Press.

Bonds, Mark Evan. 2007. Rhetoric versus Truth: Listening to Haydn in the Age of Beethoven. In *Haydn and the Performance of Rhetoric,* ed. Tom Beghin and Sander M. Goldberg, 109–28. Chicago: University of Chicago Press.

———. 2008. Listening to Listeners. In *Communication in Eighteenth-Century Music,* ed. Danuta Mirka and Kofi Agawu, 34–52. Cambridge: Cambridge University Press.

Bregman, Albert S. 1990. *Auditory Scene Analysis.* Cambridge, MA: MIT Press.

Brower, Candace. 1993. Memory and the Perception of Rhythm. *Music Theory Spectrum* 15/1: 19–35.

Brown, Clive. 1999. *Classical and Romantic Performing Practice 1750–1900.* Oxford: Oxford University Press.

Brown, Howard Mayer, and Claus Bockmaier. 2008. Tactus. In *Grove Music Online,* ed. Laura Macy; www.grovemusic.com, accessed 24 May.

Budday, Wolfgang. 1983. *Grundlagen musikalischer Formen der Wiener Klassik: An Hand der zeitgenössischen Theorie von Joseph Riepel und Heinrich Christoph Koch dargestellt an Menuetten und Sonatensätzen (1750–1790).* Kassel, Germany: Bärenreiter.

Burney, Charles. 1782. *A General History of Music from the Earliest Ages to the Present Period.* Vol. 2. London: Printed for the author and sold by T. Becket, J. Robson, and G. Robinson.

Burnham, Scott. 2005. Haydn and Humor. In *The Cambridge Companion to Haydn,* ed. Caryl L. Clark, 61–76. Cambridge: Cambridge University Press.

Burstein, Poundie. 1999. Comedy and Structure in Haydn's Symphonies. In *Schenker Studies 2,* ed. Carl Schachter and Heidi Siegel, 67–81. Cambridge: Cambridge University Press.

Caplin, William. 1978. Der Akzent des Anfangs: Zur Theorie des musikalischen Taktes. *Zeitschrift für Musiktheorie* 9/1: 17–28.

———. 1983. Tonal Function and Metrical Accent: A Historical Perspective. *Music Theory Spectrum* 5/1: 1–14.

———. 1987. The "Expanded Cadential Progression": A Category for the Analysis of Classical Form. *Journal of Musicological Research* 7/2: 215–57.

———. 1998. *Classical Form: A Theory of Formal Functions for the Instrumental Music of Haydn, Mozart, and Beethoven.* Oxford: Oxford University Press.

Christensen, Thomas. 1993. Music Theory and Its Histories. In *Music Theory and the Exploration of the Past,* ed. Christopher Hatch and David W. Bernstein, 9–39. Chicago: University of Chicago Press.

Cohn, Richard. 1992a. The Dramatization of Hypermetric Conflicts in the Scherzo of Beethoven's Ninth Symphony. *19th-Century Music* 15/3: 188–205.

———. 1992b. Metric and Hypermetric Dissonance in the Menuetto of Mozart's Symphony in G minor, K.550. *Integral* 6: 1–33.

———. 2001. Complex Hemiolas, Ski-Hill Graphs and Metric Spaces. *Music Analysis* 20/3: 295–326.

Cone, Edward T. 1962. The Uses of Convention: Stravinsky and His Models. *Musical Quarterly* 48/3: 287–99.

———. 1968. *Musical Form and Musical Performance.* New York: Norton.

———. 1985. Musical Form and Musical Performance Reconsidered. *Music Theory Spectrum* 7/1: 149–58.

Cook, Nicholas. 1987. The Perception of Large-Scale Tonal Closure. *Music Perception* 5/2: 197–95.

Cooper, Grosvenor, and Leonard B. Meyer. 1960. *The Rhythmic Structure of Music.* Chicago: University of Chicago Press.

Corrigan, Vincent. 1992. Hemiola in the Eighteenth Century. In *Johann Sebastian: A Tercentenary Celebration,* ed. Seymour L. Benstock, 23–32. Westport, CT: Greenwood Press.

Cramer, Carl Friedrich, ed. 1787. *Magazin der Musik* 2. Hamburg: Musicalische Niederlage.
DeBellis, Mark. 1995. *Music and Conceptualization*. Cambridge: Cambridge University Press.
Dies, Albert Christoph. 1810. *Biographische Nachrichten von Joseph Haydn*. Vienna: Camesinaische Buchhandlung.
Dowling, W. Jay. 1984. Development of Musical Schemata in Children's Spontaneous Singing. In *Cognitive Processes in the Perception of Art,* ed. W. Ray Crozier and Antony J. Chapman, 145–63. Amsterdam: North-Holland.
Dowling, W. Jay, and Dane L. Harwood. 1986. *Music Cognition*. Orlando, FL: Academic Press.
Drake, Carolyn, Amandine Penel, Emmanuel Bigand, and Luca Stefan. 1997. Tapping in Time with Musical and Mechanical Sequences. In *Proceedings of the Third Triennal ESCOM Conference, Uppsala, June 7–12,* 286–91. Uppsala, Sweden: ESCOM.
Einstein, Alfred. 1945. *Mozart: His Character, His Work*. New York: Oxford University Press.
Eisen, Cliff. 2003. Mozart's Chamber Music. In *The Cambridge Companion to Mozart,* ed. Simon P. Keefe, 105–17. Cambridge: Cambridge University Press.
Fink, Gottfried Wilhelm. 1808–9. Über Takt, Taktarten, und ihr Charakteristisches. *Allgemeine musikalische Zeitung* 11 (28 December–11 January): cols. 193–98, 209–18, and 225–31.
Finscher, Ludwig. 2000. *Joseph Haydn und seine Zeit*. Laaber, Germany: Laaber-Verlag.
Fitzgibbons, Peter J., Andrew Pollatsek, and Ian B. Thomas. 1974. Detection of Temporal Gaps within and between Perceptual Tonal Groups. *Perception and Psychophysics* 16: 522–28.
Fodor, Jerry. 1983. *The Modularity of Mind: An Essay on Faculty Psychology*. Cambridge, MA: MIT Press.
Fraisse, Paul. 1963. *Psychology of Time*. New York: Harper.
———. 1980. Les synchronisations sensori-motrices aux rythmes. In *Anticipation et comportement,* ed. Jean Requin, 233–57. Paris: Éditions CNRS.
———. 1982. Rhythm and Tempo. In *The Psychology of Music,* ed. Diana Deutsch, 149–80. New York: Academic Press.
———. 1987. A Historical Approach to Rhythm as Perception. In *Action and Perception in Rhythm and Music,* ed. Alf Gabrielsson, 7–18. Stockholm: Royal Swedish Academy of Music.
Franěk, Marek, and Jiří Mates. 1997. Tempo Modulation Task. In *Proceedings of the Third Triennal ESCOM Conference, Uppsala, June 7–12,* 298–301. Uppsala, Sweden: ESCOM.
Fux, Johann Joseph. 1725. *Gradus ad parnassum*. Vienna: Ghelen.
Gerber, Ernst Ludwig. 1813. Eine freundliche Vorstellung über gearbeitete Instrumentalmusik, besonders über Symphonien. *Allgemeine musikalische Zeitung* 28 (14 July): cols. 457–63.
Gjerdingen, Robert O. 1988. *A Classic Turn of Phrase: Music and the Psychology of Convention*. Philadelphia: University of Pennsylvania Press.
———. 2007. *Music in the Galant Style: Being an Essay on Various Schemata Characteristic of Eighteenth-Century Music for Courtly Chambers, Chapels, and Theaters, Including Tasteful Passages of Music Drawn from Most Excellent Chapel Masters in the Employ of Noble and Noteworthy Personages, Said Music All Collected for the Reader's Delectation on the World Wide Web*. New York: Oxford University Press.
Grave, Floyd. 1984. Common-Time Displacement in Mozart. *Journal of Musicology* 3/4: 423–42.
———. 1985. Metrical Displacement and the Compound Measure in Eighteenth-Century Theory and Practice. *Theoria* 1: 25–60.
———. 1995. Metrical Dissonance in Haydn. *Journal of Musicology* 13/2: 168–202.
———. 2001. Concerto Style in Haydn's String Quartets. *Journal of Musicology* 18/1: 76–97.
Grave, Floyd, and Margaret Grave. 2006. *The String Quartets of Joseph Haydn*. New York: Oxford University Press.

Griesinger, Georg August. 1810. *Biographische Notizen über Joseph Haydn*. Leipzig: Breitkopf und Härtel.

Haimo, Ethan. 1995. *Haydn's Symphonic Forms: Essays in Compositional Logic*. Oxford: Clarendon.

Handel, Stephen. 1989. *Listening: An Introduction to the Perception of Auditory Events*. Cambridge: Cambridge University Press.

Handel, Stephen, and Gregory Lawson. 1983. The Contextual Nature of Rhythmic Interpretation. *Perception and Psychophysics* 34/2: 103–20.

Handel, Stephen, and James S. Oshinsky. 1981. The Meter of Syncopated Auditory Patterns. *Perception and Psychophysics* 30/1: 1–9.

Hasty, Christopher. 1997. *Meter as Rhythm*. Oxford: Oxford University Press.

Haydn, Joseph. 1978. *Streichquartette "Opus 64" und "Opus 71/74."* Ed. Georg Feder and Isidor Saslav, in collaboration with Warren Kirkendale. *Joseph Haydn Werke*. Ser. 12, vol. 5. Munich, Germany: Henle.

———. 1985. *Quartetto B-Dur Op. 50, No. 1, Hob. III:44*. Ed. H. C. Robbins Landon. *Streichquartette. Urtext-Ausgabe*. Vienna: Doblinger.

———. 1986. *Klaviertrios, 3. Folge*. Ed. Irmgard Becker-Glauch. *Joseph Haydn Werke*. Ser. 17, vol. 3. Munich, Germany: Henle.

———. 1987a. *Quartetto A-Dur Op. 55, No. 1, Hob. III:60*. Ed. H. C. Robbins Landon. *Streichquartette. Urtext-Ausgabe*. Vienna: Doblinger.

———. 1987b. *Quartetto f-Moll Op. 55, No. 2, Hob. III:61*. Ed. H. C. Robbins Landon. *Streichquartette. Urtext-Ausgabe*. Vienna: Doblinger.

———. 2003. *6 String Quartets Opus 50, Hoboken III:44–49*. Ed. Simon Rowland-Jones. London: Edition Peters.

———. 2004. *6 String Quartets Opus 54/55, Hoboken III:57–62*. Ed. Simon Rowland-Jones. London: Edition Peters.

Hepokoski, James, and Warren Darcy. 1997. The Medial Caesura and Its Role in the Eighteenth-Century Sonata Form Exposition. *Music Theory Spectrum* 19/2: 115–54.

———. 2006. *Elements of Sonata Theory: Norms, Types, and Deformations in the Late Eighteenth-Century Sonata*. New York: Oxford University Press.

Horlacher, Gretchen. 1992. The Rhythms of Reiteration: Formal Development in Stravinsky's Ostinati. *Music Theory Spectrum* 14/2: 171–87.

Houle, George. 1987. *Meter in Music, 1600–1800: Performance, Perception, and Notation*. Bloomington: Indiana University Press.

Hoyt, Peter A. 1997. Review-Essay: Haydn's New Incoherence. *Music Theory Spectrum* 19/2: 264–84.

Huron, David. 2006. *Sweet Anticipation: Music and the Psychology of Expectation*. Cambridge, MA: MIT Press.

Huron, David, and Matthew Royal. 1996. What Is Melodic Accent? Converging Evidence from Musical Practice. *Music Perception* 13/4: 489–516.

Imbrie, Andrew. 1973. "Extra" Measures and Metrical Ambiguity in Beethoven. In *Beethoven Studies*, ed. Alan Tyson, 45–66. New York: Norton.

Irving, Howard. 1985. Haydn and Laurence Sterne: Similarities in Eighteenth-Century Literary and Musical Wit. *Current Musicology* 40: 34–49.

Irving, John. 1998. *Mozart: The "Haydn" Quartets*. Cambridge: Cambridge University Press.

Jackendoff, Ray. 1987. *Consciousness and the Computational Mind*. Cambridge, MA: MIT Press.

———. 1991. Musical Parsing and Musical Affect. *Music Perception* 9/2: 199–230.

———. 1992. Musical Processing and Musical Affect. In *Cognitive Bases of Musical Communication*, ed. Mari Riess Jones and Susan Holleran, 51–68. Washington, DC: American Psychological Association.

Jahn, Otto. 1891. *Life of Mozart*. Trans. Pauline D. Townsend. 3 vols. London: Novello, Ewer.
James, William. 1890. *The Principles of Psychology*. Cambridge: Cambridge University Press.
Junker, Karl Ludwig. 1776. *Zwanzig Componisten: Eine Skizze*. Bern: Bey der typographischen Gesellschaft.
Kaminsky, Peter M. 1989. Aspects of Harmony, Rhythm and Form in Schumann's *Papillons, Carnaval* and *Davidsbündlertänze*. Ph.D. diss., University of Rochester.
Keefe, Simon P. 2007. *Mozart's Viennese Instrumental Music: A Study of Stylistic Re-Invention*. Woodbridge, UK: Boydell.
Keller, Hans. 1956. The Chamber Music. In *The Mozart Companion*, ed. H. C. Robbins Landon and Donald Mitchell, 90–137. London: Rockliff.
Kirkendale, Warren. 1979. *Fugue and Fugato in Rococo and Classical Chamber Music*. Trans. Margaret Bent and Warren Kirkendale. Durham, NC: Duke University Press.
Kirnberger, Johann Philipp. 1771–79. *Die Kunst des reinen Satzes*. 2 vols. Vol. 1, Berlin: Rottmann, 1771. Vol. 2, secs. 1–3, Berlin and Königsberg: Decker und Hartung, 1776, 1777, and 1779.
———. 1782. *Anleitung zur Singekomposition*. Berlin: Decker.
———. 1982. *The Art of Strict Musical Composition*. Trans. David Beach and Jurgen Thym. New Haven, CT: Yale University Press.
[Kirnberger, Johann Philipp, and Johann Abraham Peter Schulz]. 1794. Rhythmus. In Johann Georg Sulzer, *Allgemeine Theorie der schönen Künste*, 4th ed., 4:90–105. Leipzig: In der Weidmannschen Buchhandlung. Reprint, Hildesheim, Germany: Georg Olms, 1967.
Koch, Heinrich Christoph. 1782–93. *Versuch einer Anleitung zur Composition*. 3 vols. Vol. 1, Rudolstadt: 1782. Vols. 2 and 3, Leipzig: Adam Friedrich Böhme, 1787 and 1793. Reprint, Hildesheim, Germany: Georg Olms, 1969.
———. 1802. *Musikalisches Lexikon*. Frankfurt-am-Main: August Hermann der Jüngere. Reprint, Kassel, Germany: Bärenreiter, 2001.
———. 1983. *Introductory Essay on Composition*. Trans. Nancy Kovaleff Baker. New Haven, CT: Yale University Press.
Komar, Arthur. 1971. *Theory of Suspensions*. Princeton, NJ: Princeton University Press.
Kramer, Jonathan. 1988. *The Time of Music: New Meanings, New Temporalities, New Listening Strategies*. New York: Schirmer.
Krebs, Harald. 1987. Some Extensions of the Concepts of Metrical Consonance and Dissonance. *Journal of Music Theory* 31/1: 99–120.
———. 1999. *Fantasy Pieces: Metrical Dissonance in the Music of Robert Schumann*. Oxford: Oxford University Press.
Krummacher, Friedhelm. 2001. *Das Streichquartett*. Handbuch der musikalischen Gattungen 6. Vol. 1: *Von Haydn bis Schubert*. Laaber, Germany: Laaber-Verlag.
Küster, Konrad. 1996. *Mozart: A Musical Biography*. Trans. Mary Whittall. Oxford: Clarendon.
Landon, H. C. Robbins. 1978. *Haydn: Chronicle and Works*. Vol. 2: *Haydn at Eszterháza 1766–1790*. London: Thames and Hudson.
Large, Edward W., and Mari Riess Jones. 1999. The Dynamics of Attending: How We Track Time-Varying Events. *Psychological Review* 106/1: 119–59.
Large, Edward W., and John F. Kolen. 1994. Resonance and the Perception of Musical Meter. *Connection Science* 6/1: 177–208.
Large, Edward W., and Caroline Palmer. 2002. Perceiving Temporal Regularity in Music. *Cognitive Science* 26/1: 1–37.
LaRue, Jan. 1970. *Guidelines to Style Analysis*. New York: Norton.
Lee, Christopher S. 1991. The Perception of Metrical Structure: Experimental Evidence and a Model. In *Representing Musical Structure*, ed. Peter Howell, Robert West, and Ian Cross, 59–127. New York: Academic Press.

Lerdahl, Fred. 1988. Tonal Pitch Space. *Music Perception* 5/3: 315–50.
———. 1989. Atonal Prolongational Structure. *Contemporary Music Review* 4/1: 65–87.
———. 2001. *Tonal Pitch Space*. Oxford: Oxford University Press.
Lerdahl, Fred, and Ray Jackendoff. 1983. *A Generative Theory of Tonal Music*. Cambridge, MA: MIT Press.
Lester, Joel. 1986. *The Rhythms of Tonal Music*. Carbondale: Southern Illinois University Press.
Levy, Janet M. 1981. Gesture, Form, and Syntax in Haydn's Music. In *Haydn Studies*, ed. Jens Peter Larsen, Howard Serwer, and James Webster, 355–62. New York: Norton.
———. 1982. Texture as a Sign in Classic and Early Romantic Music. *Journal of the American Musicological Society* 35/3: 482–531.
———. 1992. "Something Mechanical Encrusted on the Living": A Source of Musical Wit and Humour. In *Convention in Eighteenth- and Nineteenth-Century Music: Essays in Honor of Leonard G. Ratner*, ed. Wye J. Allanbrook, Janet M. Levy, and William P. Mahrt, 225–56. Stuyvesant, NY: Pendragon.
Lewin, David. 1981. On Harmony and Meter in Brahms's Op. 76, No. 8. *19th-Century Music* 4/3: 261–65.
London, Justin. 1993. Loud Rests and Other Strange Metric Phenomena, or Meter as Heard. *Music Theory Online* 0/2; http://mto.societymusictheory.org/issues/mto.93.0.2/mto.93.0.2.london.art.
———. 2001. Rhythm. In *The New Grove Dictionary of Music and Musicians*, 2nd ed., ed. John Tyrrell and Stanley Sadie, 21:277–309. London: Macmillan.
———. 2004. *Hearing in Time: Psychological Aspects of Musical Meter*. Oxford: Oxford University Press.
Longuet-Higgins, H. Christopher, and Christopher S. Lee. 1982. The Perception of Musical Rhythms. *Perception* 11/2: 115–28.
———. 1984. The Rhythmic Interpretation of Monophonic Music. *Music Perception* 1/4: 424–41.
Margulis, Elizabeth Hellmuth. 2007. Silences in Music Are Musical Not Silent: An Exploratory Study of Context Effects on the Experience of Musical Pauses. *Music Perception* 24/5: 485–506.
Marpurg, Friedrich Wilhelm. 1760–63. *Kritische Briefe über die Tonkunst*. 2 vols. Berlin: Birnstiel. Reprint, Hildesheim, Germany: Georg Olms, 1974.
Mattheson, Johann. 1722. *Critica Musica*. Hamburg: Author.
———. 1739. *Der vollkommene Capellmeister*. Hamburg: Herold.
———. 1981. *Der vollkommene Capellmeister*. Trans. Ernest C. Harriss. Ann Arbor: UMI Research Press.
Maurer Zenck, Claudia. 2001. *Vom Takt: Untersuchungen zur Theorie und kompositorischen Praxis im ausgehenden 18. und beginnenden 19. Jahrhundert*. Vienna: Böhlau.
———. 2008. "Mannichfaltige Abweichungen von der gewöhnlichen Sonaten-Form": Beethoven's "Piano Solo" Op. 31 No. 1 and the Challenge of Communication. In *Communication in Eighteenth-Century Music*, ed. Danuta Mirka and Kofi Agawu, 53–79. Cambridge: Cambridge University Press.
Meyer, Leonard B. 1956. *Emotion and Meaning in Music*. Chicago: University of Chicago Press.
———. 1967. *Music, the Arts and Ideas*. Chicago: University of Chicago Press.
———. 1973. *Explaining Music: Essays and Explorations*. Chicago: University of Chicago Press.
———. 1989. *Style and Music: Theory, History, and Ideology*. Philadelphia: University of Pennsylvania Press.

———. 1998. A Universe of Universals. *Journal of Musicology* 16/1, 3–25.
Michaelis, Christian Friedrich. 1807. Über das Humoristische oder Launige in der musikalischen Komposition. *Allgemeine musikalische Zeitung* 9 (12 August): cols. 725–29.
Monelle, Raymond. 2006. *The Musical Topic: Hunt, Military and Pastoral*. Bloomington: Indiana University Press.
———. 2007. The Orchestral String Portamento as Expressive Topic. Paper delivered at the Eighteenth International Congress of the International Musicological Society, Zurich, 10–15 July.
Mozart, Leopold. 1756. *Versuch einer gründlichen Violinschule*. Augsburg: Lotter.
Mozart, Wolfgang Amadeus. 1961. *Streichquartette, Band 3*. Ed. Ludwig Finscher. *Neue Mozart Ausgabe*. Ser. 8, gr. 20, sec. 1. Kassel, Germany: Bärenreiter.
———. 1967. *Streichquintette*. Ed. Ernst Hess and Ernst Fritz Schmitz. *Neue Mozart Ausgabe*. Ser. 8, gr. 18, sec. 1. Kassel, Germany: Bärenreiter, 1967.
———. 1975. *Duos und Trios für Streicher und Bläser*. Ed. Dietrich Berke and Marius Flothuis. Ser. 8, gr. 21. Kassel, Germany: Bärenreiter, 1975.
Muffat, Georg. 1698. *Florilegium secundum*. Passau.
Narmour, Eugene. 1977. *Beyond Schenkerism: The Need for Alternatives in Music Analysis*. Chicago: University of Chicago Press.
Parncutt, Richard. 1994. A Perceptual Model of Pulse Salience and Metrical Accent in Musical Rhythms. *Music Perception* 11/4: 409–64.
Paul, Steven E. 1980. Wit, Comedy, and Humour in the Instrumental Music of Franz Joseph Haydn. Ph.D. diss., Cambridge University.
———. 1981. Comedy, Wit, and Humor in Haydn's Instrumental Music. In *Haydn Studies: Proceedings of the International Haydn Conference, Washington, D.C., 1975*, ed. Jens Peter Larsen, Howard Serwer, and James Webster, 450–56. New York: Norton.
Povel, Dirk-Jan. 1981. Internal Representation of Simple Temporal Patterns. *Journal of Experimental Psychology: Human Perception and Performance* 7/1: 3–18.
———. 1984. A Theoretical Framework for Rhythm Perception. *Psychological Research* 45/4: 315–37.
Povel, Dirk-Jan, and Peter Essens. 1985. Perception of Temporal Patterns. *Music Perception* 2/4: 411–40.
Povel, Dirk-Jan, and Hans Okkerman. 1981. Accents in Equitone Sequences. *Perception and Psychophysics* 6: 565–72.
Printz, Wolfgang Caspar. 1696. *Phrynis mitilenaeus, oder Satyrischer Componist*. Dresden: Mieth.
Quantz, Johann Joachim. 1752. *Versuch einer Anweisung, die Flöte traversiere zu spielen*. Berlin: Johann Friedrich Voß.
Rameau, Jean-Philippe. 1726. *Nouveau système de musique théorique*. Paris: Ballard.
Ratner, Leonard. 1949. Harmonic Aspects of Classic Form. *Journal of the American Musicological Society* 2/3: 159–68.
———. 1980. *Classic Music: Expression, Form, and Style*. New York: Schirmer.
Reichardt, Johann. 1782. *Musikalisches Kunstmagazin*. Berlin: Verlag des Verfassers.
———. 1810. *Vertraute Briefe geschrieben auf einer Reise nach Wien und den österreichischen Staaten zu Ende des Jahres 1808 und zu Anfang 1809*. Vol. 1. Amsterdam: Kunst- und Industrie-Comtoir.
Riepel, Joseph. 1752–68. *Anfangsgründe zur musicalischen Setzkunst*. 5 vols. Vol. 1: *De Rhythmopoeia oder von der Tactordnung*. Augsburg: Emerich Felix Bader, 1752. Vol. 2: *Grundregeln zur Tonordnung insgemein*. Frankfurt-am-Main and Leipzig: 1755. Vol. 3: *Gründliche Erklärung der Tonordnung insbesondere*. Frankfurt-am-Main and Leipzig: 1757. Vol. 4: *Erläuterung der betrüglichen Tonordnung*. Augsburg: Johann Jacob Lotter, 1765. Vol. 5: *Unentbehrliche Anmerkung zum Contrapunct*. Regensburg: Jacob Christian Krippner, 1768.

[Rochlitz, Friedrich]. 1805–6. Über den zweckmässigen Gebrauch der Mittel der Tonkunst. *Allgemeine musikalische Zeitung* 8 (2 October 1805–15 January 1806): cols. 3–10, 49–59, 193–201, 241–49.

Rosen, Charles. 1971. *The Classical Style: Haydn, Mozart, Beethoven*. New York: Norton.

Rosenthal, David. 1992. Emulation of Human Rhythm Perception. *Computer Music Journal* 16: 64–76.

Rothstein, William N. 1989. *Phrase Rhythm in Tonal Music*. New York: Schirmer.

———. 1995. Beethoven with and without *Kunstgepräng*: Metrical Ambiguity Reconsidered. In *Beethoven Forum IV*, ed. Christopher Reynolds, Lewis Lockwood, and James Webster, 165–93. Lincoln: University of Nebraska Press.

———. 2008. National Metrical Types in Music of the Eighteenth and Early Nineteenth Centuries. In *Communication in Eighteenth-Century Music*, ed. Danuta Mirka and Kofi Agawu, 112–59. Cambridge: Cambridge University Press.

Rushton, Julian. 2006. *Mozart*. New York: Oxford University Press.

Samarotto, Frank. 1999a. Strange Dimensions: Regularity and Irregularity in Deep Levels of Rhythmic Reductions. In *Schenker Studies 2*, ed. Carl Schachter and Heidi Siegel, 222–38. Cambridge: Cambridge University Press.

———. 1999b. A Theory of Temporal Plasticity in Tonal Music: An Extension of the Schenkerian Approach to Rhythm with Special Reference to Beethoven's Late Music. Ph.D. diss., City University of New York.

Schachter, Carl. 1976. Rhythm and Linear Analysis: A Preliminary Study. In *The Music Forum 4*, ed. Felix Salzer and Carl Schachter, 281–334. New York: Columbia University Press.

Scheibe, Johann Adolph. 1745. *Critischer Musikus*. Leipzig: Breitkopf.

Schick, Hartmut. 1994. Ein Quintett im Diskurs mit dem Streichquartett. Mozarts Streichquintett C-Dur, KV 515. In *Mozarts Streichquintette: Beiträge zum musikalischen Satz, zum Gattungskontext und zu Quellenfragen*, ed. Cliff Eisen and Wolf-Dieter Seiffert, 69–101. Stuttgart, Germany: Franz Steiner.

Schmalfeldt, Janet. 1992. Cadential Processes: The Evaded Cadence and the "One More Time" Technique. *Journal of Musicological Research* 12/1–2: 1–52.

[Schulz, Johann Abraham Peter]. 1794. Takt. In Johann Georg Sulzer, *Allgemeine Theorie der schönen Künste*, 4th ed., 4:490–502. Leipzig: In der Weidmannschen Buchhandlung. Reprint, Hildesheim, Germany: Georg Olms, 1967.

———. 1800. Über die in Sulzers Theorie der schönen Künste unter dem Artikel Verrückung angeführten zwey Beyspiele von Pergolesi und Graun. *Allgemeine musikalische Zeitung* 2 (15 January): cols. 273–80.

Schwindt-Gross, Nicole. 1989. Einfache, zusammengesetzte und doppelt notierte Takte: Ein Aspekt der Takttheorie im 18. Jahrhundert. *Musiktheorie* 4/3: 203–22.

Seidel, Wilhelm. 1975. *Über Rhythmustheorien der Neuzeit*. Bern: Francke.

Sisman, Elaine. 1993. *Haydn and the Classical Variation*. Cambridge, MA: Harvard University Press.

———, ed. 1997. *Haydn and His World*. Princeton, NJ: Princeton University Press.

———. 2005. Haydn's Career and the Idea of Multiple Audience. In *The Cambridge Companion to Haydn*, ed. Caryl L. Clark, 3–16. Cambridge: Cambridge University Press.

Snyder, Joel, and Carol L. Krumhansl. 2001. Tapping to Ragtime: Cues to Pulse Finding. *Music Perception* 18/4: 455–89.

Somfai, László. 1981. Haydn's London String Quartets. In *Haydn Studies: Proceedings of the International Haydn Conference, Washington, D.C., 1975*, ed. Jens Peter Larsen, Howard Serwer, and James Webster, 389–91. New York: Norton.

Spitzer, Michael. 2004. *Metaphor and Musical Thought*. Chicago: University of Chicago Press.

Steedman, Mark. 1977. The Perception of Musical Rhythm and Meter. *Perception* 6/5: 555–70.

Steinbeck, Wolfram. 1984. Mozarts "Scherzi": Zur Beziehung zwischen Haydns Streichquartetten op. 33 und Mozarts Haydn-Quartetten. *Archiv für Musikwissenschaft* 41/2: 208–31.

Sulzer, Johann Georg. 1792–94. *Allgemeine Theorie der schönen Künste*. 4th ed. 4 vols. Leipzig: In der Weidmannschen Buchhandlung. Reprint, Hildesheim, Germany: Georg Olms, 1967.

Sutcliffe, W. Dean. 1992. *Haydn: String Quartets, Op. 50*. Cambridge: Cambridge University Press.

Temperley, David. 1995. Motivic Perception and Modularity. *Music Perception* 13/2: 141–69.

———. 1999. What's Key for Key? The Krumhansl-Schmuckler Key-Finding Algorithm Reconsidered. *Music Perception* 17/1: 65–100.

———. 2001. *The Cognition of Basic Musical Structures*. Cambridge, MA: MIT Press.

———. 2003. End-Accented Phrases: An Analytical Exploration. *Journal of Music Theory* 47/1: 125–54.

Temperley, David, and Christopher Bartlette. 2002. Parallelism as a Factor in Metrical Analysis. *Music Perception* 20/2: 117–49.

Temperley, David, and Daniel Sleator. 1999. Modeling Meter and Harmony: A Preference-Rule Approach. *Computer Music Journal* 23/1: 10–27.

Toiviainen, Petri. 2001. Real-Time Recognition of Improvisations with Adaptive Oscillators and a Recursive Bayesian Classifier. *Journal of New Music Research* 30/2: 137–48.

Tovey, Sir Donald Francis. 1935. *Essays in Musical Analysis*. Vol. 1: *Symphonies*. London: Oxford University Press.

———. 1949. Haydn's Chamber Music. In *Essays and Lectures on Music*, 1–64. London: Oxford University Press.

Triest, Johann Karl Friedrich. 1801. Bemerkungen über die Ausbildung der Tonkunst in Deutschland im achtzehnten Jahrhundert. *Allgemeine musikalische Zeitung* 3 (1 January–25 March): cols. 225–35, 241–49, 257–64, 273–86, 297–308, 321–31, 369–79, 389–401, 405–10, 421–32, and 437–45.

Türk, Daniel Gottlob. 1789. *Klavierschule, oder Anweisung zum Klavierspielen für Lehrer und Lernende*. Leipzig: Schwickert und Hemmerde. Reprint, Kassel, Germany: Bärenreiter, 1997.

———. 1982. *School of Clavier Playing or Instructions in Playing the Clavier for Teachers and Students*. Trans. Raymond H. Haggh. Lincoln: University of Nebraska Press.

Vogler, Georg Joseph. 1778. *Betrachtungen der Mannheimer Tonschule*. Vol. 1. Mannheim. Reprint, Hildesheim, Germany: Georg Olms, 1974.

Vos, Piet G. 2000. Tonality Induction: Theoretical Problems and Dilemmas. *Music Perception* 17/4: 403–16.

Weber, [Friedrich August]. 1800. Über komische Charakteristik und Karrikatur in praktischen Musikwerken. *Allgemeine musikalische Zeitung* 3 (26 November–13 December): cols. 138–43, 157–62.

Weber, Gottfried. 1821. *Versuch einer geordneten Theorie der Tonsetzkunst zum Selbstunterrichte*. Vol. 3. Mainz: Schott.

Webster, James. 1991. *Haydn's "Farewell" Symphony and the Idea of Classical Style: Through-Composition and Cyclic Integration in His Instrumental Music*. Cambridge: Cambridge University Press.

———. 2007. The Rhetoric of Improvisation in Haydn's Keyboard Music. In *Haydn and the Performance of Rhetoric*, ed. Tom Beghin and Sander M. Goldberg, 172–212. Chicago: University of Chicago Press.

Wheelock, Gretchen A. 1992. *Haydn's Ingenious Jesting with Art*. New York: Schirmer.

Wheelock, Gretchen A. 2003. The "Rhetorical Pause" and Metaphors of Conversation in Haydn's Quartets. In *Haydn und das Streichquartett,* Eisenstädter Haydn-Berichte 2, ed. Georg Feder and Walter Reicher, 67–85. Tutzing, Germany: Schneider.

Whitmore, Philip. 1991. *Unpremeditated Art: The Cadenza in the Classical Keyboard Concerto*. Oxford: Clarendon.

Willner, Channan. 1991. The Two-Length Bar Revisited: Handel and the Hemiola. *Göttinger Händel-Beiträge* 4: 208–31.

———. 1996. More on Handel and the Hemiola: Overlapping Hemiolas. *Music Theory Online* 2/3; http://smt.ucsb.edu/mto/issues/mto.96.2.3/mto.96/2.3.willner.html.

———. 1999. Sequential Expansion and Handelian Phrase Rhythm. In *Schenker Studies 2,* ed. Carl Schachter and Heidi Siegel, 192–221. Cambridge: Cambridge University Press.

———. 2005. Durational Pacing in Handel's Instrumental Works: The Nature of Temporality in the Music of the High Baroque. Ph.D. diss., City University of New York.

———. 2007a. Kirnberger's 4/4 Meters and Handel's Basic Paces: The Growth of Temporal Narrativity across Four Decades of Composition; www.channanwillner.com/online.htm, accessed 1 December.

———. 2007b. Metrical Displacement and Metrically Dissonant Hemiolas; www.channanwillner.com/online.htm, accessed 2 December.

Wundt, Wilhelm. 1874. *Grundzüge der physiologischen Psychologie*. Leipzig, Germany: Engelmann.

Yeston, Maury. 1976. *The Stratification of Musical Rhythm*. New Haven, CT: Yale University Press.

Zbikowski, Lawrence M. 2008. Dance Topoi, Sonic Analogues and Musical Grammar: Communicating with Music in the Eighteenth Century. In *Communication in Eighteenth-Century Music,* ed. Danuta Mirka and Kofi Agawu, 283–309. Cambridge: Cambridge University Press.

Zuckerkandl, Victor. 1956. *Sound and Symbol: Music and the External World.* Trans. Willard R. Trask. New York: Pantheon.

INDEX OF COMPOSITIONS BY HAYDN AND MOZART

Page numbers in bold refer to musical examples.

HAYDN, JOSEPH
Piano Trio No. 45 in E-flat major, Hob. XV:29, iii, 206–7n24
string quartets
Op. 2 No. 4 in F major, iv, 250
Op. 9 No. 2 in E-flat major, i, 306; iv, 306
Op. 9 No. 3 in G major, ii, 133, 136, 305
Op. 9 No. 5 in B-flat major, ii, 306; iv, 306
Op. 9 No. 6 in A major, i, 306
Op. 17 No. 1 in E major, ii, 306
Op. 17 No. 2 in F major, iv, 306
Op. 17 No. 3 in E-flat major, 230n37
Op. 17 No. 4 in C minor, ii, 306
Op. 17 No. 5 in G major, i, 179, 305–6
Op. 17 No. 6 in D major, i, 306
Op. 20 No. 1 in E-flat major, ii, 306; iv, 306
Op. 20 No. 3 in G minor, i, 179, 305–6
Op. 20 No. 4 in D major, ii, 306; iii, 136, 305; iv, 306
Op. 20 No. 6 in A major, i, 307
Op. 33 No. 1 in B minor, i, 84n68, 307
Op. 33 No. 2 in E-flat major, "The Joke," iv, 111
Op. 33 No. 3 in C major, "The Bird," i, 156; iii, 146
Op. 33 No. 4 in B-flat major, i, 34n6
Op. 33 No. 5 in G major, i, 34n6, 306, 307; iii, 147, 305
Op. 33 No. 6 in D major, ii, 118
Op. 50 No. 1 in B-flat major, i, 34n6, 120–22, **121**; ii, 212–14, **214**, 231; iii, 173–74, **173**, 197–98, **198**; iv, 111, **112**, 204, 205
Op. 50 No. 2 in C major, i, 249, 254–73, **255–56**, **261–62**, **265**, **269–70**, **272**, **274**, 286, 298, 307; ii, 118, 154n20; iii, 103–4, **104**, 113, 236n47
Op. 50 No. 3 in E-flat major, i, 111, 146, 147, **148**; iii, 236n47; iv, 175–76, **177–78**, 179, 185, 199, **199**, 240–41, 243, 249, 251, 252, 254, 273n29, 275, 305, 307
Op. 50 No. 4 in F-sharp minor, 260n10; iii, 126, **126**, 142–43, **143**, 251
Op. 50 No. 5 in F major, "The Dream," i, 99–100, **100**, 111, 124–25, **125**, 180, **181**, 307; ii, 71–72, **73**; iii, 139–40, **140**, 142, 147, 208, 230, 245n59, 250, 251, 253; iv, 147, 238–40, **240**, 253, **253**
Op. 50 No. 6 in D major, "The Frog," i, 33–35, **34**, 205; ii, 212–13, **213**, 231; iii, 54–56, **54**, 57, 60, 67, 104–6, **105**, 164, 169–70, **170–71**, 199, 306; iv, 37–38, **37**, 60, 179, **179–80**, 232n45
Op. 54 No. 1 in G major, i, 166, **167**; iii, 143–44, **145**, 147; iv, 116, **117**, 118, **119**, 236n47
Op. 54 No. 2 in C major, i, 103, **103**, 185–86, **186–87**, 189, 252, 298, 305, 307; iv, 111, 305
Op. 54 No. 3 in E major, i, 53, **53**, 67, 166–67, **167**, 203, **203–4**, 252; iii, 219–20, **220**, 224
Op. 55 No. 1 in A major, i, 124, **125**, 154n20, 214–17, **215**, **217**, 300; ii, 153, **153–54**; iii, 236n47; iv, 111
Op. 55 No. 2 in F minor, "The Razor," 230n37; ii, 111–12; iii, 118; iv, 147, 249, 275–95, **276**, **281**, **284**, **288–89**, **292**, **293**, 298–99, 300, 305, 307
Op. 55 No. 3 in B-flat major, 90n73; i, 150; iii, 109–10, **109**; iv, 85–88, **86**, 90, 118, 300
Op. 64 No. 1 in C major, ii, 150
Op. 64 No. 2 in B minor, i, 83–85, **85**, 100–101, **101**, 140, 232, 250; iii, 106, **107**; iv, 112, 118
Op. 64 No. 3 in B-flat major, i, 180–81, **182**, 195–96, **196**, 307; iii, 62, **63**, 106, **107**, 111, 150, **150**, 166; iv, 37–38, **37**, 60–61, **61**, 111, 232, 306
Op. 64 No. 4 in G major, ii, 61–62, **62**

Op. 64 No. 5 in D major, "The Lark," i, 183, **184**, 189, 208, 307; iii, 141, **141**, 147, 187–89, **188**, 236n47, 252; iv, 154, **155**, 304
Op. 64 No. 6 in E-flat major, i, 82, **83**, 196, **197**, 202–3, **202**, 250; iii, 150, 236n47, 237–38, **239**; iv, 107–8, **108**, 114–15, 127, 205, 230, 304
Op. 71 No. 1 in B-flat major, i, 34n6, 307; iv, 307
Op. 71 No. 2 in D major, i, 307
Op. 71 No. 3 in E-flat major, i, 34n6, 307; iv, 264n20
Op. 74 No. 1 in C major, i, 34n6; ii, 307
Op. 74 No. 2 in F major, iv, 307
Op. 74 No. 3 in G minor, "The Rider," i, 307
Op. 76 No. 2 in D minor, "Fifths," iii, 191n17
Op. 76 No. 3 in C major, "Emperor," i, 115n22
Op. 76 No. 4 in B-flat major, "Sunrise," iv, 298n9, 307
Op. 76 No. 5 in D major, iii, 139n8; iv, 307
Op. 76 No. 6 in E-flat major, iii, 62n42; iv, 179, 307
Op. 77 No. 1 in G major, i, 307
Op. 77 No. 2 in F major, i, 140n10; iv, 115n22
Symphony No. 45 in F-sharp minor, "Farewell," i, 204
Symphony No. 60 in C major, "Il Distratto," 300
Symphony No. 65 in A major, iii, 145n15
Symphony No. 98 in B-flat major, iv, 299n11
Trumpet Concerto in E-flat major, Hob. VIIe:1, 140n10

MOZART, WOLFGANG AMADEUS
Divertimento for String Trio in E-flat major, K. 563, iii, 147, 150; v, 147, **147**
Don Giovanni, K. 527, 164
Eine kleine Nachtmusik, K. 525, iii, 172, **172**
Ein musikalischer Spass, K. 522, 89
Piano Concerto in B-flat major, K. 238, ii, 285n42
Piano Concerto in D minor, K. 466, i, 204
Piano Sonata in C major, K. 330, i, 247n68
Piano Sonata in A major, K. 331, i, 16n27, 77n57, 231n41
Sonata for Piano and Violin in F major, K. 377, ii, 231n41
string quartets
K. 387 in G major, i, 304; ii, 61–62, 304; iv, 225, 229–30, 231, 245n59
K. 421 in D minor, i, 226, 245n59; iv, 303
K. 428 in E-flat major, ii, 162, 304; iii, 162; iv, 304n22
K. 464 in A major, i, 162, 303; ii, 304n22; iv, 302, 303
K. 465 in C major, "Dissonance," i, 263n17; iii, 62n42; iv, 304n22
K. 575 in D major, i, 115–16, **115**, 205, 226, **226**, 230, 231, 245n59, 251; iii, 147, **148**, 221n19; iv, 190, **191**, 205, 303
K. 589 in B-flat major, i, 138, **138**, 146, 147, **171**, 172, 205, 252, 253, 303; ii, 151–52, **151**, 154n20; iii, 162–63, **162**, 253, **254**; iv, 304, 305
K. 590 in F major, 90n73; i, 90–91, **91**; ii, 162, 163, **163**; iv, 154, **155–56**, 156, 205, 304
string quintets
K. 406 in C minor, iii, 191n17
K. 515 in C major, 308; i, 214n8, 251, 304; ii, 146, 148, **149–50**, 167, **168**, 303; iii, 63–65, **65**, 66, 71, 150–51, **151**, 220–21, **222**, 224, 231, 250, 303; iv, 304
K. 516 in G minor, 308; i, 126, **127**; ii, 127–29, **128**, 162, 304; iii, 115n22; iv, 88–89, **89**, 91, 151–52, **152**, 304–5
K. 593 in D major, 308; i, 68, **69**, 72, 81n64, 304, 305; ii, 205; iii, 150, 190–95, **194–95**, 249, 303; iv, 114, **114**, 127, 226–27, **227**, 245n59, 304
K. 614 in E-flat major, 299n11, 308; i, 66, 304; ii, 66; iii, 65–67, **66**, 220–22, **223**, 224, 231, 250; iv, 114–15, **114**, 127, 205, 304
Symphony No. 40 in G minor, K. 550, i, 243–44; iii, 164
Symphony No. 41 in C major, K. 551, "Jupiter," iv, 241n52

GENERAL INDEX

Absatz (phrase ending), 76, 79–81, 87, 211, 238n48, 259n7
  Grundabsatz, 79, 238n48, 259n8
  Quintabsatz, 79, 110n16, 117n25, 238n48, 259n9
Abteilungspunkte (points of division), 7, 75–77. See also *Ruhepunkte* (resting points)
accent
  durational (length), 38–40, 42–45, 64n45, 67, 94, 123, 124, 126, 131, 165, 208, 246n63 (*see also* Metrical Preference Rules [MPRs], MPR 5)
  dynamic (stress), 4, 6–7, 38–42, 43, 47, 67, 94, 123, 126, 130, 131, 165, 208 (*see also* Metrical Preference Rules [MPRs], MPR 4)
  "grammatical," 41, 71, 123–24
  harmonic, 57, 126 (*see also* harmonic salience)
  initial, 39, 44, 45–46, 48, 51, 67n49, 69 (*see also* Metrical Preference Rules [MPRs], MPR 2)
  melodic, 38–39, 47–49, 59, 174, 208
  metrical, 4–5, 8, 10–12, 14, 16, 22–23, 41, 42, 43, 47, 69
  "oratoric," 41
  "pathetic," 41
  phenomenal, 5, 14, 22–23, 38–39, 41, 42, 43–45, 48, 61n41, 69, 120, 123, 139, 174
  structural, 38–39, 69 (*see also* cadence)
  subjective, 5, 35–38, 39, 44–45, 60, 61n41
  terminal, 39, 44, 45, 48, 67n49, 69
  textural, 39, 58
accompaniment
  "oom-pah-oom-pah," "oom-pah-pah," 176, 254
  syncopated, 204–5, 251
affects, 102, 224–25, 229. *See also* topics
Affektenlehre, 225
Allanbrook, Wye J., xii, 77n57, 84, 224–25, 229–30, 231, 250, 297n8
alla zoppa, 251
amateur (*Liebhaber*), xi, 193. *See also* connoisseur (*Kenner*)
anticipation (*Vorausnahme*), 200–201, 251
appendix (*Anhang*)
  to cadence (*Kadenz*), 79
  as a means of phrase expansion, 214n9, 238, 259
artful imitation of musical bungling
  of incompetent performers, 89, 152–53, 185, 295, 298–99
  of an inept composer, 88–89, 216–17, 279, 283, 285, 292, 294, 300–301, 305

Bach, Carl Philipp Emanuel, 60, 222
Bach, Johann Sebastian, 17–18, 245n62
Baker, Nancy Kovaleff, 83n65, 93n1, 279n37
Bartlette, Christopher, 137, 139, 142
bass, 59–60, 61–62, 63, 72, 95–97, 128, 201
Beethoven, Ludwig van, 219, 222, 301, 302n19
  Piano Sonata in G major, Op. 31 No. 1, 299n11
  Piano Sonata in F minor, Op. 57, "Appassionata," 227n30, 238n49
  Piano Sonata in E major, Op. 109, i, 223n22
  Symphony No. 5 in C minor, Op. 67, i, 246–47
  Symphony No. 9 in D minor, Op. 125, i, 247n66; ii, 223–24
  Thirty-Three Variations on a Waltz by Diabelli in C major, Op. 120, 244
Beghin, Tom, 299n11
Bellman, Jonathan, 156n21, 275n32
Berger, Karol, xii
Bergson, Henri, 28
Berry, Wallace, 39n14, 57, 58, 241n53, 244
Bindung (tie). See *ligaturae* (ties)
Bonds, Mark Evan, xii, 252, 296n4, 301n15, 302n19
bourrée, 225, 229, 250, 298n9
Brahms, Johannes, Intermezzo in A Minor, Op. 76 No. 7, 223n22
Bregman, Albert, 57
brilliant style, 250

Brower, Candace, 22n37, 32n4, 152n19
Budday, Wolfgang, 241n50, 258n6
Burney, Charles, 296
Burnham, Scott, 296n4
Burstein, Poundie, 296n4

cadence, 38–39, 69–70, 72–74, 77, 79, 140
  deceptive, 107, 113, 259n8, 285n43
  evaded, 217n13, 260n12, 262n14, 264n21
  "feminine," 74, 80, 81 (*see also* feminine ending [*weiblicher Ausgang*])
  as the limit of short-term musical memory (STMM), 21–22
  "masculine," 74
  See also cadence (*Kadenz, Tonschluss*); Metrical Preference Rules (MPRs), MPR 7
cadence (*Kadenz, Tonschluss*), 111, 113, 118, 147–50, 161–62, 205, 251, 300
  concept of, 79
  metrical position of, 74, 76, 79, 130n38, 211, 262n13, 285
  and musical form, 258, 290
  and phrase structure, 259
cadenza, 118, 153, 250
caesura
  decorations of, 79–82, 236–37
  metrical position of, 74–78, 130n38, 211, 236–37
Caplin, William, 45–46, 51, 52, 56, 213n6, 260n12
categorization, 120n33
chorale, 250
church style, 225, 230, 231, 251
Cohn, Richard, 12n21, 158–59, 163, 164n31, 182n12, 224n23
comic music, 74, 89, 185, 295, 299, 301n17, 305, 306. *See also* humorous music
Cone, Edward T., ix, 13n22, 305n23
  "sonata principle," 294n51
connoisseur (*Kenner*), xi, xii, 77, 82, 83, 88, 102, 182n12, 193, 221n20, 230, 294, 301–2. *See also* amateur (*Liebhaber*); "historical listener"
consciousness, 19, 29–30, 169, 174. *See also* processing, central
contredanse, 84, 225, 230, 231, 250
conversation, 102, 299, 300
Cook, Nicolas, 207n26
Cooper, Grosvenor, ix, 13, 14n23, 41n16, 113, 245n60
cyclic integration, 252–53, 257n3, 286n45

Darcy, Warren, 110n17
deferral, 36, 145–46
  structural vs. contextual, 146
Dies, Albert Christoph, 296
displacement (*Versetzung*), 137
distraction, 102, 300–301
Dittersdorf, Carl Ditters von, 301n16, 308
double measures (*Doppeltakte*), 217–20, 230, 232
  criteria in identification of, 219
  reasons for using, 222–25, 227n29
Dowling, W. Jay, 21n36, 242n57
durational determinacy, 32, 33n5
  flexibility of, 120, 122
dynamic markings 41–42, 57, 303–4

Einschnitt (incise) (ending formula), 31, 76, 79nn61–62, 211, 235
  identification of, 236–37
Eisen, Cliff, 299n11
"elongated upbeat," 219–20, 221. *See also* "incorrect upbeat"
"empty bar," 218–19
ending formulas. See *Absatz* (phrase ending); cadence (*Kadenz, Tonschluss*); caesura; *Einschnitt* (incise); *Ruhepunkte* (resting points)
entrainment, 22, 98, 246n64
Erlebnis, 28, 29
Essens, Peter, 26n41, 44n22
Esser, Michael Ritter von, 299
expectation
  formal, 108–9, 300n13, 305n23
  temporal, 19–20, 25, 28, 93, 122–23, 138, 296
  See also surprise; unexpected, the

"false end," 111
feminine ending (*weiblicher Ausgang*), 80, 87. *See also* overhang (*Überhang*)
fermata, 116–20, 153, 251, 259n9, 297
  embellished, 118
  and general pause, 119–20
  as a resting point, 116
finger slides, 275, 299
Fink, Gottfried Wilhelm, ix, 130n39
Finscher, Ludwig, 296n4
Fodor, Jerry, xi, 17, 24n39, 30, 109n15, 309n26
folk band, parody of, 89, 152, 156, 275, 278–79, 294, 298, 304–5. *See also* artful imitation of musical bungling, of incompetent performers
"Fonte," 144, 280n39
form, musical
  concept of: as a thematic process, 251–52; as a tonal process defined by cadential closures, 108, 252
  and metric manipulations, 251–52, 300; changes of the metrical level of *Taktteile*,

225–26, 251; fermatas, 117–18; general pauses, 108–9, 110–11; hemiola, 161; *imbroglio*, 147–51, 251; metrical dissonances, 251; submetrical grouping dissonances, 151, 251; syncopated accompaniment, 205
and metrical strategies, 252; consisting of metrical dissonances, 252; involving metrical modulation, 185
See also rondo; small two-reprise form; sonata form; variations
"free fall," 139–41, 196, 297
fugue subject, 267, 268n25
Fux, Johann Joseph, 198, 200n20

gavotte, 66, 226, 229–30, 231
generative theory of tonal music (GTTM), 14, 17, 21, 25–26, 39, 58, 169, 244
Gerber, Ernst Ludwig, 302
Gjerdingen, Robert O., xii, 144n12, 278n36
grammar, musical, xi–xii, 249, 251, 308
Graun, Carl Heinrich, *Der Tod Jesu*, 159, *160*, 161
Grave, Floyd, 133, 139–40, 144, 145, 207n24, 230, 250, 263nn15, 17, 286n45, 291n48
"free fall," 139
displacement in compound meters, xi, 215n10, 264n20, 268n26
Grave, Margaret, 263n15, 263n17, 286n45, 291n48
Griesinger, Georg August, 296
grouping
meter as, 14n24, 76–77 (*see also* metrical hierarchy, principle of grouping)
vs. meter, 14, 31, 38, 51, 73, 76–77, 175n10
as a preference factor of metric perception, 38–39, 44, 45, 48–49, 51, 67n49, 69–70, 174, 189, 208, 246, 299 (*see also* accent, initial; accent, terminal; Metrical Preference Rules [MPRs], MPR 2)
preference factors of: proximity, 44, 45, 48, 49n30, 58, 67n49 (*see also* Grouping Preference Rules [GPRs], GPR 2); similarity, 45, 48, 58 (*see also* Grouping Preference Rules [GPRs], GPR 3)
Grouping Preference Rules (GPRs), 44, 45
GPR 2 (proximity), 44, 45n26
GPR 3 (change), 45, 48
GPR 7 (time-span and prolongational stability), 45n26
Grouping Well-Formedness Rules (GWFRs), 15n25, 58

Haimo, Ethan, 252, 253n2
half cadence (*Halbkadenz*), 110–11, 113, 117–18, 147, 150, 151, 153, 205, 251, 300
concept of, 110n16, 259n9
Handel, Stephen, 47, 48, 168n3
harmonic change, 38–39, 50–52, 208
in the bass, 59–60
in the melody, 59
See also harmonic rhythm
harmonic rhythm, 50, 51, 72, 81n64, 161, 241, 247. *See also* syncopations, harmonic
harmonic salience, 39, 57, 277n33. *See also* accent, harmonic
harmonic stability, 38–39, 50, 52–53, 56n34, 57, 277n33
in a sequence, 141, 144, 173, 287
of the tonic, 52–53, 56, 57, 71, 122
harmony, 38, 45, 165, 246. *See also* harmonic change; harmonic rhythm; harmonic salience; harmonic stability
Harwood, Dane L., 242n57
Hasse, Johann Adolf, *I pellegrini*, 135, 139
Hasty, Christopher, ix, x, 6n9, 24n38, 27–30, 59n40, 64n45, 120n32
deferral, 36
durational determinacy, 32, 33n5, 120, 122
hiatus, 120
"silent beginning," 36n9
"too early" vs. "too late," 146n16
Hauptmann, Moritz, 30, 45
Hauptperiode (main period), 110n16, 290
Haydn, Joseph, 91, 122, 207, 275, 295–301, 305–7, 308
anticipation, 306
concerto-like conception of the string quartet, 118
cyclic integration, 252, 253n2
direct metrical dissonance, 142
elementary motives, 187, 299, 307
embellished fermatas, 118
general pauses, 102, 103, 106, 113, 120
hemiolas, 162
imitation in displacement dissonances, 195, 297
interruption of *Metrum*, 113
ligaturae, 306
minuets, 102, 250, 296–98; contrapuntal means in, 306
monothematic sonata form, 260
playful use of caesuras, 88
preparation of metrical dissonance, 171–72
retardation, 306
slurred motives, 299, 306–7
trick of opening with a closing gesture, 34, 61
hemiola, 128, 129, 158, 159–61, 251
before the cadence, 162–63
combined with *imbroglio*, 162–63

hemiola (*continued*)
combined with pauses, 129
formal function of, 161
vs. *imbroglio*, 159–62
in non-cadential context, 164
replaced by *imbroglio*, 162
"hemiolisch," 159n25
Hepokoski, James, 110n17
high vs. low, 273, 296, 298
"low comic," 251
"low pastoral," 275
"historical listener," x, xii, 30, 77, 309
Horlacher, Gretchen, 139n9
horn calls, 150, 280. *See also* hunting style
Houle, George, 8n12, 10n16, 41n17, 43n20, 67n47, 94n2, 225
Hoyt, Peter, 253n2
human pace. *See* natural pace
humor (*Laune*), 301n17. *See also* wit (*Witz*)
humorous music, 295–302. *See also* comic music
hunting style, 66, 282. *See also* horn calls
Huron, David, 47, 49n30
Imagination–Tension–Prediction–Reaction–Appraisal (ITPRA), 303n20, 309n26
Husserl, Edmund, 28n45
hypermeter, 13n22, 111, 183n13, 224n23, 227n29, 246, 264n20, 267n22, 268n26, 271, 293n49
in eighteenth-century music theory, xi, 11, 130n39

Imbrie, Andrew
"radical" vs. "conservative" hearing, 183n13
imbroglio, 133, 135–39, 142, 145–46, 151–52, 297
combined with hemiola, 162–63
combined with sequence, 139, 141, 143, 144, 147, 173, 287–89, 291
formal functions of, 147–51, 251
vs. hemiola, 159–62
and the quartet cycle, 146–47
and topics, 150, 250, 298
See also "free fall"
imitatio per thesin et arsin, 190, 268n26, 298n9
imitation, 139, 189–90, 195, 251, 297. *See also* artful imitation of musical bungling
improper harmonization (*uneigentliche Begleitung*), 80–81, 237
of an appoggiatura, 80–81, 237
of an overhang, 80, 237
improvisation, 118, 153–54, 201, 250–1
incise (*Einschnitt*) (melodic section), 31, 79nn61–62, 95, 116, 236, 238n48
imperfect (*unvollkommener*), 83, 235
perfect (*vollkommener*), 83, 222
See also *Einschnitt* (incise)
"incorrect upbeat," 219, 220n18. *See also* "elongated upbeat"
intraonset interval (IOI), 43–44, 48
Irving, Howard, 296n4
Irving, John, 304n21

Jackendoff, Ray, x, 17–24, 26–27, 29–30, 35, 169
correspondence rules vs. formation rules, 15n25
integrative processors vs. translation processors, 17n28
See also Lerdahl, Fred, and Ray Jackendoff; processor, metric
Jean Paul [Johann Paul Friedrich Richter], 296n4
Junker, Karl Ludwig, 296

Kaminsky, Peter, 134n2
Kirkendale, Warren, 267n24, 268n25
Kirnberger, Johann Philipp, 51, 52–53, 60, 74, 200n20, 229n33, 245n62, 258
meter, 3–5, 8–12, 40, 42, 45–46, 47, 130nn38–39, 218n14, 224n25, 225, 230, 236, 241, 242
metric notation, 216
nonessential dissonances, 51–52
parenthesis, 259
prohibited harmonic progressions, 193, 279
Rhythmus, 31–32, 95
Ruhepunkt (resting point), 70
tempo giusto, 225
Koch, Heinrich Christoph, 32, 43, 83n65, 115–16, 137n5, 159n25, 204, 219n16, 220n18, 235, 245, 264n19, 279, 285n43, 290, 300, 302
Abteilungspunkte (points of division), 7, 75–76
accent: "grammatical," 41, 123–24; "oratoric," 41; "pathetic," 41
anticipation, 200
Bindung (tie), 199, 206
ending formulas, 79–82, 216n11, 237, 238n48, 259n9, 285
fermata, 116–18, 119
general pause, 101, 119
hemiola, 159, 160
imbroglio, 133, 136
imitatio per thesin et arsin, 190
meter, 4, 6–12, 67, 224n25, 238n49
metric notation, 49–50, 74–76, 87, 218–19, 222, 224, 228–29, 231
metrical position of caesura, 74–76, 78, 211
Metrum, 93–99, 101, 128, 157, 232–34
parenthesis, 105n14, 210, 242, 259n7
phrase structure, 83, 210, 211n4, 218–19, 222, 238, 259nn7–8, 282n41

retardation, 200
Rosalia, 279
Rückung (shift), 123, 136, 159, 165, 199
Ruhepunkte (resting points): *des Geistes* (of the spirit), 76, 78, 235, 237; *der Vorstellung* (of imagination), 6–8, 10, 41, 76
Sospiren, 200
syncopation, 123–24, 165
Komar, Arthur, ix, 13n22
Kramer, Jonathan, ix, 14n24
Krebs, Harald, ix, x, 133–34, 142, 156–59, 161, 165, 167n2, 171–72, 174–75, 176n11, 204, 205, 206–7, 208, 244n58, 254
"corrective accent," 207n27
metric cycle, 139n9
See also metrical dissonance

Ländler, 89n71, 166, 260, 273, 298
language
metaphor of music as, xi–xii, 40, 70, 249
processing of music and, 17, 21, 70
qualitative principle of German, 40, 42, 94
quantitative principle of Latin, 42, 93–94
See also grammar, musical; rhetoric, musical
Lawson, Gregory, 168n3
learned style, 199, 251, 272–73, 286
Lee, Christopher S., 26nn40–41
Lerdahl, Fred, 52, 56n35, 58–59, 207n26
melodic attractions vs. metrical attractions, 113, 130
sensory consonance vs. sensory dissonance, 57
surface tension, 57
tonal pitch space, 113, 130, 137n6
See also Lerdahl, Fred, and Ray Jackendoff
Lerdahl, Fred, and Ray Jackendoff, ix, x, xi, 14–17, 19, 23, 26, 27, 28–30, 38–39, 43–45, 46, 48, 52, 56, 57–58, 60, 69, 72, 76–77, 142n11, 176n11, 183n13, 241, 243–44, 307. *See also* generative theory of tonal music (GTTM); Grouping Preference Rules (GPRs); Grouping Well-Formedness Rules (GWFRs); Metrical Preference Rules (MPRs); Metrical Well-Formedness Rules (MWFRs); tactus
Lester, Joel, ix, 39n14, 51, 58, 224n23, 245n60, 246
Levy, Janet, xii, 104n13, 120, 250
Lewin, David, 182n12
ligaturae (ties), 198–200, 251
ligaturae consonantiae, 198
ligaturae dissonantiae, 198 (*see also* nonessential dissonances [*zufällige Dissonanzen*])
Lolli, Antonio, 295, 299
London, Justin, 6n9, 14n23, 22–23, 98, 113, 168n3, 210n1, 246–47
metric malleability, 67n48
Longuet-Higgins, H. Christopher, 26nn40–41
"loud pauses," 113, 127

march, 66–67, 140, 230, 250, 278n35
"exalted," 84, 226, 250
Margulis, Elizabeth Hellmuth, 113n20
Marpurg, Friedrich Wilhelm, 3, 10, 74n53, 78n59, 94, 159n25, 211n4
Mattheson, Johann, 3, 7, 8, 10, 11, 13n22, 74n53, 93, 200n20, 228n31, 245n62
Maurer Zenck, Claudia, 90n72, 94n2, 95n4, 130n38, 164n31, 237, 238n49, 258n5, 296n6, 299n11
changes between compound and simple meters, 212, 226,
double measures (*Doppeltakte*), 217, 218n14, 219, 223, 232n44, 235, 247n66
medial caesura, 110n17
melodic contour, 49, 174, 189, 299. *See also* accent, melodic
melodic motives, elementary, 183, 187, 307
default metrical properties of, 176, 182, 187
pitch alternation, 183
pitch repetition, 183, 187, 256, 257, 259–60, 262–64, 268–71, 273
slurred motives, 175–76, 178, 179, 183, 185–86, 187–89, 197–98, 275–82, 283–87, 290–91, 294, 299 (*see also* finger slides)
melodic stepwise motion, 67, 70
in parallel sixth-chords, 71–72
in parallel thirds, 54, 63, 65, 67
melody. *See* accent, melodic; melodic contour; melodic motives, elementary; melodic stepwise motion
memory
long-term musical, 21, 70, 189
short-term musical (STMM), 19, 21, 26n42, 34n8, 70
Mestrino, Niccolò, 275n31
meter, concept of
in the early eighteenth century, 3; parallels with the contemporary concept of meter, 13n22
in the late eighteenth century, ix, x, 3–8, 134; as "double uniformity," 4, 13–14; parallels with the contemporary concept of meter, 12–14, 16; and the primitive series of beats, 4–8, 13, 32n3, 40, 42, 67, 159, 202
See also *Takt* (meter)
meter–key analogy, 52, 113, 130–31, 205, 207

meters (*Taktarten*)
and affects, 224–25, 227–29
classification of, 8–12
compound (*zusammengesetzte*), 9, 11–12; "hierarchical," 11, 12n20, 130n39; "notational," 11
mixed (*vermischte*), 9, 10
simple (*einfache*), 9, 10
simple vs. compound: changes between, 82–88, 140, 209–11, 212–17; distinction between, 11–12, 78, 81n64, 82, 211, 215, 237
2/1 vs. 4/2, 9, 224n25
2/2 vs. 4/4, 9, 12, 78, 83, 84, 215, 229n35, 236, 237
2/8, 9, 231n39, 241
4/4, 9, 12, 78, 130n39, 245n62
6/8, 9, 11–12, 78, 163–64, 236
6/8 vs. 3/4, 70–71, 72
12/8, 9, 12, 238n49
metric cycle, 139n9
metric notation, 49–50, 74–76, 228–29, 230–31
incorrect, 87–88, 216, 218–19
metric representation, states of, 29, 36n9
ambiguity, 169, 174
clear sensation of meter, 16, 20–21, 29, 169, 174
vague sensation of meter, 16, 20–21, 23, 29, 169, 174
metrical consonance
primary, 133, 205, 207, 248n69
theory of, 247–48
metrical dissonance, 131, 133–34, 244n58
activation of, 175–76, 179, 182n12, 248n69, 252
direct, 142, 144, 166–67, 168, 190, 208, 297; merged, 143, 166; split, 143, 166, 168
displacement, 134, 139, 165–69, 172, 174, 190, 198, 206, 208, 251, 252, 297
grouping, 133, 136, 139, 172–73, 206–7, 208, 252, 297 (see also *imbroglio*)
indirect, 142, 144, 166–67, 168, 206–7, 208, 273
intensification of, 175, 248n69
intensity of, 167; contextual, 167n2, 244n58; inherent, 167n2, 203–4
low-, mid-, and high-level, 134, 156
perceivability of, 167n2, 174–75
preparation of, 171–73
resolution of, 207
subliminal, 205, 206–7, 208
submerging of, 208, 248n69
surfacing of, 208, 248n69
theory of, 133–34, 156, 157–59, 248; and eighteenth-century music theory, x, 134, 142, 144, 174, 203, 273; two traditions in the, 157–59, 161
See also rhythmical dissonance; submetrical dissonance
metrical hierarchy, 8, 12, 14–15, 19, 52, 77–78, 113, 129–30, 133–34, 157–59, 158–59, 161, 202, 209, 243–47
characteristics of: density, 246–47; depth, 36n11, 246; strength of articulation of metrical levels, 247
principle of division: of a series of beats, 7, 40, 47, 76–77; of time-spans, 3, 7–8, 13n22, 15, 157–59, 161, 163–64
principle of grouping, 3n1, 7–8, 10, 15, 67, 76–77, 133–34, 136, 152, 157–59, 161
See also projective hierarchy
metrical induction, 23, 32, 52, 57, 69n50, 137, 139
and key induction, 56
metrical modulation
as a change of the metrical level of *Taktteile*, 82–84, 88, 182n12, 226
as a change of phase, 182–83, 189, 197; formal functions of, 185; and the quartet cycle, 186–87
Metrical Preference Rules (MPRs), x, 16, 19, 38–39, 56, 57, 58, 243
MPR 1 (parallelism), 39, 137
MPR 2 (strong beat early), 35, 39, 44–45
MPR 3 (event), 26–27, 38
MPR 4 (stress), 39
MPR 5 (length), 39, 43–45, 46, 48n29, 50–51
MPR 6 (bass), 39, 60, 61
MPR 7 (cadence), 39, 69, 72, 77
MPR 8 (suspension), 39, 51
MPR 9 (time-span interaction), 56n34
MPR 10 (binary regularity), 36, 39, 145
Metrical Well-Formedness Rules (MWFRs), x, 15, 18
MWFR 1, 15, 26, 27
MWFR 3, 15, 33
MWFR 4, 15, 19
Metrum
based on *Taktglieder*, 95, 99, 157, 242
based on *Taktteile*, 95, 157
change of the metrical level constitutive of, 234
concept of, 93–94
continuity of, 94–97, 128, 152, 157, 232
criterion in identification of the metrical level constitutive of, 99
interruption of, 97–101, 115, 116, 124, 157, 232
and phrase structure, 95
and *Rhythmus*, 95, 297
and tactus, 99n6, 242n57
and *Takt*, 93n1, 94
See also musical motion, continuity of
Meyer, Leonard B., ix, xii, 13, 14n23, 38n12, 41n16, 113, 245n60, 296n5, 302, 303n20
"gap-fill melodies," 48n28
implication–realization model, 19

Michaelis, Christian Friedrich, 295, 296, 301n17
military style, 66
minuet, 62, 74n53, 111, 146, 187, 219n16, 231, 236n47, 296–98
  canonic, 191n17
Monelle, Raymond, 230n38, 275
"Monte," 144n12, 278–79, 280n39, 287n46
Mozart, Leopold, 67n47
Mozart, Wolfgang Amadeus, 91, 301–5, 308
  complexity, 301–3; harmonic, 172, 302, 303–4; polyphonic, 190, 303
  double measures, 219
  dynamic markings, 303–4
  fermatas, 304
  general pauses, 113–15, 304
  Haydn's influence, 90, 114–15, 304–5
  hemiolas, 162
  imitatio per thesin et arsin, 190
  interruption of *Metrum*, 113
  playful use of caesuras, 88
  preparation of metrical dissonance, 172
  time signatures, 90n72
Muffat, Georg, 67n47
musette, 251
musical motion, continuity of, 32, 98n5, 297. See also *Metrum*

Narmour, Eugene, 19
natural pace, 241–42
Neumann, Friedrich, 30
nonessential dissonances (*zufällige Dissonanzen*), 51–52, 130n38, 199. See also *ligaturae* (ties)
notation. *See* metric notation
notes inégales, 41n17, 43

Okkerman, Hans, 44, 45, 90
ongherese, 156n21. See also *style hongrois*
oscillators, 27n43
Oshinsky, James S., 168n3
overhang (*Überhang*), 79, 80, 237
  incorrect, 87, 117n25, 218–19

pantomimic effect, 109, 146, 147n17, 152, 258–59, 273
parallelism, 39, 61n41, 137
  in imitation, 189–90
  in metrical displacement dissonance, 169
  in metrical grouping dissonance, 136–39, 142, 145–46, 151, 161, 172
  recognition of, 137–38, 142, 145, 172
parameters
  statistical, 38–39, 45, 50, 246
  syntactical, 38–39, 57, 59, 246
parenthesis (*Parenthese*), 105n14, 210, 259
Parncutt, Richard, 14n24, 26n41, 36n11, 43–44, 246n63
parody. *See* artful imitation of musical bungling; comic music; folk band, parody of
pastorale, 251
Paul, Steven, 296nn4–5
pauses, 120, 297
  general, 101–16, 251, 297, 300; and fermatas, 119–20
  short, 96, 97–98; under fermatas, 116, 119–20; and resting points, 235
  strength of surprise elicited by, 112–13
  See also "loud pauses"; *Sospiren* (sighs)
performance nuance
  bowing, 66–67
  dynamics, 6–7, 41–42, 57, 66–67, 71, 126, 130, 205–6, 207n24
  timing, 43, 66–67, 67n48, 119–20
period (*Periode*), 79. See also *Hauptperiode* (main period)
phenomenology, 28
phrase, 69–70, 76–77
  as the span of short-term musical memory (STMM), 21–22
  See also accent, structural; phrase (*Satz*)
phrase (*Satz*), 31, 70, 75–76, 79, 83, 95, 103, 113, 116, 128, 219n16, 236, 238n48, 259
  closing (*Schlußsatz*), 79
  compound (*zusammengesetzter*), 282n41
  connecting of two phrases (*Zusammenketten zweyer Sätze*), 81
  expanded (*erweiterter*), 221–22
  internal (*Absatz*), 79; *Grundabsatz*, 79n61; *Quintabsatz*, 79n61
  See also *Absatz* (phrase ending); phrase structure (*Satzbau*)
phrase structure (*Satzbau*), xi, 83, 221–22, 236, 259, 297
  and bass, 128
  and changes of the metrical level of *Taktteile*, 240
  garbled, 216, 283, 291
  and general pauses, 102–3, 112–13, 116
  and *Metrum*, 95
  misrepresented in double measures, 218–19
  represented in compound meter, 210, 211n4
physical motion, disturbance of, 62, 102, 103, 296–98
poetic feet (*Füsse*), 8, 93–96
poetic meter, 94
polonaise, 74n53
"Ponte," 144n12
Povel, Dirk-Jan, 26n41, 44, 45, 90

preference rule approach, 21, 142n11, 169, 174, 189
preference rules. *See* Grouping Preference Rules (GPRs); Metrical Preference Rules (MPRs)
"primacy effect," 35, 44. *See also* Metrical Preference Rules (MPRs), MPR 2
"principle of economy," 26, 122
Printz, Wolfgang Caspar, 43, 94
processing
  central, xi, 77, 109n15, 309n26
  modular, xi, 17, 24n39, 27, 30, 77, 109n15, 207, 309n26
processor, metric
  parallel multiple-analysis model of,17–27, 29–30, 32–33, 34n8, 35–36, 58, 70, 78, 93, 123, 166, 168–69, 182, 247; "bewilderment," 20, 21–22; "hearing the music without effort," 20, 21, 25; "retrospective analysis," 20, 21–22, 25, 35, 70; "retrospective reanalysis," 20–22, 26n42, 70; selection function, 19, 20–21, 25, 29, 33, 34n8, 35, 36n10, 58, 70, 123, 166, 168–69
  serial indeterministic model of, 17–18, 70n51, 168
  serial single-choice model of, 17–18, 26n40, 29, 36, 168
projection, 19, 24–29, 32–33, 35–36, 58, 93, 118–20, 122–23, 166, 168, 182–83, 187, 189, 206–7, 208
  duple vs. triple, 36, 145–46
projective hierarchy, 19, 33, 35, 36n11, 77–78, 83, 99, 122–23, 247
prosodic features, 39–40
prosodic notation, 8, 14
psychological present. *See* memory, short-term musical (STMM)

quantitas extrinseca, 94
quantitas intrinseca, 43, 94
Quantz, Johann Joachim, 43, 118n26

Rameau, Jean-Philippe, 52
Ratner, Leonard G., xii, 89n71, 144n12, 231n40, 250, 252, 278nn35–36
Ravel, Maurice, *Valses nobles et sentimentales*, No. 1, 173n7
Reichardt, Johann Friedrich, 295, 296, 299, 301
  Ariadne auf Naxos, 223
repetition
  in a basic phrase, 83
  as a criterion in delineation of incises, 241n50
  as a means of phrase expansion, 214n9, 221–22
  in metrical modulation, 182
  types of: inversion (*Umkehrung*), 137n5; literal (*Wiederholung*), 137; translation, 137; transposition (*Transposition*), 137; variation (*Variation*), 137, 138, 142
representation. *See* metric representation, states of
retardation (*Zurückhaltung*), 200–201, 251
rhetoric, musical, xi–xii, 53n33, 108, 249, 251, 252
rhetoric pause, 102
rhythmical dissonance, 131, 138, 139n8, 165–66, 167, 169, 171–72, 252, 297. *See also* metrical dissonance; syncopations
Rhythmopoeia, 94n2
Rhythmus, 31–32, 94n2, 104, 110, 122
  and *Metrum*, 95, 297
  as *Rhythmopoeia*, 31n1 (see also *Taktordnung*)
  and *Takt*, 31
Riemann, Hugo, ix, 52
Riepel, Joseph, 53n33, 70–71, 74, 79n60, 94n2, 157, 164, 214, 236n47, 238n49, 242
  changes between compound and simple meters, 209–10, 211n5
  "Fonte," 144n12
  general pause, 102–3
  imbroglio, 135
  metric notation, 218, 228
  "Monte," 144n12, 278–79
  musical motion, 32, 96, 98n5
  "Ponte," 144n12
Robertson, Thomas, 106
Rochlitz, Friedrich, 295, 296n6
rondo, 111, 278. *See also* sonata form, rondo turning into
Rosen, Charles, 84n68, 91, 115, 296n4, 299
Rosenthal, David, 26n41
Rothstein, William, ix, xi, 74n53, 77n57, 84n67, 101n9, 168n4, 223n22, 224n23, 238n48, 264n20
  "elongated upbeat," 219, 220n17, 221n19
  "successive downbeats," 293n49
Royal, Matthew, 47, 49n30
Ruhepunkte (resting points), 70
  des Geistes (of the spirit), 76, 78, 235, 237
  der Vorstellung (of imagination), 6–8, 10, 41, 76
  See also *Abteilungspunkte* (points of division)
Rückung (shift), 123, 136, 159, 165, 199. *See also* hemiola; *imbroglio*; metrical dissonance; rhythmical dissonance; syncopations

Samarotto, Frank, 14n23, 63n44, 67n49, 120n33
  "shadow meter," 168
  temporal plane, 244–45, 247n65

Schachter, Carl, 14n23
Scheibe, Johann Adolph, 3, 10, 94
Scheinpflug, Christian Gotthelf, 232, *233–34*
Schick, Hartmut, 154
Schmalfeldt, Janet
  evaded cadence, 217n13, 260n12, 262n14, 264n21
  "one more time" technique, 262n14
Schubert, Franz, 212
Schulz, Johann Abraham Peter, 3–5, 8nn13, 15, 12nn19–20, 40, 43, 45–46, 47, 72, 73, 218n14, 225, 230, 236, 241, 242
Schumann, Robert, 133
  "Dein Bildnis wunderselig," from *Liederkreis*, Op. 39, 26n42
Schwindt-Gross, Nicole, 3n2
Sechter, Simon, ix
Seidel, Wilhelm, 3n1, 8n14, 32n3, 94n2
sensibility (*Empfindsamkeit*), 201, 251
serious vs. comic. *See* high vs. low
siciliano, 163, 231
"singing allegro," 230
singing style, 226, 230, 250
Sisman, Elaine, xii, 137n5, 301n15
Sleator, Daniel, 44n21
slurred motives. *See* melodic motives, elementary
small two-reprise form, 278–79, 282
sonata form, 225, 252, 290, 294n51
  equivalences with small two-reprise form, 286–87, 292–93
  and general pauses, 109, 110–11
  rondo turning into, 278, 282, 291, 300
Sospiren (sighs), 200, 251
Sperling, Johann Peter, 228n31
Spitzer, Michael, 77n57
standing on the dominant, 111, 117, 150, 251
Sterne, Laurence, 296n4
streaming, 38–39, 57–60, 61, 143, 176
Sturm und Drang, 204–5, 251
style hongrois, 275, 291. See also *ongherese*
"subjective rhythmization," 5, 35–37
submetrical dissonance, 298
  displacement, 189, 201–2, 250
  division,156–59
  grouping, 151–53, 156–59, 202, 250, 251, 298
  See also metrical dissonance
Sulzer, Johann, ix, 3–4, 32n3, 72, 242, 295, 299
surprise, 20, 25, 102, 106, 108, 111
  feeling of, 116, 309n26
  strength of, 112–13, 129
  See also expectation; unexpected, the
suspension. *See* caesura, decorations of; *ligaturae* (ties); nonessential dissonances (*zufällige Dissonanzen*); syncopations, ties
Sutcliffe, Dean, 111n18, 179, 257n3, 258, 267n24
synchronization, 120n32
syncopations, 123–24, 130–31, 165, 251, 297
  durational (length), 123–24, 126, 131, 165
  dynamic (stress), 123, 126, 131, 165
  harmonic, 91, 126–27, 131, 165
  performance of, 41, 205–6
  strength of surprise elicited by, 129
  ties, 96–97, 124. See also *ligaturae* (ties); nonessential dissonances (*zufällige Dissonanzen*)

tactus, 15–16, 245n61
  change of, 210n1, 241, 242–43, 245
  factors influencing perception of, 241–42, 243, 247
  and *Metrum*, 99n6, 242n57
  and *Taktteile*, xi, 15–16, 241–43
Takt (meter), 3–8, 31–32, 40
  dissolution of, 23, 178–79, 251, 305
  interruption of, 116, 119
  irregularity of, 222–24
Takte (measures), 7–12, 35, 36, 78, 136, 159–60, 163, 218, 247
  counting of, 209–10, 218–19, 220n18, 221–22
  incomplete, 222–23
  See also double measures (*Doppeltakte*)
Taktgewicht, 101, 124. See also *Metrum*
Taktglieder (members of the measure), 8, 151, 159
  articulation of, 95–96, 99, 110
  changes of the size of, 152
  and tactus, 242n57
Taktnoten (notes of the measure), 8, 151, 159
  articulation of, 99n6
Taktordnung, 94n2
Taktteile (parts of the measure), 8–12, 159, 202, 218, 225, 231, 247, 264n19
  articulation of, 32, 35, 82, 95–97, 99, 110
  caesura as the criterion in identification of the metrical level of, 77–78, 81n64, 210–11, 215, 219, 232, 236, 236–37, 245n62, 262n13
  changes of the metrical level of, 82–88, 140, 209–16, 231, 251; and changes of tactus, 242–43; and changes of temporal planes, 245; and changes of topics, 225–27, 229–30, 231, 250, 251, 300–301; as nonnotated changes of tempo, 229–30
  changes of the size of: in hemiola, 160, 163; in submetrical grouping dissonance, 152, 159
  perceptual factors in identification of the metrical level of: absolute speed, 242; harmonic rhythm, 235; the lowest metrical level consistently articulated by attacks, 82–83, 232–34; range of rhythmical values, 236; size of melodic segments, 83, 235
  shifts of, 202

Taktteile (parts of the measure) (*continued*)
and tactus, xi, 15–16, 241–42
and *Takte*, 8, 12, 35, 36, 78, 136, 159, 163–64
tarantella, 147n17, 226
Temperley, David, 27n44, 44n21, 56n36, 58–59, 137, 139, 142, 169, 267n22
tempo, 44n23, 49, 95, 187, 241–42, 246, 260n11. See also *tempo giusto*
tempo giusto, 225, 227–29, 236
tempo markings, 229, 258n5
tempo rubato, 136n4. See also *imbroglio*
time signatures, 224–25, 227–29, 230–31. *See also* meters (*Taktarten*)
"too early" vs. "too late," 145–46
topics
as context for metric manipulations, 102, 303n20
as motive of metric manipulations, xii, xiii, 66–67, 84, 89n71, 140, 150, 199, 201, 204, 224–27, 229–30, 231, 250–51, 273, 286, 298, 300
types vs. styles, 231n40
topoi. *See* topics
Tovey, Donald Francis, 84n68, 296n4
Triest, Johann Karl Friedrich, 301
Türk, Daniel Gottlob, 41–42, 43, 46, 118n26, 126, 159, 166n1, 205–6, 222–23, 224, 303
anticipation, 201–2
imbroglio, 135–36
retardation, 201–2

unexpected, the, 296–97
as a source of meaning and emotion, 302–3
See also expectation; surprise

Vanhal, Johann Baptist, 308
variations, 201, 278n35
Verwirrung. See *imbroglio*
Vogler, Georg Joseph, 62n43, 264n20, 297
Vos, Piet G., 56n36

waltz, 254, 267, 268
Weber, Friedrich August, 295, 299–300, 301n17
"comical caricature," 295
"instrumental mimicry" (*Instrumental-mimik*), 299
"vocal mimicry" (*Singmimik*), 299
Weber, Gottfried, ix, 52n31
Webster, James, 252–53, 299n11, 305n23
Wheelock, Gretchen, xii, xiii, 62, 102, 109n15, 145n15, 146, 250, 296–300, 301n17, 308–9
Whitehead, Alfred North, 28n45
Willner, Channan, 174–75n10
basic pace, 245, 247
figural paces, 245
grouping paces, 245
hemiolas, 164n30; contraction hemiola, 161n27, 162n29; expansion hemiola, 161n27, 162n29; cadential hemiola, 128n37, 161n27
wit (*Witz*), 301n17. *See also* humor (*Laune*)

Yeston, Maury, ix, 13–14, 59, 139n9, 158–59, 163, 241n50
"rhythmic dissonance," 131, 133, 158n24

Zbikowski, Lawrence, 298n9
Zuckerkandl, Victor, 145n14